THE
STORY
of
MONASTICISM

THE
STORY
of
MONASTICISM

RETRIEVING *an* ANCIENT TRADITION
for CONTEMPORARY SPIRITUALITY

GREG PETERS

B

Baker Academic

a division of Baker Publishing Group
Grand Rapids, Michigan

Published by Baker Academic
a division of Baker Publishing Group
P.O. Box 6287, Grand Rapids, MI 49516–6287
www.bakeracademic.com

Printed in the United States of America

Library of Congress Cataloging-in-Publication Data

Peters, Greg, 1971–
    The story of monasticism : retrieving an ancient tradition for contemporary spirituality /
Greg Peters.
        pages cm
    Includes bibliographical references and index.
    ISBN 978-0-8010-4891-3 (pbk.)
    1. Monasticism and religious orders. 2. Spirituality—Christianity. I. Title.
BX2432.3.P48 2014
271—dc23   2015007081

15   16   17   18   19   20   21   7   6   5   4   3   2   1

To my sons, Brendan and Nathanael,
for giving me great hope
in the church's future

Contents

Acknowledgments

As with all books, this one would not have been possible without the assistance of many people. My interest in and study of Christian monasticism continues to benefit from my friendship with the monks and oblates of St. Andrew's Abbey, Valyermo, especially Fr. Luke Dysinger, OSB, and Fr. Cassian DiRocco, OSB. The past and present faculty, staff, and students of the Torrey Honors Institute at Biola University continue to stimulate my thinking on monasticism through their insightful questions and comments. I am thankful to the administration of Biola University for awarding me a sabbatical during which I began writing this book. I appreciate my research assistant Nadia Poli for dutifully retrieving articles and books and for moments of levity in an otherwise stressful environment. The members of Anglican Church of the Epiphany, La Mirada, have been gracious in supporting me, their priest, through this and all writing projects. My wife, Christina, continues to support me unconditionally, creating a home that is both conducive to and a refuge from the ups and downs of writing. I am truly thankful for her companionship and love. Lastly, I give thanks for Brendan and Nathanael, to whom I dedicate this book. I am blessed that God called me to be their father.

Introduction

The Monastic Impulse

It seems sensible to suppose that there are at least two reasons why you might be reading this book: (1) you already have an interest in monasticism and are wondering what this book has to say about the history and institution of the monastic religious life; or (2) you have no idea about monasticism and want to learn what it is. I hope, in either case, that this book will be of value to you. But first I will need to speak to those who do not know too much about monasticism, which is the exact position that I was in nearly twenty years ago. Being raised a Southern Baptist in Virginia in the 1970s and 1980s did not give me a good grounding in the finer points of monastic life and history. Having received a decent public school education, I do not ever recall reading about monks and nuns, though it seems reasonable to suppose that I did at some point. It was not until I took a church history class that included the Middle Ages and the Reformation era during my final semester at a Christian college that I was finally introduced, in a proper manner, to monasticism. My introduction came through the charismatic and important figure Bernard of Clairvaux, a twelfth-century Cistercian monk (of whom more will be said later). I recall asking myself, What is a monk? What is a Cistercian? Several months and a few books later, I knew that I had discovered my academic area of interest. Not only was I captivated by the personality of Bernard of Clairvaux, but everything about monasticism was fascinating to me. I am probably the only graduate from Dallas Theological Seminary who has on

1

his transcript an arranged course titled "Medieval Monastic History"! From there I went to St. John's School of Theology in Collegeville, Minnesota, to study monks with monks. Needless to say, I was hooked and I continue to be hooked. Hence, a book on the history of Christian monasticism geared toward a *ressourcement* of the tradition for the twenty-first century.[1]

The untranslatable French word *ressourcement* is most often used in connection with the theological movement known as the *nouvelle théologie* (new theology), a reaction among younger Roman Catholic theologians of the early twentieth century to the theological dominance of neo-Thomism.[2] Since then, however, the task of *ressourcement* has come to be viewed as the recovery by contemporary Christian scholars of insights from the church's past. Thus it is appropriate to speak of a biblical *ressourcement* or a liturgical *ressourcement*. The Roman Catholic theological milieu after the Second Vatican Council is often described holistically as a climate of *ressourcement*. Semantically the idea of *ressourcement* falls within the range of other words that speak to a recovery or retrieval, which are common themes in monastic history—particularly during the Middle Ages—as will be seen below.

Ressourcement is not just a rediscovery or recovery of the past for the past's sake, but it is a rediscovery and recovery of the past *in order to* give fresh expression to contemporary faith. In the words of French philosopher Charles Péguy (d. 1914), "A [true] revolution is a call from a less perfect tradition to a more perfect tradition, a call from a shallower tradition to a deeper tradition, a backing up of tradition, an overtaking of depth, an investigation into deeper sources; in the literal sense of the word, a 're-source.'"[3] Martin Luther's recovery of the apostle Paul's teaching that justification is by faith alone, an insight that led to the Protestant Reformation, becomes in hindsight (and anachronistically) a moment of *ressourcement*. Likewise, as we will see below (in chap. 14) in the Vatican II decree *Perfectae Caritatis*, the council fathers commended the recovery of ancient sources as a way to imagine the future. The decree explicitly states that the way forward for monasticism is by looking to its past and by appropriating the good that is found there. Though paradoxical, in order to move forward in faith, one has to go backward first. This sentiment, that the future lies in the past, is not only a Roman Catholic

1. It should be noted that the institution of monasticism is not unique to Christianity. Buddhist forms of monasticism predate Christian monasticism by about 2,500 years. Good introductions to non-Christian forms of monasticism can be found in William M. Johnston, ed., *Encyclopedia of Monasticism*, 2 vols. (London: Fitzroy Dearborn, 2000).

2. See Hans Boersma, *Nouvelle Théologie and Sacramental Ontology: A Return to Mystery* (Oxford: Oxford University Press, 2009).

3. Cited in Marcellino D'Ambrosio, "*Ressourcement* Theology, *Aggiornamento*, and the Hermeneutics of Tradition," *Communio* 18 (Winter 1991): 537.

sentiment but has also drawn the attention of evangelical scholars, including myself.[4] This book, therefore, is a work of monastic *ressourcement*.

Defining Monasticism

When considering monasticism it is always important to start with definitions since many forms of religious life are oftentimes wrongly labeled "monastic." The English word "monk" comes from the Latin word *monachus*, which is a transliterated form of the Greek word *monachos*. The original meaning of *monachos* may or may not been equivalent to the English word "solitary," that is, one who lives alone. By the fourth century, however, as evidenced in a letter of Jerome to a woman named Eustochium, the term was also applied to those monks who lived in communities.[5] Later, around the sixth century, Pseudo-Dionysius the Areopagite, a Syrian monk and theologian, retains a sense of *monachos* as solitary when he writes that some were given the name "'monks,' because of the purity of their duty and service to God and because their lives, far from being scattered, are monopolized by their unifying and sacred recollection which excludes all distraction and enables them to achieve a *singular mode* of life conforming to God and open to the perfection of God's love."[6] Thus "monasticism" refers to those men and women who either live alone, in a solitary manner, or to a group of men or women who live together in community.[7] By this definition, however, many institutions could be labeled monastic that are certainly not monastic, such as prisons, boarding schools, or even live-in drug rehabilitation centers. Thus something more needs to be added to this definition; not only does the community live together, but they also live together according to a rule of life that includes some form of vows—an explicit institutionalization of the contours of their shared life and apostolate. In addition, it seems reasonable that monastics would have a self-understanding that would define them as monastic. This is another way of saying that one does not become a monastic by accident but

4. See, for example, Chris Armstrong, "The Future Lies in the Past," *Christianity Today*, February 2008, 22–29.

5. See Jerome, *Letter* 22.34. Monks who live in community are known historically as cenobites, with their form of life termed cenobitic. "Cenobitic" has its roots in the Greek words *koinos* (common) and *bios* (life); therefore, cenobitism means "life in common." See Greg Peters, "Cenobitism," in *The Oxford Dictionary of the Middle Ages*, ed. Robert E. Bjork (Oxford: Oxford University Press, 2010), 2:418.

6. Pseudo-Dionysius the Areopagite, *Ecclesiastical Hierarchy* 6.1.3; Colm Luibheid, trans., *Pseudo-Dionysius: The Complete Works* (New York: Paulist Press, 1987), 245, emphasis added.

7. See Greg Peters, "Monasticism," in *Zondervan Dictionary of Christian Spirituality*, ed. Glen G. Scorgie (Grand Rapids: Zondervan, 2011), 618–20.

by intention. Consequently, *monasticism refers to those who intentionally live alone or in a community under a rule of life and vows that give shape to their daily routine and shared mission in life.*

Historically, however, there have been monastic types who do not self-identify per se as monks or nuns. The most prevalent example is the friars. While I was a student at St. John's in Minnesota, my primary church history professor was a Franciscan friar. One day he said to me, "I'm not a monk; I'm a friar." This was news to me. As we will see later in chapter 1 on the formation of the friars, they were (and are) distinct from cenobitic monks, but I would argue that they are monastic inasmuch as they meet the definition of monasticism sketched above. For the purposes of this book I will consider the orders of friars to be a kind of monasticism, though I will always refer to them as friars and not as monks and/or nuns. In doing this I beg forgiveness of the friars.

With a definition in place it is now possible to move forward, seeking to answer the question, why would/should any evangelical Christian today care about monasticism? Hence, this introduction will analyze the latent reality of religious vocation in the Old and New Testaments. The intended purpose of this examination is to demonstrate that in the Scriptures a religious vocation—understood today to be, essentially, an active way of life as a pastor, missionary, or evangelist—was not always understood in a purely active sense but also included a contemplative aspect. Additionally, communal life and vows (not to mention such monastic practices as hourly prayer) were all accepted and relatively common spiritual practices in ancient Israel and the earliest Christian communities. My examination is not intended to argue that evangelicals ought to reinstitute monasticism outright, but I hope that it will break down any overt and covert rejection of monasticism as an aberration, as is often done in many Protestant circles.[8] This introduction is not an exercise in looking for support from the Scriptures for a practice that has already come into existence in order to somehow justify the presence of monasticism in the Christian church;[9] rather, it is a general investigation into the biblical nature of religious vocation (or, in common Protestant terminology, religious calling).[10]

8. For examples of these rejections of monasticism by Protestants, see Greg Peters, *Reforming the Monastery: Protestant Theologies of Religious Life* (Eugene, OR: Cascade, 2014).

9. For this perspective see John Kam, "A Cursory Review of the Biblical Basis of Monastic Life," *Asia Journal of Theology* 6 (1992): 183–86.

10. For a discussion of religious vocation from a Roman Catholic perspective, see Brian Mullady, *The Call of God: A Short Primer on the Theology of Vocation* (Libertyville, IL: Institute on Religious Life, 2008). For a Protestant perspective on religious calling, see Douglas J. Schuurman, *Vocation: Discerning Our Callings in Life* (Grand Rapids: Eerdmans, 2004).

Contemplation: "With God"

Before looking to biblical examples of religious calling, however, it is important to understand the meaning of "contemplative" since I am suggesting that a contemplative aspect is a common feature of religious callings in the Christian Scriptures. The words "contemplative" and "contemplation" are very loaded terms in the Christian spiritual tradition.[11] For the purposes of this book, I will use the definition provided by Tom Schwanda: "Contemplation is a loving and sustained gaze upon God's presence in creation and God's mighty acts."[12] As well, Keith Egan explains that "the Christian tradition has also seen a life of virtue as a prerequisite for contemplation as well as a foretaste of heaven. . . . Christians perceive contemplation as a divine gift of grace."[13] Multiple texts in the Bible speak to or hint at contemplation. Psalm 27:4 says:

> One thing have I asked of the LORD,
>   that will I seek after:
> that I may dwell in the house of the LORD
>   all the days of my life,
> to gaze upon the beauty of the LORD
>   and to inquire in his temple.

Of interest here is that the word "contemplation" comes from *con* (with) and *templum* (temple), which when used together carries the connotation that one is with God in his temple, exactly what the psalmist desires. In the Psalms we also find David's confession:

> O God, you are my God; earnestly I seek you;
>   my soul thirsts for you;
> my flesh faints for you,
>   as in a dry and weary land where there is no water.
> So I have looked upon you in the sanctuary,
>   beholding your power and glory. (Ps. 63:1–2)

And perhaps the most vivid biblical testimony, discussed again below, comes from the apostle Paul, who writes, "I know a man in Christ who fourteen

11. See Jules Lebreton et al., "Contemplation," in *Dictionnaire de Spiritualité*, vol. 2, ed. Marcel Viller, Charles Baumgartner, and André Rayez (Paris: Beauchesne, 1953), cols. 1643–2193.
12. Tom Schwanda, "Contemplation," in Scorgie, *Zondervan Dictionary of Christian Spirituality*, 371.
13. Keith J. Egan, "Contemplation," in *The New Westminster Dictionary of Christian Spirituality*, ed. Philip Sheldrake (Louisville: Westminster John Knox, 2005), 211.

years ago was caught up to the third heaven—whether in the body or out of the body I do not know, God knows. And I know that this man was caught up into paradise—whether in the body or out of the body I do not know, God knows—and he heard things that cannot be told, which man may not utter" (2 Cor. 12:2–4). One manifestation of contemplation is either talking directly with God or having some experience of face-to-face contact with God. Given this overview concerning the nature of contemplation, it is possible to turn to the concept of calling.

Religious Calling in the Old and New Testaments

In the Bible there are two primary meanings of "calling": (1) the call to membership in the people of God (e.g., Isa. 41:8–9); and (2) particular callings by God to a special work, office, or position of responsibility within his covenant community.[14] To illustrate, the word for "church" in the New Testament is *ekklēsia*, which is derived from *ek* (from, out of) and *klēsis* (calling). Thus the Greek word for church literally means "calling out of" or "called out ones." This etymology demonstrates a general call to membership in the people of God. Yet God calls out some individuals of the church (literally, out of the called-out ones) to be apostles, prophets, evangelists, shepherds, and teachers "to equip the saints for the work of ministry, for building up the body of Christ" (Eph. 4:11–12). This illustrates God's practice of "calling out" to a special work, office, or position of responsibility. In God's economy "individuals have their callings within the corporate calling."[15] Further, God is the one who calls based on his own initiative (see John 15:16), though his calling almost always comes through mediators. Some callings are to specialized roles in church and society, and others are to particular duties within these spheres. Douglas Schuurman sums it up well when he writes:

> The Bible has two basic meanings for vocation or calling. Each of these has two forms. The first is the one call all Christians have to become a Christian and live accordingly. Of this there is a general form, where the proclaimed word echoes the voice of creation calling all away from folly and into the wisdom that is Jesus Christ, and there is a specific form, where this call becomes existentially and personally felt. The second meaning is the diverse spheres of life in and through which Christians live out their faith in concrete ways. Of this there

14. See Schuurman, *Vocation*, 17.
15. Ibid., 18.

is a more general form, such as being a husband, wife, child, parent, citizen, preacher, etc., "in the Lord." And there is a specific form, where it refers to the actual duties each of us takes on in our concretely occupied places of responsibility "in the Lord."[16]

In light of this, it will be necessary to look at biblical examples of those called by God and, in particular, to look at those whose calling was to the specific duty of contemplating God.

Adam

One does not have to read far into the Christian Scriptures before encountering the concept of religious vocation. In the book of Genesis, we read that "no bush of the field was yet in the land and no small plant of the field had yet sprung up" because "the LORD God had not caused it to rain on the land, and there was no man to work the ground" (Gen. 2:5). Subsequently, "the LORD God formed the man of dust from the ground and breathed into his nostrils the breath of life, and the man became a living creature" in part, it appears, to care for the land that God created (Gen. 2:7). There was no one to care for the land; consequently God created humankind to care for the land. In light of this, it would appear that the first man was created with a specific vocation given to him by God— land maintenance and stewardship. Thus humankind's initial vocation, at least in part, was to serve God by caring for his creation. Such creation care was an active apostolate, yet we must bear in mind that prior to sin and the fall, caring for creation did not so much involve toil as it involved communion with God and with all of his creation in its perfection. In the words of Basil of Caesarea (d. 379), "The world was not devised at random or to no purpose, but to contribute to some useful end and to the great advantage of all beings, if it is truly a training place for rational souls and a school for attaining the knowledge of God, because through visible and perceptible objects it provides guidance to the mind for the contemplation of the invisible."[17]

In an unfallen state with no rational impediment, Adam had the opportunity to contemplate God himself, primarily through God's unfallen creation. Thus Adam's initial vocation of caring for creation was in reality also a calling to contemplate God; specifically, it was a religious vocation.

16. Ibid., 40–41.
17. Basil of Caesarea, *On the Hexaemeron* 1.6; Agnes Clare Way, *Saint Basil: Exegetic Homilies* (Washington, DC: Catholic University of America Press, 1963), 11.

Abraham

The most widely know calling of an individual in the Old Testament is that of Abram/Abraham, a resident of Ur of the Chaldees: "Now the LORD said to Abram, 'Go from your country and your kindred and your father's house to the land that I will show you'" (Gen. 12:1). For many students of the Scriptures it is tempting to rush past this opening verse of Genesis 12 in order to get to the actual promises made to Abraham in verses 2–3, which play such a vital role in subsequent Old and New Testament history and theology. Yet verse 1, like God's calling of Adam in Genesis 1, provides us with a description of God's activity of calling people to overtly religious vocations. Like Adam, Abraham's calling is to a particular land for a particular purpose. Whereas Adam's responsibility was to steward God's creation, Abraham's was to relocate to a land from which God would create a nation to be his special people. Adam's role was stewardship; Abraham's role was fatherhood. Throughout the remainder of the Old and New Testaments we are reminded more than once that Abraham was called by God:

> You are the LORD, the God who chose Abram and brought him out of Ur of the Chaldeans and gave him the name Abraham. (Neh. 9:7)

> Look to Abraham your father
>   and to Sarah who bore you;
> for he was but one when I called him,
>   that I might bless him and multiply him. (Isa. 51:2)

> The God of glory appeared to our father Abraham when he was in Mesopotamia, before he lived in Haran, and said to him, "Go out from your land and from your kindred and go into the land that I will show you." Then he went out from the land of the Chaldeans and lived in Haran. (Acts 7:2b–4a)

> By faith Abraham obeyed when he was called to go out to a place that he was to receive as an inheritance. And he went out, not knowing where he was going. (Heb. 11:8)

Like Adam, Abraham was called to be in communion with God, and we see this communion worked out through God's promise to Abraham and in God's faithfulness to his promises from one generation to another: "I will make of you a great nation, and I will bless you and make your name great, so that you will be a blessing" (Gen. 12:2). According to the Danish theologian Søren Kierkegaard (d. 1855), Abraham was a great and godly man for three reasons: what he loved, what he expected, and what he strove with.

Abraham was great because he loved God, because he expected the impossible (i.e., that God would give him and Sarah a son in their great age; Gen. 17:15–27), and because he strove with God.[18] Abraham's calling was not just to be the father of a great nation in the sense of creating a nation-state; his primary calling was to a life lived in communion with and contemplation of God. Abraham's calling was to a life of faith: "He left behind his worldly understanding and took with him his faith."[19] As a father, he was to lead an entire people in worship and contemplation of God. This understanding of Abraham as a person of contemplation is well known in Jewish tradition. According to Jewish legend, Abraham's mother gave birth to him in a cave and then abandoned him for twenty days. When she returned he had already grown into a young man, able to speak. Upon seeing this, his mother's surprise is tempered only by Abraham's response to her: "O my mother, it is made known unto thee that there is in the world a great, terrible, living, and ever-existing God, who doth see, but who cannot be seen. He is in the heavens above, and the whole earth is full of His glory."[20] The point of this apocryphal account is to demonstrate that even before Abraham was called by the true God to found a nation, he was already a searcher after God and one who sought to be in communion with the true God. As an apocryphal account this proves nothing definitively, but it demonstrates a long history of understanding that Abraham was one who contemplated God.

Moses

One of the most illustrious examples of someone in the Old Testament who is called and who also experiences contemplation of God is Moses. Moses's calling is recounted in the book of Exodus:

> Now Moses was keeping the flock of his father-in-law, Jethro, the priest of Midian, and he led his flock to the west side of the wilderness and came to Horeb, the mountain of God. And the angel of the LORD appeared to him in a flame of fire out of the midst of a bush. He looked, and behold, the bush was burning, yet it was not consumed. And Moses said, "I will turn aside to see this great sight, why the bush is not burned." When the LORD saw that he turned aside to see, God called to him out of the bush, "Moses, Moses!" And

18. Søren Kierkegaard, *Fear and Trembling*, trans. Alastair Hannay (London: Penguin, 1985), 50.
19. Ibid.
20. Louis Ginzberg, *Legends of the Jews*, vol. 1 (Dulles, VA: Jewish Publication Society, 2003), 171.

he said, "Here I am." Then he said, "Do not come near; take your sandals off your feet, for the place on which you are standing is holy ground." And he said, "I am the God of your father, the God of Abraham, the God of Isaac, and the God of Jacob." And Moses hid his face, for he was afraid to look at God. (Exod. 3:1–6)

Notice that Moses speaks to and sees God, both evident signs of contemplation. God continues speaking to Moses, explaining to him that he has heard the cry of his people, the Israelites, who are being held as slaves by the Egyptians. God's purpose for appearing to Moses is to call him to go to the Egyptians and free the Israelites: "Come, I will send you to Pharaoh that you may bring my people, the children of Israel, out of Egypt" (Exod. 3:10). After a time of insisting that he is not the right person for the job, Moses acquiesces to God's calling, ultimately delivering the Israelites from their bondage. Throughout the remainder of his life Moses not only continues to lead the Israelites but also continues to have intimate, contemplative encounters with God:

[The Israelites] came into the wilderness of Sinai, and they encamped in the wilderness. There Israel encamped before the mountain, while Moses went up to God. The LORD called to him out of the mountain. (Exod. 19:2b–3)

On the morning of the third day there were thunders and lightnings and a thick cloud on the mountain and a very loud trumpet blast, so that all the people in the camp trembled. Then Moses brought the people out of the camp to meet God, and they took their stand at the foot of the mountain. Now Mount Sinai was wrapped in smoke because the LORD had descended on it in fire. The smoke of it went up like the smoke of a kiln, and the whole mountain trembled greatly. And as the sound of the trumpet grew louder and louder, Moses spoke, and God answered him in thunder. The LORD came down on Mount Sinai, to the top of the mountain. And the LORD called Moses to the top of the mountain, and Moses went up. (Exod. 19:16–20)

Now Moses used to take the tent and pitch it outside the camp, far off from the camp, and he called it the tent of meeting. And everyone who sought the LORD would go out to the tent of meeting, which was outside the camp. Whenever Moses went out to the tent, all the people would rise up, and each would stand at his tent door, and watch Moses until he had gone into the tent. When Moses entered the tent, the pillar of cloud would descend and stand at the entrance of the tent, and the LORD would speak with Moses. And when all the people saw the pillar of cloud standing at the entrance of the tent, all the people would rise up and worship, each at his tent door. Thus the LORD used to speak to Moses face to face, as a man speaks to his friend. (Exod. 33:7–11a)

When Moses came down from Mount Sinai, with the two tablets of the testimony in his hand as he came down from the mountain, Moses did not know that the skin of his face shone because he had been talking with God. . . . And when Moses had finished speaking with them, he put a veil over his face. Whenever Moses went in before the LORD to speak with him, he would remove the veil, until he came out. (Exod. 34:29, 33–34a)

In short, Moses's relationship with God is summed up nicely in Deuteronomy 34:10: "And there has not arisen a prophet since in Israel like Moses, whom the LORD knew face to face." From these texts we see that Moses was both called by God into service and had frequent recourse to communion with and contemplation of God—so much so that Moses became paradigmatic of the contemplative life. Gregory of Nyssa (d. ca. 395), in his *Life of Moses* from the fourth century, writes, "I have briefly written for you, tracing in outline like a pattern of beauty the life of the great Moses so that each one of us might copy the image of the beauty which has been shown to us by imitating his way of life."[21]

Elijah

Another great prophet called by God and given the grace of contemplation is Elijah, who arrives on the biblical scene rather abruptly but leaves an indelible mark. There is no explicit mention of Elijah's calling to be a prophet of God, but it is reasonable to suppose that Elijah's prophetic ministry was the result of a calling by God similar to that of other prophets. In general, prophets were called as a result of some sort of confrontation. For Moses it was the enslavement of the Israelites by the Egyptians, and for Gideon it was Israelite oppression from the Midianites (Judg. 6:11–14). Elijah's calling was prompted by King Ahab's disobedience to God: "Ahab did more to provoke the LORD, the God of Israel, to anger than all the kings of Israel who were before him" (1 Kings 16:33b). Thus God called Elijah onto the scene to warn of impending divine judgment, including drought and famine. Moreover, Elijah was called by God to demonstrate to the Israelites (and the world) that the God of Israel was greater than the false god Baal (see 1 Kings 18:20–40). Not only was Elijah called as a prophet, but he was also a contemplative, a traditional understanding that flourished in the Middle Ages. Sometime between 1379 and 1391, a Carmelite friar named Felip Ribot (d. 1391) wrote a book titled *The Ten Books on the Way of Life and Great Deeds of the Carmelites*. This

21. Everett Ferguson and Abraham J. Malherbe, trans., *Gregory of Nyssa: The Life of Moses* (New York: Paulist Press, 1978), 136.

work, a purported history of the founding of the order of Carmelite friars (which views Elijah as the first eremitical monk),[22] offers a novel interpretation of 1 Kings 17:3: "Depart from here and turn eastward and hide yourself by the brook Cherith, which is east of the Jordan." According to Ribot, "The goal of this [monastic and prophetic eremitical life] is twofold . . . to offer God a pure and holy heart, free from all stain of sin . . . [and] to taste somewhat in the heart and to experience in the mind the power of the divine presence and the sweetness of heavenly glory, not only after death but already in this mortal life."[23] Elijah, by Ribot's standards, was certainly a contemplative, but the Bible says as much when it records that Elijah spoke directly with God: "And when Elijah heard [a low whisper], he wrapped his face in his cloak and went out and stood at the entrance of the cave. And behold, there came a voice to him" (1 Kings 19:13). Like Adam, Abraham, and Moses, Elijah enjoyed direct encounter and conversation with God.

Paul

There are two important New Testament examples of individuals who were called by God and also graced with an experience of contemplation. The first is Jesus at the transfiguration, and the second is Paul, who experienced being taken up to the third heaven. Given the uniqueness of Jesus's life and calling, I will focus only on the apostle Paul's experience. The Renaissance painter Michelangelo Merisi da Caravaggio painted two scenes of the conversion of Paul. The one installed in the Cerasi Chapel of the Santa Maria del Popolo Church in Rome is the more dramatic and visually striking of the two. In this painting three objects draw the viewer's attention. The most vivid, because it is the most illuminated, is the figure of Paul on the ground, lying on his back with his eyes closed, perhaps having just been thrown from his horse; his arms and hands are extended, palms outstretched toward God, who cannot be seen but is obviously the source of light in the painting. Standing directly over Paul—and unnaturally contorted so as to create an intense perspective—is Paul's horse. The horse is looking down at the ground and does not look like he has been startled. His front right hoof is raised above Paul so as to appear that he might step on him. To the horse's left and in the

22. "Eremitical" is the most common designation of monks who live solitary lives or in loose-knit communities. They are also known as anchorites from the Greek *anachōreō*, meaning "to separate oneself, withdraw." "Eremitical" comes from the Greek word *erēmos*, meaning "desert," which is also the root of the English word "hermit."
23. Felip Ribot, *The Ten Books on the Way of Life and Great Deeds of the Carmelites*, trans. Richard Copsey (Faversham, UK: Saint Albert's Press, 2005), 9.

poorly lit background is a servant who has taken the horse's reins and bridle in hand to lead the horse, presumably, away from Paul. This image contains all the emotion latent in the biblical account of Paul's conversion:

> Now as he went on his way, he approached Damascus, and suddenly a light from heaven shone around him. And falling to the ground he heard a voice saying to him, "Saul, Saul, why are you persecuting me?" And he said, "Who are you, Lord?" And he said, "I am Jesus, whom you are persecuting. But rise and enter the city, and you will be told what you are to do." The men who were traveling with him stood speechless, hearing the voice but seeing no one. (Acts 9:3–7)

Like Moses's encounter with God in the burning bush, Paul was given a powerful and life-changing experience of God. Formerly a persecutor of the church and her believers, Paul was now called to a life of active service. Paul's calling was to be a founder and overseer of churches throughout the Roman Empire. On more than one occasion, Paul is forced into defending his calling, and these defenses allow us to hear Paul's own explanation of his calling.

One of his most impassioned apologies is found in 2 Corinthians 10–13. In his second letter to the church in Corinth, Paul continues to call the Corinthians out on their immoral behavior and to admonish them to a lifestyle of greater holiness. His justification for being able to do this is dependent on his standing as an apostle of Jesus Christ. He defends his ministry by making several important claims. First, the Corinthian church would not even exist, nor would the Corinthians have come to faith, had it not been for God's calling of Paul as an apostle: "For we are not overextending ourselves, as though we did not reach you. For we were the first to come all the way to you with the gospel of Christ. We do not boast beyond limit in the labors of others. But our hope is that as your faith increases, our area of influence among you may be greatly enlarged" (2 Cor. 10:14–15). Second, Paul did not charge the Corinthians for bringing the gospel to them, which is a sign that he did it because of his calling, not because he sought any form of gain: "Or did I commit a sin in humbling myself so that you might be exalted, because I preached God's gospel to you free of charge? I robbed other churches by accepting support from them in order to serve you. And when I was with you and was in need, I did not burden anyone, for the brothers who came from Macedonia supplied my need. So I refrained and will refrain from burdening you in any way" (2 Cor. 11:7–9). Third, Paul lists his credentials, reminding his readers that he has shared in the sufferings of Jesus Christ:

> Are they Hebrews? So am I. Are they Israelites? So am I. Are they offspring of Abraham? So am I. Are they servants of Christ? I am a better one—I am

talking like a madman—with far greater labors, far more imprisonments, with countless beatings, and often near death. Five times I received at the hands of the Jews the forty lashes less one. Three times I was beaten with rods. Once I was stoned. Three times I was shipwrecked; a night and a day I was adrift at sea; on frequent journeys, in danger from rivers, danger from robbers, danger from my own people, danger from Gentiles, danger in the city, danger in the wilderness, danger at sea, danger from false brothers; in toil and hardship, through many a sleepless night, in hunger and thirst, often without food, in cold and exposure. And, apart from other things, there is the daily pressure on me of my anxiety for all the churches. (2 Cor. 11:22–28)

Fourth, Paul boats in his weakness, something that the false prophets of the day would not do, thereby demonstrating to the Corinthians that Paul was one sent from God: "If I must boast, I will boast of the things that show my weakness" (2 Cor. 11:30). It is in this testimony of boasting that Paul also reports that he had been called up to the third heaven. He writes, "I know a man in Christ who fourteen years ago was caught up to the third heaven—whether in the body or out of the body I do not know, God knows. And I know that this man was caught up into paradise—whether in the body or out of the body I do not know, God knows—and he heard things that cannot be told, which man may not utter" (2 Cor. 12:2–4). Though Paul speaks of this event in the third-person singular, the history of scholarship concludes that the event must have happened to Paul himself or he would have no grounds for boasting, which is the very reason Paul is recounting this event to the Corinthians. Thus we see that Paul was called by God to serve him as an apostle (see also 2 Cor. 13:10), but we also see that Paul's calling (like the callings of Adam, Abraham, Moses, and Elijah) was to contemplation.

We must note, however, that in none of these examples do we see a calling only to an active life or only to a contemplative life. Rather, what the Bible pictures for us is that God calls people to active ministries (Adam is to care for the garden; Abraham is to be the founder and leader of a great nation; Moses is to deliver the Israelites from Egyptian oppression; Elijah is to prophesy against evil rulers; and Paul is an apostle sent to start and shepherd churches) *and* to a life of contemplation. Biblically, the active life and the contemplative life are not in tension with each other but are meant to complement each other. This has not always been the case in the history of the Christian church, where oftentimes the so-called contemplative life was valued much greater than the so-called active life. Putting aside this imbalance, however, does not change the biblical revelation that presents a calling to active ministry coupled with the expectation that active ministry serves and complements contemplative ends. The Bible not only depicts God calling people to a particularly active apostolate—such as pastor, missionary, or evangelist—but it also depicts individuals called to the practice of lovingly gazing on God's presence, most often evidenced in a direct one-to-one encounter with God. The dynamic of these two callings, active and contemplative, has been discussed historically within the context of the Mary and Martha narrative of Luke 10 and John 12.

Mary and Martha

From as early as the late second century, the biblical narrative of Mary and Martha was interpreted as an allegory of the active life (Martha) and the contemplative life (Mary) or, perhaps more accurately, the active-contemplative life. Pertinent to this book is the statement of Giles Constable: "Monastic authors were particularly attracted to the view of Mary and Martha as two contrasting but complementary, and not necessarily mutually exclusive, types of life or of people."[24] This, I would suggest, is consistent with the biblical witness that we have already investigated above. A good illustration of this truth comes from John Cassian, a fifth-century monk and theologian (whom we will encounter again). In his *Conferences*, Cassian asserts that the *telos* (final end) of the monastic life is eternal life, whereas the *scopos* (this-worldly end) of monastic life is purity of heart.[25] Cassian writes, "Whatever therefore can direct us to this *scopos*, which is purity of heart, is to be pursued with all our strength, but whatever deters us from this is to be avoided as dangerous and harmful."[26] A sign of purity of heart, for Cassian, is that one's mind is always attached to divine things and to God. This being the case,

> Martha and Mary are very beautifully portrayed in the Gospel as examples of this attitude and manner of behavior. For although Martha was indeed devoting herself to a holy service, ministering as she was to the Lord himself and to his disciples, while Mary was intent only on spiritual teaching and was clinging to Jesus' feet. . . . Yet it was she [Mary] whom the Lord preferred, because she chose the better part, and one which could not be taken from her. . . . You see, then, that the Lord considered the chief good to reside in *theoria* alone—that is, in divine contemplation.[27]

24. Giles Constable, "The Interpretation of Mary and Martha," in *Three Studies in Medieval Religious and Social Thought* (Cambridge: Cambridge University Press, 1995), 16.

25. For a brief introduction to John Cassian, see Greg Peters, "Cassian, John (c. 360–432)," in Scorgie, *Zondervan Dictionary of Christian Spirituality*, 339–40.

26. John Cassian, *Conferences* 1.7.2; Boniface Ramsey, trans., *John Cassian: The Conferences* (New York: Paulist Press, 1997), 44.

27. Cassian, *Conferences* 1.8.1; Ramsey, *The Conferences*, 47, emphasis added.

Though Cassian, like many others, interprets Jesus's words ("Mary has chosen the good portion") to elevate the contemplative life above the active life, Constable reminds us that "Cassian rejected the radical dichotomy [proposed by other exegetes] . . . and accepted the need for action, in the form of caritative [charitable] as well as ascetic and apostolic work, in the monk's progressive struggle towards perfection."[28] An even stronger positive evaluation of the role of Martha (that is, the active life) comes from the eleventh-century poet Marbod of Rennes (d. 1123). In a work dedicated to the miracles of the monk Robert of La Chaise-Dieu (d. 1067), Marbod writes that Robert did not begin the active life and then ascend to the contemplative life; rather, he moved in the opposite direction. Robert did not think of the active life as less good than "the good portion" of Mary (i.e., contemplation), but he thought of Mary and Martha, both the active and contemplative life, as the same. For Robert, explains Marbod, engaging in contemplation that then causes one to act is a sign of the love that one has for one's neighbor. Again, action is not inferior to contemplation, but the two together equal the most God-honoring life.[29] Perhaps the apostle Paul's life is the most illustrative biblical example of this reality. Paul was engaged in the active life before being called up to the third heaven, and afterward he entered back into the active life of planting, guiding, and shepherding churches.

From this brief examination we can conclude that the Bible, as well as some in the Christian tradition, do not view the active and the contemplative life as being at odds. There are certainly many authors in the history of the church who unashamedly elevate the contemplative life far above that of the active life, even disparaging those who did not live a life conducive to contemplation. The moral of the story is that there have been many who have seen the monastic life as the pinnacle of Christian living, going so far as to refer to it as the "angelic life."[30] Yet the examples cited above must give us obvious warning that this is certainly not the conclusion of the biblical testimony. Of course, on the other side are those who would elevate an active life far above the "uselessness" of contemplation. In many ways this has been the besetting sin of much of the theologizing that comes out of the Protestant tradition with its emphasis on finding God's will for one's life. "Finding God's will" is often code for "what job/ministry/vocation should I have?" At worst,

28. Constable, "Interpretation of Mary and Martha," 17.
29. Ibid., 41.
30. See Karl Suso Frank, *Angelikos Bios: Begriffsanalytische und begriffsgeschichtliche Untersuchung zum "engelgleichen Leben" im frühen Mönchtum* (Münster im Westfalen: Aschendorff, 1964).

there exists an overriding perspective in evangelical culture that God has a permissive will and a perfect will. God's permissive will allows the believer to engage in any job/ministry/vocation that does not compromise biblical teachings. As long as a believer is not sinning against God in her choice of work or ministry, then God is pleased, though God might have a different perfect will for her. According to this view, God, by way of his permissive will, might be perfectly fine with me working as a professor at a Christian university. Yet if God wills that I should be a church pastor, then I need to figure that out, get on board, and stop being a professor. If God's perfect will is for me to be a pastor, then being a professor means that I am not living in God's perfect will. I might not be sinning, but I am certainly not living into God's ideal plan for my life.[31] At its best, the evangelical tradition is insistent that our first and primary calling is to be in relationship with God, and from that we are able to discern further callings of God on our life. In the words of John Calvin, "We ought first to cleave unto him so that, infused with his holiness, we may follow whither he calls."[32] Support from the biblical record would seem to indicate that Calvin is right on the mark in this regard. Adam, Abraham, Moses, Elijah, and Paul all received a direct calling from God. Moreover, they were also given the graces of contemplation, suggesting that there is no distinction between contemplative and active lives but rather that every Christian's life is an active-contemplative life.

Communal Life, Vows, Hourly Prayer

Contemplation, which is so often tied to the monastic vocation, is not the only monastic-related aspect found in the Bible. Other practices that are essential to the monastic vocation (including communal life, vows, and hourly prayer) are also biblical. Communal life is evidenced most obviously in Acts 2:43–45: "And awe came upon every soul, and many wonders and signs were being done through the apostles. And all who believed were together and had all things in common. And they were selling their possessions and belongings and distributing the proceeds to all, as any had need." This is reiterated in Acts 4:32: "Now the full number of those who believed were of one heart and soul, and no one said that any of the things that belonged to him was

31. For a discussion of these issues, see Garry Friesen, *Decision Making and the Will of God: A Biblical Alternative to the Traditional View* (Colorado Springs: Multnomah Books, 2004).

32. John Calvin, *Institutes of the Christian Religion* 3.6.2; John T. McNeill, ed., *Calvin: Institutes of the Christian Religion,* vol. 1, trans. Ford Lewis Battles (Philadelphia: Westminster, 1960), 686.

his own, but they had everything in common." Communal living is also witnessed in Jesus's own life with his disciples. They most often moved together as a group (Matt. 8:23; Mark 6:1), took meals together (Matt. 12:1), prayed together (Luke 22:39), and ministered together (John 6:1–15).

Though there is wide disparity among monastic authors regarding the exact theology and nature of vows, in essence monastic vows can be defined as a deliberate and free promise made to God about a possible and better good. Furthermore, the vows must be fulfilled by reason of the virtue of religion. Such an understanding seems consistent with James 5:12, which says, "But above all, my brothers, do not swear, either by heaven or by earth or by any other oath, but let your 'yes' be yes and your 'no' be no, so that you may not fall under condemnation." This is an echo of Jesus's own words: "Let what you say be simply 'Yes' or 'No'; anything more than this comes from evil" (Matt. 5:37). The Bible also has examples of individuals taking vows, such as the Nazarite vow of Numbers 6:1–2, the purpose of which was to separate oneself to the Lord. Samson (Judg. 13:5), John the Baptist (Luke 1:15), and Paul (Acts 18:18) each took the Nazarite vow.

Finally, fixed hours for prayer (known as the canonical hours in monastic history) are also witnessed to in the Bible, having been adopted by the early Christians from Jewish practice (see Ps. 119:164 and Dan. 6:13). Peter and John's healing of the crippled man on the temple steps happened while they were on their way to pray at a fixed hour: "Now Peter and John were going up to the temple at the hour of prayer, the ninth hour" (Acts 3:1). Likewise, Peter's vision of the unclean and clean animals occurred at the sixth hour, when he went to the rooftop to pray (Acts 10:9).

Without much argument, then, it is obvious that the Bible teaches the good practices of living with others communally, taking vows to God, and praying at fixed times. These practices, which later become staples of monasticism, have biblical precedent. Again, this is certainly not a sufficient argument for the wholesale reintroduction of monastic life into the evangelical church writ large, but it assuredly indicates that the institution of monasticism must not be rejected simply because it adopts and values these practices.

Ressourcement: Religious Vocation

If the active and contemplative lives were what constituted the full range of monastic life, sprinkled with some communal living, vow-taking, and fixed times of prayer, then the Bible certainly commends the monastic life. It is not necessary to go that far, though there are those who do believe that the

Scriptures advocate a monastic life above all other kinds of life[33] or, at best, provide examples of differing kinds of monastic life,[34] suggesting that the Bible plainly supports monasticism. At the least this survey has shown that a religious vocation is a biblically based way of life. Inasmuch as Adam, Abraham, Moses, Elijah, and Paul were called to specific vocations and duties, they were also called to contemplate God in his person and in his creation. Each of them had some sort of a direct, contemplative encounter with God: Adam in the garden during the cool of the day; Abraham in Moriah by way of an angel (Gen. 22:1–13); Moses at the burning bush on Horeb; Elijah at the mouth of a cave in Cherith; and Paul on the road to Damascus. It is likely the case that no Christian doubts that the concepts of calling and vocation are biblically centered. What is more likely to be doubted by Christians today, though not necessarily by Christians in the past, is that some believers are called to unique contemplative vocations. In the Christian churches where monasticism continues to exist, this questioning of a contemplative vocation is not necessarily the case. But in many Protestant traditions, especially the evangelical church, there is doubt whether God would call someone to an explicit contemplative vocation. This is certainly changing, and it *must* change given that the Bible unquestionably supports religious vocations that consist of contemplative callings.

Because there is a great diversity of religious vocations, including becoming a contemplative, today's church needs to be ready to help its members in their quest to hear God's directive voice. This is not to say that each person has one specific calling and it is now their job to somehow read God's mind on the matter so that they can be doing God's perfect will.[35] Rather, God has equipped each person with a range of talents, skills, and gifts, coupled with things that they like to do and things that they do not like to do. Just because one is good at math does not mean that one has been called to be an accountant. Or, just because someone has a "heart for the lost" does not mean that she should necessarily become a missionary. This being the case, the church needs to take seriously its role in helping its members discern God's will in their lives. When I felt called to become an Anglican priest, the first step that my local parish took was to assemble a group of church members into

33. The reasoning is as follows: Jesus was celibate. Celibacy is a defining trait of monasticism. Therefore, monasticism is more Christlike and thereby more biblical. In place of celibacy, one could also use the example of poverty.

34. For example, see Greg Peters, "Spiritual Marriage in Early Christianity: 1 Corinthians 7:25–38 in Modern Exegesis and the Earliest Church," *Trinity Journal* 23 n.s. (Fall 2002): 211–24.

35. The theology behind such erroneous thinking is summarized in and challenged by Friesen, *Decision Making and the Will of God*.

a Parish Discernment Committee. This committee was tasked with taking time to meet with me on a number of occasions to help me discern if I did, in fact, have a vocation to the priesthood and how I envisioned that vocation would manifest itself in light of my also being a university professor. In short, I discerned my vocation corporately, not independently.

Thus today's church should assist its members in discovering their vocations, perhaps especially if those vocations are religious ones. If it is determined that a person has a religious vocation (and perhaps even a vocation to the contemplative life), then the church should do all in its power to support that person in his or her vocation. This is illustrated well in the Book of Common Prayer's rite for marriage when the officiant asks the congregation, "Will all of you witnessing these promises do all in your power to uphold these two persons in their marriage?" The congregation responds with a hearty "We will," signaling their understanding that because this couple is called to the vocation of marriage, the church now has a responsibility to support them in this vocation.[36] At the same time, individual believers need to submit themselves to the process of corporate discernment and not act individualistically, for we do not always know what is right and best for us. The modern focus on individuality has created a culture in which I know what is best for me, so I am the primary agent for discerning God's will for my life. The hazard in this mentality, however, seems clear: I, acting individually, am most likely to discern poorly because of my blind spots about myself and my selfishness. There is, I believe, a greater chance for God's voice to be heard correctly when a group of believers are discerning together. In the end, the church has a responsibility to its members, and its members should be able to count on that support as they discern and live out their vocations. While this is true for all vocations, it is certainly true for religious vocations, including those of a contemplative nature.

36. A similar congregational affirmation occurs in the ordination of a deacon and priest, signaling that the congregation affirms the person's calling to holy orders.

Part I

ANTONY

to

BENEDICT

1

The Origins of Christian Monasticism

What came first, the chicken or the egg? So goes one of the most well-known proverbial questions. Monasticism has an equivalent question: What came first, monastics or the institution of monasticism? Answering this question is not easy, and it might actually be unanswerable. Thus this chapter will explore the origins of Christian monasticism, seeking to answer the following questions: What were the motivations for such a practice? What were the earliest manifestations of Christian monasticism? What was the Christian monastic pattern drawing on religiously, and what were its influences? Why did it start when it did? Though these questions do not always have clean-cut answers, this chapter will strive to answer them inasmuch as they are in fact answerable. There is not enough space in one volume to address all the monastic movements and tendencies that existed in earliest Christianity (or in any Christian era for that matter), but this chapter will highlight some of the most pertinent and influential movements while also investigating one of the more obscure movements that appears to have biblical precedent.

Pre-monastic Impulses

To begin, the pre-monastic impulses of the Qumran community and *syneisaktism* will be examined to show that a kind of "monastic" impulse was present in those movements that most influenced Christianity as well as in the earliest manifestations of Christianity itself.

The Qumran community of Essenes was a Jewish ascetical group of the Second Temple period (515 BCE–70 CE) whose life was rooted in the teachings of the Hebrew Bible. They spent their days praying, working, and copying manuscripts. At night they held liturgical gatherings similar to synagogue Sabbath worship, with the exception that the Essenes had a common meal at which they shared bread and wine. The Essenes were divided into two well-defined groups. One group, like that at Qumran, lived in strict community, following a rule. The other group was made up of families who also lived in the wilderness in spiritual communion with the others. In order to adhere to the teachings of their scriptures, they lived a communal way of life, practicing "celibacy (at least for a major segment of the movement), a materially simple life free of private possessions, temperance in food and drink, avoidance of oil, simplicity of dress, reserve in speech, desert separatism (for those at Qumran), [and] strict rules of ritual purity and of Sabbath observance."[1] Philo of Alexandria (d. ca. 40), the great Hellenized Jewish writer, referred to them as the athletes or practitioners of virtue, and they have often been viewed as a precursor and model for early Christian monasticism (though this is not without debate). Within the community were a group called the *yaḥad*, that segment of the sect that was governed by the Community Rule. It is this group in particular that has often been labeled "monastic" and seen as a precursor to Christian monasticism.[2] Some scholars have gone so far as to argue that John the Baptist was an Essene.[3] However, others have rejected this connection between the Qumran community and early Christian monasticism, arguing that the ascetical *yaḥad* are a "voluntary association" of the kind that dotted the ancient Mediterranean landscape and are not precursors to Christian monasticism.[4] If this is the case, as Matthias Klinghardt has argued, then there is no evidence of cenobitic monasticism until the rise of Christian cenobitism in the fourth century. However, this does not mean that there was *no* monasticism earlier than the fourth century but only that

---

1. Steven D. Fraade, "Ascetical Aspects of Ancient Judaism," in *Jewish Spirituality: From the Bible through the Middle Ages*, ed. Arthur Green (New York: Crossroad, 1986), 266.

2. See Edmund F. Sutcliffe, *The Monks of Qumran* (Westminster, MD: Newman, 1960); and Magen Broshi and Hanan Eshel, "Was Qumran Indeed a Monastery? The Consensus and Its Challengers: An Archaeologist's View," in *Bread, Wine, Walls and Scrolls*, ed. Magen Broshi (London: Sheffield Academic, 2001), 259–73.

3. C. Marvin Pate, *Communities of the Last Days: The Dead Sea Scrolls, the New Testament and the Story of Israel* (Downers Grove, IL: InterVarsity, 2000).

4. Matthias Klinghardt, "The Manual of Discipline in the Light of Statutes of Hellenistic Associations," *Annals of the New York Academy of Sciences* 722 (1994): 251–67.

monasticism in community (i.e., cenobitism) arose in the fourth century. This seems to support the extant Christian literary witness that will be discussed in chapter 2. Also, even if the *yaḥad* were not the immediate forebears of cenobitic monasticism, it seems obvious that the Essenes must have influenced early Christian monasticism.[5]

A form of monastic life that was in existence as early as the first century CE and known to the apostle Paul is *syneisaktism*. *Syneisaktism* (spiritual marriage) is a term for the practice of "female Christian ascetics who lived together with men, although both parties had taken the vow of continency, and were animated with the earnest desire to keep it."[6] In the Greek-speaking church the participants of this practice were termed *syneisaktoi*, *agapētai*, or *agapētoi* (beloved), and in the Latin-speaking church the participants were known as *agapetae* or *virgines subintroductae* (virgins secretly introduced).[7] In most scholarly English writings, the practice is referred to by its Greek name *syneisaktism* or "spiritual marriage," and the participants are referred to by the Latinized Greek term of *agapetae*. The earliest nonbiblical reference to the practice is from the first century, and there are numerous references to the practice from the second century on. Both orthodox and heterodox ecclesiastical authors, as well as secular emperors,[8] were familiar with the practice, which had spread to most church provinces in ancient Christianity by the fourth century.[9] Although references to the practice are scarce in comparison to other ancient ascetic phenomena, it is certain that celibate men and women lived together in chaste relationships for mutual support and encouragement. The praxis of asceticism was embraced by both Christian men and women,[10] but

5. Juan María Laboa, "Old Testament Monasticism," in *The Historical Atlas of Eastern and Western Christian Monasticism* (Collegeville, MN: Liturgical Press, 2003), 20.

6. Hans Achelis, "Agapetae," in *Encyclopedia of Religion and Ethics*, ed. James Hastings (New York, 1910), 177.

7. Antoine Guillaumont, "Le Nom des 'Agapètes,'" *Vigiliae Christianae* 23 (1969): 30–31. See also Rosemary Rader, *Breaking Boundaries: Male/Female Friendship in Early Christian Communities* (New York: Paulist Press, 1983), 62n2; P. R. Coleman-Norton, *Roman State and Christian Church: A Collection of Legal Documents to AD 535*, vol. 2 (London: SPCK, 1966), 613n1; and V. Emmoni, "Agapètes," in *Dictionnaire d'histoire et de geographie eccclesastiques*, vol. 1, ed. Alfred Baudrillart, Albert Vogt, and Urbain Rouziès (Paris: Letouzey et Ané, 1909), 892–93.

8. "Letter of Honorius and Theodosius II on Clerical Cohabitation and on Delation about Rapists of Consecrated Virgins," in Coleman-Norton, *Roman State and Christian Church*, 612–14.

9. The number of references to the *agapetae* shows that the practice was rather common since it drew the attention of so many writers. Additionally, the geographical locations of these writers suggest that *syneisaktism* was common in most territories of the antique world.

10. See Susanna Elm, *"Virgins of God": The Making of Asceticism in Late Antiquity* (Oxford: Clarendon, 1994), 137–83.

"the fervor with which large numbers of early Christian women pursued lives of asceticism and renunciation is a curious fact in the history of women in late antiquity."[11] It has been suggested that the renunciation of marriage and family life presented women with the opportunity to move outside the restraints of both society and family, extending to them a degree of self-determination that was unavailable to them in marriage.[12] This arrangement was necessary since they were unable to obtain such support and encouragement outside marriage in the prevailing Roman culture.

In Roman society, marriage was a private act that did not require the sanction of a public or religious authority.[13] A marriage that was contracted according to the civil laws of the time was recognized by the Christian church. The undertaking of this private act was primarily for legal purposes since ultimate proof of a marriage often rested on the intention of the parties involved and not on the vows performed.[14] Within this custom of marriage women found themselves in a difficult situation. Since they were often married at a very young age, they were unable to avoid the demands of married life that included the pains of childbirth, nursing, and, at times, the death of their infant children.[15] Besides these burdens there was also the double standard for men and women concerning adultery. It was accepted that men would have intercourse with women other than their wives.[16] However, married women were not permitted similar indulgences. As Peter Brown writes, "Despite harsh laws punishing married women for adultery, infidelity by their husbands incurred no legal punishment and very little moral disapprobation."[17] Therefore, the adoption of a celibate life allowed women the opportunity to free themselves from this double standard. With the renunciation of marriage

11. Elizabeth Castelli, "Virginity and Its Meaning for Women's Sexuality in Early Christianity," *Journal of Feminist Studies in Religion* 2 (1986): 61.

12. Rader, *Breaking Boundaries*, 70: "The practice of *syneisaktism* or celibate cohabitation was an external expression of the Christians' belief in a new age which allowed an expression of the normative male/female husband/wife relationship. While under the protection of a male celibate partner the female celibate was accorded a freedom, a dignity, and an importance not granted to her married woman-counterpart."

13. See Susan Treggiari, *Roman Marriage:* Iusti Coniuges *from the Time of Cicero to the Time of Ulpian* (Oxford: Oxford University Press, 1991).

14. Gillian Cloke, *"This Female Man of God": Women and Spiritual Power in the Patristic Age, AD 350–450* (New York: Routledge, 1995), 101–9; see also Willy Rordorf, "Marriage in the New Testament and in the Early Church," *Journal of Ecclesiastical History* 20 (1969): 209–10; and David Hunter, trans. and ed., *Marriage in the Early Church* (Minneapolis: Fortress Press, 1992).

15. Most girls were married by the age of sixteen. See Gillian Clark, *Women in Late Antiquity: Pagan and Christian Lifestyles* (Oxford: Clarendon, 1993), 14.

16. Ibid., 28–29. These women were often of the lower servant classes.

17. Peter Brown, *The Body and Society: Men, Women, and Sexual Renunciation in Early Christianity* (New York: Columbia University Press, 1988), 23.

they were able to move outside the restraints of the social and sexual expectations associated with it. It was within this milieu that *syneisaktism* developed and flourished.

Scholars have argued that the origin of *syneisaktism* can be found in the famous passage on virginity in 1 Corinthians 7:25–38, in particular, verses 36–38: "If anyone thinks that he is not behaving properly toward his betrothed, if his passions are strong, and it has to be, let him do as he wishes: let them marry—it is no sin. But whoever is firmly established in his heart, being under no necessity but having his desire under control, and has determined this in his heart, to keep her as his betrothed, he will do well. So then he who marries his betrothed does well, and he who refrains from marriage will do even better." Hans Achelis suggests that the situation here involves two persons of the opposite sex living in a difficult situation. Though they initially agreed to live together in a celibate marriage, they are tempted beyond their limits of control. The question is then raised, "Can such a virgin, vowed to virginity in a spiritual marriage, be free to marry?" Paul concludes that the virgin can marry if necessary, and in this she would not be sinning. This understanding of the text holds that Paul was familiar with *syneisaktism* and, because he does not condemn it, grants his approval.[18]

Historically, there have been at least four ways to interpret 1 Corinthians 7:36–38: (1) Paul is writing about a young man and his fiancée; (2) Paul is writing about a father and his virgin daughter; (3) Paul is discussing a levirate marriage (in which a man marries his brother's widow); or (4) Paul is describing spiritual marriage.[19] Though there is not space to discuss these four views here,[20] the view that is the most ancient and that is frequently accepted by modern commentators is that Paul is describing spiritual marriage. Antiquity and consensus, of course, are not the only criteria for deciding whether a view is correct or incorrect, but for the purposes of this book the antiquity of this particular view allows us to see that it supports an early form of monastic life. The spiritual marriage view was first set forth in the modern era by Carl von Weizsäcker,[21] expanded by Eduard Grafe,[22] and exhaustively set forth by

18. Hans Achelis, *Virgines Subintroductae: Ein Beitrag zu I Kor. VII* (Leipzig: J. D. Hinrich, 1902).

19. For a summary of these four positions, see Roland H. A. Seboldt, "Spiritual Marriage in the Early Church: A Suggested Interpretation of 1 Cor. 7:36–38," *Concordia Theological Monthly* 30 (1959): 103–19.

20. See Greg Peters, "Spiritual Marriage in Early Christianity: 1 Corinthians 7:25–38 in Modern Exegesis and the Earliest Church," *Trinity Journal* 23 (Fall 2002): 211–24.

21. Carl von Weizsäcker, *The Apostolic Age of the Christian Church*, vol. 2, trans. James Millar (London: Williams and Norgate, 1895), 371, 388, and 396.

22. Eduard Grafe, "Geistliche Verlöbnisse bei Paulus," *Theologische Arbeiten aus dem rheinischen wissen-schaftlichen Prediger-Verein*, N. F. III (1899): 57–69.

Achelis. Though many commentators reject the spiritual marriage view primarily because the earliest known noncanonical reference to the practice is from the second century CE,[23] Weizsäcker holds that 1 Corinthians 7 *is* the first reference to the practice. Simply put, he contends that because the practice existed only in Corinth, there would be no other references to the practice at this time. Achelis goes so far as to conclude that the apostle Paul was the one who developed the practice of *syneisaktism*.[24] Twentieth- and twenty-first-century commentaries continue to conclude that the spiritual marriage view is the best interpretive option. The opinion of many modern interpreters is that (1) *syneisaktism* existed in the Corinthian church; (2) Paul was aware of the practice and allowed it to continue, and therefore, Paul fully supported *syneisaktism*; and (3) the earliest reference to *syneisaktism* is not the second century but possibly circa 50 CE or earlier, depending on the dating of 1 Corinthians. I believe that the practice was not only known and developed by Paul but that it was known to other early Christian authors such as Philo, the author of *The Shepherd of Hermas* (second century), and Ephrem the Syrian (d. 373).[25] In particular is the comment of Ephrem in his commentary on the epistles of Paul. He writes that if "there is someone who perhaps has a virgin, and he remains for a certain time, as long as she be in her vow, and he realizes in himself, 'I am not suitable,' he should not feel ashamed about time that has already passed. However, one who is steadfast in his conviction, and has fallen into danger of lust and has chosen in his heart to keep his virgin, does good. So the one who gives up his virgin does good, and the one who does not give her up and is continent does good."[26] Ephrem believes that a man who gives up his virgin is good, but just as good is one who does not give her up and remains celibate. From this we can conclude that Ephrem supports the practice of spiritual marriage. Thus, with the possible exception of 1 Corinthians itself, this is the earliest reference explicitly supporting *syneisaktism*, and we are able to see that from the first century of the Christian era there were monastics. They might not have adopted the more common lifestyles that we now associate with monasticism, but this does not make them any less monastic based on the definition given in the introduction. Of particular note is Ephrem's

---

23. For example, see J. Massingberd Ford, "Levirate Marriage in St. Paul (I Cor. 7)," *New Testament Studies* 10 (1963/64): 363; C. K. Barrett, *The First Epistle to the Corinthians* (New York: Harper & Row, 1968), 183; Colin Brown, ed., *The New International Dictionary of New Testament Theology*, vol. 2 (Grand Rapids: Zondervan, 1976), 588; and Leon Morris, *The First Epistle of Paul to the Corinthians* (Grand Rapids: Eerdmans, 1958), 121.

24. Achelis, *Virgines Subintroductae*, 26.

25. See Peters, "Spiritual Marriage in Early Christianity," 222–24.

26. *S. Ephraemi Syri Commentarii in Epistulas Divi Pauli a patribus Mekhitaristis in latinum sermonem translati* (Venice: Typogr. S. Lazari, 1893), 62.

reference to vows: "as long as she be in her vow." This suggests that the practice of *syneisaktism* was more organized than expected. That women were taking vows to live this kind of lifestyle is suggestive of the institutionalization of the practice and its early establishment.

What is evident from this brief analysis of both the Qumran community and *syneisaktism* is that there was, certainly, a kind of "monastic" impulse in these movements that influenced the early development of Christianity. Christianity received an inheritance where asceticism and monasticism were established practices, thereby giving shape to early Christian practices along similar lines. It should be kept in mind that the institution of monasticism is not unique to Christianity and even predates Christianity by nearly a millennium. For example, as far back as the sixth or seventh century BCE there were holy men called "wanderers" who practiced extreme fasting, wandered around naked so as to be exposed to the elements, submerged themselves in freezing rivers during the winter, meditated in the hot summer sun while surrounded by fires, went years without speaking, and adopted contorted bodily postures when seated. The Buddha himself rejected many of these extreme forms of asceticism, developing a middle way between normal social practices and the extraordinary ascetical life. This form of Buddhist life resulted in the formation of monastic communities. The rule for these communities was based on the four cardinal practices of Buddhist asceticism: (1) sexual continence, (2) nonviolence, (3) poverty, and (4) no pretension to spiritual attainment. These monks took only one meal a day, dressed in death shrouds, changed their names, abolished all ties with family and class affiliation, and had their speech and bodily deportment strictly controlled.[27] Though these Buddhist monasteries, as far as we know, did not exercise direct influence on Christian monasticism, it is possible that Christian missionaries and others had come into contact with these monks and nuns. If the apostle Thomas did evangelize the Kerala region of India, as tradition states, then he would have come into some contact with Buddhists who first settled in southern India in the third century BCE. Therefore, Buddhism might be an indirect influence on the rise and structure of Christian monasticism, though the most direct sources of influence were certainly Jewish.

Motivations

Having seen that there were pre-Christian forms of monasticism and that the institution of monasticism itself sprang up in the first-century church of

27. Robert A. F. Thurman, "Tibetan Buddhist Perspectives on Asceticism," in *Asceticism*, ed. Vincent L. Wimbush and Richard Valantasis (New York: Oxford University Press, 1995), 108–18.

Corinth, we can now ask the question, what were the motivations for such a practice in the Christian church? Despite the impossibility of knowing the hearts and minds of the earliest Christians on this matter, we perhaps can begin to form an answer to this question from the words of Jesus himself: "For there are eunuchs who have been so from birth, and there are eunuchs who have been made eunuchs by men, and there are eunuchs who have made themselves eunuchs for the sake of the kingdom of heaven. Let the one who is able to receive this receive it" (Matt. 19:12). In this saying of Jesus we see that there are three kinds of eunuchs or, to put it in today's parlance, three kinds of celibate persons.[28] First, there are some who are born with physical and/ or biological issues that cause them to be unable to engage in sexual activity. Second, there are those who have been harmed by others to such an extent (whether physically or emotionally) that they are then unable to engage in sexual activity. Finally, and most important for this book, are those who have made themselves celibate. In the King James Version of the Bible this verse says that they make themselves eunuchs "for the kingdom of heaven's sake." In other words, the kingdom of heaven has already come by way of the incarnation and ministry of Jesus Christ. Therefore, seeing that the kingdom has arrived causes these men to become eunuchs out of thanksgiving for the kingdom. However, the English Standard Version seems to get it right with its rendering of "for the sake of the kingdom of heaven." The subtle yet important distinction in this translation is that those making themselves celibate are not doing so because the kingdom has arrived but because they want to help build the kingdom on earth. They are celibate for the sake of the kingdom, not because of the kingdom. These eunuchs want to be involved in establishing the kingdom of God on earth and have chosen celibacy as a way to help make this happen. They are not *responding* to the work of God but *cooperating* with the work of God. In this reading and rendering, Jesus's words do not so much report an event (i.e., some have made themselves eunuchs) as prescribe a way of life.[29] These words, falling on the ears of Jesus's first-century hearers, who were more familiar with intentional virginity (e.g., the Essenes), would

---

28. In its original context there is no doubt that Jesus was referring to traditional eunuchs, those who were castrated. However, the Greek word *eunouchia* (masculine) can also mean abstention from sexual intercourse, or celibate. In this usage it corresponds to *parthenia* (virginity or celibacy; feminine). For example, Athenagoras of Athens, *A Plea for the Christians* 33.3, writes: "If the remaining in virginity and in the state of a eunuch brings nearer to God, while the indulgence of carnal thought and desire leads away from Him, in those cases in which we shun the thoughts, much more do we reject the deeds." Or another way to say it: "If the remaining as a female celibate and as a male celibate. . . ."

29. Jerome Kodell, "Celibate because of the Kingdom," *Tjurunga: An Australasian Benedictine Review* 81 (2011): 23–27.

not have sounded strange but would have sounded like a rallying cry to serve on Jesus's team. What were the motivations for early Christian monasticism? First and foremost it was the call of Jesus Christ to be celibate for the sake of the kingdom of God. Again, celibacy is not the sine qua non of monasticism, but Jesus's call to such a life must have caused a movement that led individuals to begin adopting monastic lifestyles, which we see described and manifested elsewhere and which certainly included the practice of celibacy on occasion.

Another motivation for early Christian monasticism brings us back to our discussion of *syneisaktism*, which Paul approves of in 1 Corinthians 7. Not only was Jesus preaching a message that encouraged his hearers to live monastic lifestyles, but it appears his disciples preached this message too. Making such a statement needs to be counterbalanced by another statement: there is no biblical support for monasticism. Let me explain. If a believer wants to find biblical precedent for something, then she needs to know what she is looking for. Someone might ask if smoking cigarettes is prohibited in the Bible. Well, cigarettes are never mentioned in the Bible directly, so one has to either conclude that the Bible has nothing to say on this matter or approach it from a different angle, such as care for one's body, which is made in the image and likeness of God. This same principle applies to overt theological issues as well. For instance, the Bible never explicitly dictates the way in which a person should be baptized. Should it be by immersion, sprinkling, or pouring? Or could the answer be "all of the above"? To come to conclusions regarding the manner of baptism, theologians approach the topic not only biblically but systematically as well. One's theology of baptism oftentimes dictates one's mode of baptism. Let's return to the topic of monasticism. If one goes to the Scriptures, one will never find a command as direct as the command from the mouth of Hamlet: "Get thee to a nunn'ry." Rather, one needs to know what one is looking for in order to find it. If one's definition of monasticism explicitly states that vows and celibacy are essentials, then one will go to the Scriptures looking for explicit teaching about vows and celibacy. Looking for a biblical definition of monasticism is an instance of looking for a definition of something that you have already defined. That said, I suggest that the Bible does give us enough to go on when it comes to monasticism, such as Jesus speaking of persons who are celibate for the sake of the kingdom and Paul's encouragement of *syneisaktism*, as well as other examples and hints.

Further biblical texts that likely served to encourage early Christians to become monastics include the communal living and communal property passages of Acts 2 and 4 (mentioned above). Monasticism, as a flight into the desert or wilderness, finds inspiration in the wilderness wanderings of the nation of Israel depicted in the Pentateuch and in Jesus's own flight into the desert after his baptism (e.g., Matt. 3:13–4:1).[30] Another frequent element of monastic life is the concept of exile and/or pilgrimage. The Israelite wilderness wanderings and the call of Abraham to leave Ur would have provided biblical precedent and motivation, as would the missionary journeys of the apostles in the book of Acts.[31] The Old and New Testaments are littered with examples of people who lived in fidelity to God and intentionally consecrated themselves to him: "And I raised up . . . some of your young men for Nazirites" (Amos 2:11). Poverty, as a monastic virtue, finds biblical precedent in Luke 12:33a ("Sell your possessions, and give to the needy") and Matthew 6:19a ("Do not lay up for yourselves treasures on earth").[32] Together, these texts show that the earliest Christians were inundated with examples and admonitions toward the monastic life. In the words of Columba Stewart, "These traces of early ascetic attitudes pointed the way toward later developments in theology and practice."[33] This was certainly enough to help first-century believers begin adopting monastic lifestyles.

Beginnings

Having seen some of the biblical and pre-Christian examples and motivations for monasticism, we must still ask, why did monasticism start when it did? Why, within approximately twenty years of the death and resurrection of Jesus Christ, did Christians begin to adopt monastic lifestyles? Here I am thinking in particular about the practice of *syneisaktism*. Though it is not until the fourth century that cenobitic (communal) monasticism began to flourish (something that will be discussed in the next chapter), there were a plethora of non-cenobitic forms of monasticism within decades of Jesus's own life. I would suggest that there are two primary reasons for the appearance and rise of monasticism in these early years of the Christian church's life. First, the first-century context in which monasticism arose influenced the timing of its appearance. Second, monasticism is a movement of the Holy Spirit; therefore, it started at this particular time because of divine appointment.

We know from the biblical text itself that the first century was not an easy era for Christian believers. The apostle Paul, known as Saul before his conversion, was a persecutor of Christians: "But Saul was ravaging the church,

30. Antoine Guillaumont, "La conception du desert chez les moines d'Égypte," *Revue de l'Histoire des Religions* 188 (1975): 3–21.

31. Emmanuel Lanne, "La xeniteia d'Abraham dans l'oeuvre d'Irénée: Aux origines du theme Monastique de la 'peregrinatio,'" *Irénikon* 47 (1974): 163–87.

32. Andrée Emergy, "On Religious Poverty," *Communio* 9 (1982): 16–21.

33. Columba Stewart, "Monasticism and the New Testament: An Absent Phenomenon in Early Christianity," in Laboa, *Historical Atlas*, 24.

and entering house after house, he dragged off men and women and committed them to prison" (Acts 8:3). Furthermore, the Christians were persecuted
by not only Saul but also the whole Jewish community: "When it was day,
the Jews made a plot and bound themselves by an oath neither to eat nor
drink till they had killed Paul" (Acts 23:12). The Romans were also active in
the persecution of the Christians, something that did not stop until the fifth
century. The church historian Eusebius of Caesarea (d. ca. 339), writing in
the fourth century, describes early persecution this way:

> When [Emperor] Nero's power was now firmly established he gave himself up to
> unholy practices and took up arms against the God of the universe. To describe
> the monster of depravity that he became lies outside the scope of the present
> work. Many writers have recorded the facts about him in minute detail, enabling
> anyone who wishes to get a complete picture of his perverse and extraordinary
> madness, which led him to the senseless destruction of innumerable lives, and
> drove him in the end to such a lust for blood.[34]

It is into this environment of persecution and trial that the earliest Christians
were thrust on a daily basis. To take up their cross in imitation of the Savior
was a reality each day. Such a sense of imminent persecution, not to mention
the possibility of death, could and likely does account for an early Christian's
flight from the world.[35] While some Christians certainly fled from fear or self-
protection, others likely found solace in the desert, not so much because they
were looking to avoid persecution but because they wanted to choose persecution
on their own terms. That is, fleeing civilization and moving into the so-called
wilderness or desert was a Christlike form of self-denial, a kind of self-controlled
persecution of one's desires, anxieties, and sinful self-will. In the words of Bernard McGinn, "Withdrawal, like asceticism, was viewed primarily as a means
for the reintegration of the self through deeper knowledge (gnôsis) and more
ardent love (agapê)."[36] Such flight was seen as honorable and an imitation of
Jesus's own retreat into the wilderness to fight the demons. Accordingly, it is
logical to conclude that monasticism arrived in the church so quickly because
the monastic life was a way to live in light of possible persecution and death,
as well as a means to pursue persecution on one's own terms.

34. Eusebius of Caesarea, *The History of the Church* 2.25; G. A. Williamson, trans., *Eusebius: The History of the Church from Christ to Constantine*, ed. Andrew Louth (London: Penguin, 1989), 62. Nero reigned from 54 to 68 CE.
35. On the theme of monasticism as a flight or withdrawal from the world, see Bernard McGinn, "Withdrawal and Return: Reflections on Monastic Retreat from the World," *Spiritus: A Journal of Christian Spirituality* 6 (2006): 149–72.
36. Ibid., 150.

Related to this is the reality that some in the earliest church wrongly assumed that Jesus's return was going to be imminent; therefore, some believers chose to live lives that were not attuned to the culture but stood against cultural expectations. Though this motivation is not exactly a positive motivation, it seems to have existed. Although the eschatological expectation of the parousia (the second coming of Christ) enunciated by Paul and other New Testament writers began to diminish with the end of the persecutions by Emperor Diocletian in 305 CE, during the first three hundred years of the church Christians anticipated, oftentimes in a very intense manner, the immediate and unexpected return of Christ. Around 50 CE, Christians—including the apostle Paul and those in Thessalonica—were already eagerly awaiting the return of Jesus: "For the Lord himself will descend from heaven with a cry of command, with the voice of an archangel, and with the sound of the trumpet of God. And the dead in Christ will rise first. Then we who are alive, who are left, will be caught up together with them in the clouds to meet the Lord in the air, and so we will always be with the Lord" (1 Thess. 4:16–17). They assumed that Jesus's return was impending, so they recommended diligence in being ready and prepared (see 1 Thess. 5:6). However, these same believers appeared to have taken an extra step soon thereafter—they stopped working and began waiting full time for Jesus's return. Paul alludes to these individuals when he writes, "For even when we were with you, we would give you this command: If anyone is not willing to work, let him not eat. For we hear that some among you walk in idleness, not busy at work, but busybodies. Now such persons we command and encourage in the Lord Jesus Christ to do their work quietly and to earn their own living" (2 Thess. 3:10–12). From this we can see that there were early Christian believers who were so convinced of Christ's return that they began to live lives that were countercultural, but in all the wrong ways. It is conceivable that some of these individuals were the ones who would adopt a monastic lifestyle, giving up societal expectations and norms to live in expectation of the imminent coming of the Lord. If persecution likely accounts for believers choosing to live as monks and nuns, then so does the expectation of Christ's return.

Others began to live monastic lives because they were moved to do so by the Holy Spirit.[37] We have already seen how God is in the business of calling people to particular vocations, so we should not be surprised that some are called to live monastically. Such a position is not so much based on a biblical text as it is in a robust theology of calling or vocation. (A brief discussion is found in the introduction, but any further elaboration is beyond the scope of

37. It is hoped that all persons who enter the monastic life have done so because of the Holy Spirit's call!

this book.) What is obvious is that "the monastic life presupposes the grace by which God calls a man or woman to love and serve him in the monastic way."[38] From the survey in the introduction to this book of calling stories and other stories in the Bible, we can conclude that there are four common features in biblical vocation narratives: (1) God's elective love; (2) God's assurance of his faithfulness; (3) God's demand for faith and obedience; and (4) personal growth and transformation by grace.[39] For some individuals this manifests itself in a monastic lifestyle. When this happens it is the result of God's calling on their lives, a movement of the Holy Spirit. Just as Mary's "yes" to the Holy Spirit was a response to her election as the mother of God (Luke 1:38), so is a Christian's "yes" to monastic life a response to the Holy Spirit's calling. Simply put, monasticism began in the church because God called people to live monastic lives.

Ressourcement: The Monastic Tendency in Christian History

Trinitarian theology contains a dogma about the Son of God: there was never a time when he was not. That is, the Son is eternally begotten and has always existed. His begottenness is a description or a definition of his relationship to the Father, not a reference to a time when he was born. Perhaps the same is true of monasticism in the Christian church: there was never a time when it was not. We have seen in this chapter that the monastic impulse was a part of the Christian church from its very birth. In addition to this monastic impulse, actual monastic institutions (like *syneisaktism*) are known from the earliest decades as well. Granted, there are no biblical texts that say "go and be a monastic," but that does not negate the fact that monasticism seems to be a part of the church from its very origins. Although some may think that this is simply a ploy to legitimate and justify the institution of monasticism without a biblical mandate, I am tempted to conclude that there are no biblical commands for monasticism primarily because monasticism is perfectly biblical. If there were consensus on the absolute essentials of monasticism (and there is not at this point in Christian history), nothing would go against scriptural teaching. Celibacy is biblical. Communal living is biblical. An intentional pursuit of holiness apart from society is biblical. And on and on it goes. Thus monasticism has been with the Christian church from the start, and it will likely remain until the final advent of Christ.

38. Daniel Rees et al., *Consider Your Call: A Theology of Monastic Life Today* (London: SPCK, 1978), 110.
39. Ibid., 112–14.

This being the case, it is important for the church today, especially in those ecclesial traditions that historically have not had monastic institutions (e.g., evangelical Protestantism), to recognize that not everyone is called to the institution of marriage and not everyone is called to live their lives according to the prevailing norms of Christian subculture. It has come to be viewed in many Christian traditions that marriage is the norm and singleness is something to be regretted yet accommodated. Most church ministries are built around the nuclear family, and whole ministries are dedicated to familial structures and their flourishing (e.g., Focus on the Family). This implicit "marriage is the norm" philosophy alienates those who are not married. Without doubt, several groups of celibates can be found in the church: those who are single yet desire to be married; those who are homosexual in their orientation and believe that same-sex marriage is not biblical and therefore choose to live celibately; and those who are called to be single celibates. The church needs to minister to each of these groups in ways other than simply promoting marriage: singles wishing to be married should not necessarily be encouraged to enroll in a dating site; homosexual celibates do not need to be "cured" so that they will desire heterosexual marriages; and true callings to celibacy should not be dismissed as emotionally or psychologically aberrant.

Those who are called to be celibate need to be given the space to discern this within their parish. Just as a pastor is willing to work with an engaged couple to prepare them for married life, so a pastor needs to be willing to work with individuals who are called to celibacy, helping them to affirm their calling and to discern in community how this calling will work itself out in their life and ministry. For example, could churches pair up celibates with families in the congregation who have extra space in their homes so as to lighten the financial burden of the celibate who does not benefit from a spousal income? Could Christian camps and retreat houses offer unused space to celibates for similar financial reasons? Likewise, Christian celibates should be encouraged to seek out other celibates so that they may live a common life together. Too often such arrangements are viewed with suspicion because those involved are doing something that is not "normal"—they are not marrying like others their age. The church must defend the calling of these celibates and instruct members on the merits of living according to one's vocation, including the vocation of celibacy. Though these celibate vocations might not be full-blown monastic vocations, celibacy is biblical and must therefore be honored by the church, including those traditions that have not historically supported the institution of monasticism.

2

Of Anchorites and Cenobites

One of the unique features of the Basilica of St. Paul's Outside the Walls in Rome is its series of papal portraits that rim the upper walls of the church. All of the officially accepted popes are represented (i.e., the so-called anti-popes are not pictured), and each newly elected pope's image is added to the series soon after his election. One image that is missing, however, is that of "Pope Joan." Her story first appears in the early thirteenth-century *Chronica Universalis Mettensis*, written by Jean de Mailly. In de Mailly's version of the story, Joan became pope around 1099, but by the end of the thirteenth century others had picked up on the story, altering the details. For example, Martin of Opava (d. 1278) says that she was actually pope in the mid-ninth century. The details of the story are fairly straightforward. Joan, an Englishwoman, followed a lover to Athens, clothed for some reason as a man. While there she received an enviable education that made her a much sought-after teacher. Moving to Rome, she taught the liberal arts and became teacher to a number of great masters, all the while continuing to dress as a man. Based on her reputation she was elected pope but became pregnant during her pontificate because, we are told, she continued to keep a lover. While in procession one day from the papal residence at St. John's in the Lateran, she gave birth, thus exposing herself as a woman and as a fornicator. Though some versions of the story report that she was then stoned by onlookers, others are more quiet about how she died but say she was buried in the very spot where she gave birth. This story has been known to be a forgery for many centuries, but that has not stopped some from considering it true. Some groups smell a conspiracy and think that the modern church is trying to discredit a true story simply due to its supposed misogynistic tendencies. In spite of its falseness, the story of "Pope Joan" will not go away and is considered true history by some. I would suggest that something similar has happened with the historiography of monasticism.

Having investigated the earliest manifestations of monasticism, we can now see that the Christian church has always had a monastic presence. Yet in the historiography of monasticism a lingering tradition claims that Antony of Egypt was the first monk. For example, a biblical dictionary from the nineteenth century states that the "first monks were those of St. Antony, who, toward the close of the fourth century, formed them into a regular body, engaged them to live in society with each other, and prescribed to them fixed rules for the direction of their conduct."[1] While this is not the case, it is a historiography that has dominated much of the literature. Though it is not historically accurate, there is no denying that Antony's story—along with that of his fourth-century contemporary Pachomius—forms a significant turning point in monastic history. Thus this chapter will begin by exploring the *Life of Antony*, by Athanasius of Alexandria, as paradigmatic of the anchoritic (i.e., eremitical, reclusive) lifestyle. Then I will focus on the *Sayings of the Desert Fathers*, which is also representative of the Christian eremitical impulse. I will also discuss the shift from the eremitical to the cenobitic (communal) tradition in the prominent centers of early monasticism and highlight two important monks: Pachomius and John Cassian.

Life of Antony

Athanasius of Alexandria (ca. 296–373) is best known for his spirited defense of the Christian faith as determined at the Council of Nicaea in 325 against the heterodox Arians and expounded in his *On the Incarnation*. Another of Athanasius's well-known works is his *Life of Antony*, which was also written as a defense of Nicene orthodoxy.[2] The *Life of Antony* was an instant bestseller, being influential in the spread of monastic ideals. Its influence spread far

1. Richard Watson, ed., *A Biblical and Theological Dictionary: Explanatory of the History, Manners, and Customs of the Jews, and Neighbouring Nations* (New York: B. Waugh and T. Mason, 1832), 666. See also Charles Warren Currier, *History of Religious Orders* (Boston: MacConnell Brothers, 1896), 3–4.

2. James D. Ernest, "Athanasius of Alexandria: The Scope of Scripture in Polemical and Pastoral Context," *Vigiliae Christianae* 47 (1993): 341.

beyond its original Greek-speaking audience, and it was translated into Latin by Evagrius of Antioch (d. ca. 392) and also into Coptic.[3] It is regarded as one of the catalysts that finally brought Augustine of Hippo to the Christian faith.[4]

The original Greek version of the *Life* is divided into ninety-four chapters and spans the entire life of Antony (251–356), more than a hundred years. It is arranged in a series of withdrawals and returns or, to put it in spiritual terms, *exitus* and *reditus* (exit and return). Such withdrawal lies at the very heart of the English word "anchorite," which is derived from *anachōrēsis*, the Greek word for withdrawal. Not only does this signify a physical withdrawal into the wilderness/desert (though as we will see, this is a characteristic of Antony's life), but in the words of Bernard McGinn, this withdrawal "was first used to describe separation from ordinary social bonds and retreat into the self."[5] The purpose of this nonphysical, spiritual withdrawal was to attain single-mindedness, to be able to focus all of one's love on God so that one could then return to the world and love one's neighbor properly. It was understood in the *Life of Antony* that physical withdrawal served the purpose of creating the proper space for God to purify Antony's soul. Such a purified soul would then be clear-sighted to such an extent that it could see God rightly and desire only heavenly things: "The soul is overcome by a desire for divine and future realities, and it desires to be entirely united with these beings."[6]

Antony's life follows a threefold pattern of physical retreat into the deepest desert that corresponds to his ongoing spiritual and intellectual purification. Antony first retreats to an area of tombs outside Alexandria. He then moves farther out into the desert and away from the city when he settles in the "Outer Mountain." Finally, not finding complete peace in the Outer Mountain, he moves to the "Inner Mountain." Athanasius describes the transition as follows:

> Girding himself in this way, Antony went out to the tombs that were situated some distance from the village. He charged one of his friends to supply him periodically with bread, and he entered one of the tombs and remained alone within, his friend having closed the door on him.[7]

---

3. See Tim Vivian and Apostolos Athanassakis, trans., *The Life of Antony: The Coptic Life and the Greek Life* (Kalamazoo, MI: Cistercian Publications, 2003).

4. Augustine of Hippo, *Confessions* 8.6.15 and 8.12.29.

5. Bernard McGinn, "Withdrawal and Return: Reflections on Monastic Retreat from the World," *Spiritus: A Journal of Christian Spirituality* 6 (2006): 151.

6. Athanasius of Alexandria, *Life of Antony* 35; Robert C. Gregg, trans., *Athanasius: The Life of Antony and the Letter to Marcellinus* (New York: Paulist Press, 1980), 58.

7. Athanasius, *Life of Antony* 8; Gregg, *Athanasius*, 37.

Going out the next day from the tomb, he was even more enthusiastic in his devotion to God, and meeting the old man mentioned earlier, he asked him to live with him in the wilderness. But when he declined, both because of his advanced age and because such a practice was not yet customary, Antony set out immediately for the mountain. . . . When he discovered beyond the river a deserted fortress, empty so long that reptiles filled it, he went there, and took up residence in it.[8]

But when he saw that he was disturbed by many people and was not allowed to retire as he intended and wished, apprehensive that, because of the things the Lord was doing through him, either he might become prideful or someone else might think more of him than was warranted, he considered carefully and struck out, departing into the upper Thebaid, in the direction of people who did not know him.[9]

Antony's withdrawals, however, were not permanent, because he often left his cell to minister to other monks who surrounded him or to support the Egyptian Christian populace in their ongoing struggles against the pagans.

Nearly twenty years he spent in this manner pursuing the ascetic life by himself, not venturing out and only occasionally being seen by anyone. After this, when many possessed the desire and will to emulate his asceticism, and some of his friends came and tore down and forcefully removed the fortress door, Antony came forth as though from some shrine, having been led into mysteries and inspired by God. This was the first time he appeared from the fortress for those who came out to him.[10]

After this, the persecution that then occurred under Maximin oppressed the Church, and when the holy martyrs were led into Alexandria, he also left his cell and followed saying, "Let us go also, that we may enter the combat, or look upon those who do."[11]

In this way, Antony's life is characterized by a series of withdrawals and returns, providing the very definition and paradigm of a Christian monastic hermit who seeks single-mindedness.

Yet Antony's life is paradigmatic for monasticism in other ways. First, his life is one of prayer: "He prayed constantly, since he learned that it is necessary to pray unceasingly in private."[12] Second, he practiced rigorous asceticism: "He practiced the discipline with intensity. . . . More and more then he mortified the

8. Athanasius, *Life of Antony* 11–12; Gregg, *Athanasius*, 39–40.
9. Athanasius, *Life of Antony* 49; Gregg, *Athanasius*, 67.
10. Athanasius, *Life of Antony* 14; Gregg, *Athanasius*, 42–43.
11. Athanasius, *Life of Antony* 46; Gregg, *Athanasius*, 65–66.
12. Athanasius, *Life of Antony* 3; Gregg, *Athanasius*, 32.

body and kept it under subjection. . . . So he made plans to accustom himself to more stringent practices, and many marveled, and he bore the labor with ease."[13] Third, he fought with the devil and demons, defeating them as an athlete of Christ: "Antony remained and suffered no injury from the demons, and neither did he grow tired of the contest."[14] Finally, he worked in order to support those who were poor: "He worked with his hands, though, having heard that he who is idle, *let him not eat*. And he spent what he made partly for bread, and partly on those in need."[15] Again, Athanasius provides a paradigmatic picture of Antony as one who withdraws into his cell in order to live the true eremitical life. Yet this withdrawal is not permanent but temporary, as the saint comes out on more than one occasion to assist his fellow monks and other believers. Not only does this aspect of his life become exemplary, but so do many of Antony's actions, such as his prayer life, asceticism, fighting with demons, and supporting the poor. More than any other early Christian text, the *Life of Antony* establishes the categories for thinking about institutionalized eremitical monastic life. The *Sayings of the Desert Fathers*, however, describes and defines a psychology of the eremitical life.

Sayings of the Desert Fathers

The *Sayings of the Desert Fathers*, known in Latin as the *Apophthegmata Patrum*, is a collection of short, pithy statements made by monks (and nuns) that inhabited the Egyptian desert of the fourth century. The *Sayings* has come down to us in two forms. The Alphabetical Collection comprises approximately one thousand sayings under the names of 130 monks, arranged according to the Greek alphabet. This set also contains many anonymous sayings. The Systematic Collection is made up of twelve hundred sayings and stories under twenty-one headings, such as "discernment" and "humility." In time, many more sayings emerged in the various ancient languages of the areas where Christianity established itself, including Syriac, Coptic, Armenian, and Ethiopic. Despite its linguistic diversity, the *Sayings* encapsulates and disseminates a uniquely Egyptian monastic milieu, revealing to us today the spiritual essence of the landscape in which Antony (and, as we will see, Pachomius) established himself.[16] The sayings follow a predictable pattern of

13. Athanasius, *Life of Antony* 7; Gregg, *Athanasius*, 36.
14. Athanasius, *Life of Antony* 13; Gregg, *Athanasius*, 41.
15. Athanasius, *Life of Antony* 3; Gregg, *Athanasius*, 32.
16. William Harmless, *Desert Christians: An Introduction to the Literature of Early Monasticism* (Oxford: Oxford University Press, 2004), 170–71.

one monk asking another monk for a "word," that is, for advice on how to live the monastic life and ultimately find salvation: "Father, give me a word." These sayings work together to demonstrate to the reader three aspects of desert monasticism. First, the word given by the father is not meant for all persons at all times but was meant for the monk who came to ask for the word at that time. There is specificity to each saying. Second, since the word given was meant for a particular monk at a particular time, it demonstrates the astute discernment present in the monk giving the word. Third, the effectiveness of the word depended on the obedience of the monk receiving it. If a monk did not heed a word, then it was an ineffectual word. This did not reflect badly on the monk who gave it but on the receiver of the word who failed to heed it.[17] This explains why oftentimes, though not always, it is a younger monk asking an older monk for advice. This follows the age-old monastic pattern of senior monks possessing a wisdom that is lacking in the younger monks; therefore, they are in the best position to help their younger confreres. Just as the *Life of Antony* depicts a paradigmatic form of institutional eremitical life, so too does the *Sayings*, albeit a paradigmatic spirituality of the eremitical life.

One of the foundational vices that the desert fathers sought to avoid and gain victory over was anger. The great desert ascetic and theologian Evagrius of Pontus (d. 399) explains that the "demon of anger . . . causes mutilations in the course of afflictions and attacks the soul especially and prepares the ground for the spirit of acedia [sloth] so that they may (both) darken the soul and at the same time gather up its ascetic labours."[18] For Evagrius, anger can both ruin the monk's ability to engage in ascetic activity and perturb the monk's soul so that he is unable to direct his thoughts to God. In this sense, anger is a root spiritual problem. Many early Christian writers identified two major sources as constitutive of the human personality: one was a source of desire and attraction, and the other was a source of resistance and repulsion. The vice arising from the former was lust and from the latter was anger. Lust was controlled by love for God and neighbor, whereas anger was controlled by resistance to sin and struggle against temptation.[19] In the *Sayings* the desert fathers speak often of anger, painting a vivid picture of this vice. For example,

---

17. Ibid., 172–73.

18. Evagrius of Pontus, *Eulogios* 6.6; Robert E. Sinkewicz, trans., *Evagrius of Pontus: The Greek Ascetic Corpus* (Oxford: Oxford University Press, 2003), 33. On Evagrius, see Greg Peters, "Evagrius of Pontus (c. 346–399)," in *Zondervan Dictionary of Christian Spirituality*, ed. Glen G. Scorgie (Grand Rapids: Zondervan, 2011), 434–35.

19. Columba Stewart, "Introduction," in *Purity of Heart in Early Ascetic and Monastic Literature: Essays in Honor of Juana Raasch, O.S.B.*, ed. Harriet A. Luckman and Linda Kulzer (Collegeville, MN: Liturgical Press, 1999), 13.

Abba Agathon speaks frankly when he says, "A man who is angry, even if he were to raise the dead, is not acceptable to God."[20] The proper response to anger is to flee from it. The desert father known as John the Dwarf recalls how he once encountered a camel driver who made him angry, so he did the only thing open to him—he dropped everything and "took to flight."[21] Abba Nilus went so far as to define prayer as the absence of anger,[22] and for Abba Poemen one of the defining characteristics of a monk is that he is not angry.[23] For the desert fathers anger was an issue of self-mastery; the monk who was angry gave evidence of his lack of self-control, which manifested itself in either verbal slights or pejorative physical actions: "When someone wishes to render evil for evil, he can injure his brother's soul even by a single nod of the head."[24] Such a lack of self-control would then lead one into other sins and was a sign to a monk and to his spiritual father that he was spiritually unhealthy. Anger was a sin to be avoided if one wanted to be a true monk. As William Harmless reminds us, "Modern readers often imagine that for monks, sexuality posed *the* great struggle. But ancient sources indicated otherwise. Anger, not sex, figured more prominently. The challenge was human relations."[25] Anger was always a real threat to an eremitical monk's single-minded pursuit of God.

In the literature of the desert, when one sinned one often wept, for weeping was an outward sign of inner sorrow. A theology of tears or grief (Gk. *penthos*) comes out of the desert literature and is a common theme among the desert fathers.[26] Across the literature *penthos* is seen as a godly sorrow, produced by compunction for one's sins. It is tied closely to Jesus's words, "Blessed are those who mourn, for they shall be comforted" (Matt. 5:4).[27] Perhaps the best picture of proper compunction (contrition, remorse) in the life of a monk is found in a saying of Abba Poemen: "Going into Egypt one day, Abba Poemen saw a woman who was sitting in a tomb and weeping bitterly. He said, 'If all the delights of the world were to come, they could not drive sorrow away from the soul of this woman. [Likewise] the monk would always have compunction

---

20. *Apophthegmata Patrum*, Alphabetical Collection, Agathon 20; Benedicta Ward, trans., *The Sayings of the Desert Fathers: The Alphabetical Collection* (Kalamazoo, MI: Cistercian Publications, 1975), 23. The title "Abba" means "father" in Aramaic and was applied to Jesus in the New Testament. Desert women were known as "Ammas," which means "mothers."

21. *Apophthegmata Patrum*, John the Dwarf 5; Ward, *Sayings of the Desert Fathers*, 86.

22. *Apophthegmata Patrum*, Nilus 2; Ward, *Sayings of the Desert Fathers*, 153.

23. *Apophthegmata Patrum*, Poemen 91; Ward, *Sayings of the Desert Fathers*, 179.

24. *Apophthegmata Patrum*, Alphabetical Collection, Isaiah 8; Ward, *Sayings of the Desert Fathers*, 70.

25. Harmless, *Desert Christians*, 236, emphasis in original.

26. See Irénée Hausherr, *Penthos: The Doctine of Compunction in the Christian East* (Kalamazoo, MI: Cistercian Publication, 1982).

27. The Greek word for "those who mourn" is *penthountes*.

in himself.'"[28] Monks are expected to be sorrowful people. Keep in mind that this sorrow is not a kind of depression but rather a proper response to one's sins. *Penthos* is not a psychologically unhealthy state; it is a spiritual disposition expected of all monks: "If a man does not mortify all his carnal desires and acquire compunction . . . he cannot become a monk."[29] Such a state of compunction was often accompanied by tears, a sign that a monk was truly sorrowful not only for his actual sins but also for his sinfulness. In particular, older and wiser monks knew to be sorrowful about their sinfulness:

> In his cell [Dioscorus] wept over himself, while his disciple was sitting in another cell. When the latter came to see the old man he asked him, "Father, why are you weeping?" "I am weeping over my sins," the old man answered him. Then his disciple said, "You do not have any sins, Father." The old man replied, "Truly, my child, if I were allowed to see my sins, three or four men would not be enough to weep for them."[30]

Such sorrow was a sign of a monk's dying to self while growing in his understanding of what it meant to be single-minded before God. These tears were the sign of a monk coming to the end of his own self-will and beginning to live under God's will. Tears are an indicator that a monk has fled the world: "'Flee from men,' Abba Isaiah said to him. 'What does it mean to flee from men?' The old man said, 'It means to sit in your cell and weep for your sins.'"[31] In the end, compunction was so valued by these desert fathers that it was virtually a synonym for the whole ascetic Christian life. Contrition was the goal and weeping was the means of achieving the goal.

In both the *Life of Antony* by Athanasius and the *Sayings of the Desert Fathers* we see that the eremitical life was one of withdrawal into one's cell (both real and figurative) for the purpose of returning to the world to give guidance and direction to those seeking it. In their cells these desert monks spent time in ascetical activity in order to overcome vices (especially anger) and sins, primarily through weeping and compunction. Yet the eremitical life was not the only kind of monastic life practiced in the Egyptian wilderness; it was eclipsed by monks living in communities.

28. *Apophthegmata Patrum*, Alphabetical Collection, Poemen 26; Ward, *Sayings of the Desert Fathers*, 171.

29. *Apophthegmata Patrum*, Alphabetical Collection, Poemen 71; Ward, *Sayings of the Desert Fathers*, 177.

30. *Apophthegmata Patrum*, Alphabetical Collection, Dioscorus 2; Ward, *Sayings of the Desert Fathers*, 55.

31. *Apophthegmata Patrum*, Alphabetical Collection, Macarius the Great 27; Ward, *Sayings of the Desert Fathers*, 133.

Communal Monasticism of Pachomius and John Cassian

Though cenobitic (communal) monasticism was not unheard of before Pachomius, it was forever changed after Pachomius. The size of the communities associated with Pachomius was truly phenomenal; there were so many monks living in the desert that it came to be seen as a city.[32] Palladius of Galatia (d. ca. 420s), in his *Lausiac History*, writes:

> Now I spent three years in the monasteries in the neighborhood of Alexandria with their some two thousand most noble and zealous inhabitants. Then I left and crossed over to Mount Nitria. Between this mountain and Alexandria there lies a lake called Marea seventy miles long. I was a day and a half crossing this to the mountain on its southern shore. Beyond the mountain stretches the Great Desert reaching as far as Ethiopia, Mazicae, and Mauretania. On the mountain live close to five thousand men following different ways of life, each as he can or will. Thus some live alone, others in pairs, and some in groups. There are seven bakeries on this mountain serving these men as well as the hermits in the Great Desert, six hundred in all.[33]

Pachomius (d. ca. 346) was an Egyptian convert to the Christian faith and is often credited as the founder of Christian cenobitic monasticism. Just as Antony's appellation as the founder of monasticism qua monasticism is incorrect, so is Pachomius's as the founder of cenobitism. Though Pachomius did not found Christian cenobitism, his mark on the institution is indelible. While serving in the military, Pachomius was ministered to by a group of Christians whose charity deeply affected him. When he left military service in 313, he returned to his village and received baptism, taking up the ascetical life under a local hermit. According to Pachomius's biography, *First Greek Life*, Pachomius one day traveled to Tabennesi, where he heard a voice telling him, "Stay here and build a monastery; for many will come to you to become monks."[34] Pachomius, though certain that this voice was from God, did not immediately begin to build the monastery. Soon thereafter an angel appeared to him while he prayed, saying, "The will of God is to minister to the race of men in order to reconcile them to himself."[35] Hearing this three times Pachomius was moved to accept his first disciples, testing their renunciation of the world,

---

32. See Athanasius, *Life of Antony* 14; Gregg, *Athanasius*, 42–43: "There were monasteries in the mountains and the desert was made a city by monks."

33. Palladius, *Lausiac History* 7.1–2; Robert T. Meyer, trans., *Palladius: The Lausiac History* (Westminster, MD: Newman Press, 1965), 40.

34. *First Greek Life* 12; Armand Veilleux, trans., *Pachomian Koinonia*, vol. 1, *The Life of Saint Pachomius and His Disciples* (Kalamazoo, MI: Cistercian Publications, 1980), 305.

35. *First Greek Life* 23; Veilleux, *Pachomian Koinonia*, 1:311–12.

their parents, and themselves before clothing them in the monastic habit. Now that they were living a properly cenobitic life, Pachomius developed a rule and a structure for his monastery, inspired by his military service.[36] He was soon joined by other men and women, so he built a women's monastery in a nearby village, having them observe the same rule as the men's community. In time the communities grew so much that Palladius writes:

> There were some monasteries which abided by this rule [of Pachomius] and they totaled seven thousand men. First of all there was the great monastery where Pachomius himself lived. This is the mother of all the other monasteries, having thirteen hundred men. . . . There are other monasteries, too, housing from two to three hundred persons each. I visited one of these when I went to Panapolis, a place of about three hundred monks. . . . In addition to these there was also a monastery of some four hundred women.[37]

John Cassian (who will be discussed below) also records the large number of Pachomian monastics: "Their cenobium in the Thebaid is more populous than all others inasmuch as it is stricter in its rigorous way of life, for in it more than five thousand brothers are ruled by a single abba, and this huge number of monks is subject at every moment to their elder."[38] Despite these large numbers, Pachomius's foundations, like the eremitical monks, existed for one purpose: single-minded devotion to God.

The clearest way that this single-mindedness manifested itself in Pachomian foundations was in regulations for meditation and prayer. In Pachomius's communities the monks were expected to recite memorized biblical texts, a process called *meletē* (study or exercise) in Greek. In Latin translations of this practice, the word *meditatio* (meditation) is used. This was not just a mindful recitation but was often done aloud in order "to create an atmosphere conducive to prayer."[39] Once the trumpet was sounded to call all the monks to community prayer, each Pachomian monk was to "leave his cell, reciting something from the Scriptures until he reached the door of the *synaxis* [liturgical gathering]."[40] Once the communal prayer was ended, the monk was to recite something from the Scriptures while either going back to his cell or

36. For a complete study of Pachomius's rule, see Terrence G. Kardong, *Pillars of Community: Four Rules of Pre-Benedictine Monastic Life* (Collegeville, MN: Liturgical Press, 2010), 87–146.
37. Palladius, *Lausiac History* 32.8–9 and 33.1; Meyer, *Palladius*, 94–95.
38. John Cassian, *Institutes* 4.1; Boniface Ramsey, trans., *John Cassian: The Institutes* (New York: Newman Press, 2000), 79.
39. Columba Stewart, *Cassian the Monk* (New York: Oxford University Press, 1998), 102.
40. Pachomius, *Precepts* 3; Armand Veilleux, trans., *Pachomian Koinonia*, vol. 2, *Pachomian Chronicles and Rules* (Kalamazoo, MI: Cistercian Publications, 1981), 145.

to the refectory (dining room).[41] Pachomius's monks were also expected to recite Scripture while working and fulfilling community responsibilities.[42] At liturgical gatherings soloists recited psalms while the other monks listened.[43] Men who arrived at the monastery uninstructed in monastic life were first taught what they must observe and were then expected to memorize "twenty psalms or two of the Apostle's epistles, or some other part of the Scripture."[44] Pachomius goes so far as to say, "There shall be no one whatever in the monastery who does not learn to read and does not memorize something of the Scriptures. [One should learn by heart] at least the New Testament and the Psalter."[45] All of this memorization and recitation was for the purpose of meditation. The monks heard and committed Scripture to memory for the purpose of meditating on it continually: "Let us devote ourselves to reading and learning the Scriptures, reciting them continually."[46] Such continual meditation on God's word was a complement to the communal prayer practiced in Pachomius's communities and allowed each monk to center his mind on God and the work of prayer. Meditating while working or engaging in normal daily activity—such as walking to and from the prayer room—was also a way for the Pachomian monk (or nun) to keep his mind and heart focused on God. Single-minded devotion to God was the result of intentionality and a thoughtfully constructed monastic regimen.

Pachomius legislated that his monks and nuns had to be present at or perform the communal liturgy no matter the situation: "No one shall find pretexts for himself for not going to the *synaxis*, the psalmody, and the prayer. One shall not neglect the times of prayer and psalmody, whether he is on a boat, in the monastery, in the fields, or on a journey, or fulfilling any service whatever."[47] In the so-called *Regulations of Horsiesius*, one of Pachomius's successors as head of the federation of monasteries describes in detail the liturgical horarium (liturgy of the hours) of the community: (1) the signal is given for prayer; (2) another signal is given to kneel; (3) the monk makes the sign of the cross before kneeling; (4) while lying prostrate the monk weeps in his heart for his sins; (5) all rise and make the sign of the cross again; (6) all say the "prayer of the Gospel"; (7) "Lord, instill your fear into our hearts that we may labor for eternal life and hold you in fear" is said; (8) each monk,

41. Pachomius, *Precepts* 28; Veilleux, *Pachomian Koinonia*, 2:150.

42. Pachomius, *Precepts* 36–37, 59–60, and 116; Veilleux, *Pachomian Koinonia*, 2:151, 156, and 163.

43. Pachomius, *Precepts* 6, 13, and 16–17; Veilleux, *Pachomian Koinonia*, 2:146–48.

44. Pachomius, *Precepts* 139; Veilleux, *Pachomian Koinonia*, 2:166.

45. Pachomius, *Precepts* 140; Veilleux, *Pachomian Koinonia*, 2:166.

46. Horsiesius, *Testament of Horsiesius* 51; Stewart, *Cassian the Monk*, 103.

47. Pachomius, *Precepts* 141–42; Veilleux, *Pachomian Koinonia*, 2:166.

in his heart, says prayers for purification; (9) a signal is given to be seated; (10) everyone signs themselves on the forehead with the sign of the cross; (11) all sit; (12) the Scriptures are recited; and (13) all are dismissed, reciting additional Scriptures to themselves until they reach their cells.[48] Because of the cenobitic nature of these communities the morning and evening offices were held in common by the community, whereas the all-night vigil mentioned in the Pachomian literature, lasting from just after the evening office to the morning office, was done individually as a private devotion. During the community liturgy the monks who were not appointed to read, when they were seated, continued the practice of weaving rushes together to make mats and baskets that were sold to the local populace to help support the monastery.[49] Again, all of this was intended to ensure that the monks and nuns were focusing on God alone, being single-minded in their attention and practice.

Thus far we have seen how the monastic literature of early Egyptian monasticism (the *Life of Antony* by Athanasius, the *Sayings of the Desert Fathers*, and the Pachomian literature) concerns itself with both the institutional nature of eremitical and cenobitic monasticism and also with a spirituality of the desert. Not only did these texts exert a great influence in their original contexts, but they also came to exercise a great influence over Western monasticism, chiefly through translations and especially through the writings of John Cassian (d. ca. 432).

Cassian was originally a monk in Bethlehem who then traveled throughout Egypt, living in some of the most important Egyptian monasteries and learning monastic theology from the monks of the desert. He explicates the monastic spirituality he learned in two Latin works: *The Conferences* and *The Institutes*. These works were written many years after Cassian had moved from Egypt to Gaul (modern-day France), where he founded two monasteries, one for men and one for women. The purpose of *The Institutes*, which consists of twelve books, is to assist monks in overcoming the eight principal vices. The first four books discuss monastic clothing, the canonical hours of prayer, and the virtues. The remaining eight books each discuss one of the principal vices: gluttony, fornication, avarice, anger, sadness, acedia (sloth), vainglory, and pride. *The Conferences*, in twenty-four books, supposedly details the monastic theology of fifteen Egyptian monks whose talks with Cassian and his friend Germanus were recorded for the benefit of others. In

---

48. Horsiesius, *Regulations of Horsiesius* 8–10; Veilleux, *Pachomian Koinonia*, 2:199–200.
49. Pachomius, *Precepts* 4; Veilleux, *Pachomian Koinonia*, 2:145. See Armand Veilleux, "Prayer in the Pachomian Koinōnia," in *The Continuing Quest for God: Monastic Spirituality in Tradition and Transition*, ed. William Skudlarek (Collegeville, MN: Liturgical Press, 1982), 61–66.

truth, Cassian does not really record the actual words of these desert monks as much as he presents his own spiritual theology as the monks' teaching, thereby validating his own theology. In the work Cassian constructs a unified spirituality in which the monk's *telos* (final end) is the kingdom of God (or beatitude; supreme blessedness) and his *scopos* (this-worldly end) is purity of heart, a Cassianic way of speaking about monastic perfection, including single-mindedness. The virtue of humility allows a monk to discern between that which is truly good and that which is a lesser good; such discretion leads ultimately to purity of heart. Purity of heart prepares the monk teleologically for the fullness of God's kingdom, but it also makes contemplation of God in the present life possible. For Cassian, purity of heart grows over the course of one's life, consisting of differing degrees that have three main characteristics: ascetical practice, growth in love, and tranquility of heart.[50]

Jesus said, "Blessed are the pure in heart, for they shall see God" (Matt. 5:8). With this as inspiration, Cassian took the monastic theology he learned in the Egyptian desert and developed a robust theology of the spiritual life that would, by virtue of being written in Latin, become foundational to the Western monastic tradition. Cassian's own monastic career had him living at various times in cenobitic monasteries and as an anchorite, so he was familiar with both forms of life and saw both as conducive to and supportive of the monastic pursuit of *apatheia*, or passionlessness. Though *apatheia* was originally a Greek philosophical concept, it had been baptized in the desert by Evagrius of Pontus, Cassian's greatest influence. Columba Stewart writes that Evagrius's *apatheia* is Cassian's purity of heart.[51] Yet the phrase "purity of heart" is a generic and inclusive concept for monastic perfection that "embraces Cassian's many other metaphors of perfection such as 'tranquility,' 'contemplation,' 'unceasing prayer,' 'chastity,' and 'spiritual knowledge.'"[52] I would also suggest that it includes within it the monastic concept of single-mindedness, and this is supported by Cassian's own use of the term in the first of the *Conferences*: "[In the world to come] everyone will pass over from this multiform or practical activity to the contemplation of divine things in perpetual purity of heart. Those whose concern it is to press on to knowledge and to the purification of their mind have chosen, even while living in the present world, to give themselves to this objective with all their power and strength."[53] Notice the word

---

50. See Greg Peters, "Cassian, John (c. 360–432)," in Scorgie, *Zondervan Dictionary of Christian Spirituality*, 339–40.

51. Stewart, *Cassian the Monk*, 12 and 28.

52. Ibid., 42.

53. John Cassian, *Conferences* 1.10.5; Boniface Ramsey, trans., *John Cassian: The Conferences* (New York: Paulist Press, 1997), 49.

"multiform" and the phrase "with all their power and strength." In the first stages of spiritual growth, human activity is "multiform," not single-minded, but that will not be the case forever. The monk or nun is able to move past this multitude of activity and engage in contemplation of God. The "all" suggests single-mindedness, giving one's all for a particular *telos*, which, in the case of Cassian, is purity of heart. Purity of heart spilled over into all areas of the monastic life, or, to say it differently, all areas of the monastic life had purity of heart as their earthly end (*scopos*). One controlled anger by way of the heart: "Our heart, therefore, should be enlarged and expanded, lest by being confined within the narrow limits of faintheartedness it be completely filled with the turbulent emotions of wrath."[54] One's heart is most apt to be enlarged when it is moving toward greater purity. An aid to this end is ascetical purification:

> By way of this goal I forget what is behind—namely, the vices of my earlier life— and I strive to attain to the end, which is the heavenly prize. Whatever therefore can direct us to this scopos, which is *purity of heart*, is to be pursued with all our strength, but whatever deters us from this is to be avoided as dangerous and harmful. For it is for its sake that we do and endure everything, for its sake that family, homeland, honors, wealth, the pleasures of this world, and every enjoy- ment are disdained—so that perpetual *purity of heart* may be kept. . . . For the sake of this, then, everything is to be done and desired. For its sake solitude is to be pursued; for its sake we know that we must undertake fasts, vigils, labors, bodily deprivation, readings, and other virtuous things, so that by them we may be able to acquire and keep a heart untouched by any harmful passion.[55]

Thus Cassian brings us full circle, coming back to the types of helpful ascetical activities that we witnessed in the life of Antony. By developing a system of monastic theology, Cassian bequeaths the spirituality of Antony, the desert fathers and mothers, and Pachomius to future generations, perennially connecting all of monastic history to the great flourishing of monasticism in the fourth-century deserts of Egypt.

Ressourcement: Movements of Single-Mindedness on God

At the very essence of monastic life is the concept of withdrawal and return. Early Christian monks fled to the desert for the purpose of returning to the world in order to help others achieve love of God and of neighbor. It was not

---

54. Cassian, *Conferences* 16.27.5; Ramsey, *John Cassian: The Conferences*, 575.
55. Cassian, *Conferences* 1.5.3–1.7.1; Ramsey, *John Cassian: The Conferences*, 44–45, em- phasis added.

a flight from the world based on a dualistic understanding of the flesh being opposed to the spirit. Rather, the desert served as the school in which Antony, Pachomius, and others learned how to cultivate the virtues by living alone or in community, giving themselves over to prayer, discipleship, and the ascetical pursuit of the kingdom of heaven. What these monks and nuns sought (and obtained on occasion) was an environment that gave them the opportunity and privilege of pursuing God in a less distracted manner, an environment conducive to a single-minded pursuit of God. Just as Jesus frequently retreated to isolated places to pray, so too have monastics throughout the centuries. If Jesus's example is not sufficient for twenty-first-century Christians to emulate, then the examples of monks and nuns of the earliest centuries provide additional models. In this regard, not only should we be Christlike, but we should also be monastic-like.

As seen earlier, there will always be individuals called to live celibately in today's church, and there will also be those who are called to live a lifestyle that runs against the grain of contemporary culture. Just as early monks sought out the deserts of the ancient Christian world, there are dedicated Christians today who will seek out the "desert" amid the hustle and bustle of twenty-first-century society. Such a *fuga mundi* (flight from the world) is not always religiously motivated, nor is it always done in pursuit of God (e.g., think of those who are anti-government and therefore live "off the grid" simply to buck the system and to prove that normal societal structures are unnecessary). But those who desire to live in this manner for God's sake should be given the space to do so, primarily if their motivation is to live less-distracted lives so that they can focus more attention on the adoration and worship of God.

Yet for those who do not choose such a radical countercultural lifestyle, the church should provide this experience for them. The New Testament church was countercultural, as evidenced throughout the biblical record (e.g., Rom. 12:2). Unfortunately, this countercultural posture has not always been maintained over the past two millennia. The Middle Ages are notorious for the involvement of priests and bishops in secular politics and for the influence of kings and emperors on the life of the church. Similarly, the papacy reached its spiritual nadir under the Renaissance-era Pope Alexander VI (d. 1503), whose dissolute lifestyle is notorious. Today it seems that cultural trappings present themselves in more benign ways in the life of the church, but they are there nonetheless. Worship preferences aside, it would not be difficult to argue that much of today's worship (at least in American evangelical churches) is motivated primarily by what is popular in secular entertainment—rock concert-like music and TED Talk-esque sermons. These may not be bad in and of themselves, but they are certainly not countercultural.

No matter its missional strategy, the Christian church must remain a countercultural institution, giving its members opportunity to experience God less distractedly and, therefore, more single-mindedly. It would be foolish to think that the "world" does not interfere in the Christian's worship of God. This is *not* because matter is bad but because with worldly responsibility comes reduced amounts of time and energy that can be used to cultivate one's relationship with God. The apostle Paul understood this well in relation to marriage when he writes, "I want you to be free from anxieties. The unmarried man is anxious about the things of the Lord, how to please the Lord. But the married man is anxious about worldly things, how to please his wife, and his interests are divided" (1 Cor. 7:32–34a). Paul was not against marriage (see 1 Cor. 7:28), but he knew that with marriage came responsibilities that would hinder one's service to God.

Thus the church should provide each believer with an opportunity to flee the world, even if only for a short time. The church must give its members an opportunity to focus single-mindedly on God, and it can do that, in part, by standing over against the culture, creating the necessary mental and spiritual space for focused attention on God. Not only can each church service provide this opportunity, but churches should also make use of well-planned retreats and retreat houses, which provide even longer-term opportunities for living counterculturally and less distractedly. In short, all believers need an occasional flight to the "desert" to focus more intently on God, and the church can provide this space if it so chooses, but it must do so in a way that is countercultural so as to create a single-minded devotion to God. Such a flight empowers the Christian for her return to the world in faithful service. In the words of the Book of Common Prayer, prayed after Communion and just before the dismissal:

> *Eternal God, heavenly Father,*
> *you have graciously accepted us as living members*
> *of our Son our Savior Jesus Christ,*
> *and you have fed us with spiritual food*
> *in the Sacrament of his Body and Blood.*
> *Send us now into the world in peace,*
> *and grant us strength and courage*
> *to love and serve you*
> *with gladness and singleness of heart;*
> *through Christ our Lord. Amen.*

Worship in word and sacrament empowers believers for faithful loving and serving with joy and single-mindedness.

3

The Rule

I n 312 CE Emperor Constantine the Great entered the city of Rome as the sole ruler of the Roman Empire. His ascendency was not without bloodshed—both "pagan" and Roman—nor was it without God's assistance, at least in the eyes of Constantine. Upon the death of Constantius in 306, Constantine was proclaimed emperor of Spain and Gaul in York. Not convinced that he should share imperial power with his rivals, Constantine marched to Rome and defeated Maxentius, emperor of Africa and Italy, at the so-called Battle of the Milvian Bridge. As he prepared to fight Maxentius, Constantine saw a vision in the sky of a cross inscribed with the Latin words *In hoc signo vinces* ("In this sign you will conquer"). This vision prompted Constantine to promise that he would convert to the Christian faith if he was successful in battle. He was, of course, successful in battle, so not only did he convert, but he also legalized the practice of worshiping the Christian God.[1] With this change of fortune for the Christian church, it was possible to erect permanent structures and to create the kinds of institutions that had not been possible, or at least had been more difficult, in the preceding centuries. One of those

1. There is ongoing debate about the extent or validity of Constantine's conversion in 312. Given our distance from the event and the biases of the extant documents, it will likely never be known for certain how thorough Constantine's conversion was. What is known for sure is that Constantine's legalization of Christianity made it possible for Christians to move into the public square in ways that had previously been impossible. Though all persecution of Christians did not cease with Constantine's conversion, it made such persecution rarer and kept it more localized.

institutions that could flourish in the Western portion of the empire was cenobitic monasticism. In order for cenobitic monasteries to fully develop, they
needed a rule of life, just like that given by Pachomius to his monks in Egypt.
Thus beginning in the fourth century and continuing for several centuries,
a flurry of original monastic rules were written for a range of communities
by a diverse group of men.[2] This chapter will examine the development of
monastic rules in cenobitic monasteries, exploring the idea of a monastic
rule and its place in communal life. The rules of Basil of Caesarea, Augustine
of Hippo, and "the Master" will be investigated for their institutional, legal
legislation along with their spiritual emphases. Other lesser-known rules will
be given brief attention.

Rule of Basil

Basil of Caesarea (d. 379) is one of the most significant and important early
Christian authors, indefatigably defending the Nicene Creed and uphold-
ing orthodox Christianity. As one of the Cappadocian fathers (along with
his biological brother, Gregory of Nyssa [d. 395], and friend Gregory of
Nazianzus [d. 389]), Basil helped to firmly establish Nicene Christianity,
and by way of his ascetical writings, he solidified the presence of cenobitic
monasticism throughout Asia Minor (modern-day Turkey). Basil's ascetical texts evolved in three stages. The *Morals* were written when Basil lived
as a solitary across the river from his sister Macrina in 359–360. The work
is a collection of quotations from the New Testament that seems to speak
about monastic practices and is divided into eighty topics.[3] The *Asceticon*
is known in two versions. The first was written before 370 and is known as
the *Small Asceticon*, composed of 203 questions. This version has not survived in Greek, but a translation into Latin survives. The *Great Asceticon*,
written after 370, survives in Greek and includes 313 "Short Rules" and 55
"Long Rules."[4] While the majority of the questions in the *Small Asceticon*
are repeated in the "Short Rules" of the *Great Asceticon*, the "Long Rules"
include much new material (although there is still overlap between it and

2. Though there are extant rules for women's communities, these were written by men. See
Lazare de Seilhac and M. Bernard Saïd, trans., *Règles monastiques au feminine* (Bégrolles-en-
Mauges: Abbaye de Bellefontaine, 1996).

3. Monica Wagner, trans., *Saint Basil: Ascetical Works* (Washington, DC: Catholic University
of America Press, 1950), 71–205.

4. For a translation and study of the *Asceticon*, see Anna M. Silvas, *The Asketikon of St.
Basil the Great* (Oxford: Oxford University Press, 2005). An older translation is found in W. K. L.
Clarke, trans., *The Ascetic Works of Saint Basil* (London: SPCK, 1925), 145–351.

the *Small Asceticon*), showing that Basil's work grew along with his own intellectual and monastic growth over time. Given that the "Long Rules" are Basil's most mature statement on monasticism, they allow us to discern Basil's full vision for the monastic life. As well, they have an unmistakable organization, with sections ordered as follows:

Prologue–§7	How to Love God and Neighbor
§8–§15	Renunciation
§16–§23	Asceticism/Mastery of the Appetites
§24–§36	Order in Community
§37–§42	Work
§43–§54	Duties/Conduct of the Superior
§55	Medicine

There are a number of themes in Basil's ascetical works, including motivations for becoming a monastic (love of God and neighbor), separation from the world, how to live in community, and how to engage in ascetic activity, including prayer. In the *Morals* the motivation given for entering the monastic life is to perform penance for sins. The tone in the *Morals* is quite severe, but in the *Asceticon* love of neighbor comes to the fore. Basil also changes his perspective on the renunciation of property between the *Small Asceticon* and the *Great Asceticon*. In the former a monk may administer his own property, but in the latter one's property must be managed by either the community's superior or the monk's family. This is connected to another of Basil's themes, that of separation from the world. Though Basil himself lived for a brief time as a solitary after traveling to Palestine, Egypt, Syria, and Mesopotamia to study the ascetic life, he was mostly convinced that the cenobitic life was ideal. Thus in both sets of rules Basil still advocates for withdrawal, but a withdrawal into community to serve others: "For here is a kind of stadium for the contest, a good course on which to advance, a continual training, and a practising [*sic*] of the Lord's commandments—this is *the dwelling together of brothers in unity*."[5] Having witnessed extreme forms of asceticism when traveling, Basil's legislation concerning asceticism is quite moderate. For example, "Both fasting and eating must be used in the way proper to piety; so that when we ought to be fulfilling God's commandment through fasting, we fast, and again when the commandment of God requires food to strengthen

5. Basil of Caesarea, "The Long Rules" 7; Silvas, *Asketikon of St. Basil*, 186, emphasis in original.

the body, we eat, not as gluttons, but as God's workers."[6] Such balance must also be practiced in clothing, which should be simple yet distinctive for monks and nuns, who ought to be recognized by their dress.[7] Finally, members of Basil's community were to engage in work. His lengthy explanation describes which kinds of work are appropriate for monks and is centered on one common principle: "One may recommend the choice of such arts as preserve the peaceable and untroubled nature of our life, needing neither much trouble to get the requisite material, nor much anxiety to sell what has been made, and which do not involve us in undesirable or harmful meetings with men or women."[8] From this brief survey we can see that Basil's rules concerned themselves with the main issues of the monastic life; we see a similar focus in other early monastic rules.

Rule of Augustine

The so-called *Rule* of Augustine has one of the most interesting histories of any early Christian document, which seems appropriate given that Augustine of Hippo (d. 430) has one of the most dynamic conversion stories in all of Christian history.[9] Following his conversion, Augustine returned to his hometown of Thagaste in North Africa (modern-day Algeria), setting up a monastery there in 388. Three years later he was ordained to the priesthood and set up a second monastery in Hippo. Sometime around 397 he wrote his *Rule*, but this is not the form of his rule that we have today. What is now known as the *Rule* is a document comprised of nine early documents—eight legislative texts and one letter.[10] Of these nine documents, four are addressed to men and five are addressed to women; however, there is considerable overlap and borrowing. Thus in the end there are really only three texts that make up the *Rule* of Augustine: the "Regulations for a Monastery," the "Rule" (*Praeceptum*) or the "Rule for Nuns" (*Regularis informatio*), and the "Reprimand to Quarrelling Nuns."[11] Collectively, these texts are known as the *Rule* of Augustine.

6. Basil of Caesarea, "The Short Rules" 139; Silvas, *Asketikon of St. Basil*, 348.

7. See Basil, "Long Rules" 22.

8. Basil, "Long Rules" 38; Clarke, *Ascetic Works of Saint Basil*, 210.

9. Augustine's early life and circuitous path to conversion are recounted in his *Confessions*, a theological and spiritual classic. See Henry Chadwick, trans., *Saint Augustine: Confessions* (Oxford: Oxford University Press, 1991).

10. For a list of the documents, see George Lawless, *Augustine of Hippo and His Monastic Rule* (Oxford: Clarendon, 1987), 65.

11. The "Rule" (written for men) and the "Rule for Nuns" are so closely related that one is certainly a transcription of the other, though scholars are uncertain which one came first. In his translation of the texts, Lawless translates both.

Augustine begins each text by stating the correct motivation for undertaking the monastic life:

Love God above all else, dearest brothers, then your neighbour also.[12]

The chief motivation for your sharing life together is to live harmoniously in the house and to have one heart and one soul seeking God.[13]

The more than generous grace of God . . . enables you . . . to choose "living together in harmony under the same roof," so as to have "one heart and one soul seeking God."[14]

Augustine's main inspiration for his motivation to monastic life comes directly from the practice of the earliest Christians: "Now the full number of those who believed were of one heart and soul, and no one said that any of the things that belonged to him was his own, but they had everything in common" (Acts 4:32). Using this basic biblical teaching as the foundation of his *Rule*, Augustine continues by expanding on this first principle. His *Rule* is not as detailed regarding the legislation of the monastery as the *Asceticon* of Basil or, as we will see, the *Rule of the Master*. Augustine's *Rule* tends to stick to the basics. He goes on to say that monks and nuns should pray (the standard) seven times a day and that they should engage silently in meaningful work but also be given "leisure for reading."[15] Again echoing Acts 4:32, the monastery's residents are forbidden from owning private property, and they are commanded to have all things in common.[16] The superior is to be obeyed with fidelity. While eating, the monks and nuns are to remain silent and listen to the reading of holy texts. When necessity dictates that they leave the monastery, they are to go out in groups of two, eating or drinking nothing without permission. If they are conducting monastery business, they are to do so "conscientiously and faithfully, as servants of God."[17]

The ascetical teaching of Augustine is set out best in the "Rule": "To the extent that your health allows, subdue your flesh by fasting and abstinence from food and drink. . . . Do not allow your clothing to attract attention; seek

12. Augustine of Hippo, "Regulations for a Monastery" 1; Lawless, *Augustine of Hippo*, 75.
13. Augustine of Hippo, "Rule" 2; Lawless, *Augustine of Hippo*, 81. See also Augustine of Hippo, "Rule for Nuns" 2; Lawless, *Augustine of Hippo*, 110.
14. Augustine of Hippo, "Reprimand to Quarrelling Nuns" 2; Lawless, *Augustine of Hippo*, 105.
15. Augustine, "Regulations" 3; Lawless, *Augustine of Hippo*, 75.
16. See especially Augustine, "Rule," chap. 1; Lawless, *Augustine of Hippo*, 81–82.
17. Augustine, "Regulations" 8; Lawless, *Augustine of Hippo*, 77.

to please not by the clothes you wear, but by the life you live."[18] In the "Regulations for a Monastery" there is a general concern that leaving the monastery poses a hazard for the monk or nun, but it does not go into great detail about the potential hazards. The "Rule," on the contrary, is much more explicit, demonstrating that Augustine was concerned with lust, for it is outside the monastery where one will be most tempted toward sexual sin. He is realistic that monks who leave the enclosure will see women, so he does not forbid looking at women. He states that it "is wrong, however, to desire women or to wish them to desire you. Lust for women is mutually stimulated not only by tender touches but by sight as well."[19] Augustine assumes that monks will be tempted, so he devotes a fair amount of space in the "Rule" to how to discipline an errant monk. Overall Augustine is moderate in his vision of monastic asceticism, evidenced well in his legislation in the "Rule" regarding personal hygiene. The monk is not to neglect "proper hygienic care as standards for good health require."[20] Poor hygiene was often viewed as a sign of someone's holiness, evidence of their total disregard for themselves and their single-minded focus on God. Augustine believed that monks should practice a balanced asceticism; therefore, individual monks should care for themselves in ways that are conducive to their personal health and not excessive in either direction.

Augustine was well aware of the interpersonal difficulties that could arise from living in community. Though Christians were expected to love their neighbors as themselves, Augustine knew that this would not always be the case, so he gave a fair amount of attention to relationships in the monastery. (This is perhaps most obvious in the title of one of the texts that comprises the *Rule*: "Reprimand to Quarrelling Nuns.") In the "Rule," Augustine says that monks are either to have no quarrels or, if they do, to put an end to them as quickly as possible. Following biblical teaching (Matt. 18:15–17), Augustine legislates that brothers who have offended one another must right the wrong as soon as possible. He goes so far as to suggest that a quarrelsome brother who refuses to ask pardon has no place in the monastery. In the "Reprimand to Quarrelling Nuns," Augustine is eager to restore the broken fellowship among the sisters that has resulted in "quarrelling and jealousy, angry tempers and personal rivalries, backbiting, general disorder, [and] hushed comments about one another."[21] The community must strive to get beyond these divisive

18. Augustine, "Rule" 3.1 and 4.1; Lawless, *Augustine of Hippo*, 85 and 87.
19. Augustine, "Rule" 4.4; Lawless, *Augustine of Hippo*, 89. The same likely applies to nuns who leave the enclosure, but the "Rule" is written to men; therefore, Augustine's concern in this text is with temptation from women.
20. Augustine, "Rule" 5.5; Lawless, *Augustine of Hippo*, 97.
21. Augustine, "Reprimand" 3; Lawless, *Augustine of Hippo*, 107.

behaviors, and those nuns that persist in quarrelling will bear judgment should they resist change. The historical issue afflicting this community appears to be that some sisters were desirous of replacing the superior out of some sense of protection for their "priest-superior."[22] Augustine reminds them that their (female) superior has done an excellent job growing the monastery. She has related to the nuns in her charge in the same manner as a mother nurtures her children; therefore, she should be respected and allowed to continue serving as their superior. The "Rule for Nuns" elaborates on the role of the superior in the women's communities. She is to be obeyed "as a mother," out of respect for her position.[23] Her principal job is to ensure that all the precepts of the *Rule* are observed and to correct infractions, though she does this out of love rather than through inculcating fear. In sum, the superior is to serve the community in love, being "a model of good deeds for everyone."[24]

Thus Augustine's *Rule*, like that of Basil, is a series of precepts that describes the reason for becoming a monastic (love of God and neighbor), how to live in community, and how to be moderate in ascetical activity. These early rules, which lack robust institutional decrees, were, in time, replaced with rules that concern themselves not only with the spirit of monasticism but also with the finely detailed aspects of monastic life. For example, Augustine's "Rule" talks about the monks "responsible for food, clothing, or books"[25] but does not elaborate on the nature of these offices or the qualifications of the monks who hold the offices in the way that later rules do, such as the *Rule of the Master*.

Rule of the Master

The *Rule of the Master* (RM) is anonymous, or at least partly anonymous, having been written in Latin by a Western monk who is known to us only as "the Master." The exact date of composition of the RM is unknown, though it is of early Christian provenance. It was known to Benedict of Nursia and used by him in formulating his own rule in the sixth century,[26] and it was included

22. Augustine, "Reprimand" 4; Lawless, *Augustine of Hippo*, 107. Given that women's communities were unable to celebrate the sacraments for themselves, it was common for each community to have a male priest (who was sometimes a monk) exercising some sort of authority over them. This is the case with Augustine's phrase "priest-superior."

23. Augustine, "Rule for Nuns" 7.1; Lawless, *Augustine of Hippo*, 117.

24. Augustine, "Rule for Nuns" 7.3; Lawless, *Augustine of Hippo*, 117.

25. Augustine, "Rule" 5.9; Lawless, *Augustine of Hippo*, 97.

26. There has been a spirited discussion over the past century regarding the relationship of the RM to the *Rule of Benedict*. The question mostly concerns which rule was written first and who borrowed from whom. On this discussion see Odo J. Zimmermann, "An Unsolved Problem: The Rule of St. Benedict and The Rule of the Master," *American Benedictine Review*

in Benedict of Aniane's collection of ancient monastic rules, compiled in the early ninth century. Unlike the *Asceticon* of Basil and the *Rule* of Augustine, the Master offers a very detailed monastic rule, not only speaking in general terms about the monastic life but also giving detailed legislation. For example, Basil and Augustine both give space in their rules to the primacy of prayer in the monastic life, but the Master dedicates seventeen chapters (out of ninety-five) to laying out the liturgical ethos of the monastery. He also devotes much more space to the nature and qualifications of monastic offices, such as the abbot, deans, and cellarer (who was responsible for the food and drink).

Like Basil and Augustine, the Master begins his rule by declaring the proper motivations for entering the monastic life. Unlike Basil and Augustine, however, the Master does not say that the motivation for the monastic life is love of God and neighbor or even to perform penance and engage in renunciation. Rather, the Master sees the greatest motivation for entering the monastic life to be the salvation of one's soul. In the prologue, the Master states that each person reading his rule is standing at a crossroads: going to the left leads to perdition, but going to the right, on the correct and narrow road, affords the traveler salvation and "brings loving servants to him who is their Lord."[27] The prologue places a great emphasis on death, reminding readers that they will die and that they need to be ready for their life after death: "When you are summoned by death you will not, on the day of judgment and in eternal punishment, offer God the excuse that during your lifetime no one told you about amendment."[28] Such a macabre outlook on the Christian life would seem not to hold great promise for eliciting recruits into the monastery. Yet the sixth century was a difficult era for the Italian peninsula: the population of Rome dropped below 100,000, whereas it had once numbered over one million; Emperor Justinian successfully invaded Italy, defeating the Goths, but the war lasted for twenty years; in 542 the Justinian plague ravaged Italy; and in 568 the Lombards invaded. Given these tumultuous times, it is not surprising to see the Master confront people with death and their need to secure salvation. A poor reading of the RM would be that it is teaching

---

10, no. 1 (1959): 86–106; David Knowles, "The Regula Magistri and the Rule of St. Benedict," in *Great Historical Enterprises and Problems in Monastic History* (London: Nelson, 1963), 137–95; Adalbert de Vogüé, *La Règle du Maître*, vols. 1–3 (Paris: Éditions du Cerf, 1964); idem, *La Règle de Saint Benoît*, vols. 1–6 (Paris: Éditions du Cerf, 1971–1972); idem, *Le Maître, Eugippe et saint Benoît: Recueil d'articles* (Hildesheim: Gerstenberg, 1984); and Marilynn Dunn, "Mastering Benedict: Monastic Rules and Their Authors in the Early Medieval West," *English Historical Review* 105 (1990): 567–94.

27. *Rule of the Master* (RM) Prologue 14; Luke Eberle, trans., *The Rule of the Master* (Kalamazoo, MI: Cistercian Publications, 1977), 93.

28. RM Prologue 17; Eberle, *Rule of the Master*, 93.

salvation by works. That is not the case. The Master is cognizant that all Christians owe obedience and faithfulness to God and that all believers need to grow in holiness. The Master certainly believes that the monastery is the best place for achieving these ends, though the monastery is not the *only* place for one to work out one's salvation with fear and trembling (see Phil. 2:12). The Master is not convinced that every monastic lifestyle is legitimate but elevates the cenobitic and eremitical forms of monastic life higher than other kinds (described below).

The RM begins with describing four kinds of monks. This way of proceeding is not unique to the Master; John Cassian, the Master's source, did the same in his *Conferences*. Cassian describes four types of monasticism prevalent in the middle of the fifth century: (1) cenobites, (2) anchorites, (3) sarabaites, and (4) monks of a short-lived fervor. He says that cenobites are those who "live together in a community and are governed by the judgment of one elder," and anchorites are monks and nuns "who are first instructed in the cenobia and then, perfected in their practical way of life, choose the recesses of the desert."[29] Sarabaites are those "monks" who leave their cenobitic monastery, with its authority and accountability structure, and act as individuals, caring for their own needs. Cassian has nothing good to say about this group of so-called monastics.[30] The fourth group "fancy themselves in the style and likeness of anchorites," but they soon show that they possess only a short-lived fervor, which grows lukewarm as they desire to no longer be under the rule of a monastic elder. They soon want to live by themselves in their own cells.[31]

The Master also lists four kinds of monks, three of which he shares with Cassian: cenobites, anchorites, and sarabaites. The Master calls his fourth group gyrovagues. Whereas Cassian's cenobites live in community under an authority, the Master's cenobites live in community under an authority *and* under a rule. The RM's anchorites, like Cassian's, have spent some portion of their monastic life in the monastery enclosure before being allowed to live on their own as hermits. This period of probation has taught them how to fight against the devil so that they will be well-equipped in their solitary battles against evil spirits.[32] The Master has the same disdain for the sarabaites that Cassian exhibited, describing them as "the worst." The Master would prefer not to call them monks, but since they are tonsured (their head or crown is

---

29. John Cassian, *Conferences* 18.4.2; Boniface Ramsey, trans., *John Cassian: The Conferences* (New York: Paulist Press, 1997), 637.

30. See Cassian, *Conferences* 18.7.2–18.7.8.

31. See Cassian, *Conferences* 18.8.1; Ramsey, *John Cassian: The Conferences*, 642.

32. RM 1.3–5.

shaved as a sign of renunciation of the world), he must. These individuals
are untested by any rule or obedience to a master, having "as their law the
willfulness of their own desires."[33] Notice again that obedience to a rule (or
the lack thereof on the part of the sarabaites) is important to the Master. It
appears, then, that over the course of approximately 125 years the position of
the rule in the monastic life has come to hold a central place alongside that of
the spiritual elder or superior. The Master's fourth kind of monk differs from
Cassian's. The RM's gyrovagues are wandering monks, spending "their whole
life as guests for three or four days at a time at various cells and monasteries
of others in various provinces."[34] They take advantage of others' hospitality
by eating sumptuous meals and abusing charity, acting as if they are faithful
monks whose journey has been hard and are therefore worthy of gracious
hospitality. They feign humility and essentially act as thieves, robbing their
hosts to satiate their gluttonous habits. The Master is not impressed by the
sarabaites and gyrovagues, and his writing is not for these pseudomonks.
Rather, "in accordance with our high esteem for the first kind of monks, the
cenobites, whose service and probation are the will of God, let us return to
their rule."[35]

Another area in which the Master advances beyond Basil and Augustine
is in describing the roles and qualifications of particular monastic offices,
especially the role of the abbot. The abbot, first and foremost, is "the representative of Christ in the monastery," hence the name "abbot"[36] and one who
has learned the art of leading well in the "workshop of the monastery."[37] The
abbot's responsibility, writes the Master, is to teach the law of God and hold
the community accountable to it with his words but especially with his actions. The abbot is a model monk to the others. He must perform his job well,
knowing that he will be judged by God for the actions of his monks because
whatever is "lacking in the sheep will be laid to the blame of the shepherd."[38]
The abbot is to lead all of the monks without preference or bias unless a
monk has singled himself out for his good works. For the Master all monks
are equal, whether they were formerly slaves or freemen; therefore, the same
discipline is extended to all. The abbot "must reprove the undisciplined and
troublesome; he must entreat the obedient, meek and very patient to advance

33. RM 1.3–5; Eberle, *Rule of the Master*, 105.

34. RM 1.14; Eberle, *Rule of the Master*, 106.

35. RM 1.75; Eberle, *Rule of the Master*, 110.

36. The English word "abbot" comes from the Greek word *abbas* (father), which in turn is
derived from the Aramaic word *abba*. See Mark 14:36; Rom. 8:15; and Gal. 4:6.

37. RM 2.52; Eberle, *Rule of the Master*, 115. See also RM 6.1.

38. RM 2.7; Eberle, *Rule of the Master*, 111.

in virtue"; and he must "rebuke the negligent and contemptuous."[39] When making decisions that have to do with the good of the monastery, the abbot is to gather the counsel of the brothers since good advice sometimes comes from the least likely of places. In the end, it is the abbot who makes the final decision, and the monks must obey him once the decision is made.

The office of the abbot is so important to the Master that he couples his ascetical teaching within his ongoing reflections on this office. The Master refers to the work of the abbot as "holy art," something that can be learned only in the "workshop of the monastery," though it is practiced "with the use of spiritual instruments."[40] What is this "holy art"? It is "first to believe in, to confess and to fear God the Father and the Son and the Holy Spirit, one God in Trinity, and three in one, three in the one divine nature and one in the threefold power of his majesty." To state it less theologically but more biblically: "Therefore, to love him with all one's heart and all one's soul. Then in second place to love one's neighbor as oneself."[41] How this works itself out in the monastic life is then described by the Master in the form of an extended list that includes the following:

- Keep the Ten Commandments
- Practice asceticism
  - Deny oneself (eat, drink, sleep, and speak in moderation)
  - Chastise the body (do not be slothful; hate self-will)
  - Flee pleasures
  - Love fasting
  - Be obedient to the abbot
- Engage in charitable works
  - Relieve the poor
  - Clothe the naked
  - Visit the sick
  - Bury the dead
  - Help the afflicted
  - Console the sorrowing
  - Make loans
  - Give to the needy

39. RM 2.25; Eberle, *Rule of the Master*, 113.
40. RM 2.51–52; Eberle, *Rule of the Master*, 114–15.
41. RM 3.1–2; Eberle, *Rule of the Master*, 115.

- Cultivate virtue and holiness
  - Prefer nothing to the love of Christ
  - Be humble
  - Do not be angry, wrathful, hateful, envious, or jealous
  - Keep one's heart pure
  - Be peaceful, faithful, loving, sincere, truthful, and hopeful
  - Remain single-minded
  - Bear all things patiently and be reconciled with one's enemies
  - Keep God and death before one's eyes always
  - Pray often
  - Read holy books[42]

Another main ascetical theme that the Master develops in detail is his teaching on humility, which is the ladder that the monk is expected to climb in imitation of the patriarch Jacob's own ascent to God (see Gen. 28:12). Benedict of Nursia borrows heavily from the Master's teaching on humility, so I will wait until the next chapter to explicate it fully. Such focus on humility in the RM (and subsequently in the *Rule of Benedict*) indicates the importance with which this virtue was held in the sixth-century monastic milieu. Sustained teaching on humility is absent from the rules of Basil and Augustine, though John Cassian devoted a whole book of his *Institutes* to eradicating the spirit of anger and thereby cultivating humility.[43] It seems that Cassian's ten marks of humility in the *Institutes* served as the basis for the Master's twelve degrees of humility.[44] This demonstrates again the important influence that Cassian's work, described in chapter 2, had on subsequent monastic rules.[45]

Despite the maturity of the RM in its legislation and teaching, many other rules were being written and used during these early centuries of monastic flourishing.[46] Five extant rules that are grouped together because of similarities and shared influences are the *Rule of the Four Fathers* (RIVP),[47] the *Second Rule of the Fathers* (2RP), the *Third Rule of the Fathers* (3RP),

---

42. See RM 3.3–77; Eberle, *Rule of the Master*, 115–17. See also RM 4.1–10 and 5.1–11; Eberle, *Rule of the Master*, 118–19.

43. See Cassian, *Institutes*, bk. 12.

44. See Cassian, *Institutes* 4.39.

45. Columba Stewart, *Cassian the Monk* (Oxford: Oxford University Press, 1998), 25.

46. See Adalbert de Vogüé, "The Cenobitic Rules of the West," *Cistercian Studies* 12 (1977): 175–83; and Mary Forman and Thomas Sullivan, "The Latin Cenobitic Rules: AD 400–700: Editions and Translations," *American Benedictine Review* 48, no. 1 (1997): 52–68.

47. The rule's full title is *Rule of the Holy Fathers Serapion, Macarius, Phaphnutius and Another Macarius*. It is certain, however, that these names are a literary convention in order to associate a later rule with four well-known early Egyptian monks.

the *Rule of Macarius* (Rmac), and the *Regula Orientalis* (RO). RIVP, 2RP, and 3RP are the actual minutes from a meeting of abbots and reflect regulations that are intended to address immediate needs and experiences of the abbots. Though there is debate about the exact dates and places of origin for these rules, they all were written sometime in the fifth or early sixth century in either Gaul or Italy.[48] Compared to the RM, these rules are not very detailed, but they do reveal the state of monastic legislation in the period between Augustine's *Rule* and the RM. Of these five texts the RIVP is the more developed, and its contents can be divided into five parts: (1) the essence of cenobitic monasticism; (2) the role of the superior; (3) fasting and work; (4) admission of monks from other houses and reception of guests; and (5) on correcting errant brothers.[49] There is little ascetic teaching in this rule, and the only references to prayer occur in the section stipulating that no psalmody should be performed prior to the superior's signal and that no work should be performed on Sunday, which should be given to the singing of hymns, psalms, and spiritual songs (see Eph. 5:19). 2RP redresses this omission in RIVP, suggesting that the monastery already has a set timetable of prayer: the "course of prayers and psalms and the time for meditation and work shall be observed just as it has already been established."[50] It appears, then, that the monasteries using these rules supplemented and complemented them with other texts, or at least minimally with a schedule for prayer. This is confirmed in 3RP, which states that the rule should be read to the person who wants to enter the monastery and that "all the ways of the monastery be made clear to him."[51] This distinction between the rule and the "ways of the monastery" suggests that the monasteries using this family of rules had more than one text governing their lifestyle. The Rmac and RO both can be characterized as more exhortatory than the three rules of the fathers. Their purpose seems to be to inspire monks to live a proper monastic life. Though they contain some legislative material, they are not wholly sufficient in themselves to guide a monastery. It is likely that they too were used in conjunction with some other text or texts that gathered together the "ways of the monastery." However, in every way the RM is more advanced than the other early monastic rules, and its influence (primarily through the *Rule of Benedict*) elevates it above the others.

---

48. Carmela Vircillo Franklin, Ivan Havener, and J. Alcuin Francis, trans., *Early Monastic Rules: The Rules of the Fathers and the Regula Orientalis* (Collegeville, MN: Liturgical Press, 1982), 9–12.

49. Since 2RP and 3RP are textually dependent on RIVP, they also reflect this structure.

50. 2RP 22; Franklin et al., *Early Monastic Rules*, 35. See also 3RP 5–6.

51. 3RP 1.4; Franklin et al., *Early Monastic Rules*, 53.

Ressourcement: A "Rule of Life" Directing Proper Behavior and Holiness

The great Anglican poet, priest, and theologian George Herbert (d. 1633) once wrote,

> Slight those who say amidst their sickly healths,
> Thou liv'st by rule. What doth not so, but man?
> Houses are built by rule, and common-wealths.
> Entice the trusty sun, if that you can,
>   From his Ecliptic line: beckon the sky.
> Who lives by rule then, keeps good company.[52]

Herbert says that everything in God's creation follows a rule. The only exception to this principle is humankind, and the fact that we do not is a commentary on our "sickly healths," or drunkenness, caused by sin. The same is true in the spiritual life. An individual rule of life, just like a monastic rule, serves the purpose of keeping us disciplined so that we behave properly and grow in holiness. An ordered life is not to be eschewed but pursued. Early Christian monastic rules created ordered environments so that the monks and nuns inhabiting these well-ordered monasteries could focus on what was most important—love of God and neighbor. Why should a twenty-first-century Christian life be any different? If living by a rule is good enough for the rest of God's creation, then it should be good enough for us too.

The Scriptures themselves are the primary rule of life for Christians. Whenever we speak of the canon of Scripture, we are referring to the fact that the Bible functions as a "measuring rule" or standard, for that is the very meaning of "canon." Further, within the Scriptures there are texts that seem to function as a rule within the rule. For example, the Ten Commandments and Jesus's new commandment (John 13:34–35) continue to guide and shape the Christian's life in a unique way since they are concise summations of the overall spirituality of the Bible. However, the Bible does not give clear guidance in all areas of life; therefore, it seems pertinent to adopt further guidelines for Christian living. This is often done by way of one's local church, which tends to observe a set of standards, whether implicit or explicit. Some churches, for example, prioritize the so-called quiet time, during which the Scriptures are read and prayers are offered, often with the use of a devotional guide. Other local churches place a great emphasis on its members being active in a small group. Though these ecclesial activities are rarely labeled as aspects of a rule of life, they effectively function in this capacity.

52. George Herbert, "The Church-Porch" 23; John Tobin, ed., *George Herbert: The Complete English Poems* (London: Penguin, 1991), 10.

There is room both for these churchwide activities that help to guide individuals into greater faithfulness and also for individual or corporate rules of life that complement the standards set forth in the Scriptures. For example, as part of his spiritual life an individual may choose to pray three times a day, give 20 percent of his income to the church, and read the Bible cover to cover every twelve months. None of these activities are commanded in the Scriptures with specificity, but this person has chosen to honor the Bible's teaching on praying without ceasing, giving cheerfully, and publically reading the Scriptures, whereas another believer will choose a different set of disciplines. Neither person is more right than the other since they both are living into God's will for his followers, but it is safe to say that each of them is following a different rule of life. Moreover, some Christians join communities that legislate, in greater detail, individual behavior. A Christian university student attending a school that disallows the consumption of alcoholic beverages during a term follows a rule of life that differs from another Christian university student whose institution does not have the same standard.

What is important to note is that the content of a Christian rule of life is not always the same, other than what is commanded by the Scriptures. A rule of life is a dynamic document (though it does not necessarily need to be written down) that reflects the reality of how one believer chooses, under the guidance of God, to live out her Christian life. A rule of life should be flexible enough to adjust to the realities of a person's life but firm enough to require obedience. It would likely be foolish for a married woman with three young children at home to decide that she will spend three hours each morning in prayer and meditation. My guess is that she would be disturbed more times than she could count. It may be more realistic for her to covenant with her husband that one Saturday of each month will be set aside for her to spend the day hiking on the beach or in the mountains in prayer while he watches the children. Just as monastic rules are followed by the communities that adopt them, a rule of life is meant to be followed by those who subscribe to it, whether they be individuals or a community.

Part II

BENEDICT

to

BERNARD

4

The Flowering of
Benedictine Monasticism

I n 1313 Bernard Tolomei (d. 1348), along with two friends, initiated a
reform of Benedictine monasticism that came to be known as the Benedictine Monks of St. Mary of Mount Olivet, or the Olivetans. Recognized
by the local bishop in 1319, the community began constructing its first and
most important monastery in 1393 just south of Siena, Italy, and finally
completed it in 1526. The monastery, which came to be known as Monte
Oliveto Maggiore (Mount Olivet Major), is most well known for an important series of frescoes in the great cloister. These frescoes, which are a life
cycle of Benedict of Nursia, were painted by the great Renaissance artists
Luca Signorelli (d. 1523) and Antonio Bazzi (called Sodoma; d. 1549).[1] This
series of thirty-six frescoes is inspired mostly by events recorded in Gregory
the Great's "Life of St. Benedict," which will be discussed below. The first
fresco one encounters when leaving the church is an image of Benedict of
Nursia, painted by Sodoma, on an abbatial seat and dressed anachronistically
as an Olivetan,[2] handing copies of his monastic rule to two Olivetan monks.
The meaning of this image is unambiguous: Benedict's rule is that which
will guide the Olivetan community. As an image it is a persuasive vision of

---

1. Signorelli began the cycle in 1497; it was completed by Sodoma in 1508.
2. Benedictines traditionally wore black, but the Olivetan reformers chose to wear white
habits cut in the same manner as the traditional Benedictine habit.

71

the dominance of Benedict's rule in high- and late-medieval monasticism, for no other monastic founder or rule has been as influential as Benedict of Nursia. Thus this chapter will discuss the life of Benedict as both hagiography and exemplum to its readers on how to live the Christian life. The *Rule of Benedict* (RB) will also be examined for its institutional import and spiritual theology, including the roles of hospitality (treating everyone as if they were the person of Christ), humility, and obedience in the Christian life. I will also discuss Benedict's enduring vision of the monastic institution and lifestyle. This chapter will not only look at the literary documents concerning Benedict but will also focus briefly on architectural and artistic representations of Benedict, of which numerous examples exist from the medieval and Renaissance eras.

The Life of Benedict

What is known of the life of Benedict comes from Book 2 of the *Dialogues* of Gregory the Great (d. 604).[3] The *Dialogues*, written around 593, are a collection of miracle stories composed as hagiography (Gk. *hagios*, "holy," and *graphē*, "writing"). Hagiography refers to all Christian literature that concerns the saints (i.e., the holy ones), and hagiographical elements can be found throughout different genres of writing, including biographies of saints, collections of miracle stories, canonization records, accounts of the discovery or transfer of relics, sermons, and more. The purpose of hagiography was to promote the sanctity and devotional cult of its subject. Though hagiography often contains historically accurate information, its purpose was not to communicate the "facts" of history, like that found in modern biographical writings. In hagiographical texts the saints are presented as exemplars of the Christian life; therefore, the author is more concerned with displaying the saint in a positive light than with being slavishly accurate. Readers of these texts are supposed to modify their own lifestyle in light of the saint's holy actions. Hagiographical writings should not be dismissed as fictionalized accounts, but they must be read with caution. Given that Gregory's account is our only source for Benedict's life, we have little option than to present his narrative as the "likely story" of Benedict's life.

---

3. Over the past thirty years there has been a debate about the authorship and date of the *Dialogues*. For a proposed later date and different author, see Francis Clark, *The Pseudo-Gregorian Dialogues*, 2 vols. (Leiden: Brill, 1987). For a rebuttal of Clark and a defense of Gregory's authorship, see Paul Meyvaert, "The Enigma of Gregory the Great's *Dialogues*: A Response to Francis Clark," *Journal of Ecclesiastical History* 39 (1988): 335–81.

Benedict (d. ca. 547) was born in the region of Nursia, located in central Italy. According to Gregory, Benedict was sent to Rome for his education, but seeing the grave vice of his classmates he abandoned "his literary studies and leaving his family home and inheritance, he sought to please God alone. He went looking for a monastic habit so that he could lead a holy life."[4] This led him ultimately to a cave in Subiaco, a "wild place . . . about forty miles from Rome."[5] Gregory tells us that on the way to Subiaco, Benedict met a monk named Romanus who clothed Benedict with the monastic habit. Over the next three years Romanus brought Benedict food, lowering it to him in the cave with a long rope. In time Benedict's holiness and virtue became well known, leading others to emulate his way of life. Members of a local monastery approached Benedict, asking him to become their superior. Though Benedict doubted that his lifestyle would align with those of the monks, he finally agreed to be their abbot. In time, Benedict's hesitation was proven accurate when "the monks under his rule grew furious. . . . It was hard for them to have to change their attitudes."[6] When the monks attempted to poison Benedict, he responded by leaving the monastery and returning to Subiaco "with a calm face and a tranquil mind."[7] The "Life" goes on to state that Benedict founded some number of monasteries in the vicinity of Subiaco, though he was not the abbot of these monasteries, which were populated with sons of "the pious and noble families of the city of Rome."[8] Yet, due to ongoing difficulties, Benedict "placed all the monasteries he built, with their brothers, under their superiors. Taking a few monks with him, he changed his place of residence."[9] This led Benedict to move south, where he continued to perform miracles and where he eventually died, being laid to rest in an oratory of his monastery dedicated to John the Baptist. This monastery at Monte Cassino is his most famous monastery and, as many suppose, the catalyst for his writing the RB.[10]

James Clark, in his magisterial study of the Benedictines in the Middle Ages, writes, "The men and women that followed the sixth-century customs of Benedict of Nursia (*c.* 480–*c.* 547) formed the most enduring, influential,

---

4. Gregory the Great, "The Life of St. Benedict," Introduction 1; Terrence G. Kardong, *The Life of St. Benedict by Gregory the Great: Translation and Commentary* (Collegeville, MN: Liturgical Press, 2009), 1.

5. Gregory the Great, "Life of St. Benedict" 1.3; Kardong, *Life of St. Benedict*, 7.

6. Gregory the Great, "Life of St. Benedict" 3.3; Kardong, *Life of St. Benedict*, 21.

7. Gregory the Great, "Life of St. Benedict" 3.4; Kardong, *Life of St. Benedict*, 22.

8. Gregory the Great, "Life of St. Benedict" 3.14; Kardong, *Life of St. Benedict*, 31.

9. Gregory the Great, "Life of St. Benedict" 8.5; Kardong, *Life of St. Benedict*, 42.

10. Given that Benedict used the *Rule of the Master* (RM) in creating his rule, it is not correct to say that he "wrote" the RB. In one sense he edited it or redacted it from previously existing monastic rules. For the sake of simplicity, however, I will continue to say that Benedict "wrote" the RB.

numerous and widespread religious order of the Latin Middle Ages. Their mode of life superseded the monastic codes of the early Christian fathers and before the close of the eleventh century it was the dominant form of monastic observance practised in the west."[11] So what was it that made the RB so influential that it became the monastic rule par excellence of the Middle Ages and beyond? The answer to this question is often given in two parts. First, the RB is seen as a much more balanced document than most of the earlier monastic rules. It does not contain the excesses of the *Rule of the Master* (RM), but it is not as brief as the rules of the fathers, for example. It strikes the right balance between sufficient legislative specificity and robust ascetical teaching. Second, historical circumstances were such that the RB came to be the preferred rule of Latin monasticism. We will discuss the ascendency of the RB in monastic history in later chapters. For now I will examine the legislative and spiritual teachings of the RB.

Legislative Teachings of the *Rule of Benedict*

There are seventy-three chapters in the RB, many of which borrow from the RM verbatim or are paraphrases or slight alterations.[12] Benedict begins by summoning the monks to "listen carefully . . . to the master's instructions . . . [which] will bring [them] back to him from whom [they] have drifted through the sloth of disobedience."[13] Benedict casts the monastic life as a battle, where those who serve "the true King" please God by their good work of entering the monastery, securing their salvation by attending the "school for the Lord's service."[14] Despite the difficulties of the monastic life, especially for novices, it ultimately leads to "hearts overflowing with the inexpressible delight of love."[15] Next, Benedict writes about the four kinds of monks; like the Master (and Cassian), he views cenobitism as a preparation for the eremitical life and rejects both the sarabaites and the gyrovagues. He then turns his attention "to draw up a plan for the strong kind, the cenobites."[16] Thinking in terms

11. James G. Clark, *The Benedictines in the Middle Ages* (Woodbridge, UK: Boydell Press, 2011), 1.

12. For a list of correspondences between the two rules, see Timothy Fry, ed., *RB 1980: The Rule of St. Benedict in Latin and English with Notes* (Collegeville, MN: Liturgical Press, 1981), 479–88.

13. RB Prologue 1–2; Fry, *RB 1980*, 157.

14. RB Prologue 45; Fry, *RB 1980*, 165.

15. RB Prologue 45 and 49; Fry, *RB 1980*, 165. As discussed in chap. 3, salvation was also the Master's main motivation for the monastic life.

16. RB 1.13 and 49; Fry, *RB 1980*, 171.

of legislative directives and ascetical teaching, Benedict's rule can be broken down as follows:

Legislative Directives
Role of the Abbot (chaps. 2–3, 26–27, 44, 46–47, 56, 64)
Other Monastic Offices (chaps. 21, 31–32, 35, 38, 57, 60, 62, 65–66)
Organization of the Monastery (chaps. 1, 22, 29, 34, 36–37, 48, 53, 58–59, 63)

Ascetical Teachings
The Tools of Good Works (chap. 4)
Personal Behavior (chaps. 5, 23–25, 28, 30, 43–45, 68–71)
Virtues and Discipline (chaps. 6–7, 33, 39–42, 49, 51, 54–55, 67, 72–73)
Prayer (chaps. 8–20, 50, 52)
Hospitality (chaps. 53, 61)

The rule's noteworthiness is displayed primarily in Benedict's teaching on humility, obedience, and hospitality, concepts that run across the breadth of the rule and permeate the entire text.

Benedict's teaching on humility is borrowed from the Master, who in turn based it on Cassian.[17] In the RB, obedience is primary vis-à-vis humility. In the chapter titled "Obedience," Benedict says that the "basic road to progress for the humble person is through prompt obedience."[18] Thus there is an intimate connection between humility and obedience in the RB: it claims that to progress in his spiritual life a monk must be both humble *and* obedient. Humility for the monk comes by ascending the twelve steps of the ladder of humility:

Step 1: A monk keeps the fear of God before his eyes.

Step 2: A monk does not love his own will nor takes delight in satisfying his desires.

Step 3: A monk submits out of love of God to his superior.

Step 4: If obedience to his superior becomes difficult, unfavorable, or unjust, a monk embraces suffering and does not seek to escape it.

17. See RM 10 and John Cassian, *Institutes* 4.39. Throughout this chapter I will refer to this teaching on humility as Benedict's, though it is largely the work and words of the Master. Given that Benedict adopted it wholesale also makes it his teaching, and therefore to refer to it as "Benedict's teaching" is as correct as referring to it as the "Master's teaching."

18. RB 5.1; Terrence G. Kardong, *Benedict's Rule: A Translation and Commentary* (Collegeville, MN: Liturgical Press, 1996), 103.

Step 5:   A monk does not hide private or public sinful thoughts or actions from his abbot but willingly and humbly confesses them.

Step 6:   A monk is content with low and menial treatment, regarding himself as a poor and worthless workman.

Step 7:   A monk believes and acknowledges that he is inferior to all other persons.

Step 8:   A monk only does that which is allowed by the rule of the monastery and the example of his superiors.

Step 9:   A monk remains silent unless asked a question.

Step 10: A monk is not quick to laugh.

Step 11: A monk speaks gently without laughter, seriously with modesty, briefly and reasonably without raising his voice.

Step 12: A monk is always humble inwardly and outwardly, in his heart and actions.[19]

To the modern reader some of these steps can seem incredibly harsh, too self-abasing to be of any real good. Modern readers tend to see in Benedict a self-effacement that rubs against established, wholesome psychological health. Our response simply ought to be that Benedict was writing at a different time. We know this, of course, but it is essential that this truth be borne in mind when reading the RB. What we might view as cruel and psychologically unhealthy, Christians of the sixth century viewed as spiritual and necessary for growth in holiness. This difference of understanding and chronological distance must not lead us to reading the RB poorly.

Benedict's idea of humility was one of ascending degrees. This would seem obvious from his use of the ladder motif, but this image was primarily borrowed from the Scriptures (see Gen. 28:10–22) and perhaps from other Christian literature.[20] Throughout the course of one's life in the monastery, one was to ascend the ladder of humility. The steps do not correspond directly to moments in the monk's life, but as a monk grew in his monastic and Christian maturity, he would, presumably, ascend higher on the ladder of humility. It also seems that Benedict did not think of these steps as sequential—that once one had mastered the first step one moved on to next step, no longer concerned with the teaching or emphasis of the previous step. Rather, the steps are cumulative; the monk who has advanced to the fifth step is still

19. RB 7.10–62; Fry, *RB 1980*, 193–201.

20. The most famous spiritual text to employ the motif of the ladder, though it postdates the RB, is John Climacus's *Ladder of Divine Ascent*. See Colm Luibheid and Norman Russell, trans., *John Climacus: The Ladder of Divine Ascent* (New York: Paulist Press, 1982).

practicing humility according to the first four steps. Benedict is not creating a twelve-step program akin to Alcoholics Anonymous where a step must be completed before a person is allowed to move to the next step. He is offering a fully formed theology of spirituality under the theme of humility. Once the monk has reached Benedict's last step, he has reached spiritual perfection, and he is now pure of heart (to use John Cassian's language). In the words of Benedict: "Now, therefore, after ascending all these steps of humility, the monk will quickly arrive at that perfect love of God which casts out fear."[21]

Within Benedict's spiritual theology of humility are embedded two other important teachings: on silence and the use of speech, and on obedience. Steps 9–11 (three of the top four steps) are dedicated to silence and the use of speech, which shows how important this topic is to Benedict. (Two chapters of the RB speak to the same subject.) In general, Benedict is committed to monks keeping silent at all times: "Monks should diligently cultivate silence at all times."[22] By dedicating these three steps to the topic, Benedict is laying out three principles: monks should control their speech (Step 9); monks must not be frivolous (Step 10); and a monk's speech, when necessarily used, must be moderate (Step 11). In other words, everything that comes out of the mouth must be God-honoring, which echoes Matthew 15:10–20.[23] The ninth step says that a "monk controls his tongue and remains silent, not speaking unless asked a question."[24] This is rooted, writes Benedict, in the teaching of Proverbs 10:19, in which excessive speech is said to lead to sinning. Benedict's concern is that a monk will become excessively loquacious, that is, that he will become a chatterbox.[25] To avoid this, Benedict expects a monk to speak only when spoken to. The connection to humility has to do with speech being tied to a person's sense of self-importance, his need to be heard as someone who has the answers and is wise. This is echoed in chapter 6 of the RB when Benedict says that silence is so important that even "mature disciples" should seldom be given permission to speak. Excessive talking is a problem not just for younger monks but for the older, wiser monks too—hence its appearance near the top of the ladder of humility.

Step 10 addresses the topic of silence by forbidding monks to be "given to ready laughter," for "only a fool raises his voice in laughter."[26] Though

---

21. RB 7.67; Fry, *RB 1980*, 201. Benedict is quoting 1 John 4:18.

22. RB 42.1; Fry, *RB 1980*, 243.

23. Though Benedict never quotes Matt. 15 directly, it seems reasonable that Jesus's teachings here would have influenced him. He does quote or allude to the Gospel of Matthew forty-nine other times in his rule.

24. RB 7.56; Fry, *RB 1980*, 201.

25. See Kardong, *Benedict's Rule*, 134.

26. RB 7.59; Fry, *RB 1980*, 201. Benedict quotes from the apocryphal book of Sirach 21:23.

laughter may be the best medicine, it is also a distraction in the monastery. It would not only interrupt necessary and desirable silence, but it would also distract the monks engaged in prayer, meditation, spiritual reading, and work. Whereas Benedict forbids speech because of its tendency to lead to sin, he forbids laughter because of its connection to foolishness and its propensity to be disruptive. The former is more personal, whereas the latter concerns living in community. Because the rule regarding laughter (which affects the community) is on a higher step than the rule regarding speech (which affects the person), it is possible that Benedict thinks that care for community is a higher spiritual good than care for one's personal behavior. Put another way, a monk's conduct in community is a great measure of his growth in holiness. Benedict's final words on speech in the ladder of humility are, "When a monk speaks at all, he does so gently and without laughter, humbly and seriously, with few and careful words."[27] For the Master the monk was supposed to use holy words, whereas for Benedict the word "holy" (*sancta*) has been replaced with "careful" or reasonable (*rationabilia*). The Master allowed conversation between the monks on holy topics, while Benedict wants to promote a culture of "civilized communication between all members of the community."[28] Though Step 9 calls for ongoing silence, Step 11 seems to allow the reality that monks, at times, have to engage in conversation. When this is the case, Benedict expects monks to speak in a godly manner that is in keeping with humility. Moreover, it seems that for Benedict "proper speech can manifest humility quite as well as complete silence."[29]

Also present in Benedict's ladder of humility is a strong emphasis on obedience. This is soundly supported elsewhere in the RB, with chapters dedicated to the abbot's role in obedience and correction of faults. The third step of humility is for a monk to "[submit] to his superior in all obedience for the love of God."[30] The first thing to notice is that Benedict's obedience is rooted in the greater end of the love of God. Obedience is not blind but borne out of the monk's love for God, in imitation of Jesus Christ's obedience to God the Father, even to the point of death (see Phil. 2:8). Obedience in the RB is christological, not pathological. Again, like Jesus himself and in imitation of the crucifixion, the monk must remain obedient even when it is "difficult, unfavorable, or even unjust." When this is the case, the humble monk "embraces suffering and endures it without weakening or seeking escape."[31] Monks who

27. RB 7.60; Kardong, *Benedict's Rule*, 134.
28. Kardong, *Benedict's Rule*, 157.
29. Ibid.
30. RB 7.34; Fry, *RB 1980*, 197.
31. RB 7.35–36; Fry, *RB 1980*, 197.

do this, says Benedict, are fulfilling the Lord's command to turn the other cheek when struck. Obedience is an opportunity both to imitate Christ and to satisfy Christ's commands. The most trying crucible of obedience in the RB is a monk's unquestioning obedience to his abbot. Benedict's teachings in this regard seem unbelievable to the modern reader, for monks "carry out the superior's order as promptly as if the command came from God himself," and they "follow the voice of authority in their actions."[32] The reasons for immediate obedience are twofold: (1) the monks are cultivating a love that seeks to gain everlasting life and that is in response to God's love; and (2) the monks forsake their own judgment in imitation of Christ, who came not to do his own will but the will of the Father who sent him. In the words of Terrence Kardong, "Obedience is rooted in listening to God (RB 5.5–6; Luke 10:16) and . . . the whole point of obedience is to return love to God, who loves us first (RB 5.16; 2 Cor 9:7). To combine these themes, obedience means listening to God so as to know how to respond in love to his will. RB 5 centers that response in obedience to the commands of authority."[33] Wholehearted obedience, without hesitation and with complete willingness, to one's abbot is evidence of one's love of God. To be disobedient, then, is to demonstrate a lack of love for God.

For Benedict, the abbot holds "the place of Christ in the monastery, since he is addressed by a title of Christ, as the Apostle indicates: You have received the spirit of adoption of sons by which we exclaim, abba, father."[34] Again, obedience to one's abbot is obedience to Christ; for Benedict this obedience is quite literal since the abbot is expressly christological in his role and person. The abbot in turn is not to teach or require anything that goes against the Lord's teachings because, at the day of judgment, he will be held accountable for his own conduct and for the treatment of the monks in his care. The abbot is to favor no monk above another and is to love all monks in his monastery equally. Benedict understands that abbots, though holding an important and powerful office, are ultimately responsible for the souls entrusted to them and that they must be neither too lenient nor too severe. In important matters the abbot should prudently seek the advice of the other monks, especially the elders of the monastery, though he should not neglect the advice of the younger monks, since he is unable to know through whom God might choose to speak. Less important matters of the monastery can be decided by the abbot and the older monks alone. At the end of the day, however, it is always the abbot himself who stands in the place of Christ and wields the most power.

32. RB 5.4 and 8; Fry, *RB 1980*, 188–89.
33. Kardong, *Benedict's Rule*, 115.
34. RB 2.2–3; Fry, *RB 1980*, 173. Benedict cites Rom. 8:15.

Benedict devotes a lot of space in his rule to the correction of faults and the proper attitude that monks are to have toward wayward brothers. He also provides guidelines for restoring repentant brothers. One of the most common ways that the rule envisions that monks will err is in disobedience to the abbot. The need to be obedient to one's abbot has already been mentioned, but then there is the ongoing relationship between the monk and his superior. Within the monastery there is the potential that some monks will be excommunicated from the community by their actions. Mind you, this is not excommunication from the church but excommunication from the normal routines of the monastic community due to faults. Excommunication in the monastery works as follows: (1) a stubborn, disobedient, or proud monk who despises the rule and defies his superiors is warned twice; (2) if he does not change, he is rebuked in front of the community; and (3) if he fails to reform, he is excommunicated. The RB legislates that the degree of excommunication must fit the crime, with the abbot ultimately determining the gravity of the fault. If another monk, without an order from the abbot, associates with an excommunicated brother, then he too is excommunicated. Pastorally, the abbot then assigns older monks to the excommunicated so that they can "support the wavering brother, urge him to be humble as a way of making satisfaction, and console him lest he be overwhelmed by excessive sorrow."[35] Excommunication in the RB is for the purpose of restoring the excommunicated brother, to motivate him to amend his faults. If a monk fails to do this, the RB calls for a harsher response—corporal punishment by being beaten with a rod. If this still fails to cause the monk to amend his faults, then the abbot "must use the knife and amputate" the monk from the community—that is, remove the monk from the community by sending him back into the world.[36] He is no longer a monk at this or any other monastery. At this point it is important to remember that the context of Benedict's teaching on obedience is the monastery. Benedict is not legislating for the whole Christian community but only for those who choose "to live in monasteries and to have an abbot over them."[37] While Benedict certainly sees his teaching as fully biblical, he understands it is not equally applicable to all states of life. The model monastic life for Benedict is one of mutual obedience where "obedience is a blessing to be shown by all, not only to the abbot but also to one another as brothers. . . . [For] although orders of the abbot or of the priors appointed by him take precedence, and no unofficial order may supersede

35. RB 27.3; Fry, *RB 1980*, 223.
36. RB 28.6; Fry, *RB 1980*, 225.
37. RB 5.12; Fry, *RB 1980*, 189.

them, in every other instance younger monks should obey their seniors with all love and concern."[38] Obedience is meant to permeate the monastery, creating an ethos of love of God and love of neighbor, especially love of one's fellow monk. Yet the rule considers one's "neighbor" to be not only one's fellow monk but also the literal, non-monastic neighbors of the monastery.

It is often assumed that all monks and nuns spend the bulk of their monastic lives having little contact with those outside their monastery. That is not true for the modern period, nor is it true for the medieval era. From the start, Benedict envisioned that his monks would have contact with non-monastic neighbors and other officials from the local community. In describing the qualifications of the porter of the monastery (the monk who acts as representative to the outside world), Benedict says that he will need a room at the entrance to the monastery so that he will be able to greet visitors on arrival, including monks from other communities.[39] Not only will visitors sometimes come to the monastery, but also the monks will have to leave the enclosure on monastery business. In anticipation of this, Benedict dedicates two chapters to brothers sent on a journey.[40] On leaving for their journey, these monks are to ask the abbot and the community to pray for them. If they are away for only a day, they are not to eat outside the monastery. On their return they are to lie face down on the floor at the conclusion of the canonical hours, asking for the community's prayers for their faults, "in case they may have been caught off guard on the way by seeing some evil thing or hearing some idle talk."[41] Notice that Benedict does not presume that these monks will commit faults but rather that they may have done so, whether intentionally or unintentionally. The non-monastic world is not more evil than the monastery, though there is a greater chance for sin outside the monastery.[42] Benedict is not operating out of some form of false dualism, a supposed tension between "good" spirit and "evil" matter.[43] Nor is he motivated by some arbitrary distinction between the monastery and the "world." That Benedict includes legislation on amending

38. RB 71.1 and 3; Fry, *RB 1980*, 293.
39. See RB 61 and 66.2.
40. See RB 51 and 67.
41. RB 67.4; Fry, *RB 1980*, 289.
42. Benedict's experience as a student in Rome demonstrated to him that living outside a monastery simply exposed one to more sinful temptations and opportunities, whereas life in the monastery greatly reduced these opportunities to sin. For Benedict, the "world" is set over against the monastery. Whereas the world is characterized by pride and licentiousness, the monastery is distinguished by humility and chastity. Benedict was also skeptical of the effects of "worldly knowledge"—that is, learning about and from classical authors. See Gregory the Great, "Life of St. Benedict" 1.1; Kardong, *Life of St. Benedict*, 1.
43. Though this tendency is prevalent in the Christian tradition, nothing in the RB suggests that Benedict thought in these terms.

faults and on excommunication is evidence that he believes in the sinfulness of people, regardless of whether they live inside or outside a monastery.

Chapter 53 of the RB is wholly dedicated to the reception of guests but also includes one of Benedict's most well-known teachings: to welcome all guests as if they were Christ himself.[44] In particular, those visitors of the Christian faith and those on religious pilgrimage are to be welcomed and shown appropriate hospitality. There was a protocol for the proper reception of guests: (1) the guest was announced, presumably by the porter; (2) the superior and the monks were to meet him "with all the courtesy of love";[45] (3) the visitor, superior, and monks would pray together; (4) the kiss of peace would be exchanged; (5) the Bible would be read to the guest; (6) the guest's hands would be washed by the superior and his feet by another monk; and (7) the guest would be fed. All of this was to be done in humility and with great care and concern, especially when receiving the poor or pilgrims since they, in particular, represented Christ. Because of this exuberant reception of guests, Benedictines have become known for their hospitality.

The RB still expects that the monastic precinct will be a fairly self-sufficient, self-enclosed environment: "The monastery should, if possible, be so constructed that within it all necessities, such as water, mill and garden are contained."[46] The most famous example of an ideal Benedictine monastery is that of the "Plan of St. Gall." Though this monastery was never constructed, its unknown architect envisioned an expansive enclosure. Along with the usual elements of a cenobitic monastery—such as the church, dormitory, and refectory (dining room)—the St. Gall plan imagined the presence of multiple types of houses for animals (e.g., a fowlhouse and goosehouse), a house for bloodletting, an infirmary that housed a doctor and the critically ill, a granary for the brewer along with a cooling room for beer, a laundry and bathhouse, a hostel for the traveling or poor, a school and schoolmaster's lodging, a special house and refectory for the abbot, and much more. Though an idealized monastery, the "Plan of St. Gaul" shows that Benedictines desired to have their monasteries be as self-contained as possible. Benedictines may have always been ready to welcome guests as Christ, but they were also prepared to remain cloistered.

The large-scale adoption of Benedictine monasticism across Europe will be discussed in chapter 8, but contrary to what some scholars have said, the RB was not an instant bestseller. Other monastic rules continued to be

44. See RB 53.1.
45. RB 53.3; Fry, *RB 1980*, 257.
46. RB 66.6; Fry, *RB 1980*, 289.

written, and the RB was not uniformly used in the first centuries after its composition. In time, as we will see, it became *the* monastic rule of many (if not most) of the cenobitic monasteries of the Western Middle Ages, but that was not the case in the mid-sixth century. Like Bernard Tolomei, mentioned at the beginning of this chapter, monastic founders and reformers across the centuries continued to be inspired by and adopt the RB. For example, the Cistercians are a late eleventh-century reform movement of Benedictine monasticism, as are the Camaldolese, founded by Romuald of Ravenna in the mid-eleventh century.

Since Benedict's time there has been a continuous (or near continuous) monastic presence at his cave in Subiaco. A visitor to this monastery today is treated to a beautiful and stunning site: a monastery perched carefully on the side of a mountain with the "Holy Cave" of Benedict forming the spiritual and physical center of the edifice. The walls of the church, chapels, and public spaces are covered in frescoes depicting the life of Benedict and other themes significant to Benedictine monastic life. On the ceiling of the Lower Church is a vibrant fresco of Benedict surrounded by Benedictine saints painted by Magister Conxolus, an artist of the Roman School of 1250–1300. Amid a sea of deep-blue sky sprinkled with stars, Benedict is pictured in the center of the fresco, his right hand positioned in the form of a blessing. In his left hand he holds a copy of his rule. He is surrounded by eight Benedictines: four wear their black habits and are positioned in the cardinal directions around Benedict; four others are dressed as popes or bishops, occupying the ordinal directions. Only a few of the individuals have been identified, including Gregory the Great, Sylvester, and Lawrence. The message of the image is apparent: Benedict and his rule are the sure foundation of the monastic life, and following the rule makes it possible to achieve great sanctity. A manuscript illustration from Jean de Stavelot (d. 1449), completed in 1437, reinforces this message. Stavelot's "Collection of Writings on St. Benedict" is loaded with images of events from the life of Benedict or events related to Benedict, such as Gregory the Great writing the second book of his *Dialogues*. One image is a genealogical tree of monks who are literally rooted in Benedict.[47] The trunk of the tree emerges from Benedict's gut and grows upward, depicting twelve individuals on twelve branches who are important in Benedictine history: Gregory the Great, Thomas Becket (d. 1170),[48] Robert of Molesme (d. 1111),[49]

47. Chantilly, Musée Condé, MS 738, f. 126r. Reproduced on the front cover of Clark, *Benedictines in the Middle Ages*.

48. Martyred archbishop of Canterbury who spent two years in the Cistercian abbey of Pontigny in France.

49. Abbot of Benedictine monasteries and founder of the Cistercian order.

Maurus,[50] Venerable Bede (d. 735),[51] Odilo of Cluny (d. 1049),[52] Anselm of
Canterbury (d. 1109),[53] Leodegar (d. 679),[54] Victor III (d. 1087),[55] Columbanus
(d. 597),[56] Remaclus (d. 663),[57] and Gerard of Clairvaux (d. 1138).[58] Again the
message is clear: Benedict and his rule are a sure foundation for the monastic
and spiritual life. Who would not want to be in the company of such eminent
men? For those who aspire to such a state, Benedict's rule, the fresco and illumination suggest, is a trustworthy guide.

Ressourcement: Humility, Obedience, and Hospitality—Seeing Christ in Others

On the way down a set of steps toward the Madonna Chapel at the monastery
in Subiaco, which ultimately leads to a chapel used for the funeral of monks
and their original crypt, are two frescoes on either side of the steps. On the
right is a fresco picturing Death on a horse. The horse appears to be either
riding over a group of individuals who have already died or killing them by
riding over them. Regardless, one's focus is drawn to Death's sword, striking
down two noblemen having a conversation. The meaning is unmistakable:
death will find you. The image on the left when descending the steps is also
a reminder that regardless of your station in life, you will die and, in time,
decompose. In this picture, a man (likely a monk) is speaking toward three
people of the nobility. Though two are more interested in talking to each
other, one is listening to the monk. Before the monk is an image of a deceased
nobleman in three different stages of death: "freshly" dead, beginning stages
of decomposition, and, finally, skeletal remains. The fact that two of the three
listeners are paying no attention to the preacher indicates that they likely think
they are above death, or at least that death will not visit them soon. However,

50. One of the first faithful disciples of Benedict whose deeds are recorded in the "Life of
Benedict" by Gregory the Great.

51. Monk of Wearmouth-Jarrow in England and author of *The Ecclesiastical History of
the English People*.

52. First abbot of the reformed Benedictine abbey of Cluny.

53. Abbot of the abbey of Bec in Normandy, archbishop of Canterbury, philosopher-
theologian, and author of several important theological treatises, including the *Cur Deus Homo*.

54. Spelled as Leodigan by Jean de Stavelot, Leodegar was abbot at the monastery of St.
Maxentius in Poitou, France, and later bishop of Autun. He introduced use of the RB at St.
Maxentius.

55. Abbot of Monte Cassino and pope.

56. See chap. 5.

57. Founder of the monastery of Stavelot in Belgium, where Jean de Stavelot was a monk
and produced the "Collection of Writings on St. Benedict."

58. Brother of Bernard of Clairvaux and one of the founding monks of the Cistercian
monastery of Clairvaux in 1115.

the message in this image is similar to the one on the other side of the stairs: everyone dies and everyone rots. Therefore, lay aside your worldly pleasures and live a holy life. This visual message conveys essentially the same message as the RB itself. The legislation and spiritual theology of the RB is intended for one end: to help monks or nuns following the rule become holy persons, always mindful of death's presence.

Benedict envisioned his rule to be merely a "little rule that [he has] written for beginners."[59] While he deferred to the Scriptures and other Christian writings as being better guides for the Christian life, his rule is sufficient as a starting point. His rule is a primer for the Christian life. Though written for monks, Benedict's rule speaks to us today. His insistence on cultivating the virtues of humility, obedience, and hospitality are timeless. Though we may not agree with Benedict on all points, his rule should not be ignored. Benedict has much to teach us; therefore, we should eagerly enroll in his "school for the Lord's service."

Yet Christian virtues are not in vogue these days; maybe better said, they tend not to be cultivated unless they can lead to something better. That is, virtues are not virtuous in and of themselves but are only virtuous inasmuch as they are useful for one's personal gain. In this age of stardom and super fandom there is little humility to go around but plenty of pride. Of course, a healthy self-respect is necessary for human flourishing, but the line between self-respect and pride has always been thin—even more so today, though it is important not to forget that pride has existed since time immemorial (Ezek. 28:17). Still, humility is at the heart of God's salvation history; it is the background to the narrative of Jesus Christ: "Have this mind among yourselves, which is yours in Christ Jesus, who, though he was in the form of God, did not count equality with God a thing to be grasped, but emptied himself, by taking the form of a servant, being born in the likeness of men. And being found in human form, he humbled himself by becoming obedient to the point of death, even death on a cross" (Phil. 2:5–8). Simply put, we should be humble because our salvation is rooted in God's humility. Further, our obedience to God is rooted in the Son's obedience to the Father. Humility and obedience go together; they are two sides of the same coin.

However, humility and obedience (and hospitality for that matter) do not just spring up in us unexpected; they are cultivated in us by the Holy Spirit and learned through imitation. Unlike the theological virtues of faith, hope, and love—which are infused by God into each believer—humility, obedience, and hospitality must be learned. Benedict of Nursia knew this well

59. RB 73.8; Fry, *RB 1980*, 297.

and was convinced that one of the best places to learn these virtues (if not *the* best place to learn them) was in the monastery. That most of us will not join a monastery, however, is not an impediment to our acquisition of these virtues, for we have not only the example of Jesus Christ but also the school of the Christian church to teach us. For most Christians, the local church is the "school for the Lord's service." That being the case, it is imperative that the church assists its members in acquiring the virtues; this is best done, as with any good education, through not only verbal teaching but also by word and deed. If the church is an ideal learning environment for virtue, then each believer must attend this school with faithfulness.

The church is ideally poised in society to model humility, obedience, and hospitality. How this happens in each congregation will vary, but humility and hospitality are modeled well when the church follows the teaching of the Epistle of James and shows no partiality to members, regardless of age, race, gender, socioeconomic condition, and so on. That Sunday mornings are proverbially the most segregated hour in America is lamentable, but it does not need to remain that way. Local parishes should make every effort to welcome all those who come to her doors, color- and status-blind, and churches should find creative ways to be open to all persons without compromising orthodox faith and practice. A truly inclusive church can still recognize and name sin as sin.

Obedience is best learned as the church and all her members collectively submit to God's will. Whereas in Benedict's monastery the abbot stands in the place of Christ, that role in the local church is held by the pastor (or pastors) and elders. Individual church members should submit themselves to godly, duly called church leaders. Though obedience seems old-fashioned, it is still legislated by God in the context of the local church (see Heb. 13:17). Of course, all of this is done alongside the work that the Holy Spirit is already doing in and through God's people. The monastery was never meant to supplant the church (monasteries have often been thought of as *ecclesiolae in ecclesia*, "little churches within the church"); therefore, the "monastic" virtues of humility, obedience, and hospitality are open to all Christians, particularly those who choose to participate in a local church.

5

Other Voices: Celtic, Frankish, and Eastern Monasticism

When pilgrims walk into St. Peter's Basilica in Rome, they are likely overwhelmed by the sheer size of the edifice, the grandeur of Bernini's baldachin, or the beauty of Michelangelo's *Pietà*. As they make their way around the interior of the church, they will certainly be struck by the magnificent monuments to popes and royalty, along with the many altars and relics of the saints, including those of Pope John XXIII and Pope John Paul II. What a pilgrim may not notice at first is that the basilica's piers contain thirty-nine statues of founders of religious orders. Included among these statues are several important monastic founders: Benedict of Nursia, Norbert of Xanten (founder of the Premonstratensians), Francis of Assisi, Dominic, and Bruno of Cologne (founder of the Carthusians). These thirty-nine founders are just a tiny representation of the many others that have come and gone in the two-thousand-year history of the Christian church. Charles Currier lists over two hundred in his history of religious orders, which is far from complete,[1] but clearly there have been and continue to be many, many religious and monastic orders. Though the Benedictines have historically been one of the most well known of the monastic orders, they have certainly not been alone. In medieval historiography it is often wrongly assumed that

1. Charles Warren Currier, *History of Religious Orders* (Boston: MacConnell Brothers, 1896).

Benedictine monasticism became *the* monasticism of Western Europe from at least the seventh century onward. This chapter will expose the error of this thinking and show the variation and continuity in non-Benedictine monasticism. Particular attention will be paid to the Celtic monastic tradition and its Frankish successors, but this chapter will also introduce Byzantine monastic history. Individuals discussed in this chapter include Columbanus, Chrodegang of Metz, Athanasius of Athos, and Paul Evergetinos.

Columbanus

The story of the rise of Benedictinism in the Middle Ages is complex.[2] It took centuries for the *Rule of Benedict* (RB) to become the dominant (though not exclusive) rule for medieval cenobitic monasteries, and early in its history it often competed with or was complemented by monastic rules from Ireland, especially the monastic rules of Columbanus (d. 615).[3] Columbanus spent many years of his life in the Irish monastery at Bangor but was also a missionary to continental Europe. His life was written by Jonas of Bobbio (d. ca. 665), a monk who entered the Columbanian monastery of Bobbio in northern Italy three years after Columbanus's death. Jonas purports to present the life of Columbanus as he learned it from those at Bobbio who had known Columbanus personally. Like many of the medieval monastic saints, Columbanus was destined for the monastery from a very young age. In his adolescence he was well disposed to study grammar, rhetoric, and the Scriptures. While still in his teens he took up residence at the monastery of Lough Erne to continue his studies under its famed monk Sinell. Columbanus, however, did not enter Lough Erne as a monk but instead chose to enter the monastery at Bangor, which, under Comgall (d. ca. 602), was famed for its austerity. After many years at Bangor, Columbanus received permission to leave the monastery to become a "pilgrim for Christ" (*peregrinus pro Christo*) or, in the words of Richard Woods, "a monastic evangelist."[4] In the words of Jonas: "After he had been many years in the cloister he longed to go into strange lands, in obedience to the command which the Lord gave Abraham: 'Get thee out of thy country, and from thy kindred, and from thy father's house, into a land that I will shew

---

2. For a very detailed history, see James G. Clark, *The Benedictines in the Middle Ages* (Woodbridge, UK: Boydell Press, 2011), 22–59.

3. For other Irish monastic rules, see Uinseann Ó Maidín, trans., *The Celtic Monk: Rules and Writings of Early Irish Monks* (Kalamazoo, MI: Cistercian Publications 1996).

4. Richard Woods, "Columban, St., c. 543–615," in *Encyclopedia of Monasticism*, ed. William M. Johnston (London: Fitzroy Dearborn, 2000), 321.

thee.'"[5] It was common practice in early medieval Irish monasticism for monks to undertake a pilgrimage as part of their monastic career. Given the close bonds of kinship within Irish clans, to leave home was seen as an extreme form of asceticism and as most appropriate for a mature monk. Today these monks would likely be viewed as foreign missionaries, but their primary motivation was not solely to evangelize the unconverted but also to engage in an intentional form of self-denial and asceticism.[6] Columbanus's pilgrimage would forever alter the course of Western medieval monasticism. The last twenty-five years of Columbanus's life would be dedicated to founding some of the most influential monasteries in early medieval Europe. He established monastic houses in Gaul (Annegray, Luxeuil, and Fontaines) and Italy (Bobbio), each of which followed his monastic rules. Columbanian monasticism became so successful that over the next century more than a hundred monasteries followed Columbanus's rule (often called the *Regula monastica*).

Columbanus's rule is actually two rules: the *Monk's Rule* (*Regula monchorum*), addressed to the individual monk, and the *Rule of the Monastery* (*Regula coenobialis*), which was intended to guide the communities he founded. These rules were meant to complement each other, and like the *Rule of Macarius* and the *Regula Orientalis* (discussed in chap. 3), these rules were more concerned with monastic spiritual dispositions than legislation for the monastery. The *Monk's Rule* is concerned with the spiritual to such an extent that it gives little attention to any material aspects of the individual monastic life.[7] For example, Columbanus writes that a "monk's chastity is indeed judged in his thoughts. . . . And what profit is it if he be virgin in body, if he be not virgin in mind?"[8] For Columbanus, one's physical chastity was less important than one's spiritual disposition to chastity. One's immaterial, spiritual state was as important as the actual physical practices of the monk. Thus, despite the later date of Columbanus's text, it shares much in common with the earlier rules written in Gaul. Though they lack detailed legislation, the rules of Columbanus were very successful, and competed with or complemented the RB (and other rules) for the next three centuries. This was the time of the so-called mixed rules (*regulae mixtae*).

5. Jonas of Bobbio, *Life of St. Columbanus* 9; Dana Carleton Munro, ed., *Life of St. Columban*, trans. and repr., Original Sources of European History, vol. 2, no. 7 (Philadelphia: Department of History of the University of Pennsylvania, 1895), 5.

6. See Róisín Ní Mheara, *In Search of Irish Saints: The Peregrinatio pro Christo* (Dublin: Four Courts Press, 1994).

7. Jane Barbara Stevenson, "The Monastic Rules of Columbanus," in *Columbanus: Studies on the Latin Writings*, ed. Michael Lapidge (Woodbridge, UK: Boydell Press, 1997), 206.

8. Columbanus, *Monk's Rule* 6; G. S. M. Walker, ed., *Sancti Columbani Opera* (Dublin: Dublin Institute for Advanced Studies, 1957), 129.

Monastic historian James Clark writes that a *"regula mixta* in which the *RB* was an important ingredient appears to have been formulated first in the Columbanian heartlands of Bobbio and Luxeuil."[9] This is not too surprising given that the RB disappeared from Italy at the time of the destruction of Monte Cassino by the Lombards between 577 and 589, returning to Italy in the eighth century when Monte Cassino was refounded. By then the RB was an import from Gaul, where it had been used at the monastery of Altaripa near Albi in southern Gaul during the seventh century. Most often, however, when the RB is mentioned in Gaul during the seventh century, it is mentioned in conjunction with Columbanus's *Regula monastica*.[10] A foundation charter for the monastery of Solignac in Aquitaine admonishes its monks to follow the example of the monks of Luxeuil, a Columbanian foundation, and to follow closely the rules of Benedict and Columbanus. The monastery of Rebais-en-Brie was founded, we are told, in order to gather together monks and pilgrims (note the Irish influence) "under the rule of Blessed Benedict and according to the practice of Luxeuil," that is, according to Benedict and Columbanus.[11] The formula "according to the rule of Blessed Benedict and the manner of the monastery of Luxeuil" is found again and again in seventh-century monastic foundation charters from Gaul.[12] Frankish literature of this period contains many phrases describing this mixed rule: "under a rule of the holy fathers, especially those of the abbots St. Benedict and St. Columbanus"; "in accordance with the standards of master Benedict and master Columbanus"; and "according to the rule of St. Benedict or master Columbanus."[13] And not only were *new* foundations using the mixed rule, but *existing* monasteries were being reformed and placed under the mixed rule as well.

Given that Columbanus may not have known the RB in its entirety, it is hard to know what the *regula mixta* may have legislated for the monks of Luxeuil and his other monasteries. It is possible, however, to examine how the RB was being used alongside other rules, likely demonstrating the ways that the RB was employed when paired with Columbanus's rule. The *Rule of a Certain Father to Virgins* (*Regula cuiusdam Patris ad Virgines*) is routinely designated as the "Rule of Waldebert of Luxeuil" because Waldebert (d. 670), third abbot of Luxeuil, composed a rule for the monastery of Evoriacum that

9. Clark, *Benedictines in the Middle Ages*, 27.

10. Dáibhí Ó Cróinín, "A Tale of Two Rules: Benedict and Columbanus," in *The Irish Benedictines: A History*, ed. Martin Browne and Colmán Ó Clabaigh (Dublin: Columba Press, 2005), 15.

11. Ó Cróinín, "A Tale of Two Rules," 16.

12. Friedrich Prinz, *Frühes Mönchtum im Frankenreich. Kultur und Gesellschaft in Gallien, den Rheinlanden und Bayern am Beispiel der monastischen Entwicklung (4. bis 8. Jahrhundert)*, rev. ed. (Munich: R. Oldenbourg, 1988), 269.

13. See ÓCróinín, "A Tale of Two Rules," 16 and Prinz, *Frühes Mönchtum*, 269.

liberally used, without attribution, Benedict and Columbanus. The *Rule for Virgins* (*Regula ad Virgines*) by Donatus of Besançon (d. 660), a former monk of Luxeuil, was compiled for his mother's foundation of Jussanum. In the preface to his rule, Donatus reveals that the monastery's abbess persuaded him to read and use Caesarius of Arles's *Rule*, which had been written especially for women.[14] In the words of Donatus,

> Though I am eminently aware, most precious vessel of Christ, that you live daily by the norms of the rule, nevertheless you have always wished to inquire with wise intention how you may excel yet more. For this reason, you have often urged me that, having explored the rule of the holy Caesarius, bishop of Arles, which was especially devoted to Christ's virgins, along with those of the most blessed Benedict and the Abbot Columbanus, I might cull the choicest blooms, gathering them, as I might say, into a bouquet.[15]

Donatus made use of Caesarius's *Rule* for his sections on admission, conduct, and possessions. From the RB he borrowed the well-known steps of humility and teaching on the authority of the superior. From Columbanus, Donatus developed his legislation on confession, punishments, and the liturgy. Waldebert borrowed from Columbanus in the area of discipline and from the RB on the legislation for monastic officials, such as the prioress, cellarer, and doorkeeper. Both rules stress that the abbess is to be a teacher of her nuns, an aspect from Columbanus and Benedict. It appears, then, that the *regula mixta* of seventh-century Gaul was simply a conglomeration of legislation taken from either the RB or the Columbanian rules as the monks saw fit. As will be discussed in greater detail in chapter 7, this period of *regulae mixtae* largely came to an end with the Synod of Aachen in 816, which was the result of the reforming efforts of Benedict of Aniane, whose monastery was taken under Emperor Charlemagne's royal protection in 792. With royal backing, Benedict of Aniane's monks traveled to other monasteries in the Frankish kingdom promoting the exclusive use of the RB, a move that had been gaining momentum since 800. In 802 Charlemagne ordered that a proper text of the RB be established and observed in all monasteries in an effort to unite and correct the Carolingian monasteries. With the succession to the throne of Charlemagne's son Louis the Pious, the reform was continued and strengthened because Benedict of Aniane was a

14. Marilyn Dunn, *The Emergence of Monasticism: From the Desert Fathers to the Early Middle Ages* (Oxford: Blackwell, 2000), 174.

15. Donatus of Besançon, *Rule for Virgins*, prologue; Jo Ann McNamara, *The Ordeal of Community* (Toronto: Peregrina, 1993), 32.

mentor and religious adviser to the young king. Meetings of monks, abbots, bishops, counts, and judges held in 802 and 813 ruled that all monasteries should live in accordance with the RB. In 816 and 817, synods of abbots met at the imperial residence at Aachen to produce legislation that would institute uniform monastic practice throughout the Carolingian Empire. Though it took time, the result of the synods was the gradual adoption by most Carolingian monasteries of the RB as their single guiding document, a pattern that would be repeated elsewhere.

Charlemagne's actions, which resulted in the reforming councils at Aachen, were the climax of a long series of reforming councils throughout the eighth century under the direction and oversight of Chrodegang, bishop of Metz (d. 766). Chrodegang was likely born near Liège (modern-day Belgium) around 712. He was brought up in the court of Charles Martel, mayor of the palace under the Merovingians from 718 to 741, and educated at the Benedictine monastery of St. Trond, though there is no evidence that he himself took the Benedictine monastic habit. In 741, on the death of Charles Martel, Pippin III (known as Pippin the Short) was made mayor of the palace, appointing Chrodegang as the bishop of Metz on October 1, 742.[16] In 754 Pope Stephen II conferred on him the position of archbishop of Germany. It was as archbishop that Chrodegang presided over a series of reforming synods and worked to implement his ideas of reform. He was also a man of action, instituting reform among the priests of St. Stephen's cathedral in Metz with his *Rule for Canons* (*Regula canonicorum* [RC]).

By definition a canon is a member of the clergy who lives according to the canons promulgated at ecclesiastical councils.[17] In Christian history, particularly in the West, a sharp distinction was often drawn between the canons and monks. For example, the Council of Toledo in 400 refers to clergy (*clerici*) who pretend to be monks and insists that there is a distinction between true monks (*veri monachi*) and true canons (*veri canonici*).[18] However, the Greek term *kanonikos* was used by some early Christian authors to refer to monks,[19] and Paul the Deacon (d. ca. 799), the eighth-century historian of the bishops of Metz, understood that Chrodegang "converted the sacred space within the cathedral cloister to the image of a monastery; and he instituted a rule

---

16. Pippin III would be the last "mayor of the palace." In March 752 he would become king of the Franks; therefore, the Carolingians would displace the Merovingians as the ruling dynasty.

17. Jerome Bertram, *The Chrodegang Rules: The Rules for the Common Life of the Secular Clergy from the Eighth and Ninth Centuries; Critical Texts with Translations and Commentary* (Aldershot, UK: Ashgate, 2005), 4.

18. J. D. Mansi, ed., *Sacrorum Conciliorum Nova et Amplissima Collectio, Tomus Tertius* (Venice: Antonio Zatta, 1759), 1012.

19. See Pseudo-Basil, *Constitutiones asceticae* 15.

for them."[20] Together this suggests that canons were, at least at times before the eighth century, viewed as monks. A clear and enduring distinction was achieved only at the Council of Aachen in 816, after Chrodegang's death.

There is evidence for Chrodegang's participation in five synods in the middle of the eighth century: Düren (748), Ver (755), Verberie (756), Compiègne (757), and Attigny (762).[21] These synods were local in nature (that is, they were meant to reform church life in the Frankish realms) and were in continuity with earlier church synods around Europe that were primarily concerned with reformation of the clergy. The Franks realized that there were still problems in the organizational structures of the church in their realms, so they sought to provide legislation for the clergy that would address this issue. They did not think that what they were doing was new; rather, they believed it to be in continuity with the "rules of the ancient fathers" and "the most proper norms of the holy catholic church."[22] For example, the synod at Ver promulgated twenty-five canons. The first eleven concerned themselves with contemporary issues such as reconstituting the ecclesiastical hierarchy, enforcing ecclesiastical discipline, and initiating church reforms. The final fourteen canons "are generally based on older church enactments, repeating or rephrasing edicts from Chalcedon, Antioch, Arles, and Carthage, once again adapting older norms to contemporary usages."[23] At the other councils, similar concerns arose, especially the validity or invalidity of a marriage and the proper relationship of the church to society. In the end, Chrodegang realized that there would not be a truly unified Frankish church unless its spiritual leadership was also united to one another and its bishop and clergy were well organized and spiritually exemplary. Chrodegang began this program in earnest with the writing and publication of the RC.

Though the RC was written initially for Chrodegang's clergy at the cathedral church of St. Stephen in Metz, it was likely meant to establish a pattern for others to imitate. The first thing to notice about the RC is that it is heavily dependent on the RB, quoting it in almost every chapter. That Chrodegang would make use of the RB is not surprising when one considers that he was educated at a Benedictine monastery and that his first act as a bishop was to found the monastery of Gorze.[24] Chrodegang's motivation for founding

20. M. A. Claussen, *The Reform of the Frankish Church: Chrodegang of Metz and the Regula canonicorum in the Eighth Century* (Cambridge: Cambridge University Press, 2004), 58.

21. Ibid., 47.

22. Ibid., 48.

23. Ibid., 50.

24. On Gorze and its early medieval history, see John Nightingale, *Monasteries and Patrons in the Gorze Reform: Lotharingia c. 850–1000* (Oxford: Clarendon, 2001).

Gorze is fairly traditional: to help him alleviate the inevitable heavenly consequences of his sins. The monks at Gorze are to live a life of quietness, order,
and tranquility according to the rule of "our holy father, St. Benedict." In 761
Chrodegang sent a group of monks from Gorze to found the Gengenbach
monastery, and near the end of his life he took an interest in the monastery
at Lorsch, using the RB as a guide for these communities as well.

The RC consists of thirty-four chapters broken down into sections by
M. A. Claussen as follows: a prologue; The Mechanics of Community; Sins
and Their Correction; Daily Life; and an epilogue. Further, Claussen sees a
more detailed structure to the RC:

> The Prologue introduces us to the rule, and, rehearsing a version of Christian
> history, it offers Chrodegang's interpretation of the obligations attendant on his
> office as bishop and lays out the reasons why he felt obliged to impose this new
> set of regulations on the life of the canons. The three middle sections of the rule
> are quite similarly structured, in that the first chapter of each (cc. 1, 12, and 20)
> sets forth the theme of the section, the central chapter (cc. 8, 14, and 25) is the
> most important and in a way exemplifies that theme, and the last chapters (cc. 11,
> 19, and 30) summarize the contents and goals of the section. The final section, in
> exploring the implications of the previous thirty chapters, restates and extends
> the purpose and goals of the rule which were initially set out in the Prologue.[25]

What is evident from the rule, and something that makes it distinct from
the RB, is that Chrodegang wrote to instigate reform in his readers and communities. Benedict wrote to give a particular structure to the monastic life,
not so much to reform already existing monastic life. His rule was one among
many. Chrodegang was attempting to alter current practice and to reenvision
community life as it was practiced in the Frankish kingdoms. His goal was not
just to order the life of one community but to bring *unanimitas* (unanimity)
to all the communities of canons that he oversaw.[26] Using Claussen's schema
we can see the most important emphases of Chrodegang's rule.

In his first section (chaps. 1–11: The Mechanics of Community), Chrodegang stresses the importance of humility, which is worked out practically in
the lives of the canons by attending the daily chapter meeting so that faults
can be amended and good zeal encouraged. Chrodegang reminds his readers
that God finds the proud abominable and resists them but gives grace to the
humble. The proud are sons of the devil, whereas the humble are sons of God.

---

25. Claussen, *Reform of the Frankish Church*, 60.
26. It is important to remember that the RB was originally written only for the monks at
Monte Cassino. It was not written as a rule for a "Benedictine order."

The proud will go to hell, while the humble attain everlasting life. All Christians, along with "the whole human race," should strive to be humble, but it is especially grievous for those who have "devoted themselves to the special service of God [to] leave the way of humility, and ally themselves with pride, which is the tyranny of the devil." The prideful need to return to God "through humility, through charity, through obedience and all else that is good."[27] For canons the greatest demonstration of their humility is through faithful, daily attendance at the chapter meeting. At chapter they will hear the Word of God and the RC read, and they will hear whatever commands the bishop (or his archdeacon) gives. Also, the bishop will "correct what needs correction and ensure that what needs to be done is done."[28] Each canon must come to chapter vested appropriately and act properly, according to their rank in the community. Chrodegang concludes this section by returning to the language of salvation: an evil zeal (i.e., pride) leads to hell, but a good zeal (i.e., humility) "leads to God and everlasting life."[29] Those in authority must reprove and punish pride so as to destroy it and thereby encourage "everyone to a better way of life." The one who loves his own soul in humility "keeps guard over himself, and draws others after himself to a pattern of good conduct, both by his words and his actions."[30]

The next section (chaps. 12–19: Sins and Their Correction) begins by legislating that no canon can strike or excommunicate another canon, no matter the circumstances. This is a right reserved for the superior. This section is mostly concerned with the power of those in authority—something that Chrodegang believes needs to be reformed—and he is likely influenced heavily by the RB, which spends much time on questions of authority and hierarchy in the monastery. Instead of canons excommunicating one another or administering corporal punishment (actions that receive approbation in the RB), Chrodegang recommends frequent confession and amendment of life as the remedy for sins. Using earlier Christian teaching, Chrodegang says that as soon as "any evil thought enters the heart of a servant of God . . . he should *humbly confess* it at once to his superior."[31] Structurally, however, each clergyman is to make confession to his bishop twice each year: once at the beginning of Lent and again between mid-August and November. But

27. RC 1; Bertram, *Chrodegang Rules*, 55.
28. RC 8; Bertram, *Chrodegang Rules*, 60. Themes addressed in this section's other chapters include sleeping arrangements, keeping silence, the daily offices, manual labor, and traveling outside the community. Transgressions of these standards are likely what is corrected at the chapter meeting.
29. This is a quotation from RB 72.2.
30. RC 11; Bertram, *Chrodegang Rules*, 62.
31. RC 14; Bertram, *Chrodegang Rules*, 63, emphasis in original, indicating a quotation from RB 7.

clergy can also make confession to the bishop or the bishop's representative whenever they want or need to. Regular confession allows each priest to receive the body and blood of Christ each Sunday and on principal feast days. Echoing the RB again, Chrodegang legislates that any of the clergy who fail to confess their sins to the bishop due to fear of being degraded in rank or held back from ordination, should it be found out by the bishop, are to suffer either corporal punishment (usually a beating with a rod) or imprisonment. The RC's purpose is to ensure that the "*measure of excommunication and punishment should be proportioned to the gravity of the fault, which shall be determined by* the bishop or his representatives."[32] Confession and excommunication, where necessary, are medicine for sick souls.

The final section of the RC (chaps. 20–30: Daily Life) begins with a chapter titled "Of the Observance of Lent." This would seem an odd place to begin a discussion of daily life in a community of canons except for Chrodegang's dependence here on chapter 49 of the RB. Benedict says that the life of a monk ought to be a continuous Lent, that is, austere and penitential. The RC echoes this when it says that "*the life of a* Christian *ought at all times to be* simple and sober," and even more so for those with "religious minds."[33] The overall Lenten nature of the clerical life is subjected to the oversight of the archdeacon or *primicerius*, both of whom are representatives of the bishop. As elsewhere in the RC, Chrodegang is heavily dependent here on the RB's teaching regarding the abbot (especially RB 2 and 64). These two leaders should learn to be "prudent in good and innocent of evil" by reading the Scriptures and the "canonical rules laid down by the holy fathers." They need to be adaptable to their clergy, meeting each one at his own level of spiritual development, while at the same time being stern when necessary. Furthermore, they need to be examples to the community and consult the bishop when "they cannot decide for themselves." Should these leaders be found to be "proud, pompous, argumentative or contemptuous of the canonical rule and this little rule," then they must be admonished; if they do not reform, they will be judged by the bishop.[34] For Chrodegang the canonical life is one of (1) humility, manifested in faithful chapter attendance and good zeal; (2) penance and regular confession; and (3) balanced, appropriate asceticism under the oversight of approved leadership. In many ways Chrodegang and his rule have more in common with the RB than not, though the subsequent history of canons, as we will see, diverged greatly from Benedictine monastic life.

32. RC 19; Bertram, *Chrodegang Rules*, 66, emphasis in original, quoting from RB 24.1–2.
33. RC 20; Bertram, *Chrodegang Rules*, 66, emphasis in original.
34. RC 25; Bertram, *Chrodegang Rules*, 71.

Byzantine Monasticism

While these developments were happening in the Western Middle Ages, there was an independent development of monasticism in the Byzantine Empire. Though Latin and Greek monasticism both trace their histories back to the deserts and cities of Egypt and the Holy Land, by the late fifth century the monastic life was practiced in distinct ways in the East and West. There were similarities, of course, but there were noticeable distinctions—perhaps the most obvious one being that Eastern Christian monasticism never developed into structured orders in which all observed the same rule. Eastern monasteries remained independent, though oftentimes they were affiliated with one another through a shared textual history. In Byzantium, monasteries were governed by two documents: a founder's *typikon* and a liturgical *typikon*. These *typika* governed the quotidian life of the community as well as the liturgical life of the monastery. Some *typika* became well-known and served as the model for many communities, such as the *typikon* for the Stoudios monastery in Constantinople. Two individuals and two *typika* in particular serve to illustrate the nature of Byzantine monasticism.

Between 925 and 930 Athanasius of Athos (d. 1001) was born in the Trebizond along the Black Sea. He was brought to Constantinople for studies, eventually becoming a professor in the theological academy there. Under the influence of an ascetic from Mount Olympus in Bithynia, Athanasius was attracted to the monastic life, joining the Kyminas community around 925 and remaining in this community for five years. He then moved to Mount Athos, the easternmost of the Chalcidice peninsulas, in late 957 or early 958. He lived for a year with another monk and later in a community at Karyes. Toward the end of 959 he moved into a solitary cell, and in 960 he moved to a more desolate site at the southeastern tip of the Athonite peninsula. In 962/63 he chose to construct a *lavra* (monastery) with enough cells for five solitaries, a refectory, and a communal church.[35] At this time Athanasius also drew up a *typikon* for this *lavra*. Yet in 964 Athanasius decided to adapt his community from a *lavra* to a cenobitic monastery, though the community came to be known by the misnomer the "Great Lavra."

35. Greg Peters, "Monasteries," in *The Encyclopedia of Christian Civilization*, ed. George Thomas Kurian (Malden, MA: Wiley-Blackwell, 2011), 3:1547: "The Greek word *lavra* means 'lane' or 'alley' and originally referred to the paths that connected individual monastic cells to a main, centralized church. In time, the term came to designate the whole monastic complex. In lavriotic monasteries, the monks spend the week praying, working and eating in their individual cells, coming together on Saturday and Sunday for a common liturgy. When returning to his cell, a monk would take the next week's provision of food and supplies to complete his assigned manual labor."

The *typikon* for the Great Lavra is heavily dependent on the ninth-century Stoudios *typikon*, borrowing primarily from Stoudios's liturgical regulations. As in all monastic communities, East or West, the bulk of the monk's day is spent in prayer. Athanasius took it for granted that the monks would pray at the traditional hours for prayer, so he devotes much of the space to the proper "performance" of prayer, including, for example, how many prostrations are to be done each day and how many at each service.[36] According to the *typikon*, the monks were to engage in regular manual labor including metal working, animal husbandry, shipwrighting, carpentry, wine-making, and baking.[37] The laboriousness of their work determined the amount of food that they were given each day, and it was up to the superior to determine the appropriate amount. On the days when the monks did not engage in manual labor, they were not to spend time "in idleness and laughter, but rather in prayer and reading."[38] The monks were not allowed to have any "personal property and private funds or coins or currency without the approval and knowledge of the superior."[39] Monks were not to leave the monastery without permission, and a "wise old monk" was to serve the monastery as gatekeeper, ensuring that visitors' questions were answered and that nothing was stolen from the monastery.[40] This gatekeeper served alongside several other monastic officials: the superior, a disciplinarian, someone who awakens the community at the proper time for prayer, an overseer, and a doorkeeper.[41] Athanasius's foundation and legislation was so successful that the Great Lavra still exists today. Mount Athos is a monastic republic composed of twenty monasteries, with the Great Lavra being the largest and most prominent.

Another highly influential Byzantine *typikon* was that of the monastery of the Theotokos Evergetis in Constantinople, founded by Paul of Evergetis. Though nothing is known of Paul's early life, he founded the Theotokos Evergetis between 1049 and 1054 on property belonging to his family just outside the walls of Constantinople. Given that he was already a tonsured monk when he founded the monastery, he must have first become a monk in the 1040s.[42] Paul's initial foundation consisted of only a small monastery

36. *Ath. Rule* 9; John Thomas and Angela Constantinides Hero, eds., *Byzantine Monastic Foundation Documents*, vol. 1 (Washington, DC: Dumbarton Oaks, 2000), 223.

37. *Ath. Rule* 29–31.

38. *Ath. Rule* 32; Thomas and Hero, *Byzantine Monastic Foundation Documents*, 1:228.

39. *Ath. Rule* 33; Thomas and Hero, *Byzantine Monastic Foundation Documents*, 1:228.

40. *Ath. Rule* 36; Thomas and Hero, *Byzantine Monastic Foundation Documents*, 1:228.

41. See *Ath. Rule* 17.

42. The fact that he had already received the tonsure, something that happens only after one has been a monk for some amount of time, shows that he was not a newcomer to the monastic life but someone already experienced in monastic living.

with a few cells. Sometime in the next few years, before his death in 1054, he composed a *typikon* for the monastery that was mostly administrative in nature. After Paul's death, Timothy of Evergetis became the superior, enlarging the original *typikon* (known as the *Hypotyposis*) as well as the monastery itself and composing a liturgical *typikon*.[43]

According to the *typika*, the Evergetis monastery could contain as many monks as the house could financially maintain.[44] These monks were divided into two groups: those who lived in the monastery at all times and those involved in various ministries both within and outside the monastery.[45] Some monks celebrated the canonical hours, whereas a non-liturgical group served as administrators of the monastery's properties or as cellarers, bakers, or cooks.[46] The monks were not allowed any personal possessions without the superior's permission, nor could a monk correspond with members of his family.[47] There were two monks to each cell, but all monks took their meals in common in the refectory with everyone eating the same food. Each monk also dressed the same so that there would be no physical distinction between choir monks and non-choir monks.[48] Regarding its administration, the monastery was to be a free, independent, and self-governing house, making it exempt from lay control.[49] The monastery's superior was chosen by the current superior in consultation with the preeminent monks of the house.[50] In addition to the superior, the monastery was to have a steward who handled the financial affairs of the foundation along with several treasurers.[51] Monks entering the house did not need to present an entrance gift, though the givers of these gifts were often remembered in the monastery's liturgical services.[52] In general, the Theotokos Evergetis was hostile to granting privileges to its monks, and it legislated for an egalitarian environment. In the words of Paul of Evergetis,

So then these are our wishes and are acceptable to God and the Evergetis [that is, the Virgin Mary], and they are greatly beneficial for your help; and in the

43. In this context the Greek word *hypotyposis*, like the word *typikon*, means "pattern." See Timothy of Evergetis, *Hypotyposis* 2–3.
44. Timothy of Evergetis, *Hypotyposis* 23.
45. Timothy of Evergetis, *Hypotyposis* 7.
46. Timothy of Evergetis, *Hypotyposis* 33.
47. Timothy of Evergetis, *Hypotyposis* 22.
48. Timothy of Evergetis, *Hypotyposis* 24 and 26.
49. Timothy of Evergetis, *Hypotyposis* 12. This status was necessary due to the existence of *charistikarioi*, private individuals who were granted the management of monasteries, which will be discussed in chap. 6.
50. Timothy of Evergetis, *Hypotyposis* 13.
51. Timothy of Evergetis, *Hypotyposis* 13 and 30.
52. Timothy of Evergetis, *Hypotyposis* 37.

future it will be your concern to maintain them unbroken and unchanged always. By this I mean, to carry out completely in all the *synaxeis* [i.e., liturgies]
the canonical procedure handed on to you, to preserve loyalty and honour
which is due to your *proestotes* [i.e., superior], to love one another, to be keen
each of you to surpass each other in humility, to labour with one another in
everything. . . . Look to one thing only, that is to live and conduct yourselves
virtuously and breathe in nothing else, if possible, than the word of salvation
and everything that is for the edification and benefit of the soul.[53]

Due to the balance of the *typika* and the monastery's independence from
lay control, the Evergetis foundation documents highly influenced subsequent
Byzantine monastic history. The Evergetis *typikon* "was undoubtedly the most
influential Byzantine founder's *typikon* ever written. . . . It was through the
borrowing of its *typikon* rather than through the development of any kind
of monastic order that *Evergetis* saw its institutions and customs introduced
into many of the most influential monasteries of later Byzantium."[54]

Ressourcement: Variations in the Ordered Life with Unity of Purpose

In short, Byzantine monasticism, like monasticism in Western Europe, flourished in a variety of ways during the Middle Ages. Despite monasticism's
earliest history, there was never one standardized form of monasticism to
which all monks and nuns conformed. There was diversity among regions,
orders, individual houses, and different monastic rules. Even among those
houses of the same order (like Benedictine monasteries) or those living under
a *typikon* that borrowed heavily from a preexisting *typikon* (like the monks
of the "Great Lavra"), there was still great diversity. This diversity, at least
in the West, was given expression in monastic customaries—collections of
regulations that were specific to an individual house. In Byzantine monasticism, which lacked monastic orders, distinct practices were spelled out in
the monastery's original foundation document, the *typikon*. This variety in
practice was not a sign of disunity but was, rather, a sign of the many ways
in which the shared values of monasticism (prayer, community, orderliness,
growth in holiness, etc.) could be expressed in a diversity of customs. Though
there was always variation in the ordered life of monasticism, there was also
always unity of purpose amid such diversity.

53. Paul of Evergetis, *Typikon* 42; R. H. Jordan and Rosemary Morris, *The Hypotyposis of
the Monastery of the Theotokos Evergetis, Constantinople (11th–12th Centuries): Introduction,
Translation and Commentary* (Farnham, UK: Ashgate, 2012), 238.
    54. Thomas and Hero, *Byzantine Monastic Foundation Documents*, 2:468, emphasis in original.

Few Protestant Christians, I would guess, likely view the plethora of denominations that exist as a good thing. The disunity among Christians that has given rise to many of these churches is sinful and certainly not in conformity with Jesus's prayer that we may all be one as he and the Father are one (John 17:21). Yet diversity of practice is not sin even if division and disunity are often sinful. Though the individualism that is rampant in the Christian church is to be regretted and resisted, the diversity of practices should mostly be welcomed. When God made humankind, he saw fit to ensure, by way of genetic constitution, that no two humans would be exactly the same. Though identical twins may look alike and even act alike, they are still two distinct persons. God is not interested in unity to the point of uniformity, for he delights in diversity (see Rev. 7:9–10).

It is this diversity among humankind that legitimates the many different forms of worship that manifest themselves in the Christian churches. Contrary to the historical and theological fiction that God ordained one way of worship and that way is best represented by church N., the reality is that even in the New Testament we see theological univocity amid liturgical diversity. Though this diversity presented difficulties for the earliest Christians (see Acts 15), the solution was not to legislate uniformity but to settle on theological essentials and to exercise charity in nonessentials. It appears that God delights in our worship of him in the beauty of holiness even if the form varies from one local church or denomination to another. What the monastic tradition demonstrates is that there are agreed-upon practices that all monasteries have in common even if they are practiced differently from one community to another. The same is true in local churches.

First Timothy 4:13 is one of the few biblical texts that seems to envision the essence of a Christian worship experience: "Devote yourself to the public reading of Scripture, to exhortation, to teaching."[55] How this reading is done and how this exhortation and teaching are accomplished is, apparently, left up to the discretion of the worshiping community, since the author provides no clear prescriptions. Though this is an argument *ex silentio*, it seems reasonable to suppose that God is happy when we worship him according to our unique giftings, assuming that it is done decently and in order and for the building up of the body of Christ (see 1 Cor. 14:26–40). Thus for some this will manifest itself in a structured church service (e.g., an Anglican service done according to the Book of Common Prayer), whereas for others a less

---

55. To this I would add 1 Cor. 11:17–34, which appears to says that the Eucharist is a regular feature of Christian worship: "when you come together as a church" (i.e., *when* you come together, not *if*).

structured, spontaneous service will be preferable (e.g., the "silent waiting" of Quakerism). Yet none of these styles should be seen as more right or authentic to the Christian tradition, nor should these ways of worshiping be seen only as preferences that fit one's personality. Instead, each congregation should strive to live into the diversity that God has gifted to his church. Worship style should never be equated with church identity or missional strategies, for these are found only in the never-changing truth of the person and gospel of Jesus Christ. Liturgical diversity exists to exalt the one God: Father, Son, and Holy Spirit. And God delights in our God-given diversity.

6

Challenges of Christendom

There has always been an interest in monasticism by those who are not monks or nuns themselves. Throughout much of Christian history, this took (and continues to take) the form of monastery visits and financial support.[1] Yet this support and visitation were not always beneficial to the monastery, often disrupting the daily regimen. For example, in 1376 the Premonstratensian canons at Alnwick, England, entertained Henry Percy, the earl of Northumberland and their patron, along with thirteen of his knights and 1,020 parishioners, who ate in the cloister.[2] Though the chronicler who recorded this event does not necessarily state that it was burdensome to the canons, it is certainly shocking to imagine so many non-monastics enjoying themselves in areas of the abbey that were supposed to be reserved for the monks alone. As well, such an extravagant meal must have taken a number of weeks to plan and execute, suggesting that some number of the canons at the abbey were likely more involved in the plans for the meal than in the daily discipline of the monastery. And this is just one example among thousands in extant sources from both the Byzantine Empire and the Western monastic tradition, spanning the entire range of the Middle Ages. In both Eastern and Western monasticism there was a movement around 1000 when laypersons and non-monastics became heavily involved in the lives of monasteries, not

---

1. See, for example, Karen Stöber, *Late Medieval Monasteries and Their Patrons: England and Wales, c. 1300–1540* (Woodbridge, UK: Boydell Press, 2007).
2. Ibid., 75.

only as patrons, but also sometimes as lay abbots and abbesses and oftentimes as founder-benefactors. This did not always bode well for the monasteries individually or for the institution of monasticism generally. This chapter, therefore, will examine the rise of non-monastic involvement in monasticism, especially the *charistikē* in the Byzantine Empire and the practice of commendatory abbots and abbesses in Latin monasticism during the Middle Ages, showing that such connections between monastics and lay monastics often had negative consequences and even devastating results.

Non-monastic Involvement in Monasticism

During the eleventh and twelfth centuries, monasticism in the Byzantine Empire and the Latin West underwent an intense period of reform and renewal (see chaps. 7 and 8). This included the influence of the monastic founders Christodoulos of Patmos (d. 1093), Nikon of the Black Mountain (d. ca. 1110), Lazarus of Mt. Galesion (d. 1053), and Timothy of the Theotokos Evergetis (d. after 1067) in the Christian East, and the rise of the Carthusians, Cistercians, Gilbertines, and other eremitic and cenobitic monastic movements and orders in the Western church. This fervor of new foundations continued unabated into the twelfth century.[3] One of the main reasons that Byzantine monasticism needed to be reformed throughout the eleventh and twelfth centuries was due to the pervasive existence of private religious foundations throughout the Byzantine Empire. The rise of these institutions is well documented but complex.[4] What is important to note, however, is that by the later tenth century and into the early eleventh century "benefactors [of religious institutions] . . . would prefer to found a church or monastery of their own rather than contribute toward the maintenance or repair of an existing foundation. That way the benefactor would gain for himself [or herself] the prestigious title of *ktistes*, the 'founder.'"[5] Emperor Nicephorus Phocas (963–969), though he himself was the benefactor of private institutions (especially of the Great

3. For a discussion of this reform in the Byzantine Empire, see the chapter titled "The Resurgence of the Monastic Life" in Rosemary Morris, *Monks and Laymen in Byzantium, 843–1118* (Cambridge: Cambridge University Press, 1995), 9–30; and the section titled "Monasteries and Society" in Michael Angold, *Church and Society in Byzantium under the Comneni, 1081–1261* (Cambridge: Cambridge University Press, 1995), 263–382. For the Christian West, see Giles Constable, *The Reformation of the Twelfth Century* (Cambridge: Cambridge University Press, 1996), and C. H. Lawrence, *Medieval Monasticism*, 3rd ed. (Harlow, UK: Longman, 2001), 146–206.

4. See John Philip Thomas, *Private Religious Foundations in the Byzantine Empire* (Washington, DC: Dumbarton Oaks Research Library and Collection, 1987), 157–213.

5. Ibid., 150.

Lavra on Mount Athos), stated in his *Novella de monasteriis* of 964 that there were too many private religious foundations in the empire:

> In times gone by when such institutions were not sufficient, the establishment of them was praiseworthy and very useful; surely the good done by those who established them was more abiding, for they wished to provide food and care for the bodies of men in one case, and in the other, to pay attention to the conduct of the soul and the higher life. But when their number had increased greatly and has become disproportionate to the need, and people still turn to the founding of monasteries, how is it possible not to think that this good has not mixed with evil, that darnel has not been added to the wheat?[6]

Nicephorus suggests in this *Novella* that the need for individuals to start new foundations is due to their vanity. Then as now, individuals liked to see their names on public buildings. While the newer foundations did well financially because of the generosity of their benefactors, the real issue in the emperor's eyes was that older institutions were in dire financial straits; as a result, their property had begun to physically decay because of insufficient funds:

> This is indeed obvious to anyone, for at a time when there are thousands of other monasteries which have suffered by the lapse of time and need much help we show no zeal in spending money for their rehabilitation, but turn our attention instead to the creation of new monasteries of our own. And this in order that we may not only enjoy the name of having founded something new, but also because we desire that our foundation should be clearly in evidence and be apart by itself to the end that our name may appear throughout the world and be celebrated in accordance with the divine prophecy.[7]

Realizing that something needed to be done, Nicephorus introduced legislation to try to curb the endowment of new foundations while also trying to buttress those that had a shortage of income. Though the emperor's legislation did not abolish private monasteries, he prevented the laity from endowing new foundations, making only a few exceptions. The emperor's main concern was not to initiate a reform of monastic life or to impede its growth but rather to help those monasteries that were suffering due to the practice of private endowment. He strove to direct much needed funds to older, established foundations. Nicephorus championed the monastic life by

6. Peter Charanis, "Monastic Properties and the State in the Byzantine Empire," *Dumbarton Oaks Papers* 4 (1948): 56–57, where the whole *Novella* is provided in English translation. See also Thomas, *Private Religions Foundations*, 150.

7. Cited in Thomas, *Private Religious Foundations*, 150–51; Charanis, "Monastic Properties," 57.

trying to help existing monasteries flourish rather than aiding the formation of new foundations at the expense of older monasteries. This was a laudable goal, though it proved harmful in the end.

The *Charistikē*

Unfortunately for older monasteries and for Byzantine monasticism in general, Nicephorus's law was repealed in 988 by Emperor Basil II, leaving a large number of monasteries in a desperate financial situation. To help alleviate the problems, "a public program sponsored by the emperor and the ecclesiastical hierarchy" was established in which the "management of religious institutions" was placed in the hands of private individuals.[8] This practice came to be called *charistikē* when it involved laymen and *epidosis* when it involved ordained church leaders.[9] In the words of John Thomas, "Under this program, private individuals obtained the management of an ecclesiastical foundation by appealing to the emperor, who held the rights of ownership over imperial foundations, or to the office of the patriarch, metropolitan, or bishop that had originally issued a foundation's *stauropegion*," that is, an exemption from the jurisdiction of the local bishop, putting the monastery directly subject to the highest authority of the church.[10] The purpose of this was for the laymen or churchmen to help restore and repair the monastery's property and place it on more secure financial footing, though this did not always happen in reality. The purpose of the *charistikē* was soon undermined by the awarding of monasteries to influential laymen who continued to accumulate oversight and influence in monasteries. "The turning point," writes Thomas, "occurred when the authorities began to grant out well-endowed, financially stable institutions which did not require the restorations so urgently needed by other, less financially remunerative foundations." Further, a "similar transformation in the use of *epidosis* had already occurred by the tenth century. It had always been more profitable for a patron to reap the financial rewards of administering a wealthy private monastery than to commit the capital and the property necessary to found a new monastery. Similarly, the rewards of administering a healthy monastery under the *charistikē* far surpassed those of restoring a ruined one."[11] Thus a system intended to solve a problem becomes a problem itself. Monasteries with no financial needs were given over to the management of laypersons, while new houses continued to

8. Thomas, *Private Religious Foundations*, 157.
9. For simplicity, when referring to this practice I will primarily use the word *charistikē*.
10. Thomas, *Private Religious Foundations*, 157.
11. Ibid., 158.

be founded and generously endowed, leaving little or no financial help for existing monasteries with significant financial needs.

According to John V the Oxite (d. 1100), patriarch of Antioch, by the end of the eleventh century nearly all the monasteries in the Byzantine Empire had come into the hands of the *charistikarioi*.[12] Though this is certainly an exaggeration, it does show the extent of the spread of the institution. Whereas Byzantium had once teemed with private religious institutions, including independent monasteries, there were now few such institutions. As a result, the monasteries that had come under *charistikē* or *epidosis* were now mostly under the influence of non-monastics, and most often laypersons, who began to dictate how the monastery would be run and who controlled the monastery's movable and immovable goods. Alexius Studites, patriarch of Constantinople from 1025 to 1043, was one of the first critics of the *charistikē*. A public record from November 1027 says that the purpose of the *charistikē* is for the maintenance, well-being, and enlargement of ecclesiastical foundations. He proposed that the office of his chancellor would be the centralized office through which all requests and approvals for *charistikē* would pass. He also legislated that the original recipients of the grants would not be able to transfer their rights to other persons, ensuring that no one could expect to hold a perpetual, hereditary *charistikē*. Lastly, he "forbade men to hold a *charistikē* over a convent of nuns, or women to hold one over a monastery" of men.[13] In January 1028 he issued a second document that "once again . . . decried the rapacity of evil *charistikarioi*, who appropriated the incomes of the institutions that they were supposed to protect and drove away the monks who resided in them."[14] Unfortunately, Alexius's legislation did not stop the growth or abuse of the *charistikē*.

Though caution must be used when reading and interpreting monastic reform documents, which tend to vilify existing monasteries and monastic practices in favor of reformed practices, the consistent narrative of eleventh- and twelfth-century Byzantine reform documents seems to paint an accurate picture of the abuses related to the *charistikē*. Beginning in the eleventh century, the *typika* of new monasteries began to explicitly address the problem of the *charistikē*, and the founders of these new monasteries legislated in ways that they hoped would keep the *charistikē* at bay. One of the most well known of these documents is the *typikon* of Timothy Evergetinos (discussed in chap. 5) for the monastery of the Theotokos Evergetis (the Benefactress). As stated earlier, the monastery,

12. John of Antioch, *Oratio de monasteriis laicis non tradendis* 9.
13. Thomas, *Private Religious Foundations*, 168.
14. Ibid., 169.

located in Constantinople, was founded in 1048 or 1049 by Paul Evergetinos. In time it became a highly influential institution in later Byzantine monastic history, especially by way of its *typikon*, which was written by Timothy, the so-called second founder, sometime between 1098 and 1118. This document is oftentimes heavily quoted from or even used wholesale by later monastic founders, and its insistence on the monastery's independence became a model for others to follow.

There are several ways in which the founders of the Evergetis monastery imagined that they could avoid being taken over and controlled by the *charistikē*. First, they set up the monastery to be an independent and self-governing institution. Second, there would be a way in which the house's superior would be chosen so as to ensure that he was not only suitable for the job but also that the house would not come under the governance of someone who would seek or be liable to the influence of the *charistikē*. Third, the finances of the monastery would be governed by its steward whose election was subject not only to the superior but also to the community's preeminent monks. Fourth, the monastery would be properly endowed so that it would not find itself in a difficult financial situation that might occasion involvement with a *charistikarioi*. Fifth, the foundation's properties were viewed as inalienable.

The Evergetis *typikon* states that the monastery is to be a free, independent, and self-governing monastery: "We instruct all in the name of our Lord God the Ruler of All that this holy monastery is to be independent, free of everyone's control, and self-governing, and not subject to any rights, be they imperial or ecclesiastic or of a private person."[15] Given that a *charistikarioi* could be an ecclesiastic or layperson, or even the emperor, it is no surprise that the *typikon* lists these categories of persons. Timothy viewed the monastery as under the governance and direction of the Virgin Mary, the founder Paul Evergetinos, and the monastery's duly-elected superior. Further, the monastery had received an imperial chrysobull (an official document bearing the emperor's seal) establishing its independence; thus to violate the foundation's independence would be to go against God, the founder, and the prerogative of past emperors. Perhaps realizing how difficult it would be to safeguard the monastery's independence from people as powerful as the emperor and the patriarch of Constantinople, Timothy legislated that anyone who violated the monastery's independence would be subject to grave consequences. To show

---

15. Timothy of Evergetis, *Hypotyposis* 12; John Thomas and Angela Constantinides Hero, eds., *Byzantine Monastic Foundation Documents*, vol. 2 (Washington, DC: Dumbarton Oaks, 2000), 482.

the extent and the seriousness of Timothy's insistence on the monastery's independence, it is worth quoting his warning to would-be violators in full:

> If anyone ever at any time and in any way wishes to gain control over this monastery or put it in subjection or place it under someone's power, whether he be an emperor or a patriarch or some other member of the clergy or of the senate or even the superior of this monastery himself or its steward or simply one of its brothers prompted by an attack of the devil, not only will he be held responsible for the divine body and blood of Our Lord God and Savior Jesus Christ and to the Mother of God our Lady *Evergetis*, but also "Let him be accursed" (Gal. 1:8), as the holy apostle says, and let him inherit the curse of the three hundred and eighteen Holy Fathers and become joint-heir with the traitor Judas and be counted with those who shouted "away with him, away with him, crucify him" (John 19:15), and "his blood be on us and on our children" (Matt. 27:25), because this wretched person has treated wretchedly something which was once a farm and was turned into a monastery with much sweat and toil and set up to be free by those very people who established it, placing it with malicious and deceitful intent, perhaps under the power of corrupt and wicked men who look to nothing else but pernicious gain.[16]

Those outside the monastery who transgress Timothy's *typikon* will be accursed by God, considered another Judas, and thought of in terms of the disobedient Israelites. In addition, the Evergetis *typikon* warns those inside the monastery that they need to keep the rule in all its points as well, for a monk who transgresses the *typikon* will be "taught and instructed in a brotherly way." Thus the Evergetis *typikon* sees that individuals both within and outside the monastery can transgress the founder's wishes, but only those outside should be accursed and condemned.

One way to help keep the monastery independent was to provide unambiguous legislation regarding the house's superior. Originally the monastery was to have two superiors, one a reclusive hermit and the other "unconfined." When the hermit superior died, the "unconfined" superior would retire to the hermitage, and a new "unconfined" superior would be appointed. Timothy, in time, thought better of this and legislated that there should be only one superior for the monastery. This superior could choose to be a recluse, but it would not be required of him; if he chose to live in an "unconfined" manner,

---

16. Timothy of Evergetis, *Hypotyposis*, 12; Thomas and Hero, *Byzantine Monastic Foundation Documents*, 2:482. The "three hundred and eighteen Holy Fathers" is a common reference in Byzantine monastic foundation documents and refers to the Council of Nicaea in 325, which was attended, it is said, by 318 church officials. Thus Timothy warns of an anathema from the apostles and the Nicene fathers upon the violators.

he was limited to leaving the monastery only to visit the area surrounding the monastery and its nearby estates. He could also leave the monastery if summoned by the emperor or patriarch. Though the reason given for this legislation is not explicit, one cannot help but wonder if Timothy was making it nearly impossible for the superior to meet people who would then desire to exercise some sort of control over the monastery. The seriousness of Timothy's legislation can be judged in this warning: "If [the superior] should ever transgress this instruction, treating it as of no account, he will be excommunicated."[17]

In order to ensure that the right person was chosen as superior, Timothy legislated that upon the death of the current superior, the monastery's steward should be promoted to the office. In this way the monks would have a first-hand knowledge of the fitness of their next superior because they would have observed him in the office of steward: "If this steward carries out his office faultlessly, proving to be reliable in the sight of God and you . . . the [dying superior] should appoint him to leadership over you, since his faultless actions as steward have already been enough to act as a test." In turn, the new steward was to be elected by the newly appointed superior in concert with a few of the monks "who always surpass the others in their conduct, manners, intellect, character, discipline, and their spiritual state and way of life." Together they were to appoint a steward "who surpasses everyone in all these points."[18] Should the elected steward fail in his task, he is to be removed from office. One of the areas of potential failure concerned the subjection of the monastery's property (by the steward) to someone else's control—that is, a *charistikarioi*. Timothy writes, "If time proves him to be unqualified and unsuitable, either . . . because he has been doing favors for his relatives or has been appropriating some of the monastery's property . . . or has been betraying or subjecting the monastery's property to anyone's control . . . then another person should be found."[19] In short, the *typikon* is designed to ensure that the monastery has no superior who will be prone to letting the monastery come under the *charistikē*. This is done not only by electing the right person to the office of steward, who will in turn become the superior, but also by examining how that steward handles the monastery's finances. If he betrays the monastery, then he is removed from office as steward, long before he becomes the superior.

17. Timothy of Evergetis, *Hypotyposis* 13; Thomas and Hero, *Byzantine Monastic Foundation Documents*, 2:484.

18. Timothy of Evergetis, *Hypotyposis* 13; Thomas and Hero, *Byzantine Monastic Foundation Documents*, 2:484.

19. Timothy of Evergetis, *Hypotyposis* 14; Thomas and Hero, *Byzantine Monastic Foundation Documents*, 2:485.

Thus the offices of superior and steward are ideally held by men who will resist any advance of the *charistikē* toward the monastery.

Timothy legislated another way to resist the *charistikē* by ensuring that the monastery was properly endowed. This, of course, was the goal of most (if not all) Christian monasteries from the very beginnings of the institution itself. In order for monks and nuns to live properly monastic lives, they needed the financial freedom to do so. That is not to say that monastics never engaged in money-making activities.[20] Rather, with financial stability and freedom came the option of living lives according to the community's own rule or customs with little or no interference from the non-monastics beyond the foundation's walls. Timothy's *typikon*, written early in the community's history, gives evidence to the fact that the monastery possessed dependencies, such as St. Andrew's in Constantinople, as well as "some small pieces of immovable property."[21] The *typikon* also legislates commemoration for those who have "left or will leave something worthy of remembrance to the monastery."[22] By establishing themselves on a strong financial footing, the monks would not be placed in a position to seek the assistance of outside persons who may then co-opt the monastery's leadership and property.

Regarding the monastery's possessions, both movable (such as sacred vessels, icons, and books) and immovable, Timothy states that they are in essence inalienable, "and not only inalienable but also completely safe from removal and theft by anyone at all."[23] Those who do remove the monastery's property are acting sacrilegiously and are subject to any lawful penalties. The only reason given for removing property or giving it to another is a calamity, such as a fire or earthquake that destroys the monastery, after which the foundation's property may be sold to save the monastery or rebuild it. Even this alienability of property, however, must be done with full knowledge of the superior, steward, ecclesiastical officials, and other "preeminent officials [who] have gathered together for this purpose."[24] The items are to be removed in the sight of all the people and duly reflected in the monastery's inventory.

---

20. As mentioned above vis-à-vis Pachomius's monks, early monastics in the Egyptian desert often plaited reeds into baskets that they then sold to commercial tradespeople and other monastics.

21. Timothy of Evergetis, *Hypotyposis* 34; Thomas and Hero, *Byzantine Monastic Foundation Documents*, 2:493.

22. Timothy of Evergetis, *Hypotyposis* 36; Thomas and Hero, *Byzantine Monastic Foundation Documents*, 2:494.

23. Timothy of Evergetis, *Hypotyposis* 19; Thomas and Hero, *Byzantine Monastic Foundation Documents*, 2:488.

24. Timothy of Evergetis, *Hypotyposis* 19; *Byzantine Monastic Foundation Documents*, 2:489.

From the aforesaid, we can see that the legislation of the Evergetis monastery confirms that the main areas in which the *charistikē* were violating
monastic principles were oversight and financial (mis)management. The ac-
curacy of the picture painted by the Evergetis's legislation is confirmed in
other monastic foundation documents throughout the eleventh and twelfth
centuries. Had the *charistikē* not been liable to these accusations, then why
the need for legislation against such ongoing abuses? That which needs to
be legislated against proves its existence and its pervasiveness. The *charistikē*
became such a problem that at its height the institution enjoyed the right
to nominate and appoint the clergy in their institutions as well as put laypersons, some of whom lived in the monastery itself, on the payrolls of the
monasteries that they held. Even if a *charistikarioi* received a financially well-
endowed monastery that was operating according to its founder's wishes,
he often took it upon himself to redistribute the incomes of the monastery
for personal gain. Ultimately the *hēgumenoi* (abbots/abbesses) lost control
of the daily administration of the monasteries, especially oversight of the
house's finances. Discipline among the monks and nuns also broke down
due to the presence of the *charistikē*. If a monk or nun did not agree with
his or her superior, then he or she would petition the *charistikē*, who often
overstepped his boundaries. To put it bluntly, despite the good intentions of
those who introduced the *charistikē*, the institution was abused and became
a source for the devolution of Byzantine monasticism, bringing about the
need for a monastic reform movement in the eleventh- and twelfth-century
Byzantine church.

Similar stirrings and developments can be witnessed in the Western monastic tradition, though with different results. The starting point of the *charistikē*
was a noble one—to ensure that older monasteries would survive into the
future. In Western monasteries many of the problems began not with a gov-
ernmental plan implemented to help monasteries but with a loosening of
discipline from within monasteries. This was not always the case, but a general
picture does emerge from the evidence.

In his rule for monks, Benedict of Nursia noticed and addressed an issue
that would be detrimental to cenobitic monastic life—private property. He
writes, "Above all, this evil practice must be uprooted and removed from
the monastery. We mean that without an order from the abbot, no one may
presume to give, receive or retain anything as his own, nothing at all—not a
book, writing tablets or stylus—in short, not a single item."[25] Granted, not

---

25. *Rule of Benedict* (RB) 33.1–3; Timothy Fry, ed., *RB 1980: The Rule of St. Benedict in
Latin and English with Notes* (Collegeville, MN: Liturgical Press, 1981), 231.

all monasteries in Western Europe followed the *Rule of Benedict* (RB), but Benedict was not the only monastic legislator who saw the potential pitfalls of private property in the monastery and therefore legislated for individual as well as corporate poverty.[26] Udalric, a monk of Cluny writing in the eleventh century, said that the monk's attitude toward all things is that they are "ours." The only thing that a monk could call his own was his father and mother, and this applies to the abbot as well.[27] Legislation concerning the prohibition of monastics owning any private property even entered into general codes of canon law, including that of Pope Gregory IX in the thirteenth century and the conciliar decrees of both Lateran III (1179) and Lateran IV (1215), among other councils.

Commendatory Abbots and Abbesses

By the turn of the first millennium, however, the legislation was loosened so that monks could own private property. The statutes of the English Benedictines from 1219 to 1225 defined proprietaries, that is, those who possessed *proprietas* (private property), as "those who, without knowledge of their abbot (or of their prior if there be no abbot) possess anything to themselves which the abbot has not given or permitted."[28] Notice that this appears to support the initial prohibition against private property given in the RB, but by the thirteenth century it was often the abbot himself who was most likely to possess private property—a trend that had started centuries earlier. In earliest Christian monasticism, the whole community was seen as the owner of the monastery's properties and goods. The abbot controlled the goods on behalf of the monastery, but he did not own them himself. This changed, however, when monasteries began to make a distinction between that part of the monastery's income that should be designated for the sustenance of the monks or nuns versus that part meant to sustain the physical fabric and other needs of the monastery. In the tenth century that part designated for the sustenance of the monks and nuns came to be called the "table" (*mensa*).[29] At times this division in the monastery's resources protected the monks from

26. See Adalbert de Vogüé, "Poverty in Western Monasticism: Fourth to the Eighth Century," *Monastic Studies* 13 (1982): 99–112.

27. G. G. Coulton, *Five Centuries of Religion*, vol. 3, *Getting and Spending* (1936; repr., New York: Octagon Books, 1979), 359. The following pages are heavily indebted to Coulton's exposition.

28. Ibid., 363.

29. See Emile Lesne, *L'Orgine des menses dans le temporal des églises et des monasteries de France au IXᵉ siècle* (Lille/Paris: Rene Giard/Honoré Champion, 1910). An English summary of Lesne can be found in Coulton, *Five Centuries of Religion*, 3:364–67.

unsavory abbots, but in the judgment of Emile Lesne the division of resources into *mensa* and non-*mensa* is a sign of the relaxation of monastic discipline.[30] G. G. Coulton concludes,

> However this partition [of resources] may have begun at the wish of the breth-
> ren, abbots soon began to bend it to their own purposes. It left them, in many
> cases at least, more economic freedom: the earmarking of one portion for the
> community implied a similarly definite allocation of the rest to the abbot, and
> gave them the less opportunity of protest; so long as their own portion was
> paid, he might more easily apply all the rest to his own personal purposes.[31]

This division of the monastery's goods into two different accounts, if you will, made it easy to identify which houses were, in particular, the wealthiest. This led, on some occasions, to laypeople setting themselves up as overseers of the monastery for the purpose of appropriating the monastery's wealth for their own ends. This was the beginning of the *commendam* system in Western monasticism.

When a person held an ecclesiastical benefice, whether an office or a prop-erty, *in commendam*, he or she was entitled to the revenues of the office or property. In the history of monasticism,

> Monasteries were subject to papal grants *in commendam*, under which terms
> the house passed into the hands of a secular [that is, non-monastic], or occa-
> sionally a lay, beneficiary, who became titular abbot. Generally the *commen-*
> *dam* abbot exercised authority over the temporal and spiritual possessions of
> the monastery but did not govern it directly. Therefore, such grants invariably
> undermined the material condition of the monastery and led to indiscipline,
> depopulation and even desertion.[32]

Though known occasionally in the earliest church, the practice of *commen-dam* became much more commonplace in the tenth century and flourished in the later Middle Ages. For example, Adelaide of Burgundy (d. 999), former wife of Lothair II of Italy and future wife of Otto I the Great, Holy Roman Emperor, was given in 938 "the *commendam* of certain abbeys in Tuscany." Church officials also held ecclesiastical benefices *in commendam*, such as Hatto (d. 913), the tenth-century archbishop of Mainz, who is said to have held twelve monasteries *in commendam* at one time. Even Pope Gregory VII (d. 1085)

30. Lesne, *L'Orgine des menses*, 48.
31. Coulton, *Five Centuries of Religion*, 3:365.
32. James G. Clark, *The Benedictines in the Middle Ages* (Woodbridge, UK: Boydell Press, 2011), 294.

granted abbeys *in commendam* to bishops and laypersons alike. This continued at such a pace that "in the twelfth and thirteenth centuries it befell frequently that bishops, either by their own authority or by that of the pope, retained abbacies for themselves under the title of *commendam* or administration."[33] For example, Cardinal Giovanni Gaetano Orsini (d. 1335) was made prior of the monasteries of Marestay and St. Jean d'Angeliac, both in southwestern France, by Pope John XXII on the same day (July 25, 1317). Ten years later he was made commendatory abbot of the Benedictine monastery of Santa Maria in Florence by the same pope.[34]

In time, as individual monasteries grew more lax (or at least were perceived to be lax and/or accused of relaxing their discipline), church officials would request that such monasteries be given to them *in commendam* under the pretext that they were going to reform and restore them. Rarely, however, did this bode well for the monastery. In the words of Zeger Bernard van Espen, "These abbots commendatory were occupied with the one single concern of increasing their revenues; whence it followed that they left little or nothing for the maintenance of the monks, the celebration of the divine service, the exercise of hospitality, the relief of the poor, and the upkeep or repair of the fabric [of the monastery]."[35] By the late Middle Ages one monastic chronicler, Thomas Walsingham (d. ca. 1422), monk of St. Albans Abbey north of London, describes the state of monastic life (at least in England) in the mid- to late-fourteenth century as follows:

> In the last day of this Abbot [Thomas de la Mare (d. 1396)], the Church of the Exempt was reduced to such servitude in the Kingdom, that the Pope presumed to quash elections duly made, and set up other [Abbots] at his own pleasure, until the King and his Council assumed a more lively spirit and decreed to resist such great evils. . . . So the most experienced men feared lest, if the Pope had free power to dispose of the churches of this realm . . . he would confer the wealthiest abbeys upon his own Cardinals or familiar servants, who would strive not to increase Religion or augment the numbers of monks, but rather to destroy.

Walsingham continues by describing that these commendatory prelates would not allow the monasteries to maintain large communities because they wanted the monks or nuns to die off so that "the possessions of such monasteries [would] come wholly into the hands of the [commendatory]

33. Coulton, *Five Centuries of Religion*, 3:430.
34. B. R. Beattie, *Angelus pacis: The Legation of Cardinal Giovanni Gaetano Orsini, 1326–1334* (Leiden: Brill, 2007), 217–18.
35. Quoted in Coulton, *Five Centuries of Religion*, 3:431.

Cardinals." Eventually, writes Walsingham, all of the monasteries would be reduced to "granges or stalls for beasts."[36] The extant documents of the abbey of Carbone near Bari, Italy, which came under *commendam* in the fifteenth century, record that the commendatories "filched all that was valuable in the way of pictures or manuscripts: the monastery buildings and churches went to ruin; the offices and ceremonies could not be kept up for want of vestments and books; the monks starved and were forced to go from place to place begging for sustenance."[37] In short, the late medieval landscape, littered as it was with commendatory abbots and abbesses, was the fruit of the seed of practices that had been sown many centuries earlier. Though some houses that fell under *commendam* profited from fit leadership and were even reformed,[38] the more common story is one of laxity and dissolution.

Ressourcement: Countercultural Practices and Ideals

Walter Capps writes that monasticism is the "most powerful and enduring instance of counter-culture."[39] The Christian church itself is ideally countercultural and is certainly shown to be in the Acts of the Apostles, but there are times when even the church needs an institution that calls it to return to its countercultural nature. Monasteries are ideally positioned to serve in this capacity since they are, by design, set apart from the prevailing culture. They are a part of culture while serving as a beacon to the countercultural nature of the gospel of Jesus Christ. From its earliest beginnings, the institution of monasticism often sought to distance itself from the larger life of the church and from non-monastic believers. Yet it is important to bear in mind that this was rarely articulated as an absolute distancing. For example, Benedict of Nursia advocated that monks and nuns exercise hospitality, and many early monasteries ran, on their own property and at their own expense, hospitals and hostels. At times this desire to be distanced from the non-monastic world was justified by erroneous reasoning (e.g., women, by nature, are always a source of sexual temptation to men), whereas at other times the sentiment was well founded, as the history of the *charistikē* and of the *commendam* system demonstrate. It was not a foregone conclusion from early monastic legislators that interaction with non-monastics would have a detrimental or

36. G. G. Coulton, *Five Centuries of Religion*, vol. 4, *The Last Days of Medieval Monachism* (Cambridge: Cambridge University Press, 1950), 663.

37. Ibid., 65.

38. See Clark, *Benedictines in the Middle Ages*, 295.

39. Walter Capps, *The Monastic Impulse* (New York: Crossroad, 1983), 7.

even devastating effect on monasteries. Yet history demonstrates that an overly close interaction between monasteries and non-monastics can and often does have negative results, and the issue is repeatedly exacerbated by the financial status of a monastery. Monastic history teaches us that if a monastery is valuable, then it often becomes an object of desire for those who hope to gain from its success. Monasteries, however, do not exist to be objects of desire for those who would squander the house's resources; rather, they are meant to stand in opposition to such a perspective and to serve as places of renewal and godly living. Monasteries remind us that instead of giving in to our temptations toward sinful acculturation, we should stand over against them. Monasticism reminds us that it is possible to be countercultural à la the early Christian church.

As discussed earlier, the ways in which monasteries have been countercultural are also ways in which the Christian church in general should strive to be countercultural. Churches that overly accommodate themselves to culture cease, in time, to be true Christian churches; often, they become just another part of the cultural fabric (e.g., any number of "mainline" Protestant churches in the United States that have been in deadly decline for many years), or they become cultural magnets that fail to make deep, godly disciples (e.g., the seeker-sensitive church movement). Monasteries are not inherently immune from cultural accommodation, but, as evangelical theologian Donald Bloesch envisions, they can serve as countercultural institutions for the purpose of giving churchgoers a place in which to withdraw from the world for a season in order to return to the church and the world, engaging them on a deeper level.[40] Monasteries do not displace the church but complement it. Because both are called to counterculturalism, monasteries can serve as centers for renewal within the church; they are uniquely placed to serve as the church's conscience, calling it out of any cultural accommodation to faithful living. The church, of course, can and should do the same for monasteries; both stand against prevailing cultural trends that compromise the gospel and mission of God.

---

40. See chap. 13 for a full discussion of Bloesch's monastic vision.

7

The Road to Reform

All organizations and institutions experience seasons of renewal. This does not always mean that they have degenerated in quality or vision, though that is often a reason for renewal. On a positive note, some renewal is the result of re-visioning. The old structures were no longer working, so new ones are created and put into place, thereby rejuvenating the organization. In the corporate world, the turnaround of Apple Computer under Steve Jobs beginning in 1997 is a great example of a company revisioning itself and becoming hugely successful despite near failure. Sometimes renewal is necessary because the organization or institution has lost its way and become something that its founders could have never imagined. In corporate America one thinks of Kodak, a company that failed to see the future in digital photography, delaying renewal until it was too late.[1] Like these examples from the business world, the Christian church has experienced seasons of decay and decline as well as seasons of renewal.[2] As would be expected, the history of monasticism also contains stories of renewal that were prompted

1. Ironically, Kodak invented the digital camera but waited too long to put enough energy and research dollars into improving and marketing the technology.
2. On renewal in Christian church history, see Christopher M. Bellitto, *Renewing Christianity: A History of Church Reform from Day One to Vatican II* (Mahwah, NJ: Paulist Press, 2001); and Christopher M. Bellitto and David Zachariah Flanagin, eds., *Reassessing Reform: A Historical Investigation into Church Renewal* (Washington, DC: Catholic University of America Press, 2012).

by both renewed vision and decay. Beginning in the tenth century, there was large-scale movement in the institution of monasticism that resulted in the creation of large monastic orders and congregations of affiliated monastic houses. As well, Benedictine monasticism took root (again) in the British Isles. This chapter will investigate the "ordering" of Benedictine monasticism in Western Europe associated with the Carolingian reforms, particularly the work of a monk named Benedict of Aniane. Further, the history of the rise of the Cluniac "order" will be distilled, and the history of the refoundation and re-formation of English Benedictinism will be surveyed as a case study in monastic renewal.

Benedict of Aniane

Benedict of Aniane (née Witiza; d. 821) is known in monastic history as Benedictus Secundus, the "second Benedict."[3] Benedict was born around 750 in southern France, and was sent by his father to the royal court of Pippin the Short (d. 768) and then Charlemagne (d. 814), eventually serving as the king's cupbearer.[4] In his mid-twenties he witnessed his brother's accidental drowning, providing, it appears, the catalyst for his conversion and withdrawal from the world. In 774 he joined the Benedictine community of St. Seine, near Dijon, where he remained for six years. Though surely somewhat of an exaggeration, Benedict's vita records that he "proceeded to damage his body with incredible fasting," which did not necessarily endear him to his fellow monks.[5] Furthermore, and perhaps most interesting, is that this "second Benedict" did not put much stock into the *Rule of Benedict* (RB) as a guide for the monastic life at this time. Benedict declared "that the Rule of blessed Benedict was for beginners and weak persons. . . . However much the Benedictine Rule might regulate possible things for paltry people . . . [Benedict of Aniane] perennially explored more impossible things."[6] Yet, as Benedict's biographer Ardo is quick to remind his readers, "divine favor decreed that [Benedict] was to become an example of salvation for many and would be inflamed with love for the Rule of Benedict."[7] Until that time,

---

3. See Hieronymus Frank, ed., *Capitula qualiter observations sacrae in nonnullis monasteriis habentur quas bonae memoriae Benedictus secundus in coenobiis suis alumnis habere instituit* (Siegburg: Schmitt, 1963), 353.

4. Ardo, *Life of Abbot Benedict of Aniane* 1.1; Allan Cabaniss, trans., *Benedict of Aniane: The Emperor's Monk* (Kalamazoo, MI: Cistercian Publications 2008), 65.

5. Ardo, *Life of Abbot Benedict of Aniane* 2.3; Cabaniss, *Benedict of Aniane*, 67.

6. Ardo, *Life of Abbot Benedict of Aniane* 2.5; Cabaniss, *Benedict of Aniane*, 68.

7. Ardo, *Life of Abbot Benedict of Aniane* 2.5; Cabaniss, *Benedict of Aniane*, 69.

and seeking a more challenging monastic life (perhaps to escape election as the abbot of St. Seine), Benedict moved to his family estate near Montpellier, eventually erecting a full-fledged monastery near the brook of Aniane. Initially Benedict's monastery at Aniane was modest and somewhat crude, wholly devoted to extreme asceticism and care for others. In time, however, Benedict relaxed his asceticism; this was reflected in the construction of more permanent, beautiful structures.

The reason for Benedict's relaxation of his discipline is not wholly clear, but it is certainly tied to a request from Charlemagne in 782 that Benedict construct a cloister large enough to house one hundred monks as well as a new church of similar size and grandeur. In this newly remodeled monastery (and in all of the monasteries established by Benedict thereafter), the RB, "the one rule," as Benedict of Aniane liked to call it, shaped life in the community.[8] In the words of Ardo, "Let anyone who seeks to read or listen to this biography, realize that Aniane is the head of all monasteries, not only of those erected in the regions of Gothia, but also of those erected in other areas at that time or afterwards according to its example and enriched with the treasures of Benedict. . . . [Benedict of Aniane] gave his heart to studying the Rule of blessed Benedict."[9] Two aspects of this quotation deserve notice: (1) Benedict of Aniane had so adjusted his understanding and judgment of the RB that he adopted it for all of his monasteries; and (2) the monastery at Aniane functioned as the "head of all monasteries," that is, a motherhouse for other houses founded by the second Benedict. This, in particular, sets up the larger monastic reform movement instituted under Charlemagne.

By 792 the monastery at Aniane was under the royal protection of Charlemagne, and monks from Aniane were being sent to other monasteries to promote the RB. Though most monasteries at this time followed not just one rule but some combination of various rules (e.g., the *Rule of Columbanus*), Benedict of Aniane argued for the faithful observance of the RB. In his *Concordia regularum* (*Harmony of Rules*) Benedict of Aniane insisted on the harmony of the precepts of the RB with other existing rules. That is, the RB was not superior to other monastic rules; it was completely in accordance and of one mind with the other rules. In matters not addressed directly by the RB, Benedict assembled a set of customs based on observances at various other houses. As a result of this work, Benedict's "holiness reached the ears

---

8. See chap. 5 for the so-called *regulae mixtae*, "mixed rules," of this period over against the "one rule" of Benedict of Nursia.

9. Ardo, *Life of Abbot Benedict of Aniane* 18.1; Cabaniss, *Benedict of Aniane*, 79.

of the emperor [Charlemagne]," and "moved by pious consideration, Charles granted possession of the monastery to Benedict by charter."[10] That is, Charlemagne favored Benedict with privileges and gifts so that he was then able to reform additional monasteries in the area along the strict lines of the RB, coupled with the customs of Aniane: "Out of love of charity and in order to secure the salvation of many, he visited the cells of others and explained the obscurities of the holy Rule."[11] Benedict's influence among the Frankish monasteries grew when, in 813, a council was convened by the emperor in Arles, at which Benedict was able to teach and instruct bishops, abbots, and monks about the monastic life. As a result, the "throng of monks engaged in God's service so increased that there were more than three hundred. Because of the extraordinary company, Benedict ordered a bigger house to be built, one able to hold a thousand or more men. . . . And because other places could not hold them, he constructed cells at suitable locations at which he placed brothers with teachers to direct them."[12] This dispersion of monks (who were influenced by the second Benedict) to newly built monasteries around the empire meant that the RB's influence on monastic life continued to grow steadily, gaining further impetus and influence under Charlemagne's successor, Louis the Pious (d. 840).

Louis and Benedict had known each other for over thirty years when Louis acceded to the Frankish throne. Louis's agenda as king vis-à-vis the monasteries in his realm was to bring them into greater uniformity, and the person to do this, in Louis's estimation, was Benedict. Thus Louis made Benedict abbot of the monastery at Inden, near the royal court at Aachen, giving Louis more immediate access to Benedict. Louis's next move was to call a series of reforming church councils at Aachen in 817 and 818–819.[13] As discussed in chapter 5, these councils drew a line of distinction between the orders of canons (e.g., Chroedegang of Metz) and the order of monastics. Already in 802, however, Charlemagne had convoked a synod and called for the establishment of a correct text of the RB (i.e., one that would contain the same wording as Benedict's original), legislating that it was to be adopted throughout the Frankish kingdom. This was reiterated at the Council of Châlons in 813. Thus the councils in 817 and 818–819 outlined further the obligations of the RB on the lives of both monks and nuns, elaborated on the liturgical requirements of the RB, and addressed how the monasteries were to be governed in

---

10. Ardo, *Life of Abbot Benedict of Aniane* 18.2; Cabaniss, *Benedict of Aniane*, 79.
11. Ardo, *Life of Abbot Benedict of Aniane* 20.1; Cabaniss, *Benedict of Aniane*, 83.
12. Ardo, *Life of Abbot Benedict of Aniane* 22.1; Cabaniss, *Benedict of Aniane*, 85.
13. To read Ardo's account of the role played by Benedict of Aniane at the Aachen councils, see *Life of Abbot Benedict of Aniane* 36.1–2; Cabaniss, *Benedict of Aniane*, 97–98.

relationship to royal and episcopal authority.[14] According to Mayke de Jong, several main issues were addressed at the Aachen councils: "Acceptance of the [Benedictine] Rule as the one law governing monastic life was not the problem; predictably, it was the uniform interpretation of it that met with most resistance."[15] The main issues were (1) the "general and uniform compliance" of Carolingian monasteries with the stipulations of the daily office in the RB over against the common observance of the Roman office; (2) whether the Carolingian monasteries would observe the continual singing of psalms year round (resulting in the daily recitation of 450 psalms with members of the community taking turns around the clock) or would adopt the plan laid out by Benedict of Aniane, in which only 138 psalms would be sung daily (which is still three times the number of psalms legislated by the RB for daily recitation); and (3) the relationship between the community and its abbot.[16] By the early ninth century the abbatial office was one of power and prestige wherein many abbots lived aristocratic lifestyles with abbots' houses being built separate from the monastery so that the abbot could entertain important guests. The council of Aachen legislated that the abbots were not to receive these special privileges but were to live and eat with the rest of the community.[17]

Scholars are divided over the success of the Aachen reforms. An older, outdated historiography says that henceforth from the Aachen reforms all monasteries in the Frankish realm were faithfully following the RB. This, however, was certainly not the case. Though the second Benedict's "one rule" was never fully realized, the RB "did gain preeminence: though local custom varied widely, the *Regula Benedicti* became the foundation of monastic identity."[18] Not only did the canonical regulations effect change, causing many monasteries to become resolutely Benedictine, but Benedict of Aniane continued to exert influence. Ardo tells us that bishops, "hearing reports of Benedict's sanctity and the holy reputation of his flock," requested monks from Benedict's houses to come and serve as examples to monasteries within their dioceses.[19] Benedict's response was to send twenty monks to each loca-

14. James G. Clark, *The Benedictines in the Middle Ages* (Woodbridge, UK: Boydell Press, 2011), 36–37.

15. Mayke de Jong, "Carolingian Monasticism: The Power of Prayer," in vol. 2 of *The New Cambridge Medieval History, c. 700–c. 900*, ed. Rosamond McKitterick (Cambridge: Cambridge University Press, 1995), 632.

16. For a description of less important issues among the different monasteries that were addressed by Benedict's customs, see Ardo, *Life of Abbot Benedict of Aniane* 37.1–38.7; Cabaniss, *Benedict of Aniane*, 98–101.

17. De Jong, "Carolingian Monasticism," 632–33.

18. Ibid., 633.

19. Ardo, *Life of Abbot Benedict of Aniane* 24.1; Cabaniss, *Benedict of Aniane*, 85.

tion along with a "teacher," so that they could establish proper Benedictine monasticism. Though this was happening even before the councils at Aachen, it certainly continued after the councils when Louis "set Benedict over all monasteries in his realm."[20] But by the time of Benedict's death in 821 there was still much work to be done, and it would be another several hundred years before the RB became the primary rule of monastic communities across continental Europe. However, the task of re-forming the monasteries had begun. The RB's prominence was given a further boost with the founding of the monastery of Cluny in 909.

Monastery of Cluny

Cluny is indirectly the product of the reforming efforts of Benedict of Aniane and the Aachen councils because its customs were based on those of the monastery at Baume, which had adopted Benedict's reforms (of which more will be said below).[21] Further, Berno (d. 927) was abbot of Baume before being selected to also serve as Cluny's founding abbot by Duke William I of Aquitaine (d. 918), the monastery's founder and first patron.[22] On September 11, 909, William signed the founding charter of Cluny. From all of William's lands, Berno had picked a remote location to avoid the political struggles of the day. Berno, an ardent monastic reformer, had entered the monastery of St. Martin in Autun in 880. Several years later he left to found his own community at Gigny and received, in 894, a papal bull allowing the monks of Gigny to elect their own abbot without any lay or episcopal interference. Though Gigny was not alone with this privilege, it foreshadows an indispensable element of Cluniac monasticism—independence from local secular and ecclesial persons. William's foundation charter contains two important elements: (1) Cluny is vassal to no one (not the local lord or the local bishop); and (2) the monastery is placed directly under the jurisdiction of St. Peter, that is, the Holy See. Thus the Cluniac community is free to observe the RB strictly and free to follow their own rhythm of prayer and work. It was on this foundation that Odo was elected second abbot in 926.

20. Ardo, *Life of Abbot Benedict of Aniane* 36.1; Cabaniss, *Benedict of Aniane*, 97.

21. David Appleby, "Benedict of Aniane, St. c. 750–821," in *Encyclopedia of Monasticism*, ed. William M. Johnston (London: Fitzroy Dearborn, 2000), 1:128.

22. By the time of his death in 927, Berno was the abbot of a number of monasteries. Under canon law at that time he was able to leave the abbacies of Baume and Gigny to his nephew and the abbacies of Cluny, Massay, and Deols to Odo of Cluny. See Gerard Sitwell, trans. and ed., *St. Odo of Cluny: Being the Life of St. Odo of Cluny by John of Salerno and the Life of St. Gerald of Aurillac by St. Odo* (London: Sheed and Ward, 1958), 41n1.

Odo (d. 942) was born around 879 and at the age of eighteen entered St. Martin's at Tours as a canon, followed by time in Paris, before settling at the monastery of Baume under Berno, future abbot of Cluny.[23] While still a canon, living in a small cell about two miles from the tomb of St. Martin and engaged in regular biblical commentary and study, Odo discovered the RB. His biographer, John of Salerno, relates the importance of this event:

> In reading various books [Odo] came on the Rule of St. Benedict, and while he was going quickly through it he came on that place in which monks are ordered to sleep clothed [chap. 22]. But not understanding this passage aright, for three years he lay down in his clothes, and not yet a monk he bore the mild yoke of monks. He took care to obey the precepts of the one saint [Benedict of Nursia], and desired to imitate the life of the other [Martin of Tours]. For the Lord Jesus cast then the simple seed in the bare earth from which He foresaw yield a hundredfold.[24]

In time Odo was joined by Adhegrinus, who was also a monk and who moved into Odo's small cell. John tells us that in spite of their attempts to find a monastery to join, "nowhere could they find a religious house in which they felt inclined to remain." Thus Adhegrinus decided to make a pilgrimage to Rome; on the way he came to the monastery at Baume, where he stayed for some time so "that he might get to know their way of life and the customs of the place."[25] This "way of life" and these "customs" were none other than those established by Benedict of Aniane for St. Martin's at Autun, from which Berno was sent to reform Baume. St. Martin's itself was reformed around 870 by monks from St. Savin near Poitiers, and St. Savin was a daughter house of Aniane. Thus there is a direct line of influence from Benedict of Aniane to Baume and even to Odo himself before he was a monk at Cluny. As a result of his experience at Baume, Adhegrinus called for Odo, and they both joined the community, with Odo becoming the master of the monastery's school; he was later ordained a priest.

When Berno died, Odo left Baume to become the second abbot of Cluny. John of Salerno tells us that some of the senior monks of Baume followed him to Cluny, giving the newer monastery a good number of monks experienced in the reformed monasticism of the second Benedict. Like the older Benedict of Aniane, Odo's first task as abbot was to build proper buildings for the monastery, using money brought from Baume as well as that collected

23. John of Salerno, *Life of St. Odo of Cluny* 1.3; Sitwell, *St. Odo of Cluny*, 6.
24. John of Salerno, *Life of St. Odo of Cluny* 1.15; Sitwell, *St. Odo of Cluny*, 18.
25. John of Salerno, *Life of St. Odo of Cluny* 1.22; Sitwell, *St. Odo of Cluny*, 24–25.

for this purpose. Odo spent much of his time as abbot of Cluny traveling to other monasteries in the area to persuade more abbots about the advantages of following the RB. As well, whenever any kings, bishops, and local lords "built [monasteries] in their territories they handed them over to his rule that he might reform and regulate them according to [Cluny's] customs."[26] His strategy to help instigate reform along the lines of the RB was to leave some Cluniac monks behind at each monastery that he visited so that they could help implement reforms.[27] To support this activity, Pope John XI (d. 935), in 931, gave Cluny's abbot the right to take over and reform any monastery that requested his assistance. The same pope also gave Odo (and future abbots) the right to admit any monk to Cluny if their own monastery rejected reform. These actions created a family of monasteries that were united together in a community of intention, that is, a community that strove to observe the RB in all its details. Odo's concern was spiritual in that he wanted other houses to observe the RB. He was not motivated by any sense that he was structurally uniting a group of previously independent and disparate monasteries into a monastic "order," though a few monasteries did choose to give up their own abbots and place themselves under the abbot of Cluny. In this sense, therefore, Odo is to some extent responsible for the later rise of the full-fledged monastic "order" centered at Cluny.[28]

What is important from Odo's life and tenure at Cluny is the pattern he established of taking Cluniac customs (many of which were also common to Benedict of Aniane) to other monastic houses, which were then reformed along Cluniac lines and may have even surrendered themselves to the abbot of Cluny or at least elected a Cluniac monk as their next abbot. Under Majolus (d. 994), who was abbot from 954, Cluny's outward influence continued with the reformation of existing monasteries, the founding of new monasteries, and the multiplication of *cellae*—houses without their own abbot who were therefore under the direct jurisdiction of the abbot of Cluny. The high point of Cluniac monasticism, however, came with the abbacies of Odilo (994–1049), Hugh of Semur (1049–1109), and Peter the Venerable (1122–1156).

In 998 Pope Gregory V (d. 999) granted the abbey church autonomy so that no one, including the pope or local bishop, could interfere with Cluniac usages. This was extended in 1024 by Pope John XIX (d. 1032) and, according to Dominique Iogna-Prat, "John's measure marked the real birth of the *Ecclesia cluniacensis* (the Cluniac Church) as an ecclesiastical network of abbeys

26. John of Salerno, *Life of St. Odo of Cluny* 2.23; Sitwell, *St. Odo of Cluny*, 66.
27. For example, see John of Salerno, *Life of St. Odo of Cluny* 3.7.
28. On monastic orders, see Greg Peters, "Monastic Orders," in *The Encyclopedia of Christian Civilization*, ed. George Thomas Kurian (Malden, MA: Wiley-Blackwell, 2011), 3:1551–55.

and priories with the Burgundian sanctuary at its center."[29] Though Cluny's influence remained largely regional up through the abbacy of Odilo, under Hugh it became a European monastic force. During the abbacy of Peter the Venerable, Cluny's size was such that it was necessary to convene a general chapter at Cluny of all the abbots and priors of the Cluniac dependencies. Between 1199 and 1207 abbot Hugh legislated that the general chapter should be a yearly affair. Henceforth, "it is possible to speak of an 'order' structured by provinces whose establishments received periodic visits."[30] To summarize the rise of Cluny into a reformed monastic order:

> Under its early abbots, from Berno to Majolus, Cluny was a relatively informal network of establishments linked to the person of the abbot. . . . [B]eyond this first circle is a shifting, uncertain realm of monastic establishments that the abbot of Cluny reformed, spreading to them the models of discipline and liturgy in use at Cluny, although these houses did not become possessions of Cluny. . . . Much later, under Hugh of Semur's governance, the abbot of Cluny was functionally an *archiabbas* [archabbot]. . . . Cluny went from being a "Reformzentrum" (center of reform) to being a "Kongregationsmittelpunkt" (center of a congregation). . . . The Cluniac "body" was a hierarchic structure consisting of a head . . . and members (abbeys and priories) of regional importance, to which in turn other priories or subpriories were subordinate at the local level.[31]

Peter the Venerable gave final order to this development by mandating yearly general chapters. In short, Cluny showed the medieval world how a monastic order could arise that would then become a dominant force, not only in its own time, but in its ongoing influence on monastic organization and history. It showed how a re-formation of monasticism begun under Benedict of Aniane in the ninth century could reach its full flowering in the twelfth century.

England

While these developments were taking place on continental Europe, something similar, yet distinct, was happening in England. There is a fair bit of uncertainty surrounding both the arrival of Christianity *and* monasticism to the British Isles. Though it is impossible to determine the exact origins of

29. Dominique Iogna-Prat, *Order and Exclusion: Cluny and Christendom Face Heresy, Judaism, and Islam (1000–1150)*, trans. Graham Robert Edwards (Ithaca, NY: Cornell University Press, 2002), 27.

30. Ibid., 30.

31. Ibid., 55 and 57.

Christianity in England, we know that Venantius Fortunatus, a Gallic poet and bishop writing in the latter half of the sixth century, says that the apostle Paul evangelized England.[32] Clement of Rome (fl. ca. 96) states that the apostle Paul came to "the boundary of the West," which could be a reference to England since the Roman Empire stretched up into England.[33] A Welsh legend tells how Bran the Blessed went to Rome as a hostage for his son and became a Christian during his time there, bringing the faith back to Britain. Yet the most famous legend related to the conversion of England is that of Joseph of Arimathea, who is said to have arrived in Britain with twelve companions in 63. This tradition says that Joseph brought with him the Holy Grail and built the first British church at Glastonbury, but the story first appears in the writings of the twelfth-century writer William of Malmesbury (d. ca. 1143). Given its late origin, this account is likely not historically accurate. Post-Reformation Roman Catholic authors made much of a Roman tradition of sixth-century origin where in 167 Lucius, king of the Britons, requested that Pope Eleutherus send missionaries to his country. According to the Venerable Bede the mission was a success, and the Britons preserved their faith uncorrupted until the time of Emperor Diocletian (284–305).[34]

However, it was probably in the second half of the second century that the Christian faith was introduced to the province of Britain, and this was likely the result of individual commercial and military contacts between Britain and Gaul that resulted in a "natural germination of Christianity" in England. Evidence for this second-century arrival includes the writings of Tertullian around 200, which include the Britons in a list of peoples who have accepted Christ and which say that Christianity has penetrated the remotest parts of Britain.[35] Later in the third century Origen of Alexandria (d. 254) says that Christianity has secured adherents in Britain, though most Britons have not yet heard the gospel.[36] In the fourth century Eusebius of Caesarea says that Christianity crossed over to the British Isles,[37] and in the early fifth century Theodoret of Cyrus (d. ca. 457) states that the apostles and earliest disciples successfully evangelized the Romans and other nations, including the Britons. Finally, and perhaps most important, the church in Britain sent three bishops (of London, York, and Lincoln) to the Council of Arles in 314, and at the

32. The following is dependent on C. J. Godfrey, *The Church in Anglo-Saxon England* (Cambridge: Cambridge University Press, 1962), 9–12.

33. Clement of Rome, *Epistle to the Corinthians* 1.5.

34. See Venerable Bede, *A History of the English Church and People* 1.4 and 5.24.

35. Tertullian, *Against the Jews* 7.

36. Origen of Alexandria, *Homilies on Luke* 6.

37. Eusebius of Caesarea, *Demonstratio Evangelica* 3.3.

Council of Ariminum in 360 there were at least three British bishops present. That these councils had English episcopal representatives demonstrates a level of organization that suggests a second-century arrival of Christianity in England. What is apparent, however, is that a native monasticism existed prior to the arrival of Augustine of Canterbury (d. ca. 604) in 597.

In 590 Gregory the Great became pope. According to Bede, along with a biography of Gregory written in Northumbria in the eighth century, around 585 Gregory witnessed in the Roman Forum the sale of Anglo-Saxon boys as slaves, giving him a desire to "evangelize" Britain.[38] In or about 595 Gregory sent a priest to Gaul to help manage his estates in that country, also instructing him to buy English slave-boys aged seventeen or eighteen and to place the boys in monasteries. This appears to be the first step by Gregory to evangelize the Anglo-Saxons. Gregory's plan was to train these native boys in monasticism so that they could return to England, set up monasteries, and use these houses as centers of evangelism. Thereafter, Gregory chose the prior of his monastery on the Caelian hill in Rome to lead this mission: Augustine. In the spring of 596 Augustine and several companions set out from Rome, eventually arriving and settling in Kent. Soon after their arrival these missionary monks were given a monastery by king Æthelbert (d. 616), which was dedicated to Sts. Peter and Paul, thus establishing a Roman-style monastery in England (over against the Celtic monasteries flourishing in the north). With this foundation, monasticism took off, so much so that it "is clear that by 700 a large number of monasteries of one kind or another were in existence amongst the Anglo-Saxons."[39] Monastic historian David Knowles affirms this: "The first half of the eighth century saw the Anglo-Saxon monasticism at the highest point of its development and influence. . . . Indeed, during the greater part of the eighth century the monasteries of England possessed a life, and exercised an influence, more powerful than those of any other monastic *bloc* in Europe."[40] Yet Knowles laments that "all available evidence from the reign of Alfred [871–899] points to a collapse of monasticism [in England] by the end of the ninth century."[41] The reasons for this collapse are many, complicated, and debated. Within a two-hundred-year span monasticism in England went

38. Venerable Bede, *A History of the English Church and People* 2.1. Gregory was apparently unaware of the Christian presence already in England.

39. Henry Mayr-Harting, *The Coming of Christianity to Anglo-Saxon England* (University Park: Pennsylvania State University Press, 1991), 148.

40. David Knowles, *The Monastic Order in England: A History of Its Development from the Times of St. Dunstan to the Fourth Lateran Council 913–1216* (Cambridge: Cambridge University Press, 1950), 23.

41. Ibid., 33.

from being a robust, ubiquitous institution to "an act of private devotion."[42] This collapsed state of monasticism is reflected in contemporary texts as well. The *Regularis Concordia*, written around 970, says that "the holy monasteries in all quarters of [Edgar's] kingdom" were "brought low, and almost wholly lacking in the service of our Lord Jesus Christ."[43] The vita of Oswald of Worcester (d. 992) claims that "in those days there were no monks, nor any men of the sacred rule in England."[44] This all changed, however, with the monastic careers of Dunstan of Canterbury (d. 988), Æthelwold of Winchester (d. 984), and Oswald of Worcester.

Dunstan was born in 909 near Glastonbury, and though monastic life had ceased at this popular pilgrimage site (reputed to contain the relics of Sts. Patrick and Bridget), he obtained an excellent education and was ordained into minor orders (acolyte, lector, etc.). Under the influence of his relative Aelfheah "the monk" in Winchester, and after a severe illness, Dunstan became a monk and was subsequently ordained a priest. He returned to Glastonbury where, next to the church, "he built a tiny cell for himself," and "he dwelt, prayed, sang psalms there, and did with his hands whatever things the narrow space allowed."[45] Around 939, when Edmund became king, Dunstan entered into his service. As a result of a near-death experience and in repentance for a wrong that he committed against Dunstan, the king gave Dunstan the property at Glastonbury. Dunstan then "began to lay the foundations there for the expansion of the church, to construct cloisters and workplaces, and to build there whatever was necessary for the monks who serve Christ the Lord. After these things had been done and many were brought together with him, he was appointed abbot of that place. Thereafter the monastery increased in size both inside and out."[46] According to Knowles, this marks the beginning of the monastic revival in England. Moreover, according to one biographer (the so-called priest "B"), Dunstan based monastic life at Glastonbury on the RB,[47] though it was likely supplemented with other monastic customs and the verbal reports of English monks who had spent time in continental monasteries.[48]

42. Ibid., 36.

43. *Regularis Concordia* 1; Thomas Symons, trans., *The Monastic Agreement of the Monks and Nuns of the English Nation* (London: Thomas Nelson and Sons, 1953), 1.

44. Clark, *Benedictines in the Middle Ages*, 43.

45. Eadmer of Canterbury, *Life of St. Dunstan* 11; Andrew J. Turner and Bernard J. Muir, eds. and trans., *Eadmer of Canterbury: Lives and Miracles of Saints Oda, Dunstan, and Oswald* (Oxford: Clarendon, 2006), 67.

46. Eadmer of Canterbury, *Life of St. Dunstan* 11; Turner and Muir, *Eadmer of Canterbury*, 81.

47. *Vita auctore B* 15; William Stubbs, ed., *Memorials of Saint Dunstan, Archbishop of Canterbury* (London: Longman, 1874), 25.

48. Knowles, *Monastic Order in England*, 38.

One of Dunstan's early disciples was Æthelwold, whom Dunstan had known in Winchester and who had also been ordained by Aelfheah. In the words of Æthelwold's biographer, "He profited greatly by Dunstan's teaching and eventually received the habit of the monastic order from him, devoting himself humbly to his rule."[49] Æthelwold was then made dean of the monastery and, around 954 after Eadred ascended to the throne, was given the monastery at Abingdon. Despite the poor condition of the buildings but "with the consent of Dunstan, it came about that the man of God Æthelwold took charge of this place, with the aim of establishing monks there to serve God according to the rule." He was joined by others from Glastonbury, and soon thereafter he was elected abbot of "a flock of monks."[50] In 963 Æthelwold was elected bishop of Winchester and in due time dismissed the dissolute canons from the minster and replaced them with "monks living according to the Rule [of Benedict]."[51] He next established a women's community at Winchester and men's communities at Ely, Peterborough, and Thorney. In short, "thanks both to Dunstan's counsel and activity and to Æthelwold's unremitting aid, monasteries were established everywhere in England, some for monks, some for nuns, governed by abbots and abbesses who lived according to the Rule."[52] Like Æthelwold, Dunstan was made a bishop, first of Worcester in 957 and additionally of London in 958. In 960 he was made the archbishop of Canterbury. As bishop and archbishop he continued to oversee the foundation of new monasteries or reform existing monasteries, such as Bath, Malmesbury, Westminster, and St. Augustine's and Christ Church, Canterbury.

The final important monastic reformer of this century was Oswald. Oswald was the nephew of Oda (d. 958), archbishop of Canterbury, from whom he received a good education. While still a youth, he entered the rank of canons at Winchester but was put off by the lifestyle of the canons: "Those men despised the teaching of their own order and led their lives following the impulses of their hearts." In response, Oda sent Oswald to the monastery of St. Benedict at Fleury-sur-Loire in Gaul because Oswald desired "to observe the Rule of blessed Benedict obediently."[53] The main reason, it appears, that

---

49. Wulfstan of Winchester, *Life of St. Æthelwold* 9; Michael Lapidge and Michael Winterbottom, eds., *Wulfstan of Winchester: The Life of St. Æthelwold* (Oxford: Clarendon, 1991), 15.

50. Wulfstan of Winchester, *Life of St. Æthelwold* 11; Lapidge and Winterbottom, *Wulfstan of Winchester*, 21.

51. Wulfstan of Winchester, *Life of St. Æthelwold* 20; Lapidge and Winterbottom, *Wulfstan of Winchester*, 37.

52. Wulfstan of Winchester, *Life of St. Æthelwold* 27; Lapidge and Winterbottom, *Wulfstan of Winchester*, 43.

53. Eadmer of Canterbury, *Life of St. Oswald* 5; Turner and Muir, *Eadmer of Canterbury*, 225 and 227.

Oswald was sent to Fleury was to learn the monastery's customs so that he would be able to return to England and teach them to others. Oswald returned to England around 958 and was named the bishop of Worcester in 961. Like Dunstan and Æthelwold, Oswald was an active founder and reformer of monastic houses, such as Ramsey (where he centered his reforming activities), Westbury-on-Trym, Winchcombe, and Pershore. In 971 Oswald was elevated to the archbishopric of York, placing him in a position, along with Dunstan and Æthelwold, to permanently influence Benedictine monastic life in England. This was accomplished primarily through the *Regularis Concordia* (RC).

Around 970 there were a number of significant reformed monastic foundations as well as a recognition that the new movement needed to be organized; or, to say it in the words of the RC itself, there was a need to harmonize the differences of the various houses in accordance with the RB: "When therefore the Rule of the holy Father Benedict had been accepted with the greatest goodwill, very many of the abbots and abbesses with communities of monks and nuns vied with one another in following the footsteps of the saints; for they were united in one faith, though not in one manner of monastic usage." Thus King Edgar called a council to be held at Winchester in which "he urged all to be of one mind as regards monastic usage, to follow the holy and approved fathers and so, with their minds anchored firmly on the ordinances of the Rule [of Benedict], to avoid all dissension, lest differing ways of observing the customs of one Rule and one country should bring their holy conversation into disrepute."[54] In response, the English monastic leaders obtained the monastic customs of the abbeys of Fleury-sur-Loire (which was reformed in 930 by Odo of Cluny and where Oswald had learned Benedictine customs; see above) and of St. Peter in Ghent. The response of those gathered at Winchester was to make "a solemn vow to our Lord Jesus Christ, confirming their oath with a spiritual pact, that, living all their life under the yoke of the Rule, they would carry out these selfsame monastic customs [i.e., the RC] openly and with one uniform observance."[55] In conclusion, the abbots and abbesses resolved to "uphold by every means in our power those things which have been handed down to us from our Father Benedict. . . . Solicitously and according to our ability and as the grace of the Holy Ghost shall dictate, we shall set forth plainly in writing those customs of the Holy Rule which have been constantly and everywhere observed both by the aforesaid Benedict and by his holy followers and imitators after

54. *Regularis Concordia* Proem; Symons, *Monastic Agreement*, 2–3.
55. *Regularis Concordia* Proem; Symons, *Monastic Agreement*, 4.

deep consideration and examination."[56] In short, the monastic re-formation of England was along the lines of the RB and in continuity with monastic reform movements on the continent.

Ressourcement: Continual Re-formation

The church is always being reformed, whether by its own initiative (e.g., the calling of church councils) or by a direct, unexpected outpouring of the Holy Spirit (e.g., the Azusa Street Revival). There are, of course, different reasons why the church needs to be reformed, not all of which indicate a significant doctrinal or spiritual decline. A pattern that emerges from two thousand years of Christian history is that the life and vitality of the church will ebb and flow from time to time and from place to place. When East Africa was experiencing intense revival in the 1920s and 1930s, the church in the United States, at least the mainline Protestant church, was shifting toward a theological liberalism that resulted in its steady numerical decline. Yet it is not just the church qua church that needs reformation; individual members need to be reformed as well. In one sense the biblical narrative is one of formation and re-formation—God creates, judges through destruction, and re-creates. Or, looking at the book of Romans, our minds are depraved, but thanks to the redeeming work of Jesus Christ we are able to be renewed (see Rom. 12:1–2). Just like the pattern of Christian history generally, monastic history shows itself to be one of ebb and flow, creation and re-creation—not only because of decline (though that is true of England) but also because of personal initiative and ongoing mission. Historically monasticism has always evolved and reformed itself, and that continues even today. Christians should expect to see this pattern not only in their own lives but also in the institution of the church itself. Just like God's word, the church is living and active, and therefore it will need to be constantly re-formed.

Ecclesial re-formation and re-creation should not always be initiated by individuals, though this is often the case; it also ought to be the product of a healthy church as well as a sign of a healthy church. Theologically speaking, ecclesial renewal is always a work of God; it is not the work of God's followers pulling up their proverbial bootstraps and getting the job done. In that sense, it is impossible to predict, much less bring about, ecclesial or personal reformation. Oftentimes the Christian church attempts to affect reformation in herself and in members by way of particular programs, some of which are

56. *Regularis Concordia* Proem; Symons, *Monastic Agreement*, 8–9.

bold enough to even adopt the name RENEW. Though these programs have often met with some success at the local level, they often fail to translate to the national or international level. For example, though the Anglican Alpha Course has been employed in many parishes of the Church of England to great effect, it has failed to turn the tide on the Church of England's theological liberalism and numerical decline. Programs and human strategy alone cannot guarantee that the church will undergo a season of reform. That should not, however, cause such despair among the church's leadership that they do not strive for renewal. Rather, the church's leadership should recognize that institutional reformation is usually (though not always) the result of reformation in its members first, who then cause larger, institutional change. We see this time and again throughout the church's history. Thus it seems reasonable and wise to strive for renewal in the life of individual Christians who will effect institutional change. Nonetheless, individual reformation can actually be the result of ecclesial initiative, demonstrating that renewal is cyclical and not necessarily linear. That is, personal and ecclesial reform is reciprocal between the institutional church and its members; it is perichoretic in imitation of the Holy Trinity.

A good example is the liturgical renewal of the past fifty years. This renewal has been witnessed primarily in the Roman Catholic Church as a result of the changes instituted by the Second Vatican Council, which met from 1962 to 1965. Before Vatican II, no Roman Catholic Christians worshiped in their native tongue; instead priests recited the liturgy in Latin, and only those fortunate enough to have been well catechized could understand what was being said. By the late 1960s or early 1970s, however, the primary services of the church's liturgy were translated into the vernacular. Likewise, the oldest Christian liturgical documents were studied so as to remove the centuries of unnecessary accretions. The liturgy was restored to its more primitive form, and most Roman Catholic worshipers benefited immensely. Soon thereafter, the Roman Catholic Church's liturgical renewal began to affect other churches, especially the Protestant churches. Before long even evangelical Christians were discovering the riches of the liturgy, with many following it to the Anglican Communion, walking the so-called Canterbury Trail.[57] By the early 2000s even Pentecostals, known more for their spontaneity than their commitment to liturgical forms, were students of ancient liturgical practices.[58] This recovery of liturgical worship led to a renewed sense of the role of the church in the

57. See Robert Webber, *Evangelicals on the Canterbury Trail: Why Evangelicals Are Attracted to the Liturgical Church* (Waco: Word Books, 1985).

58. See, for example, Simon Chan, *Liturgical Theology: The Church as Worshiping Community* (Downers Grove, IL: IVP Academic, 2006).

life of the believer (e.g., the weekly observance of the Lord's Supper) and to a renewed vision of the spiritual life. In this case, the church's rediscovery of ancient practices led to individual renewal, which has since led to ecclesial renewal (e.g., the renewal of Anglicanism in the United States with the birth of the Anglican Church in North America in 2009). Thus re-formation is both personal and institutional; the one affects the other. Monastic history bears this truism out again and again.

Part III

BERNARD
to
LUTHER

8

The Cistercians, Carthusians, and Other Reforming Orders

Around 1760 the French painter Hubert Robert painted a picture that he titled "A Hermit Praying in the Ruins of a Roman Temple." The painting shows the disrepair of the Roman temple—a collapsing roof, birds flying around inside, and disintegrating marble. Yet the hermit prays, using a discarded piece of marble as his prie-dieu, complete with crucifix, rosary, skull, and hourglass—a reminder that time flies and that death is always near. Moreover, his house of prayer is not very private; four women have entered this hallowed space, with one stealing a flower from a side altar and another attempting to annoy the hermit by hitting him with tree branches. All in all, the hermit's chosen location is ideal for its lack of attention to the things of the world, even if he is occasionally bothered by bored and less-than-devout young women. The painting now hangs in the J. Paul Getty Museum in Los Angeles, a magnificent structure at a cost of $1.3 billion. If the hermit in the painting were alive, he would probably not be happy about "living" in such an expensive museum. Similarly, many of the monasteries of eleventh-century France (and Italy) associated with Cluny had grown in influence and in wealth. Because of the liturgical emphasis of the Cluniac monasteries, it makes sense that they owned quite a bit of precious metal and costly fabrics, but they were also prone to construct new houses or renovate existing houses in grand style.

The famous Cistercian Bernard of Clairvaux, in 1125, wrote his *Apologia* to abbot William of Saint-Thierry in which he ridicules Cluniac excesses in food, clothing, and buildings. Regarding Cluniac buildings he writes, "I shall say nothing about the soaring heights and extravagant lengths and unnecessary widths of the churches, nothing about their expensive decorations and their novel images, which catch the attention of those who go in to pray, and dry up their devotion."[1] Such rhetoric lay behind much eleventh- and twelfth-century vitriol as one monastic order hurled accusations (not always false) at another order. In short, historiographies of monasticism often speak of the degenerate nature of "ordered" monasticism near the turn of the eleventh century, pointing fingers, à la Bernard of Clairvaux, especially at the Cluniac-affiliated Benedictines. This chapter will examine the nature of two so-called reformed orders of the late eleventh and early twelfth centuries: the Cistercians and the Carthusians. The goals of the founders of these orders, as well as the early foundation documents, show the exact nature of the "reform" envisaged by these renewal movements. Brief attention will also be paid to other reformers and reformed orders of monasticism, including Romuald of Ravenna and the Camaldolese, and John Gualbert and the Vallombrosans.

The Cistercians

The Cistercians were founded in 1098 by the Benedictine monk Robert of Molesme (d. 1111). Robert spent time in several monasteries, serving as both abbot and prior, before following a more eremitical vocation and moving into the woods in 1074. Here he was joined by like-minded monks who chose Robert as their spiritual leader. Under his direction they agreed to follow the *Rule of Benedict* (RB) with an accent on asceticism and poverty. This led to the foundation of the monastery at Molesmes in Burgundy, but soon thereafter the fame of the community's sanctity attracted many donations, causing dissension in the community. The twelfth-century ecclesiastical historian Oderic Vitalis (d. ca. 1142) records the tension:

> [Robert] made a careful examination of the Rule of Saint Benedict, and once he had consulted the documents of other holy fathers, he called the brothers together. . . . "Dear brothers, we made profession according to the Rule of our holy father Benedict. But . . . we are not keeping it fully. We observe many things

---

1. Bernard of Clairvaux, *Apologia ad Guillelmum* 12.28; Michael Casey, trans., *Cistercians and Cluniacs: St. Bernard's* Apologia *to Abbot William* (Kalamazoo, MI: Cistercian Publications, 1970), 63.

which are not enjoined in it and we negligently omit many of its precepts. We do not work with our hands, as we read that the holy fathers did. . . . I recommend therefore that we keep the Rule of Saint Benedict absolutely, being careful to deviate from it neither to the right nor to the left. . . ." With these statements the community of monks did not agree.

In response, in 1098 "the abbot [Robert] . . . withdrew from them with twelve likeminded brothers who had decided to keep the Rule of Saint Benedict strictly to the letter. . . . At length Duke Odo . . . took pity on them and granted them a manor at a place called Cîteaux."[2] Though Robert was forced by the church hierarchy to return to Molesme, the "New Monastery" at Cîteaux secured a firm footing under its first abbots, Alberic (d. 1109) and Stephen Harding (d. 1134). The *Exordium cistercii*, a brief account of the early history of the monastery up to 1115, reveals that the manor of Cîteaux belonged to Reynard, viscount of Beaune, and his wife, Hodierna. The text claims that it was "for the remission of their sins and those of their forebears" that moved Reynard and Hodierna to give their manor to Robert and his companions for "observing the Rule of Saint Benedict more strictly and faithfully than they have hitherto done."[3] It was during Stephen's tenure as abbot that the Cistercian family of monasteries began to grow. The earliest documents claim that the order floundered in its earliest years until the arrival of Bernard of Clairvaux and many members of his family in 1112. Without doubt, from 1112 to 1119 a dozen new monasteries were founded, including the four chief daughter houses of Cîteaux: La Ferté (1113), Pontigny (1114), Morimound (1115), and Clairvaux (1115). By the time of Bernard's death (in 1153) there were more than 340 Cistercian monasteries. By 1200 this number grew to 500, and on the eve of the Reformation there were over 700 Cistercian monasteries throughout Christendom. Yet, like most monastic orders, the Cistercians, in time, were in need of reform. In 1335 Benedict XII, himself a Cistercian monk, promulgated a series of documents in an effort to effect a much-needed restoration of the earliest Cistercian practices. Similar efforts toward reform were carried out by popes of the fifteenth century, but the most important and wide-reaching reform of the Cistercians began in 1663 at La Trappe in France.

Returning to the earliest history of the Cistercians, however, reveals a number of motives for the Cistercian reform. Apart from the simple fact that Cîteaux itself started because one monk, Robert of Molesme, desired a more faithful (at least as he understood it) observance of the RB, the Cistercians

2. E. Rozanne Elder, ed., *The New Monastery: Texts and Studies on the Earliest Cistercians* (Kalamazoo, MI: Cistercian Publications, 1998), 20–21 and 25.
    3. Ibid., 11.

were soon to provide a range of reasons for their reform and to justify their existence. Written sometime between 1113 and 1119, the *Exordium parvum* states that the goal of Cistercian life is "the observance of the Holy Rule" and that Cistercian monks were to "sweat and toil even to the last gasp in the straight and narrow way which the Rule points out."[4] But it is in chapter 15 of the *Exordium parvum*, titled "The Institutes of the Monks of Cîteaux who Came from Molesme,"[5] that the goals of the first founders are laid out in some detail. First, as already stated, the earliest Cistercians' main goal was to keep the RB, "rejecting whatever offended against that Rule." The litany of offenses against the RB includes violations of Benedict's legislation regarding clothing, sleeping comforts, and food. These offenses are contrary to the RB "in all its purity." Thus those who did not faithfully follow the RB were going against its grain, whereas the Cistercians were matching and conforming "their steps to the footprints traced by the Rule."

Second, the Cistercians were attempting to live up to the etymology of their name as monks. That is, they desired to live a solitary life, interpreted not as living alone but rather as flight from the trappings of the things of the "secular" world: "Where the blessed father Benedict teaches that a monk should estrange himself from secular conduct, there he clearly testifies that these things should have no place at all in the conduct or in the hearts of monks." Such "secular conduct" is listed as follows: the possession of churches and altars beyond the monastery precinct that would require a priest-monk to be in residence outside the community; "offerings or burial dues"; tithes that come from owning non-ecclesiastical property (such as ovens and mills); oversight of manors and the serfs that would work the manors; and allowing women to enter or be buried inside the monastery.

Finally, the first Cistercians rejected the concept and the practice that monks should be supported by tithes given to the church. According to the *Exordium parvum*, tithes were meant to be divided into four quarters: for the bishop; for the parish priest; for guests, widows, and the poor; and for the repair of the church. So, "because they [the first Cistercians] found in this accounting no mention of the monk . . . they accordingly declined all these things as an unjust usurpation of the rights of others." In short, the Cistercians did not want to harm others by seeking their own support and sustenance.

The implication of all these goals is the view that non-Cistercian monasteries, particularly the Cluniac-affiliated houses, were not keeping the RB,

---

4. Chrysogonus Waddell, ed., *Narrative and Legislative Texts from Early Cîteaux* (Cîteaux: Commentarii cistercienses, 1999), 417.

5. The following quotations from *Exordium parvum* 15 are taken from ibid., 434–35.

not living truly as "monks" and not loving their neighbors well, by taking financial resources away from those who needed them most. This left the early community at Cîteaux facing a decision regarding how they would support both themselves and the guests of the monastery, whom they were to receive as Christ according to the RB. Their first decision was to obtain the bishop's permission to receive laybrothers (*conversi*) and "hired hands." Why? Because, in spite of their disavowal of possessing income-generating property that would keep a monk away from the monastery, the Cistercians were intent to "receive landed properties . . . vineyards and meadows and woods and streams for operating mills . . . and for fishing," "for their own use only." As well, these properties would be in different locations than the monasteries, so "they decreed that the aforesaid laybrothers, and not monks, should be in charge of those dwellings, because, according to the Rule, monks should reside in their own cloister." The Cistercian monastic vision allowed for owning non-ecclesiastical property as long as it was used only for the monks' support and was under the oversight of a laybrother or hired laborer. But who were these laybrothers? According to the *Exordium parvum* they were men whom the monks "would treat as themselves in life and death—except that they may not become monks." These laybrothers, who often came from the lowest classes of society and were illiterate (as were many people in the Middle Ages), "played a vital part in the administration of the [Cistercian] monastic estates, especially in their role as grange masters."[6] The extensive role played by laybrothers in Cistercian monastic life and history is a hallmark of the Cistercian "evolution."[7]

Not only did the Cistercians introduce the use of laybrothers so as to protect their monks from having to live away from the main monastery, but the Cistercians were also innovative when they required that all abbots of Cistercian houses would gather together annually for a chapter. The *Summa Cartae caritatis* lays out the details: "Once a year all the abbots come together to [Cîteaux] to visit with each other, to re-establish good order, to confirm peace, and by grace to safeguard charity. When things that are amiss have to be corrected there, each individual is reverently and humbly to obey the lord abbot of Cîteaux and that holy assembly."[8] Only two reasons are allowed for missing the annual chapter: illness and the need to remain at one's own monastery in order to bless an entering novice. The purpose of this legislation,

---

6. James France, *Separate but Equal: Cistercian Lay Brothers 1120–1350* (Collegeville, MN: Cistercian Publications, 2012), 4.

7. See Constance Hoffman Berman, *The Cistercian Evolution: The Invention of a Religious Order in Twelfth-Century Europe* (Philadelphia: University of Pennsylvania Press, 2010).

8. Waddell, *Narrative and Legislative Texts*, 405.

of course, was to help ensure that the Cistercians were acting in one accord and functioning not as individual houses but as an order. As well, the founders of Cîteaux knew that the annual chapter was the primary way in which to correct the faults of an errant abbot. Thus the chapter was not for the purpose of control but rather was motivated by fraternal charity and the good of the order. In other words, the abbot of Cîteaux was not a kind of lesser pope (though that does seem to be the case, at least at times, with the abbot of Cluny) but the head of a fraternal order of like-minded communities.

In the area of spirituality, the Cistercians came to exercise great influence, especially through the writings of Bernard of Clairvaux, Aelred of Rievaulx (d. 1167), and William of Saint-Thierry (d. 1148). As a reform movement of Benedictine monasticism, the Cistercians, like all Benedictines, prioritized the daily round of communal prayer (*opus Dei*), manual labor, and divine reading (*lectio divina*) as the foremost activities of its monks' spiritual lives.[9] Cistercian monks (though not the laybrothers who were expected only to pray the Our Father and other short prayers at appointed times) gathered communally for the sevenfold daily office and at least once for Mass. Regarding manual labor, the Cistercian Idung of Prüfening writes, "We all work in common, we [i.e., the choir monks], our lay brothers and our hired hands, each according to his own capability, and we all make our living in common by our labour."[10] Unlike the Cluniacs, who thought it was inappropriate for a monk to be "begrimed in dirt and bent down with rust labors," the Cistercians valued the role of manual labor as a way to avoid boredom and sloth.[11] The Cistercian Stephen of Sawley (d. 1272), however, does say that manual labor must be done in such a way as not to interfere with one's devotion to God: "When you go to work, do what has to be done in such a way that your concern for the task at hand will not divert your mind from the things of God."[12] Finally, the slow, contemplative reading of spiritual texts known as *lectio divina* was a common monastic practice from its earliest history and was a staple of Cistercian practice. Again, Stephen of Sawley offers a traditional Cistercian approach to the practice. He first suggests that the junior monk use the Cistercian "Book of Usages, our Antiphonary, the *Lives of the Fathers* and the *Dialogues* of blessed Gregory [the Great]" for his *lectio*, and only later when

9. See RB 48.1–6.
10. Idung of Prüfening, *A Dialogue between Two Monks* 2.52; Jeremiah F. O'Sullivan, trans., "A Dialogue between Two Monks," in *Cistercians and Cluniacs: The Case for Cîteaux* (Kalamazoo, MI: Cistercian Publications, 1977), 94.
11. See Janet Burton and Julie Kerr, *The Cistercians in the Middle Ages* (Woodbridge, UK: Boydell Press, 2011), 106–7.
12. Stephen of Sawley, *A Mirror for Novices* 11; Jeremiah F. O'Sullivan, trans., *Stephen of Sawley: Treatises* (Kalamazoo, MI: Cistercian Publications, 1984), 103.

he has matured should he then begin to study the Old and New Testaments. Stephen instructs the novice that the purpose of *lectio divina* is not to acquire knowledge but to "employ the Scriptures as a substitute for a mirror wherein the soul somehow finds a reflection of its own image. It sees there things that are corrupt and corrects them; and things that are beautiful which contribute to its radiance."[13] Coupled with these areas of spiritual focus (which are not unique to the Cistercians but perhaps find a proper balance with the Cistercians) is the fact that Cistercian monasteries were always constructed in out-of-the-way locations, often on reclaimed land. The Cistercians saw the need for monasteries to be somewhat isolated from the rest of society, but it was the Carthusians who perfected the idea of monastic seclusion.

The Carthusians

The Carthusians came into existence sometime between 1082 and 1084 when Bruno of Cologne (d. 1101), along with several companions, left his prominent position as cathedral canon and headmaster of the school at Reims and settled in France. Bruno left Reims because reforms regarding ecclesiastical corruption (e.g., simony—the buying of church offices) in his diocese failed. As medieval Benedictine historian Guibert of Nogent (d. 1124) recounts: "After the death of Gervais, a very famous archbishop, a certain Manasses took over the government of Reims by using simony. . . . The man's morals, not to mention his shameless and stupid behavior, had begun to horrify all decent people. Bruno, who enjoyed an excellent reputation among the churches in Gaul at this time, left Reims out of hatred for this wretched man. Several of the most noteworthy figures of the clergy of that city followed him. . . . As for Bruno, once he had left the city he decided to renounce the world."[14] In 1084 Bruno retired with six companions to the solitude of an Alpine valley near Grenoble, France, where they were welcomed by the area's bishop, Hugh, who helped them to establish the monastery of La Chartreuse ("charter house"). In the words of Guibert, they "chose to live on the promontory of a steep and truly terrifying mountain that one could reach only by way of a rugged and rarely used path."[15] There they observed a primitive form of monasticism, in imitation of the early Christian desert fathers, wearing simple clothing and eating vegetables and coarse bread while living in community. Their early

---

13. Stephen of Sawley, *A Mirror for Novices* 15; O'Sullivan, *Stephen of Sawley*, 106–7.

14. Paul J. Archambault, trans., *A Monk's Confession: The Memoirs of Guibert of Nogent* (University Park: Pennsylvania State University Press, 1996), 30–31.

15. Ibid., 31.

form of life was drawn from the statutes of the canon regulars of St. Ruf near Avignon and the RB. Guibert describes the life of the earliest Carthusians:

> They have a cloister that is well suited for the cenobitic life, but they do not live cloistered as do other monks. Rather, each has his own cell around the perimeter of the cloister, in which he works, sleeps, and eats. Every Sunday the cellarer provides each of them with food, namely, bread and vegetables; with this each makes for himself a kind of stew, which is always the same. As for water . . . they draw it from a conduit, which leads from a spring and goes around all the cells and flows into each of these little houses through holes that have been drilled for that purpose. On Sundays and great feasts they have fish and cheese. . . . They hardly ever speak. . . . They wear hair shirts next to the skin.[16]

In 1090 Bruno left the community after being called to Rome, where he acted as adviser to Pope Urban II (d. 1099), his former student in Reims.

In the 1120s the fifth prior of La Chartreuse, Guigo I (d. 1136), who is often referred to as the true founder of the community, wrote a summary of the Carthusian pattern of life that has come to be called the *Customs*. Guigo, born Guigues du Pin, entered La Chartreuse in 1106, and in 1109, at the age of twenty-six, was elected prior; thereafter, he began to further mold the character of and popularize the Carthusian manner of life. Guigo remained in the office of prior until his death. It was under Guigo's leadership that La Chartreuse expanded into a full-scale monastic order. Similar to the Cistercians, the Carthusians were divided into two classes called fathers (*fraters*) and laybrothers (*conversi*). The fathers lived in the upper house (the monastery proper), and the laybrothers lived in the lower house, working the land and managing interaction with the outside world. By the end of the twelfth century, a unique Carthusian architecture had developed around this distinction between fathers and laybrothers to support the Carthusians extreme form of monastic solitude: "It [i.e., a Carthusian monastery] comprised a series of independent stone cells ranged, like terraced houses, round a covered cloister walk. At the rear of each cell was a small walled-in plot of garden and a private lavatory. Adjacent to the cloister stood the monastic church, the kitchen, refectory, and other offices."[17] Each monk occupied a separate cell, with a bed of straw, a pillow, a woolen coverlet, and the tools for manual labor or for writing. The cell consisted of three rooms and the garden: the first room contained an image of the Virgin Mary, which the monk bowed toward as he entered his hermitage; the second room was the *cubiculum*, containing an

16. Ibid., 31–32.
17. C. H. Lawrence, *Medieval Monasticism*, 3rd ed. (Harlow, UK: Longman, 2001), 158.

oratory, study, and dining room; while the third served as a woodshed and workroom, where the monk engaged in the copying of books. The monks left their cells only for liturgical offices and the funeral of a brother, and three times a week they fasted on bread, water, and salt. In addition, several long fasts were observed during the year; meat was forbidden at all times and so was wine, unless it was mixed with water. Uninterrupted silence was enforced except on rare occasions. The monks gathered daily in the church for Vespers and the night office, while remaining in their individual cells for the other offices of the day.

After 1133, when Guigo's *Customs* received the approval of Pope Innocent II (d. 1143), the order started to expand. Existing monasteries began to adopt Carthusian customs so that during the priorship of Anthelm (d. 1178), who became Guigo I's successor in 1142, it was necessary to have a regular meeting of all priors, called the General Chapter. The prior of the original house at La Chartreuse (now known as the Grande Chartreuse) was elected by the monks of that house and served as the general of the order. With the General Chapter meeting annually, the observances of the various houses were regularized. Growth was slow, so that by 1300 there were only thirty-one Carthusian monasteries in Europe. For example, the first charterhouse (Carthusian monastery) in England was founded in Witham in 1178, with a second founded at Hinton in 1225. Around 1245 the Benedictine nuns of Prébayon in Provence, in the south of France, adopted the customs of Carthusian life, in effect creating an order of Carthusian nuns. By the time of the dissolution of the monasteries in England in the 1540s, there were only nine Carthusian monasteries in England.[18] Yet the fourteenth and fifteenth centuries were a significant time of growth for the order across Europe, so much so that in 1521 there were 206 Carthusian monasteries. Growth among the women's houses was even slower than in the men's, so that by 1400 there were only nine Carthusian women's monasteries in existence.

A wonderful example of the Carthusian monastic vision is found in Guigo's *Customs* in a chapter titled "The Praise of the Solitary Life." This chapter is really just a recitation of biblical and early Christian examples of solitude

18. Henry VIII, king of England from 1509 to 1547, ordered the closure of all monasteries in England for theological, political, and financial reasons. He further legislated that their properties and possessions must pass to the royal treasury. It began with a royal act in 1536 declaring that all religious houses with fewer than twelve members and less than £200 of income per year were to be given to the king. By 1540 Henry confiscated over eight hundred monasteries and friaries, displacing more than ten thousand monks, nuns, friars and canons. Many of these monastic properties were sold to landowners, and some became churches, such as Durham Cathedral. Most of the displaced monastics were financially remunerated and given pensions, though some resisted and were executed.

emphasizing Guigo's insistence that "almost all the greater and more profound secrets were revealed to God's friends when they were alone and not in the midst of milling crowds."[19] Further, Guigo says that "solitude is the greatest support for sweet psalmody, pious reading, fervent prayer, deep meditation, ecstatic contemplation, and the baptism of tears."[20] Guigo believes that the Carthusian way of life commends itself by its rarity and small numbers of adherents and that it is actually a better monasticism of "higher merit," for, in his estimation, "the more the members the more a form is lower and inferior."[21] Despite the dubious nature of this claim, it does show the Carthusian vision for an eremitical monasticism that was better than the cenobitism practiced by the Cluniacs and the Cistercians. Yet the Carthusians were not the only eremitical reform movement of the eleventh century and, therefore, not the only ones living according to this ideal. Nor were they the only monks to esteem the eremitic life above the cenobitic.

The Camaldolese and the Vallombrosans

Romuald of Ravenna was born into an aristocratic family circa 951. Around 973 he journeyed to the monastery of St. Apollinare in Classe, Italy, to make reparation for his father but underwent a conversion in which he joined the community. Soon, however, he became disillusioned with the disparity between the RB and the way that it was observed at Classe. After three years in the community he obtained permission to leave and became a disciple of the hermit Marino near Venice. In about 978 he went to the monastery of St. Michael of Cuxa in France, where he built a cell near the abbey, was joined by a small group of disciples, studied the early Christian monastic tradition, and was ordained a priest. He returned to Italy around 988 to reform monasteries in Tuscany and built a monastery at Bagno but was soon driven from the house by the monks, unhappy with his monetary assistance to a group of homeless monks.[22] He then settled at Pereo in 993, a solitary place in the salt marshes outside Ravenna where a small group of disciples gathered around him to share the eremitical life. After a short abbacy at St. Apollinare in Classe, Romuald headed to Monte Cassino and then to Rome, where he was joined by several

19. Guigo I, *Customs* 80; Bernard McGinn, ed., *The Essential Writings of Christian Mysticism* (New York: Modern Library, 2006), 132.
20. Ibid., 134.
21. Ibid.
22. It appears that the monks of Bagno preferred that their money be kept for their own use and not to assist the monks of other houses. Romuald's beneficence did not endear him to this community, so he continued on his way.

like-minded monastic reformers. Together they returned to Pereo in the hope of becoming missionary monks to Poland and Hungary. Romuald's disciples went to Poland, where they were martyred in 1003, whereas Romuald went to Istria, a peninsula opposite Venice. He returned to Italy and established a community of hermits and a monastery for nuns. Between 1010 and 1025 Romuald founded or reformed many monasteries in northern and central Italy before finally establishing a monastery at Camaldoli in 1023 or 1025. The original foundation consisted of five monks who built monastic cells and a church higher up the mountain as well as a guest house lower down the mountain.

The community at Camaldoli was eremitical in its orientation but was not intended as a breakaway from the Benedictine heritage so valued by Romuald. In his mind, reformed monasticism consisted of poverty, asceticism, solitude, prayer, and psalmody, set within the RB and the monastic tradition of discretion and guidance by a spiritual father. Despite the number of communities that Romuald established or reformed, his monastic ideals remained largely fixed. After a lifetime of moving frequently, Romuald died in 1027.

Commenting on Romuald's frequent movements, his biographer Peter Damian (d. 1072/73) writes, "So heartfelt was his longing to do good that he was never satisfied with what he achieved; as soon as he had one project in hand, he would rush off to start another. Anyone might have thought that his plan was to turn the whole world into a hermitage and for everyone to become monks."[23] Because vitae are written for the purpose of holding up the individual for emulation by the faithful, the details of a saint's life are sometimes altered to provide a greater model for those intending to imitate the saint. An excellent example of this is the *Life of St. Romuald* by Peter Damian, whose main purpose is to promote eremitical monastic ideals. Written around 1042, the vita was likely the first work of Damian and was written the year prior to his election as prior of Fonte Avellane, a monastery founded by one of Romuald's disciples. As Henrietta Leyser points out, "Romuald's reputation through the centuries rests on a tradition that Damian never mentions: that Romuald was the founder of the monastery of Camaldoli near Arezzo, a foundation comprising both hermitage and monastery which subsequently, in 1113, became the head of a new monastic order."[24] The question that must be asked, then, is: What is Damian's purpose in writing the vita of Romuald if

---

23. Henrietta Leyser, trans., "Peter Damian, *Life of St. Romuald of Ravenna*," in *Medieval Hagiography: An Anthology*, ed. Thomas Head (New York: Garland, 2000), 308.

24. Ibid., 295. In 1113 Pope Paschal II issued a bull that united under Camaldoli all the monasteries and hermitages founded or reformed by Romuald, as well as those who had adopted the Romualdian reform.

not to offer a direct example for Damian's own monks to follow? The answer, again according to Leyser, is as follows:

> In 1049, only six years after [Peter Damian's] election as prior of Fonte Avellane, the Council of Reims was held, an occasion conveniently and not unreasonably taken as marking the first signs of the papal reform movement that was subsequently to convulse Europe. At this council both clerical sodomy and simony were on the agenda; both were matters of close concern to Damian as his writings of the time show and as already adumbrated in his *Life of St. Romuald*. Damian's commitment to such causes led to his becoming cardinal bishop of Ostia in 1057; what is important here is to stress the ways in which the *Life of St. Romuald* was thus already programmatic. In Romuald, Peter Damian could see and doubtless to some extent create a figure of great charismatic force fearlessly and restlessly contesting conventional standards of morality while at the same time demanding that the greatest respect be paid to ordered lives. . . . The plan is to monasticize the world—to turn it all, indeed—and they are Damian's words as he describes the activities of Romuald "into a hermitage."[25]

Similarly, as Colin Phipps has remarked, "[Damian's] image of Romuald became his own model. In the process, the image seems to have become imbued for its part with the colouration of Damian's own concerns. The whole life took on a shape and a structure determined not by Damian's hard knowledge of the man but by his schematisation, his programme, of Romuald's spiritual growth. The *Life* is the vehicle of a kind of argument."[26] From Leyser's perspective, Peter Damian construed the life of Romuald so that it could serve a greater programmatic purpose, with that purpose being the very monasticization of the world! Phipps says, "The argument of the *Life* . . . is primarily a theory of eremitism, an argument as to why men should wish to associate themselves with Romuald, of how such as he serve God more effectively—as Damian believed—than all others."[27] Despite this crafting of the vita for a specific purpose, however, Damian is still concerned about the example set by Romuald. "In this little work I am not attempting to make a collection of miracle stories," writes Damian, "but rather to tell of Romuald's way of life for the edification of us all."[28]

25. Ibid., 296.

26. Colin Phipps, "Romuald—Model Hermit: Eremitical Theory in Saint Peter Damian's *Vita Beati Romualdi*, Chapters 16–27," in *Monks, Hermits and the Ascetic Tradition*, ed. W. J. Sheils (Oxford: Basil Blackwell, 1985), 65.

27. Ibid., 67.

28. Peter Damian, *Life of St. Romuald*, prologue; Leyser, "Peter Damian," 297.

The context of Damian's vita of Romuald is the tension between the cenobitic monastic tradition and emerging eremitical practices.[29] In Damian's estimation, these cenobitic monasteries did not measure up to the "glories" of ancient Egyptian and Syrian monasticism.[30] Like the Cistercians after him, Damian (and Romuald) believed that the Benedictine cenobitic monastic tradition did not need to be eliminated but, rather, reformed. He especially saw this happening along the lines laid down by Romuald at Fonte Avellane.

In chapter 18 of the vita, Damian writes that some monks from the monastery of St. Michael the Archangel in Bagno "broke into [Romuald's] cell with sticks and staves, beat him many times and having stolen everything chased him ignominiously out of the region." The reason for this, we are told, is that Romuald was taking a stand against the "evil customs" of the cenobitic monks at St. Michael's by giving generous amounts of money to those in need. The monks of the monastery, therefore, are pictured as avaricious and wrathful. Romuald's response to this episode was to go "on his way plunged in deep depression, thinking to himself that never again would he worry about the salvation of anyone else but himself." Before long, however, Romuald "decided [that] he was overcome with fear [and] that if this was really how he chose to act in [the] future then undoubtedly he would perish, damned by divine judgment." The monks, meanwhile, "behaved as if they had been liberated from a great burden and congratulated each other most heartily on their behavior."[31] The point of this story is plain: the avaricious monks represent all that needs reforming in the church, while Romuald, though tempted to give up on people, represents those appointed by God as the reformers of the church. Phipps takes this incident as "an almost explicit statement of what eremitism is not."[32]

Elsewhere, in chapter twenty-six of the vita, Damian offers a statement of how eremitism should be: "To each and to the many other brethren gathered there Romuald assigned a cell; together all observed the rigors of the eremitic way of life in such a way that everyone who came to hear of their manner of living was filled with admiration."[33] Thus, after realizing his mistake of being desirous to simply abandon others and pursue his own salvation, Romuald, writes Damian, realized that he needed to live for others. The true hermit and, by extension, the true monk lives for others, offering an example by faithfully

---

29. For helpful summaries of this tension, see Norman F. Cantor, "The Crisis of Western Monasticism, 1050–1130," *American Historical Review* 66 (1960): 47–67; and John Van Engen, "The 'Crisis of Cenobitism' Reconsidered: Benedictine Monasticism in the Years 1050–1150," *Speculum* 61 (1986): 269–304.

30. Phipps, "Romuald," 67.

31. Damian, *Life of St. Romuald* 18; Leyser, "Peter Damian," 301–2.

32. Phipps, "Romuald," 69.

33. Damian, *Life of St. Romuald* 26; Leyser, "Peter Damian," 304.

following one's appropriate "manner of living" (*conversatio*). Between these two statements of the wrong and correct forms of the eremitical life, Damian offers a rejection of unreformed cenobitism. For example, in chapter twenty-two of the vita, the emperor Otto, "wanting to reform the abbey of Classe, gave the monks the choice of electing as abbot whomsoever they pleased. Unanimously they voted for Romuald." Otto, knowing that Romuald would likely not accept the abbacy, went in person to bring news of the election. Damian tells us that the king "beseeched him to accept the abbacy. Romuald refused it outright; the king retaliated by threatening him with sentences of excommunication and anathema from all the archbishops, bishops, and the whole synod." Faced squarely with such facts, Romuald relented "and against his will took up this pastoral role." Damian, pressing home his agenda that eremitism is superior to cenobitism, writes: "He ruled the monks with strict discipline, allowing no one, however wellborn, however learned to stray from the path of righteousness. . . . When the brethren realized, rather late in the day, the character of the man they had chosen they blamed each other for having encouraged his election."[34] In this example at the monastery in Classe, Damian wants his readers or hearers to see the negative portrait of cenobitic monks that he paints and that Romuald, as an eremitical exemplar, is superior to the very cenobitism that he critiques. As Phipps states, by the end of the vita Damian's message is obvious: "Only in the hermitage can the fullest ascetic and devotional relationship with Christ be developed, away from the infection of communal sin. Only by caring for the salvation of others can the hermit love his neighbour as God commanded."[35] In his own words Damian asks, "Who indeed would not be awestruck, who would not proclaim the power of God's right hand to effect change at the sight of men who previously had been clad in silk, even in gold, surrounded by crowds of courtiers, accustomed to every luxury, at the sight of such men, I say, now content with one garment, living as recluses, barefooted, unadorned, worn out by severe abstinence?"[36] The answer is no one. Thus Damian takes the life of a man who did not reject all forms of cenobitic monasticism and makes it into a strong apologetic for the superiority of eremitism over cenobitism. The spirit of eremitism was in the air, and others would follow in the footsteps of Romuald.

John Gualbert was born in 995 near Florence, Italy. After a kinsman was murdered, it fell to John to revenge the killing. When encountered, the killer

34. Damian, *Life of St. Romuald* 22; Leyser, "Peter Damian," 302.
35. Phipps, "Romuald," 69.
36. Damian, *Life of St. Romuald* 26; Leyser, "Peter Damian," 304.

kneeled before John with his arms outstretched in the form of a cross, asking for mercy. Because it was Good Friday, John let him go free but was so shaken by the event that he visited the monastery of San Miniato in Florence. While he was there, the carving of Jesus on the crucifix in the church gave his approval of John's good deed by bowing his head. Interpreting this as a sign of God's forgiveness, John asked for and was granted admission to the Cluniac-affiliated monastery. Due to his zeal for the RB and for Benedictine life, the monks elected John abbot. However, the abbacy had already been sold through simony by Atto, bishop of Florence. John went into the marketplace of Florence to denounce the newly "elected" simoniacal abbot and the bishop, but the people turned against John; he fled the city to look for a monastery in which to faithfully observe the RB. He entered Camaldoli in 1030, but his desire to preach in the city against the prior's wishes forced him to leave. So he settled near Florence in 1036 with two companions. Approximately three years later they settled on land given to John by Itta, abbess of a neighboring monastery. John named the new monastery Vallombrosa ("shady valley").

At Vallombrosa John established a two-tier monastic system like that at Camaldoli. The first tier (or upper monastery, since it was higher up the hill) consisted of individual cells for monks whose aim was to observe the RB strictly. Their quotidian regime was one of silence, simplicity, and poverty. In addition, they refused to be ordained (so as not to receive any money for saying the Mass, contra their poverty), they rejected the Cluniac horarium in favor of the RB's order of psalmody, and they refused support from donors. The second tier (or lower monastery) existed to ensure the tranquility of the upper monastery and was administered by laybrothers (*conversi*) who did the work of the community, lived apart from the eremitical monks, dressed and were tonsured differently, and were allowed to talk when they went into town for necessities.[37]

Though the initial growth of the Vallombrosan observance was slow (there were only eight houses in 1073 when John Gualbert died), there were over 125 communities by the mid-thirteenth century. At first these communities were not linked together juridically, like the Cluniacs and later the Cistercians, but were connected "by a bond of charity and (uniform) observance."[38] In April 1090 Pope Urban II granted the Vallombrosans freedom from diocesan oversight, referring to the vigilance that the abbot of Vallombrosa exercised over the other houses. This papal bull also said that the abbot of Vallombrosa was not

---

37. The use of *conversi* by John Gualbert predates that of the Cistercians.

38. Terence Kavenagh, "Vallombrosans," in *Encyclopedia of Monasticism*, ed. William M. Johnston (London: Fitzroy Dearborn, 2000), 2:1320.

to be elected only by the monks of that house but by a *conventus abbatum*, a kind of general chapter of all the abbots of Vallombrosan communities. This early germ of a formal organization grew in the twelfth century: "The abbot of Vallombrosa was referred to as abbot major (*abbas maior*), and his power began to be juridically defined. No abbot was to be elected in any of the other monasteries without his knowledge and approval. . . . By the first half of the 13th century [the Vallombrosan congregation] began to be referred to as the Order of Vallombrosa,"[39] though this organizational structure would not survive the Middle Ages.

Ressourcement: Continual Re-formation

In Romans 12:2 the apostle Paul exhorts the Christians in Rome to "not be conformed to this world, but be transformed by the renewal of your mind." Given that scholars view chapters 12–16 of Romans as application or, in more overt theological terms, instructions in sanctification, it would appear that the spiritual life is to be one of nonconformity and renewal. Spiritual renewal is rarely, if ever, instantaneous, so it is not surprising that the institution of monasticism was not perfected in an instant but has always experienced an oceanlike ebb and flow of renewal throughout church history. At times cenobitism predominated, and occasionally eremitical forms of monasticism took center stage. In a more perfect world there would be no tension between these forms of monastic life; they would coexist in a perfect harmony supporting one another. This is the vision that Benedict laid out in chapter 1 of the RB: the anchorites or hermits are those

> who have come through the test of living in a monastery for a long time, and have passed beyond the first fervor of monastic life. Thanks to the help and guidance of many, they are now trained to fight against the devil. They have built up their strength and go from the battle line in the ranks of their brothers to the single combat of the desert. Self-reliant now, without the support of another, they are ready with God's help to grapple single-handed with the vices of the body and mind.[40]

In Benedict's monastic vision the hermit is fit to live on his own only when he has learned how to be a hermit by living in a monastic community.

---

39. Ibid.

40. RB 1.3–5; Timothy Fry, ed., *RB 1980: The Rule of St. Benedict in Latin and English with Notes* (Collegeville, MN: Liturgical Press, 1981), 169.

Yet Benedict's ideals are not always easily attained, showing that the monastery is oftentimes no different than an individual's spiritual journey. Just as monasticism at times needs to be renewed and should always be in the process of renewal, so should all believers. A community of monks or nuns in the process of renewal can only produce a monastery that is undergoing renewal. Thus, in the words of the apostle Paul: "So we do not lose heart. Though our outer self is wasting away, our inner self is being renewed day by day" (2 Cor. 4:16).

In the current evangelical church this personal renewal is, at times, along "monastic" lines. For example, as will be discussed in chapter 13, the New Monastic movement that is prominent in evangelicalism is monastic in its vision and genesis. Moreover, many evangelical Christians are strengthened spiritually by being associated with monasteries, whether formally as oblates or associates (see chap. 14) or informally as participants in short-term retreats. But monasticism's influence on evangelical renewal can also be seen in evangelicalism's adoption of the ministry of spiritual direction and retreat centers. The Institute for Spiritual Formation at Biola University's Talbot School of Theology has graduated dozens of trained spiritual directors, some of whom oversee the Evangelical Center for Spiritual Wisdom, which provides a listing of evangelical spiritual directors in North America. As well, leading evangelical publishing houses regularly publish titles on spiritual direction, and some evangelical churches now keep a spiritual director on staff. Though spiritual direction is not uniquely monastic, it flourished historically in monasteries, and up until the latter half of the twentieth century, if one wanted a spiritual director, that person was often found in the monastery.

Alongside spiritual direction, evangelicals now have a robust vision of the benefit of going on personal and corporate retreats, but it was only in the nineteenth century that Protestants began making retreats, having been viewed with suspicion as too Roman Catholic prior to that.[41] Now it is not uncommon for evangelical churches to rent out entire retreat centers (located often at monasteries) for the weekend or to encourage members to make personal retreats when they are able. An evangelical church as well-known as Saddleback Church in southern California even owns its own retreat center, complete with retreat ministry staff (including spiritual directors). Though these practices are not distinctively monastic any longer, both of these disciplines originated in the monastery and show evangelicalism's openness to

41. John Tyers, "Not a Papal Conspiracy but a Spiritual Principle: Three Early Anglican Apologists for the Practice of Retreat," *Journal of Anglican Studies* 8.2 (2010): 165–83.

spiritual disciplines that are monastic in origin. As these practices reform the individuals who observe them, those individuals in turn affect the institutions of which they are a part. Not only is monasticism always reforming and evolving, so too are those who live in the monasteries and those who engage in monastic spiritual disciplines.

9

Regular Canons, Hospitallers, and the Military Orders

I n 1991 I joined the United States Naval Reserve, becoming a member of a Naval Mobile Construction Battalion—a Seabee. I attended boot camp in San Diego and then A-school in Gulfport, Mississippi. Both San Diego and Gulfport were home to a great many military personnel in the area. When I went off base to the nearby towns, people did not act surprised to see a person in uniform. Even if I was not in uniform, they could assume from my closely cropped hair and clean-shaven face that I was in the military. However, when I returned home to Langhorne, Pennsylvania, and was assigned to a construction battalion in New Jersey near my college, things changed. I was no longer one of many Seabees out and about, and I was no longer part of a large, cloistered group of military men. I was working at a construction site—not a typical task for a military person.

Something similar happened in the Middle Ages. Just when everyone was used to monks living in large communities behind walls with their distinctive clothes, forms of nontraditional monasticism began to emerge. These monastics did not necessarily live in large groups together behind walls, and they began to engage in activities that were not typical to monks, such as building hospitals or fighting in battle.

The monastic landscape was changing. Thus this chapter will survey the foundation, growth, and spirituality of the non-cloistered orders of regular canons (particularly the Premonstratensian and Victorine canons), the Hospitaller order, and the military order of the Knights Templar. Their organization, apostolates, and spiritualities will be examined in an effort to demonstrate that the pairing of a mónastic lifestyle with a robust *vita activa* (and, in the case of the canons, a *vita apostolica*) was a viable form of the monastic life, consistent with earlier manifestations of monasticism. Though attention will be paid to foundation documents, an emphasis of this chapter will be on the institutions created by these forms of monasticism and how these institutions benefited and fit into medieval society.

The Origins of the Orders of Canons

As discussed in chapter 5, the origin and growth of the canons is somewhat historically unclear, but they were given definition and shape by Chrodegang of Metz in the eighth century. By the twelfth century there were two kinds of clerics: (1) regular canons, who were ordained clerics and lived a common life, eschewing private property, under the *Rule* of Augustine (RA; discussed in chap. 3); and (2) all other clergy, who lived communally but did not meet these requirements and who were labeled "secular clergy."[1] In essence the "canons regular were really a hybrid order of clerical monks, congregations of clergy living under a monastic rule"[2] whose reemergence is intimately tied to the Gregorian Reform program of the eleventh century.[3] Initiated by Pope Gregory VII (pope from 1073 to 1085), these reforms laid great stress on the need for the clergy to observe clerical celibacy, renounce personal property, and live in community—all in an effort to end the secularization of ecclesiastical offices brought on by practices such as simony. Before becoming pope, Gregory VII (then named Hildebrand) had argued that the New Testament "canons" were the apostles and that their lifestyle, based on Acts 2:42–47, provided the model for all future canons. This understanding of the canonical life had been endorsed by monastic reformers, such as Peter Damian (d. 1072/73). In a letter of 1051 to clerics at Fano, Damian reveals that a group of the clerics had attempted to live "by the rule in a house of canons" but that most of the others refused this way of life. In Damian's mind this refusal made no sense since a cleric living among other clerics should not

1. Caroline Walker Bynum, *Docere Verbo et Exemplo: An Aspect of Twelfth-Century Spirituality* (Missoula, MT: Scholars Press, 1979), 2.
2. C. H. Lawrence, *Medieval Monasticism*, 3rd ed. (Harlow, UK: Longman, 2001), 160.
3. See J. C. Dickinson, *The Origins of the Austin Canons and Their Introduction into England* (London: SPCK, 1952), 26.

live a secular life. A cleric's religious profession made it impossible for him to live like a layman.[4] The main issue for Damian was that the cleric would desire to accumulate wealth for himself instead of living in poverty. Also, Damian chastises his readers for their desire to live away from the church and one another, choosing the streets and marketplaces of the city over the real sanctuary of God (i.e., the church building). He writes, "These wish to have the name of canon, that is, of a regular, but not to live regularly. These seek to share in the Church's common property, but reject the idea of living in community near the church. Certainly, this is not the pattern of the Early church, and it deviates greatly from the discipline of apostolic origin."[5] In time he turns to the issue of celibacy, stating that if someone is married, then he will approach the altar of God lustfully: "How dare one in conscience approach God's altar if he is incited by greed or passion?"[6] The sacramental nature of the cleric's life demands that he eschew possessions, live in community, and forsake marriage, for "it is quite impossible . . . for one who is burdened with fiscal responsibilities, who by living among and conversing with throngs of people is daily involved in their affairs, to take part in the sacred mysteries with heart unsullied."[7] The future direction of the canons was set by this reformist agenda and given papal approval at the Lateran Councils of 1059 and 1063.

The earliest reformed house of canons was Saint-Ruf (near Avignon), founded in 1039, but a host of other houses soon followed, all with the stated goal of reforming the clerical life along the lines of the vision laid out by Gregory VII. Though canons technically are not monks, the lifestyle of the regular canons soon came to be monastic. While most writers of the time would define a "monk" as someone who followed the *Rule of Benedict* (RB) and a "canon" as someone under the RA, the differences were not always so obvious. Both monks and canons engaged in the *cura animarum* (care of souls), which included preaching and celebrating Mass; both observed a daily horarium of prayer; and both exhibited signs of adhering to a so-called monastic spirituality. The anonymous *Book of the Various Orders and Callings in the Church* (*Libellus de Diversis Ordinibus et Professionibus qui sunt in Aecclesia*) talks about two types of monks (those who live close to society like the Cluniacs and those who remove themselves from society like the Cistercians) and three types of canons (those who establish

---

4. Peter Damian, *Letter* 39.2; Owen J. Blum, *Peter Damian: Letters 31–60* (Washington, DC: Catholic University of America Press, 1990), 98–99.

5. Damian, *Letter* 39.6; Blum, *Peter Damian*, 102.

6. Damian, *Letter* 39.10; Blum, *Peter Damian*, 106.

7. Damian, *Letter* 39.10; Blum, *Peter Damian*, 107.

themselves far from society like the Premonstratensians, those who have houses near society like the Victorines, and secular canons who live among men of the world).[8]

The Premonstratensians

The *Libellus*'s first group of canons, the Premonstratensians, owe their founding to Norbert of Xanten (d. 1134). Norbert was born to a noble Christian family, and even before his birth his mother, we are told, heard a voice from heaven assuring her that Norbert would become great before God and men. After his schooling, he was ordained a subdeacon by the archbishop of Cologne but soon turned his attention away from the church. In spite of his worldliness, he was offered a canonry in the cathedral of Cologne and was then offered the bishopric of Cambrai, which Norbert refused. In the summer of 1115, Norbert experienced a profound conversion:

> He was dressed in silk, accompanied by a single servant. While he was on his way [to Freden] a dark cloud overtook him, lightning flashed, thunder roared, and—what was more inconvenient—there was no house for shelter nearby. As both he and his companion were unnerved, suddenly the terrifying sound and sight of a thunderbolt struck the ground, opening it to the depth of a man's height. From here steamed forth a putrid stench, fouling Norbert and his garments. Struck from his horse, he thought he heard a voice denouncing him. Returning to his senses and now repentant, he reflected on the words of the Psalmist: *Turn from evil and do good* (Ps. 33:15; 36:27). Thus motivated, he returned home. There, caught up in the spirit of salvation through fear of the Lord, he put on a hair shirt beneath his outer garments intending to do good deeds and penance for his past life. He went to the monastery of Siegburg.[9]

What is important to notice immediately in this account is that Norbert's conversion was a turning from materialistic private property (e.g., silk clothing) toward community living, both hallmarks of the Gregorian reform. Though Norbert went to the Benedictine abbey of Siegburg, he did not join the community but followed Benedictine values as a priest at the church in Xanten, having been ordained a priest soon after his conversion. Further, he received guidance from hermits and others: "Norbert carefully inquired into the life and

8. Giles Constable and Bernard S. Smith, eds. and trans., *Libellus de Diversis Ordinibus et Professionibus qui Sunt in Aecclesia* (Oxford: Clarendon, 1972).

9. *Vita Norberti A* 1; Theodore J. Antry and Carol Neel, *Norbert and Early Norbertine Spirituality* (Mahwah, NJ: Paulist Press, 2007), 126–27. Siegburg was a Benedictine monastery outside Cologne.

customs of anyone living under a rule—monks, hermits, and recluses—and by their example he made even greater spiritual progress."[10]

Norbert next retired to a church on his family property where he lived "as a solitary, spending his time in prayer, reading, and meditation."[11] Some, apparently jealous of his holiness, accused him before the papal legate of usurping the office of preacher and demanded to know why he wore a habit when he still lived on his own and had not entered the religious life. After defending himself, he set out as a missionary, divesting himself of his properties and possessions. Throughout his itinerant preaching ministry, he began attracting disciples, and in 1120 he and his followers settled in the valley of Prémontré near Laon. Though some advised Norbert to establish his community as a Cistercian house, he "ordered that the rule be accepted which the blessed Augustine had established for his followers. He now hoped to live the apostolic life he had undertaken by his preaching."[12] Norbert's vision for the community was for it to have both active and contemplative elements, with the canons imitating the apostles in prayer and pastoral activity. Soon after the foundation at Prémontré, the first Premonstratensian community of canonesses was founded. These Premonstratensian communities were made up of both lay and clergy members; men and women shared the same enclosure (with separate buildings for each gender) and a common church. Norbert received papal approval for the order in 1126, the same year that he was elected archbishop of Magdeburg.

Desirous to continue his preaching ministry, Norbert never served as the abbot of Prémontré. That office went to Hugh of Fosse (d. 1164), who organized the new order and oversaw its early growth and adherence to the ideals of Norbert. By 1128 there were six houses, and Hugh was functioning as the abbot general. When Hugh died, there were more than a hundred houses, and by the mid-thirteenth century there were more than five hundred houses. By this time, however, there were no longer any Premonstratensian canonesses, having been phased out over the order's first century. The emphasis of the order was placed on intellectual formation and preaching.[13] One of the Premonstratensians greatest gifts to medieval society was their emphasis on preaching and practicing what they preached: teaching in word and deed.[14] Moreover, they did this while living nearly monastic lives. Whereas

10. *Vita Norberti A* 3; Antry and Neel, *Norbert*, 128.

11. *Vita Norberti A* 3; Antry and Neel, *Norbert*, 128–29.

12. *Vita Norberti A* 12; Antry and Neel, *Norbert*, 146.

13. Bruce L. Venarde, "Premonstratensian Canons," in *Encyclopedia of Monasticism*, ed. William M. Johnston (London: Fitzroy Dearborn, 2000), 2:1043–45.

14. Borrowing from the title of Bynum's *Docere Verbo et Exemplo*.

the secular clergy were often poorly educated and "worldly" (i.e., kept concubines and possessed material possessions), the Premonstratensians were well-educated celibates who renounced personal property. It might not be too much of an overstatement to say that the Premonstratensians (and other canonical orders) were the pastoral elites of the twelfth century. According to the anonymous *Libellus*, the Premonstratensians' task was "to teach the people, take tithes, collect offerings in church, remonstrate with delinquents, reconcile the corrected and penitent to the church, and observe other duties" of clerics.[15] It should be remembered that, first and foremost, canons are pastors, and all of their contemplative activity as priests is geared toward reengaging people.

Soon after the Premonstratensians there arose another sort of canon whose life would be lived much closer to cities but oriented in the same direction as the Norbertines, that is, toward preaching and a robust combination of action and contemplation. In the words of the *Libellus*, these canons "were in the middle, being unlike those who withdraw from the company of worldly men entirely [e.g., the Premonstratensians] and unlike those who are called seculars and who share their living-quarters with other men." The purpose for this close-to-the-city lifestyle is so that they can "undertake . . . the correction of human customs, so that evil men seeing their life should be converted from evil and, being converted, may either enter upon such a life or, if they cannot enter it, in loving it and imitating it as much as they can."[16] The best example of this type of canon is the Victorines of Paris.

The Abbey of St. Victor was founded by William of Champeaux (d. 1121) in 1108. After a career of teaching in the schools of Paris, William retired to a hermitage on the Seine River to spend time in prayer and study, but soon a small community grew up around him. The community probably would have elected William its first abbot, but in 1113 he was elected bishop of Châlons, so the community elected Gilduin (d. 1155). Under Gilduin the abbey prospered, and men came from many areas of Europe to join the nascent community. Like many other reform movements (à la the Cistercians), the first monastery founded became the motherhouse of an order with its own general chapters. Having gained the support of King Louis VI (d. 1137), the community became a leading house among the emerging communities of canons. Though the Premonstratensians were also known for their learning, the Victorines became leaders in the intellectual climate of the twelfth century, exercising an immense influence due to their location just outside the walls of Paris.

15. Constable and Smith, *Libellus de Diversis*, 69.
16. Ibid., 75.

During the abbacy of Gilduin, several important men joined the abbey and emerged as intellectual bright lights. Hugh of St. Victor (d. 1141) was a German who established the Victorine tradition of theology by combining "fidelity to the monastic and poetic theology of the early Church with openness to the methods and questions of the newly emerging theology of the schools with its emphasis on order, logic, and argument."[17] Hugh wrote a number of important works, including the *Didascalicon* (a guide to reading) and *On the Sacraments* (a synthesis of theology). Adam of St. Victor (d. 1143) composed poetry and musical compositions, whereas Achard of St. Victor (d. 1170/71), from England, specialized in the writing of sermons before he left the abbey to become the bishop of Avranches. The Scotsman Richard of St. Victor (d. 1173) was a prolific author of sermons, treatises on the spiritual life, mystical texts, and biblical exegesis. Hugh and Richard have left the largest footprints and thus serve as excellent representatives of Victorine spirituality; however, we will focus on a short treatise from Hugh, which demonstrates a spirituality that is typical of the canons.

Hugh entered the abbey around 1115, and in the 1120s he was put in charge of the students and became master of the school. At the time of his death in 1141, Abbot Gilduin assembled a collection of Hugh's works, among which was a treatise titled *On the Kinds of Meditation and Their Usefulness*. According to Hugh, "Meditation is a frequent reflection investigating the manner, the cause, and the reason of each thing. The manner investigates what it is, the cause why it exists, and the reason how it exists." Further, "there are three kinds of meditations: on creatures, on Scriptures, and on moral conduct."[18] Regarding meditation on the Scriptures, first we are to read a passage so as to know the truth. Then, through meditation, we assimilate the truth. Next, prayer places it before God, and then action organizes it; finally, contemplation rejoices in it. When a person meditates on the Scriptures, she is doing it in order to determine how to put into practice what she knows: "Meditation is the reflection on the plan of how to put into practice what we know, because it is no use to know something unless we put it into practice."[19] Notice here the distinction between contemplation and action, which is typical of canonical life. For traditional monastics, like the Benedictines and Cistercians, meditation tends to be an end in itself, whereas for canons it is for the purpose of action as much as it is an end in itself. Concerning actions, Hugh states that

17. Hugh Feiss, "Victorines," in Johnston, *Encyclopedia of Monasticism*, 2:1323.

18. Christopher P. Evans, ed., *Writings on the Spiritual Life: A Selection of Works of Hugh, Adam, Achard, Richard, Walter, and Godfrey of St Victor* (Turnhout, Belg.: Brepols, 2013), 387.

19. Ibid., 388.

these too must be meditated on in order to ensure that they are being done for proper and right reasons:

> Regarding works we have to consider first whether they are done with a good intention. A good intention is one that is simple and right. . . . Thus the intention needs to be both right through discernment and simple through kindness. The second thing to consider in works is whether what was begun with the right intention also is brought to an end with the fervor of perseverance, so that neither perseverance grows numb, nor love grows tepid.[20]

Action, in and of itself, is not necessarily good unless it is done with proper motivation and disposition. Good works are motivated not just for reputation's sake but also through the prick of conscience. Again, holy action has its rootedness in contemplation.

From this brief survey of the Premonstratensians and the Victorines, we can see that the canons were neither wholly monastic nor were they non-monastic. Their inwardly focused contemplative bent shared similarities with other reformed monastic orders, such as the Cistercians and Carthusians, but their outwardly focused lives of action share greater similarities with parish priests. Institutionally, the canons' greatest contribution to medieval society and the history of monasticism was to show that contemplation and action are not in irreconcilable tension but that a lifestyle characterized by both is possible. As well, the orders of canons gave to medieval society a system of schooling for clergy that vastly improved on what had been available up to that time while anticipating the full flowering of the medieval university. Further, they helped to instantiate the goals of the Gregorian Reform, vastly improving the moral lives not only of the clergy but ultimately of all Christians who would look to their local priests and the canons as examples of how to live the *vita activa* and the *vita apostolica*. Other emerging forms of monasticism would show medieval citizens that even one of the most violent forms of vocation (i.e., knighthood) could be lived monastically.

Military Orders

Up to the twelfth century the shedding of blood by killing was always a sin requiring confession and satisfaction. Canon law forbade clerics and monks from using the sword. However, in the twelfth century a new phenomenon

20. Ibid., 389.

arose—the military orders. Prior to this, in the tenth and eleventh centuries, the church attempted to restrain an unbridled use of violence by the knightly class by creating movements called the "Peace of God" or "Truce of God." This led to the Christianization of knightly behavior and ultimately to codes of chivalry. A century later, however, the Latin church was supporting and preaching the crusades—military attempts to reclaim property from the Muslims in the Holy Land. The First Crusade (1096–1099) recaptured Jerusalem from the Muslims, placing it again under Christian control. This was made possible by a shift in theology, which said that violence against an infidel was a legitimate and Christian act. Thus it was no longer viewed as a sin, and the crusades were seen as "holy" wars. The main expression of this Christian legitimation of war as a holy act was the creation and sanctioning of the Hospitallers and the Knights Templar.

Hospitallers

Sometime between 1063 and 1070, a group of pious merchants from Amalfi in Italy, having no place to stay in Jerusalem, received from the Fatimid caliph of Egypt land in the Christian quarter of Jerusalem, next to the Holy Sepulcher. While there, it appears that they rebuilt the Benedictine monastery of St. Mary of the Latins, and soon thereafter, they built the daughter convent of St. Mary Magdalene as a shelter for female pilgrims. Due to the growing presence of pilgrims in the Holy Land, they constructed a hospice (or hospital) with its own church named for John the Baptist.[21] They must have taken monastic vows because, when Pope Paschal II (d. 1118) confirmed the hospital's independence from the abbey in 1113, he referred to them as "professed brothers." It is most likely that these first Hospitallers were made up of Benedictine "serving brothers" (conversi).[22] These newly formed monastics placed themselves under the jurisdiction of the patriarch of Jerusalem.

In 1099, the year that Jerusalem fell to the Christian Crusaders and before their papal confirmation, the master of this group, Gerard, persuaded the first rulers of the new Latin Kingdom to endow the hospice with lands and city properties in newly acquired territories so that they could found daughter houses. The Hospitallers also quickly set up hospices in key port cities

21. The words "hospital" and "hospice" were often used interchangeably since they both referred to places where a traveler could find shelter and medical care if he was sick. For a history of hospitals, see Timothy S. Miller, *The Birth of the Hospital in the Byzantine Empire* (Baltimore: Johns Hopkins University Press, 1997).

22. Jonathan Riley-Smith, *Templars and Hospitallers as Professed Religious in the Holy Land* (Notre Dame, IN: University of Notre Dame Press, 2010), 15.

of Europe, such as Pisa, Bari, and Messina. Due to their presence in these important cities, they attracted donations of land and recruits. They were quick to emphasize that their real raison d'être was the spiritual and material care of pilgrims, recognizing the "lordship" of the poor and sick while they themselves were the "serfs." Thus they were obligated to serve the poor.

The turning point for the new order occurred in 1118 when Gerard died and was succeeded by Raymond du Puy (d. 1160). The order underwent two significant changes. First, they expanded their role from care of sick pilgrims to a military apostolate as a result of a shortage of manpower (therefore, an inability to have a standing military) in the Latin Kingdom of Jerusalem. Further, an unmistakable military emphasis began in 1123 when a group of Hospitallers formed an emergency corps of mounted soldiers to help repel the Fatimid invasion from Egypt. Subsequently they were given an increasing number of military assignments alongside the newly formed Knights Templar (see below). By the mid-1030s they had been given two fortresses, and by 1180 they held twenty-five castles in Palestine. But how did the original band of charity-offering laypeople become militarized so easily? Jonathan Riley-Smith says that "the Hospital's militarization . . . seems to have been born out of the religious aspirations of para-crusading or mercenary knights in Palestine."[23] These secular knights had come to the Holy Land out of piety or for pay and then attached themselves and their ideals to the Hospitallers.

Second, sometime before 1153 Raymond had the Hospitallers switch from a Benedictine-type of rule to one that Raymond composed. This rule is a stern, practical document, lacking the inspiration and insight of other monastic founders of the period, adapted more to an active style of life as a military order. The rule called for the Hospitallers to profess poverty, chastity, and obedience and prescribed that the Hospitallers were to wear no bright colors (though it is unclear if they had a special habit); furthermore, they were to always wear a cross on their chests. The rule said nothing regarding the militaristic nature of the Hospitallers but emphasized that a sick person was to be received by letting him confess his sins to a priest and partake of the Eucharist; afterward he was carried to bed, where he could be daily refreshed with food according to the ability of the house. This role was reinforced by Pope Alexander III (d. 1181) in the 1170s when he reminded the Hospitallers that their primary obligation was to care for the poor and that their military actions should be limited to special occasions. In the pope's words, "The poor are better defended by showing them love and mercy than by force of arms."[24]

23. Ibid., 16.
24. Ibid., 18.

The order responded by insisting that the military element was essential to their life but stating that they would not stop caring for the sick.

Knights Templar

The foundation of the Knights Templar dates to the capture of Jerusalem in 1099, which was largely due to the internal division of the Muslim factions in the region. The existing government was followed by the creation of the Latin Kingdom of Jerusalem, with its dependent territories. As mentioned above, only a small skeletal force remained in the region after the Latins captured the Holy Land, so a real danger existed for defenseless pilgrims journeying to Jerusalem and the other holy places, especially along the key routes of Jaffa (the major arrival port of Western pilgrims) to Jerusalem, Jerusalem to Bethlehem, and Jerusalem to Jericho. An inability of the Latin settlers to police the roads in order to protect pilgrims led one of the crusaders, Hugh of Payens (d. 1136), a French knight possibly related to Bernard of Clairvaux, to form a small standing militia in 1119 to escort these pilgrims safely between holy sites. From the start, this group was envisioned to be more than a militia, as Hugh's intention was to form a group of religiously minded men interested in living monastically while also protecting pilgrims. Hugh was given permission by the patriarch of Jerusalem to form a group of lay knights. The Latin King of Jerusalem, Baldwin II (d. 1131), saw the group's usefulness and offered Hugh and his eight companions quarters in his palace, which he had evacuated. This palace was located south of the Dome of the Rock; hence, because it was in the temple area, this group of knights came to be called the Knights Templar or simply the Temple.

Hugh conceived of his group as something new: soldier-monks. They took monastic vows of chastity, obedience, and individual poverty (like the Hospitallers) but followed a form of cenobitic religious life as laymen, attending the Divine Office sung by canons regular at the Church of the Holy Sepulcher. The Templars represented a conjunction and logical extension of three religious phenomena: cenobitical monasticism, the Christianization of violence, and the desert tradition of the monk/hermit as a soldier of Christ (*miles Christi*). Due to their novelty and strangeness, the Templars initially drew few recruits, but in the autumn of 1127 Hugh went to Rome with several companions to seek official authorization for this new kind of religious life. He was referred to the upcoming council, which was held in 1128 in Troyes, led by the papal legate Matthew of Albano. The council approved Hugh's plan and commissioned the writing of an appropriate rule, a task (possibly) entrusted to Bernard of Clairvaux. The subsequent rule owes much to the RB but includes more rigorous practices borrowed from the Cistercians. Its mandates include: a cenobitical form of life (with a central monastery); monastic vows; simple dress (a white gown representing chastity and a hair shirt for penance); no association with women; a common dormitory and refectory; and the knight's presence for the chanting of the hours by the canons. Since many of the first knights were illiterate, they listened to others chant the offices, but in time, as the order attracted priests, they had their own services. The rule relaxed the regimen of prayer and fasting for those sent out on duty of protecting or fighting. The initial organization of the Templars reflected the class consciousness of medieval society: the knights were from aristocratic families, whereas men of more humble origins who fought alongside the knights were given the title "sergeant."

To promote the new order, Bernard of Clairvaux wrote *In Praise of the New Knighthood*, a defense of the legitimacy of combining violence for the sake of Christ with specifics of a monastic spiritual life: the knight of Christ (*militia Christi*) versus the worldly knight (*militia saeculi*). Bernard refers to his work as "words of exhortation" and sees himself as offering moral support (as opposed to material support) to the Knights Templar. Since he himself, as a Cistercian monk, cannot wield the sword, he can write a word of encouragement to those who do fight militarily "against the tyrannical foe."[25] Bernard acknowledges that this knighthood is new and says that it "wages a twofold war both against flesh and blood and against a spiritual army of evil in the heavens."[26] Thus the Templars fight both pagan humans and the satanic forces who strive against God. The human foes must be fought with human strength and the sword, whereas the satanic foes are fought with spiritual strength and the tools of monastic life. Both kinds of fights are common inasmuch as there has always been physical violence and monasticism. However, the Templars uniquely combine both into one person: this "fearless knight" is "secure on every side, for his soul is protected by the armor of faith just as his body is protected by armor of steel."[27] Moreover, this new kind of knight is worthy of praise because though the death of all holy ones is precious in the eyes of God, even more so is the death of those who die in battle with an unsullied conscience. As long as the monastic knight's intentions are sincere, then he is not a murderer.

25. Bernard of Clairvaux, *In Praise of the New Knighthood*, prologue; Daniel O'Donovan and Conrad Greenia, trans., *Bernard of Clairvaux: Treatises 3* (Kalamazoo, MI: Cistercian Publications, 1977), 127.

26. Bernard of Clairvaux, *In Praise of the New Knighthood* 1; O'Donovan and Greenia, *Bernard of Clairvaux*, 129.

27. Bernard of Clairvaux, *In Praise of the New Knighthood* 1; O'Donovan and Greenia, *Bernard of Clairvaux*, 130.

The end of worldly knighthood is one's own glory, whereas the end of the new knighthood is service to God. Bernard assures his readers that the new knights do not commit sin but instead please God: they "may safely fight the battles of their Lord, fearing neither sin if they smite the enemy, nor danger at their own death; since to inflict death or to die for Christ is no sin, but rather, an abundant claim to glory."[28] The knight of Christ can die in confidence as God's minister and a punisher of evildoers, for to kill an evildoer is not to kill a human but to kill evil. Bernard does not advocate killing but sees it as merciful and just: "I do not mean to say that the pagans are to be slaughtered when there is any other way to prevent them from harassing and persecuting the faithful, but only that it now seems better to destroy them than that the rod of sinners be lifted over the lot of the just, and the righteous perhaps put forth their hands unto iniquity."[29] Furthermore, Bernard sees in the Scriptures justification for Christian knights when he asks, "If it is never permissible for a Christian to strike with the sword, why did the Savior's precursor [i.e., John the Baptist] bid the soldiers to be content with their pay, and not rather forbid them to follow this calling?"[30] He also sees biblical support in the scriptural passages that have to do with God ransoming his people and setting them free (e.g., Isa. 35:10).

Likely because of Bernard's support and the fact that they met a practical need, the Knights Templar continued to grow and flourish. In 1139 Pope Innocent II issued a bull officially approving the rule and giving the Temple "privileged status." This forever changed the focus of the Templars from guarding pilgrims to protecting crusaders and actually going to war. As well, they were allowed to have their own oratory and burial grounds, and they did not have to pay tithes. Through the creation of the chaplain-brothers, they were directly under papal jurisdiction and did not rely on members of other monastic orders to meet their spiritual needs.[31] With such official recognition and approval, there was a sudden influx of recruits and donations, especially in the form of landed estates and the revenues earned by them, as well as profits from the foodstuffs and handiwork produced on these lands. All of this income was gathered up and sent to support the mission in the Holy

28. Bernard of Clairvaux, *In Praise of the New Knighthood* 4; O'Donovan and Greenia, *Bernard of Clairvaux*, 134.

29. Bernard of Clairvaux, *In Praise of the New Knighthood* 4; O'Donovan and Greenia, *Bernard of Clairvaux*, 135.

30. Bernard of Clairvaux, *In Praise of the New Knighthood* 5; O'Donovan and Greenia, *Bernard of Clairvaux*, 135. See also Luke 3:14.

31. The "chaplain-brothers" were full members of the community, however, their responsibility was not to fight but to provide spiritual services to the knights, such as hearing confessions, celebrating the Mass, and leading the daily offices.

Land. The later history of the Knights Templar is not necessarily a happy one. Their presence and role in the Holy Land diminished with the failure of the Second Crusade in 1149 and was forever tarnished with the fall of Acre in 1291. So they turned their attention mostly to activities in the Latin West, becoming involved in local warfare and banking. They were finally suppressed in the fourteenth century.[32]

Ressourcement: Inspiration and Ministry to Others

I often hear people say something like, "What earthly good is a monk or nun who simply spends his or her life in a monastery praying?" Such thinking is common and does not always come from someone in a non-monastic tradition; I have heard Roman Catholic Christians ask this question. This line of thinking assumes there *must* be some sort of practicality or applicability to the monastic life. To put it more bluntly, there must be some earthly good to all of this heavenly behavior. Though the "usefulness" of monks and nuns can easily be discerned in the history of the Christian church,[33] the institutions and radical change of thinking about the monastic life that resulted from the emergence of the canons regular and the military orders should go a long way in dispelling the historiographical myth that monasticism is not good for anything, at least on this side of heaven. Though no Christian today would necessarily want to see the reemergence of the military orders (much less the idea of God-sanctioned crusading), we continue to benefit from the advances in care for the sick and wounded first pioneered by the Hospitallers. We also think that believers from any religion should have the freedom to travel in safety to their respective holy sites—an idea first promulgated by the Knights Templar. Most of us, I imagine, also like the fact that pastors and priests today have access to a good seminary education before they embark on their pastoral ministries. Such radical thinking about pastoral ministry and education was highly valued by the canons regular and put into practice by the Premonstratensians and Victorines. Thus we can see from these movements that monasticism is not only inwardly focused but also outwardly focused. Of course, it is always outwardly focused in its prayer for the church and the world, but sometimes it is explicitly outwardly focused in its intention and institutionalization. The canons regular and the military orders prove this without a doubt.

32. See Malcolm Barber, *The Trial of the Templars* (Cambridge: Cambridge University Press, 1978).
33. As mentioned above, even the desert fathers and mothers of Egypt spent their prayer times plaiting baskets to be sold for business and household use.

Similarly, evangelical Christians are known for their outwardly focused activism. Historian David Bebbington even lists activism as one of the qualities of evangelicalism: "There are four qualities that have been the special marks of Evangelical religion: *conversionism*, the belief that lives need to be changed; *activism*, the expression of the gospel in effort; *biblicism*, a particular regard for the Bible; and what may be termed *crucicentrism*, a stress on the sacrifice of Christ on the cross. Together they form a quadrilateral of priorities that is the basis of Evangelicalism."[34] Consequently, evangelicalism's activism would align well with those monastic orders whose primary apostolate is ministry to others. Indeed, it could be argued that for monasticism to flourish within the evangelical church, it would need to be activist, not because there is no room for contemplative vocations within evangelicalism but because activism is a sine qua non of evangelical Christianity. Such a vision of evangelical monasticism aligns well with its history of missionary activity and social assistance (e.g., the Salvation Army). Not all monastic institutions need to be contemplative and not all need to be engaged in ministry to others, but these two foci are not mutually exclusive, and one is not more authentic to Christian monastic history than the other. Both are legitimate forms of monastic life, and they can coexist even in the same community.[35]

34. David Bebbington, *Evangelicalism in Modern Britain: A History from the 1730s to the 1980s* (Grand Rapids: Baker, 1989), 2–3.

35. Benedictine monasteries that operate universities or have responsibility for a large number of parishes are a good example.

10

The Friars

Likely no cycle of medieval paintings is more well known than the life cycle of Francis of Assisi created around 1300 by multiple painters, one of which may have been the great Florentine painter Giotto (d. 1337). Composed of a series of twenty-eight frescoes in what is now known as the "Upper Church" of the Basilica of St. Francis in Assisi, these paintings are known for their naturalism and realism (at least when compared to other paintings from the same period). Several of the frescoes, in particular, capture the ethos of the mendicant movement of the thirteenth century.[1] In order of the life cycle, the second fresco depicts Francis, a rich young man, giving his mantle to a (presumably) poor man. Several scenes later is a fresco in which Francis gives up all of his material belongings to God in order to live a life of total poverty. Francis came from a wealthy family, and one of the hallmarks of the medieval friars was their disavowal of worldly goods in favor of personal poverty and the need to live by begging for alms (i.e., mendicancy). Further into the life cycle is a depiction of Francis preaching to the birds. Just beyond this is another image of Francis preaching, but this time to Pope Honorius III

---

1. "Mendicant" refers to living on alms; these orders were not financially supported by the church, nor did they own any property. They survived on charity. As stated in the introduction to this book, friars are not historically considered monks (or nuns), though they are certainly monastic as I have defined the term. Therefore, in this chapter I will refer to them as monastics but *not* as monks and nuns, and I will call them friars and sisters (since there is no feminine equivalent of "friar" in the English language). "Friar" is derived from the Latin *frater*, which means "brother."

(d. 1227). No matter what one thinks of birds or the papacy, the point of these frescoes is to show that preaching was a task of the friars. Thus, in many ways, a friar is one who begs for his daily bread and actively preaches the Word of God. Yet the history of the medieval mendicant movement is much more than this. In short, with the arrival of the mendicant orders in the early thirteenth century, monastic history was altered forever. Focusing on the two dominant mendicant orders of the Middle Ages—the Dominicans and Franciscans—this chapter will explore the foundation history and particular charisma of these preaching and teaching orders.[2] Concerning the Dominicans, I will pay attention to Thomas Aquinas and to the unique preaching call of the Order of Preachers and their role in medieval preaching and university teaching. The place of poverty in medieval monastic mendicancy will be illustrated in the life of Francis and in the order he founded (the Order of Friars Minor). The spirituality of the friars, by way of the writings of Bonaventure, will also be examined briefly.

Beginnings of Mendicant Monasticism

In one sense, the medieval mendicant movement began before the birth of any of the first friars. Up to the mid-eleventh century, medieval society was one of feudalism, characterized by a gift economy.[3] In short, it was an economic society in which one form of treasure (e.g., food) was converted into another kind of treasure (e.g., clothing). According to Lester Little, "In a gift economy, goods and services are exchanged without having specific, calculated values assigned to them."[4] What is important, necessary, and valuable to one group of people is not necessarily what is valued by another group. Thus the value of an item was determined by its necessity to the people doing the "buying" and was not necessarily set by the "seller." Throughout much of the early medieval era, goods were traded by interested parties, both locally and, when necessary, further abroad. Though coinage never went away completely, it was only in the thirteenth century that "coin was being minted by virtually every important government in western Europe."[5] The significance of the return of coinage should not be missed. With the revival of towns and markets (due to

2. For a history of other orders of friars, see Frances Andrews, *The Other Friars: Carmelite, Augustinian, Sack and Pied Friars in the Middle Ages* (Woodbridge, UK: Boydell Press, 2006).

3. See Marc Bloch, *Feudal Society*, trans. L. A. Manyon (Chicago: University of Chicago Press, 1961); and Lester K. Little, *Religious Poverty and the Profit Economy in Medieval Europe* (Ithaca, NY: Cornell University Press, 1978).

4. Little, *Religious Poverty*, 4.

5. Ibid., 17.

the agrarian and commercial revolutions of the High Middle Ages) and the reconnection of regions by sea and roads (that is, the rebuilding of old Roman roads), trade was possible beyond one's local region, requiring a new and "neutral" means of exchange. Coin was the perfect means of exchange between geographically distant peoples, allowing them to cultivate a commercial relationship that was impossible in a gift economy. Coin is compact, mobile, and storable and is suitable to a mercantile economy of manufactured goods. In this way, a new phenomenon entered the picture. In a barter exchange, things of relatively equal value are traded, but in a mercantile economy things are traded with coin. Merchants can therefore inflate the value of their goods, gaining a profit from what they sell. Thus the mercantile economy leads to a money economy that leads to a profit economy.

This rise of the profit economy was met with unease by the church, fearing that this "new prosperity" would lead to an obsession with things of the world. Yet such newfound prosperity was highly unstable and unpredictable; people moved from rural manors into cities, creating social dislocation due to a lack of housing and employment. This gave rise to the economically poor who were truly destitute, resulting in the rise of crime, violence, and prostitution. In short, there are two related problems with a money economy. First, a profit mentality arises, in which a seller charges a buyer more than a product is worth. Such transactions were calculated to earn the seller a profit to be used for investments, a higher standard of living, and so on. The church saw these transactions as unjust because they involved dishonest gain at the buyer's expense; anything unjust was immoral and thus forbidden. Second, money repaid to a creditor becomes more than was given out. The medieval church considered this theft and therefore forbidden. In moral terms it was usury, a practice prohibited by Pope Leo I (d. 461) in the fifth century and reiterated in later collections of canon law.

The effects of this new economy on spirituality are best seen in a shift in the identification of the chief vice. Prior to the eleventh century, the church considered the chief vice to be pride (raising oneself up in strength against weaker people); yet during the eleventh century, the chief vice became avarice (greed). This shift was due directly to the new money economy. The response to this shift gave rise to the mendicant monastic movement.

The immediate context for the genesis of the Order of Preachers (also known as the Dominicans) was the proliferation of heresy, especially the Cathar (or Albigensian) heresy. Like other heretical movements before it, Catharism was a dualistic heresy. It was common practice in Christian theology and church life to ask, "How do you explain the presence of evil in a world created by an allegedly good God?" Two answers were often given. The first is that God made a good, even perfect, creation where some created beings (usually angels) go bad. A second answer, more radical than the first, is that there are two creative principles: the good God who is spiritual and the evil God who is material. The latter answer was based in an exaltation of the spiritual and the denigration of matter, the most common form of dualism in Christian history.

In 1143 Eberhard of Steinfield reported that there was a group of "new heretics" in Cologne. He stated that these heretics held antimaterial ideas, evidenced in a disdain for marriage, sexuality, and food produced through sexual generation. Sacramentally they advocated against the Eucharist and rejected baptism with water. Eberhard reported that they developed a church structure with three orders of commitment: *auditor* (hearer/inquirer), *creditor* (believer), and *perfectus* or *cathar* (perfect or pure one). These *cathari* believed that they received the Holy Spirit through the laying on of hands and in response pledged to live the remainder of their lives in total purity. All authority was vested in these pure ones. In Cologne, these "new heretics" were burned at the stake by a crowd of orthodox believers. However, a remnant settled in southern France near the city of Albi.

The Dominicans

At approximately the same time, a Spaniard named Dominic de Guzmán (d. 1221) was establishing his ecclesiastical career.[6] Dominic was born around 1170 near Castile, and by 1196 he was a canon at the cathedral in Osma under the episcopal oversight of Bishop Diego. In 1199 the cathedral canons were reformed, and the *Rule of Augustine* (RA) was adopted, an event that would prove providential. Because of his close relationship with Diego, Dominic traveled with the bishop to Denmark in 1203 to arrange a royal marriage. On their way through Toulouse, they stayed at the inn of a Cathar deacon. While discussing the Cathar's reasons for leaving the church, Dominic was able to bring him back to orthodox faith, an encounter that had a profound impact on Dominic.

The matter of the royal marriage required a second trip to Denmark in 1205, and during this trip Dominic noted the need for missionaries in the region. But Rome denied him permission to preach, so he turned for home. On his return he made a side trip to visit the Cistercians at Cîteaux and also

6. For a general history of the mendicant movement in the Middle Ages, see C. H. Lawrence, *The Friars: The Impact of the Early Mendicant Movement on Western Society* (London: Longman, 1994).

went to Montpellier to meet Cistercian missionaries combatting the Cathars. The Cistercians asked Diego and Dominic how to proceed in winning the Cathari back to orthodox faith. Dominic told them that the message is only as believable as the messenger; therefore, the Cistercians should go to the Cathari in humility—barefoot and without gold or silver in imitation of the apostles. Further, suggested Dominic, the Cistercians should get rid of their horses and fine clothes, both of which were offensive to the antimaterialistic heretics. In response to this advice, the Cistercians invited Dominic and Diego to assist them in their mission, an invitation they both accepted. After some success among the Cathari, Diego returned home and died in December 1207.

Dominic, however, set up a mission in 1206 at Prouille whose purpose was twofold: to provide a place of rest for his growing group of antiheresy preachers and to serve as a monastery for converted Cathar women evicted from their families. These women in return saw to the needs of the preachers and in time formed the core of the Dominican sisters. In 1214 Dominic was invited to preach in Toulouse, which had just been militarily retaken from the Cathars. He converted a man named Peter who then joined Dominic and gave the group of preachers his house, a major turning point in Dominican history. Due to their success, Bishop Fulk of Toulouse (d. 1231) asked Dominic to lead a group of preachers in his diocese. In preparation, Dominic sent men to study theology at the cathedral school. He then petitioned Rome for permission for this emerging group of itinerant preachers. He was given permission but with the stipulation that they act as clerics supported by tithes and not by begging. In 1215 Dominic, alongside Bishop Fulk, attended the Fourth Lateran Council in Rome. The council stated that the bishops by themselves were not up to the task of combating heresy or instructing the faithful in their dioceses. As well, another conciliar canon stipulated against the creation of new monastic orders and stated that should they be given approval, they must adopt an existing monastic rule. Thus Dominic returned to Toulouse, choosing to adopt the RA (along with Premonstratensian customs) for his group.[7] Regarding poverty—the hallmark virtue of the mendicant orders—these first Dominicans retained ownership of the property of their churches and houses and received revenue if needed. In December 1216 a papal bull from Honorius III approved their manner of life, recognizing them as canons regular of the Toulouse diocese. This was quickly followed by a second bull (dated January 21, 1217) that referred to them for the first time as an order of preachers (*ordo praedicatorum*). This

---

7. Dominic lived under the RA as a canon in Osma, so it is not surprising that he chose this flexible rule for his order of preachers.

bull had far-reaching consequences as it created a supradiocesan order of preachers—that is, a universal order of preachers for the whole church. This bull was then sent to all Latin Christian bishops, ordering them to welcome and support these preachers.

By 1217 Dominic had gathered sixteen friars at Prouille, so he dispersed friars from Toulouse to Paris, Orleans, Bologna, and elsewhere. Dominic's primary motivation for this dispersal was to extend the nascent order's mission of doctrinal preaching. By being sent to the university towns, the friars would engage in advanced studies in theology and be ideally placed to recruit new members who would be well educated. After this dispersal, Dominic spent his time traveling to new communities to visit the friars, while making Bologna his center of activity. In 1220 Dominic met Francis of Assisi, who immediately deepened Dominic's appreciation of poverty. For the Dominicans, poverty was never an absolute but was always a means to an end, a "weapon" to be used to make their message acceptable and credible to heretics. For Dominic, the *cura animarum* (the care of souls) by way of preaching was more important than poverty qua poverty. To this end, as the order developed, they legislated that each priory must have its own teacher; that is, every convent became a school. Subsequently it was decided that every province would have its own house of studies and that the order itself would have a *studia generalia*, a general house of studies open to students of the order from across Europe. These houses of study would, in time, come to complement the education received by the Dominicans at the newly founded universities.

The rise of medieval universities was a long (and not always straightforward) process, but by 1200 there were several major universities in existence in Paris, Bologna, and Oxford. From the start, the mendicant orders saw the universities as ideal places from which to recruit new friars. Jordan of Saxony (d. 1237), master general of the Dominican order from 1221 to 1237, wrote that the universities were ideal places for a "good catch" of new recruits. Even more telling was a later comment by the Congregation of Masters at the University of Oxford:

> It is commonly said, and we have learned from experience, that noble persons of this kingdom, gentlemen, and even those of common birth desist from sending their sons or relatives or others dear to them to the university in their youth, when they would make most progress in the primary stages of learning, because they are very fearful that the friars will entice them into joining the Mendicant Orders.[8]

8. Lawrence, *The Friars*, 127.

Not only were the universities full of potential friars, but they were also ideal locations in which to place friars as professors in order to influence theological discussions (especially about poverty) and promote the mendicant monastic lifestyle. Because the Dominicans existed for the purpose of preaching, they highly valued a university education. Even before his death, Dominic pushed his friars to be well educated (hence the development of Dominican *studia*), and the Franciscans came to recognize the value of a good education soon after Francis's death.

The first Dominicans sent to the University of Paris in 1218 acquired a hostel in which they held all their classes. They were taught by a secular master of theology until one of their own, Roland of Cremona (d. 1259), inaugurated a chair in theology at Paris, a position held by other Dominicans throughout the thirteenth century. Before long, the mendicants occupied a host of university teaching positions, a fact that bothered the secular masters so much that in February 1252 the University of Paris limited the number of chairs that the friars could hold to one per order. Further, between 1254 and 1256 William of St. Amour (d. 1272), a Parisian secular master, published a series of works denouncing the mendicant orders.[9] Yet the mendicants were in the universities to stay, and in time they produced some of the greatest medieval theologians. From the Dominicans, the brightest light was Thomas Aquinas (d. 1274).

Thomas Aquinas

Thomas was born into an aristocratic family in 1226. At the age of five or six he was given to the Benedictine monks of Monte Cassino (where his father hoped that one day Thomas would become abbot) to be raised for an ecclesiastical career. However, in 1235 or 1236 Thomas left the abbey due to the political problems of the time and the general unrest surrounding the abbey.[10] In addition, the monks at the monastery had recommended to Thomas's father that Thomas study at the recently founded University of Naples. It was there that Thomas was introduced to the Dominicans, whose Neapolitan priory had been founded in 1231. It appears that Thomas was drawn to the Dominicans because of their commitment to study and to preaching, and against his parents' wishes he entered the Dominican order around 1242. Thomas then left Naples for study in Paris. Before he reached

---

9. See Michel-Marie Dufeil, *Guillaume de Saint-Amour et la polémique universitaire parisienne, 1250–1259* (Paris: Picard, 1972).

10. Angelus Walz, *Saint Thomas Aquinas: A Biographical Study* (Westminster, MD: Newman Press, 1951), 17–18.

Paris, however, Thomas was "kidnapped" by his own family in an attempt to convince him to abandon his Dominican profession and rejoin the Benedictine monks at Monte Cassino. Though his family failed to convince him to leave the Dominicans for the Benedictines, it is estimated that Thomas's captivity lasted for two years.[11]

After his release, Thomas finally arrived in Paris to study under the Dominican master Albert the Great (d. 1280). After one year in Paris, he accompanied Albert to Cologne for additional studies. It was at Cologne that Thomas's incredible intellectual abilities were first realized by both fellow students and his teacher. Thomas's five-year stay in Cologne ended when he was sent back to Paris to begin the process of becoming a master in theology. He incepted as a master in 1256 at the age of thirty, five years below the minimum age for this degree.[12] The remainder of Thomas's life was spent teaching at either the University of Paris or the *studium* in Rome and ministering as *lector* (reader) in his province of Orvieto.

Though the complete list of Thomas's philosophical, theological, and biblical works is immense, none were as influential as his *Summa theologiae*. Begun in 1266, the *Summa* was unfinished at the time of his death. Leonard Boyle has argued that the *Summa* is primarily a work "born of Aquinas's desire to improve the education of fellow Dominicans in moral theology, so crucial for pastoral activity (preaching and sacramental activity)."[13] This being the case, Thomas's theological magnum opus was meant to train Dominicans in the tasks to which they were called as Dominicans—the *cura animarum*—and in particular the task of preaching.

Revival of Orthodox Preaching

At nearly the same time that Dominic was founding the Order of Preachers, Pope Innocent III was calling priests, bishops, and theologians together in 1215 for the Fourth Lateran Council. As stated above, one of the purposes (if not the main purpose) of the council was to reform the education, morals, and abilities of local parish priests: "By this inviolable constitution we decree that prelates of churches should prudently and diligently attend to the correction of their subjects' offences especially of clerics, and to the

---

11. See Simon Tugwell, *Early Dominicans: Selected Writings* (New York: Paulist Press, 1982), 206–7.

12. Ibid., 210–11.

13. Cited in Joseph P. Wawrykow, *The SCM Press A–Z of Thomas Aquinas* (London: SCM Press, 2005), ix. See Leonard Boyle, "The Setting of the *Summa theologiae* of Saint Thomas," in *The Gilson Lectures on Thomas Aquinas* (Toronto: PIMS, 2008), 19–45.

reform of morals. Otherwise the blood of such persons will be required at their hands."[14]

Further, there was explicit intentionality at the council that orthodox preaching be revived in the church at large:

> Among the various things that are conducive to the salvation of the Christian people, the nourishment of God's word is recognized to be especially necessary, since just as the body is fed with material food so the soul is fed with spiritual food. . . . It often happens that bishops by themselves are not sufficient to minister the word of God to the people, especially in large and scattered dioceses, whether this is because of their many occupations or bodily infirmities or because of incursions of the enemy or for other reasons—let us not say for lack of knowledge, which in bishops is to be altogether condemned and is not to be tolerated in the future. We therefore decree by this general constitution that bishops are to appoint suitable men to carry out with profit this duty of sacred preaching, men who are powerful in word and deed and who will visit with care the peoples entrusted to them in place of the bishops, since these by themselves are unable to do it, and will build them up by word and example.[15]

So while there was a move in the thirteenth-century church to improve the quality and effectiveness of preaching, the formation of the Dominican friars addressed this need directly. Here, for the first time, was a congregation of priests devoted especially to the apostolate of preaching, so much so that in his *Postilla super Genesim* the Dominican theologian Hugh of Saint-Cher (d. 1263) writes, "First the bow is bent in study, then the arrow is released in preaching." For Hugh, study had one purpose: preaching. This high calling to preach is explained well by the Dominican Humbert of Romans (d. 1277) in his *Treatise on the Formation of Preachers*:

> To see what a noble job preaching is, we must notice that it is an apostolic job: it was for this job that the Lord chose the apostles. "He appointed twelve to be with him and to be sent out to preach" (Mark 3:14). It is also an angelic job. "I saw a mighty angel, preaching with a loud voice" (Apoc. 5:2). And was he not preaching who said, "See, I bring you good news of a great joy" (Luke 2:10)? And there is nothing surprising in angels being called preachers, since their mission is for the sake of those who are to inherit salvation, just as preachers are sent out for the salvation of men. Further, it is a divine job. God became man precisely to do this job. "Let us go into the neighbouring villages and towns

---

14. Fouth Lateran Council, Canon 7; Norman P. Tanner, ed., *Decrees of the Ecumenical Councils*, vol. 1, *Nicea I to Lateran V* (Washington, DC: Georgetown University Press, 1990), 237.

15. Fourth Lateran Council, Canon 10; Tanner, *Decrees of the Ecumenical Councils*, 1:239–40.

so that I may preach there too, because it was for this purpose that I came" (Mark 1:38). Now, the apostles are the most outstanding of all the saints, the angels are the most outstanding of all creatures, and in all that exists, nothing is more outstanding than God. So a job which is apostolic, angelic and divine must indeed be outstanding![16]

The history of the Dominican order demonstrates that it was founded for one primary purpose: preaching (whether to bring heretics back into the church or to edify the laity). It was a true Order of Preachers. The Order of Friars Minor, however, began primarily as a direct response to the new economy—as an order dedicated to a poverty of wealth and power.

Order of Friars Minor and Saint Francis

Francis Bernardone was born around 1181 to a wealthy cloth merchant in Assisi, Italy, during a time when the Italian city-states were subject to party strife and there was ongoing tension between the empire and papacy. Assisi's main foe was Perugia, and the young Francis was unable to avoid the culture of hostility and warfare that was characteristic of his time. Furthermore, the ideals of knighthood expressed in the French *chansons de geste* (songs of heroic deeds) and in crusading literature contributed to Francis's bellicose youthfulness. Around 1201 the city of Assisi found itself in a civil war. The resulting warfare brought death and destruction, and Francis himself was captured at the battle of Collestrado in November 1202. The resulting imprisonment in Perugia, followed by a prolonged sickness, gave Francis time to think and reevaluate his life. The end of this process was radical conversion and a new orientation in life.

Behind the hagiographical nature of the biographies of Francis (written by Thomas of Celano and Bonaventure; see below), Michael Robson notes that Francis's conversion occurred in three stages. First, while praying before a crucifix at the church of San Damiano, Francis "was startled by a voice from the cross commanding him to rebuild the church."[17] Francis interpreted this command literally and began to rebuild the church of San Damiano. Later, however, Francis would come to understand that this command was not to rebuild one particular church but to renew the universal church. Seeing that wealth could be used for the good of the church and others, Francis traveled

16. Tugwell, *Early Dominicans*, 184–85.
17. Michael Robson, *The Franciscans in the Middle Ages* (Woodbridge, UK: Boydell Press, 2006), 13.

to a fair in Foligno with the purpose of illicitly selling his father's fine cloth and his own horse and clothes, signs of power. These events are the beginning of Francis's adoption of extreme poverty, which included not only material poverty but a poverty of power. Second, around 1206 Francis encountered a leper, a common occurrence in the Middle Ages. As Francis writes, "While I was in sin, it seemed very bitter to me to see lepers,"[18] and he went out of his way to avoid leper houses. Yet, upon encountering this leper, "he behaved with a typical generosity and spontaneity by kissing the leper, the symbol of contagion and rejection."[19] In Robson's estimation this reveals Francis's move toward self-mastery and an obvious love for others. Third, having repaired the church of the Portiuncula ("small portion of land"),

> Francis attended Mass in the tiny chapel, [and] the Gospel assigned to the Mass struck him with a new force and clarity. . . . Francis responded in the most literal manner, laying aside his shoes, staff and leather girdle. The habit of the hermit was swapped for the dress of an apostle: bare feet, a single tunic and a small cord. A new form of dress announced the radical change in the life of Francis. The two years of uncertainty gave birth to a new conviction and confidence: the *imitatio Christi* ("imitation of Christ") would illuminate and animate his life.[20]

In short, Francis's conversion was a conversion to material and immaterial poverty, to unconditional love of others (including those who are considered unlovable), and to a literal imitation of Christ and his disciples.

From the start, Francis's newfound religious lifestyle drew others to him. By 1210 he and a handful of followers had worked out their form of life and were actively engaged in local penitential preaching missions. Though meeting with some success, their way of life came under scrutiny, so Francis obtained papal approval from Pope Innocent III in 1216. By 1212 there were also Franciscan sisters founded by Clare of Assisi, and in 1221 three thousand friars gathered together, demonstrating the quick and tremendous growth of the order.[21] Though written just before his death in October 1226, Francis's *Testament* is a good source of information regarding the practice of these early Franciscans. Beyond their embrace of poverty, the brothers prayed the daily office in imitation of all priests (the non-ordained Franciscan lay brothers

18. Francis of Assisi, *Testament* 1; Regis J. Armstrong and Ignatius C. Brady, trans., *Francis and Clare: The Complete Works* (New York: Paulist Press, 1982), 154.

19. Robson, *Franciscans in the Middle Ages*, 15.

20. Ibid. According to Bonaventure's *Legenda maior*, the Gospel passage was Matt. 10:9–10: "Acquire no gold or silver or copper for your belts, no bag for your journey, or two tunics or sandals or a staff, for the laborer deserves his food."

21. Armstrong and Brady, *Francis and Clare*, 3.

recited the Lord's Prayer at the canonical hours). They engaged in active work for the purpose of avoiding idleness and as an example to others. They lived by begging and were forbidden to receive churches or any properties built for them, and they were to obey the minister general and any guardian placed over them by the minister general. Though the *Testament* does not mention preaching explicitly, from the start the Friars Minor were expected to preach. The rule of 1221 (the *Regula non bullata*) dedicated an entire chapter to the vocation of preaching, stating that (1) none of the brothers' preaching can be contrary "to the form or regulations of the holy Church," and a brother cannot preach without permission from the minister; (2) preaching is not only in words but by deeds; and (3) a brother should stop preaching if he is told to do so. The basis of preaching, according to the rule, is humility and mortification of the flesh.[22]

As the order grew, however, it became apparent that a good education was also necessary for effective preaching, and because of their success in university towns, the Franciscans experienced a large influx of well-educated recruits. It is likely that Francis would not have been too keen on the more learned direction of the order, for he himself had once said, "Those brothers of mine who are led by curiosity for knowledge will find themselves empty-handed on the day of reckoning."[23] A house of studies established in Bologna in 1219 was nearly closed by Francis, but by the 1230s the second generation of Franciscan leadership was actively pursuing university-level education. Around 1236 Alexander of Hales (d. 1245), an English theologian who held a chair of theology at Paris, entered the Franciscans, immediately giving the order a position in theology at the university. Having arrived in England in 1224, the English Franciscans at Oxford were taught by secular masters for two decades before a brother, Adam Marsh (d. 1259), finally incepted as a doctor in the theology faculty. Henceforth, the Franciscans, like the Dominicans, became an order of the schools, turning out such notable theologians as Bonaventure.

Bonaventure

Bonaventure (née John; d. 1274) was born in Bagnoregio, north of Rome, around 1217. Though little is known of his childhood, it is possible that Bonaventure received his initial education from the Franciscan friars in his

22. Ibid., 122–23. When Innocent III approved the order, he did so based on a *propositium vitae* (plan of life), but in 1223 Pope Honorius III approved the Second Rule (the *Regula bullata*).
23. Thomas of Celano, *The Remembrance of the Desire of a Soul* 2.147; Regis J. Armstrong, J. A. Wayne Hellmann, and William J. Short, eds., *The Francis Trilogy of Thomas of Celano* (Hyde Park, NY: New City Press, 2004), 290.

hometown. About 1234 he entered the University of Paris, and in 1243 he entered the Franciscan order, studying theology under Alexander of Hales. Known for his holiness and his intellect, Bonaventure became rector of the Franciscan school at Paris in 1253/54, teaching there until he was elected minister general of the order in 1257. Despite his responsibilities as head of the order, Bonaventure continued to produce scholastic treatises, spiritual writings, and lecture series. Two of his most well-known and influential spiritual treatises are *The Soul's Journey into God* and the *Life of St. Francis*. The former work was influenced by the thought of Pseudo-Dionysius the Areopagite, a sixth-century Syrian author writing in Greek who claimed to be the convert of Paul in Acts 17, and the latter was influenced by the long history of saints' lives, but especially the biographies of Francis composed by Thomas of Celano (d. 1260).

The Soul's Journey into God provides an itinerary of conversion that begins with contemplating God's reflection in the material world and ends with contemplating God as he is in himself. As Ewert Cousins notes, "Bonaventure's division of the journey into six stages is a refinement of a larger division of three stages . . . : meditation on nature, on the soul and on God."[24] Though this tripartite division is found in the thought of early monastic authors, such as Evagrius of Pontus, Bonaventure likely encountered it in his reading of Pseudo-Dionysius. In *The Soul's Journey into God* Bonaventure offers six stages that the soul must pass through on its way to union with God, basing these on his belief that the human mind has "three principal perceptual orientations"—exterior material objects, within itself, and above itself.[25] The six stages are (1) contemplating God in his vestiges in the universe; (2) contemplating God in the sense world; (3) contemplating God through his image stamped on humankind's natural powers; (4) contemplating God in his graced, reformed image in us; (5) contemplating the divine unity through its being; and (6) contemplating the Trinity in its name, which is the Good. Having progressed through these stages the mind is then able to enter into ecstasy when one's affection passes over into God.

In 1228 the Franciscan Thomas of Celano was given the task of writing the first biography of Francis of Assisi, which he finished the following year. During the course of his lifetime, however, Thomas would write another biography of Francis. In 1260 Bonaventure was asked by the general chapter to write a biography of Francis, making use of the biographies already in

24. Ewert Cousins, trans., *Bonaventure: The Soul's Journey into God, The Tree of Life, The Life of St. Francis* (New York: Paulist Press, 1978), 20.
25. Bonaventure, *The Soul's Journey into God* 1.4; Cousins, *Bonaventure*, 61.

existence. Bonaventure's goal was to "gather together the accounts of his virtues, his actions and his words."[26] What he accomplished, though, was a biography structured in accordance with the ancient tripartite schema of purgation, illumination, and perfection.[27] This tripartite division incorporates the virtues that Francis cultivated in his life, which Bonaventure details in nine chapters. In the purgative stage Francis cultivated mortification, humility, and poverty. In the illuminative stage he cultivated piety, charity, and prayer. The stage of perfection is evidenced by his understanding of the Scriptures and his gift of prophecy, his effective preaching and healing abilities, and his receiving the stigmata (the sacred wounds of Jesus on his hands, feet, and side). For Bonaventure, Francis truly imitated Christ, attaining the height of spiritual perfection.

Ressourcement: Complete Reliance on God for Sustenance and Strength

The central characteristic of the medieval friars was their commitment to poverty in order to be freed up to do the work that God had given them to do, especially the *cura animarum* by way of preaching. This poverty was not just a poverty of material possessions but a poverty of power, authority, influence, and thinking of oneself as higher than others. By having no worldly attachments, the friars strove to be completely free to follow Christ: *nudus nudum Christum sequi* (follow naked the naked Christ). Though the Franciscan ideal of absolute poverty ultimately was unsustainable and divided the order soon after Francis's death,[28] the goal of living life unencumbered so that one is more free for service is not only Dominican and Franciscan, but is also biblical (e.g., Luke 6:20). Though poverty is not fashionable and money and commerce are necessary elements in life, the way in which we choose to stand in relation to these realities speaks volumes as to where our treasure lies, which in turn shows the condition of our heart. Though absolute poverty of material possessions may not be completely possible in the twenty-first century, and though poverty of power and influence proves elusive, we must nonetheless be willing, like the medieval mendicants, to acknowledge our role in the world's power dynamics and imbalances. Money and power in and of themselves are not sinful, but what we do with them can easily tend in that direction, so

---

26. Bonaventure, *The Life of St. Francis*, prologue 3; Cousins, *Bonaventure*, 182–83.

27. See Cousins, *Bonaventure*, 42–44; and Regis J. Armstrong, "The Spiritual Theology of the *Legenda Major* of Saint Bonaventure" (PhD diss., Fordham University, 1978).

28. See David Burr, *The Spiritual Franciscans: From Protest to Persecution in the Century after Saint Francis* (University Park: Pennsylvania State University Press, 2001).

we should strive to live in poverty. In the words of Francis, directed to Clare and her sisters, "I, brother Francis, the little one, wish to follow the life and poverty of our most high Lord Jesus Christ . . . and to preserve in this until the end; and I ask and counsel you, my ladies, to live always in this most holy life and in poverty. And keep most careful watch that you never depart from this by reason of the teaching or advice of anyone."[29]

In developed nations such as the United States, Canada, and England, evangelicalism is mostly a middle-class to upper-middle-class religion. Though this is not true in Africa or South America, it is certainly true of the evangelical church in the West. Again, money and power—and the things that accompany them—are not inherently sinful, but what is done with them can be. North American evangelicalism seems to sit somewhat uncomfortably with the reality that it is a rich church that exercises great power. By and large the Protestant missionary movement of the past three centuries was not only undertaken historically by evangelical Christians, but it was also funded by affluent evangelicals. In the United States evangelical power has shown itself repeatedly on the political landscape (e.g., the Moral Majority) and in the entertainment industry, where Christian bands and movies compete with their "secular" counterparts for quality and influence. Though it is not always successful in these venues, the fact remains that evangelicalism has power and money. This does not make the evangelical church sinful, but it does increase its potential to misuse these God-given resources. Unlike the Roman Catholic Church and the Eastern Orthodox Church, which have monastic orders dedicated to poverty in order to (theoretically) counterbalance this affluence, the evangelical church lacks such a counterweight and leavening influence.

Knowing how much is too much is not always an easy discernment process for Christian believers. The need to finance one's retirement in old age seems reasonable, as does the desire to provide for one's family. The child Jesus himself received gifts from the Magi, so gift-giving is biblical and should not be neglected. Rising to the top of one's profession can be evidence of hard work and even God's graciousness, so the power and salary that come with such promotions should not be scorned. But how much is too much? How big is too big? And how many is too many? If a three-bedroom house is modest, is a five-bedroom home too lavish and thereby sinful? If a small nest egg is resourceful, is a beach house in Maui immoderate and thereby sinful? How many pairs of shoes can I own before I cross the line? Or to make it more personal, how many books am I allowed to possess before my collection is labeled extreme?

29. Armstrong and Brady, *Francis and Clare*, 46.

There aren't clear-cut answers to any of these questions since the biblical witness lacks such specificity. Yet monastics who have taken vows of poverty can provide the model for all believers as they seek not only to be good stewards of God's gifts but also to honor God with their money, possessions, and power or influence. Without such an example it seems that most Christians choose to do what is right in their own eyes with their hard-earned money and things, even while giving lip service to God as the one who provides such bounty. Though the church can preach against such excess, it has too often compromised itself in this regard and often fails to be a credible voice.[30] Consequently, evangelical believers should not only be aware of their wealth and power, but they also should strive to control them and use them for God's glory, looking to monastic simplicity as the model.[31] An evangelical monasticism that embraces poverty should be welcomed for its ability to show believers a different way of using money and power.

30. Though the Christian church is no longer the largest landowner in Europe, as it once was in the Middle Ages, it is still a wealthy institution when global poverty rates are taken into consideration. Likewise, most megachurches in North America have property mortgages that rival, if not exceed, local for-profit businesses.

31. Though many historic (and contemporary) monasteries were actually quite wealthy, their humblest members faithfully observed their vows of poverty, to the point that the historical record is littered with examples of monks and nuns who died from malnutrition and from their community's lack of resources, especially during times of persecution and duress. That some monasteries have been and are wealthy does not detract from the value of monastic poverty as a sign to non-monastic Christians of how they could divest themselves of money and power.

11

Decline or Development?
Lay Piety and Religious Life
in the Late Medieval Era

There has been, for many years, a romantic nostalgia attached to monastic ruins, especially in the British Isles, and this is evidenced most patently with the ruins of Tintern Abbey in Wales. Founded in 1131 as a Cistercian monastery, the abbey was suppressed by King Henry VIII in 1536. For 450 years the remains of the abbey have either been in the hands of private owners or, during the past century, under the protection of the government. The ruins were made most famous by poet William Wordsworth's "Lines Written a Few Miles above Tintern Abbey," composed while he was on a tour of Wales in July 1798. More than a decade earlier, however, the watercolorist and landscape gardener William Gilpin had already written that the abbey was "a very inchanting [*sic*] piece of ruin. Nature has now made it her own. Time has worn off all traces of the rule: it has blunted the sharp edges of the chisel; and broken the regularity of opposing parts."[1] Such nostalgia for ancient monastic sites was captured throughout the eighteenth and nineteenth centuries in prose writings, poems, and paintings. These reminisces harken back to a golden age of monastic life, one that may be more the stuff of

1. William Gilpin, *Observations on the River Wye*, 2nd ed. (London: R. Blamire, 1789), 48.

fiction than fact—so much so that historians of the Reformation have often struggled to understand the religious reorientation of the sixteenth-century in relationship to late medieval religious practice and devotion, searching for both continuities and discontinuities with the medieval tradition. Recent scholarship has shown that late medieval monastic life was not as corrupt or debased as suggested in the polemical texts of the Protestant Reformers, especially in the writings of Martin Luther. In an attempt to illustrate that even late medieval monasticism still strove in many ways to honor God and worship him devoutly, this chapter will investigate the actual state of monasticism and the rise of lay piety on the eve of the Reformation, focusing in particular on England. I will seek to show that both forms of spirituality—monastic and non-monastic—existed side by side, each contributing in its own way to the evangelization and sanctification of the late medieval church.

Historiographical Schools of Thought

When one attempts to evaluate the relationship between late medieval Christianity in England and the Reformation, one is immediately met with (at least) two distinct historiographical schools of thought. The first was established by A. G. Dickens and the second by Eamon Duffy. In 1964 Dickens published *The English Reformation*, in which he argued that little value could be found in the late medieval church and therefore the Reformation was a vast improvement in the theology and spirituality of the English church. He succinctly stated that "English Catholicism, despite its gilded decorations, was an old, unseaworthy and ill-commanded galleon, scarcely able to continue its voyage without the new seamen and shipwrights produced . . . by the Counter-Reformation."[2] Simply put, the Dickensian school of historiography states that late medieval Christianity was bankrupt and listless, desperately in need of reform. In Dickens's account, the Reformation was prefaced by John Wycliffe and the Lollards, who were not only forerunners of the Reformation but who proved to be England's first converts to reformed thinking. In short, the healthiest pre-Reformation Christians in England were the so-called heretical Lollards, whose only sin was a desire to preach and read the Bible in the vernacular. That they could be seen as heretics shows the depraved state of the late medieval English church.

In direct contrast to Dickens is the second historiographical school of thought, presented by Duffy. In the second edition of *The Stripping of the*

2. A. G. Dickens, *The English Reformation*, 2nd ed. (University Park: Pennsylvania State University Press, 1989), 129.

Altars, Duffy writes that his purpose for writing the book was "to contribute a shovelful of history to the burial of the venerable historiographical consensus" held and defended by such people as Dickens.[3] In Duffy's estimation, "late medieval Catholicism exerted an enormously strong, diverse, and vigorous hold over the imagination and the loyalty of the people up to the very moment of the Reformation. Traditional religion had about it no particular marks of exhaustion or decay, and indeed in a whole host of ways . . . was showing itself well able to meet new needs and new conditions."[4] For Duffy, late medieval English Christianity was alive and flourishing, meeting the needs of its people; it was not longing for reformation. The Reformation did not reform religion in necessarily helpful ways but rather "dug a ditch, deep and dividing between the English people and their past."[5] The Reformation harmed late medieval theology and spirituality in England, which took many years to recover. Without siding with either Dickens or Duffy, I believe late medieval religious life (both monastic and non-monastic) possessed much that was commendable and much that needed to be reformed. As with most historical investigations, the result is both/and, not either/or. In the words of G. W. Bernard, late medieval English monasticism was a "combination of vitality and vulnerability."[6] That being the case, it is imperative to assess the spiritual practices in late medieval England, beginning with the institution of monasticism and then turning to non-monastic practices and their connection to monasticism.

Monastic Recruitment

There are (at least) several ways in which one can judge the vitality of monasticism in late medieval England: recruitment, intellectual life (including the printing of books), and the care of souls. Concerning recruitment, at the turn of the sixteenth century there were approximately 900 monastic houses in England with nearly 12,000 monks, nuns, canons, and friars. This number was up from a total of approximately 6,500 monastics in 1400.[7] The total

3. Eamon Duffy, *The Stripping of the Altars: Traditional Religion in England 1400–1580* (New Haven: Yale University Press, 2005), xiv.

4. Ibid., 4.

5. Ibid., xiv.

6. G. W. Bernard, *The Late Medieval English Church: Vitality and Vulnerability before the Break with Rome* (New Haven: Yale University Press, 2012), 164.

7. James G. Clark, "The Religious Orders in Pre-Reformation England," in *The Religious Orders in Pre-Reformation England*, ed. James G. Clark (Woodbridge, UK: Boydell Press, 2002), 7. It should be borne in mind, however, that the Black Death in 1348–1349 had killed between

population of England at the time was half a million people; therefore, there was one monastic for every forty-two people. Statistics from individual houses show the slow yet steady growth of monasticism in the two centuries leading up to the dissolution of the monasteries under King Henry VIII (d. 1547).[8] For example, there were only thirteen monks at Carlisle in 1366, but that number had grown to twenty-three in 1540. Romsey Abbey had ninety-one nuns in 1333 but only eighteen in 1478 (due in part to the devastation wrought by the Black Death). By 1521 the number had grown to forty. Finally, there were fifty-nine Benedictine monks at Durham in 1483 and seventy-four in 1532. In 1535, on the eve of the dissolution, they recruited eight monks, suggesting, in Durham at least, that the monastic life was not dying but thriving.[9] According to James Clark, "The comparative prosperity of many if not all of the monasteries in pre-Reformation England is borne out in their levels of recruitment."[10]

A charge often leveled at late medieval monasticism is that it was a dumping place for men of low estate who did not wish to be monks, whereas most nuns were the daughters of the nobility and gentry. This is an inaccurate assessment but a belief that continues to endure. What is true is that most monasteries attracted recruits from the immediately surrounding area. For example, of the monks who entered Durham between 1383 and 1446, most of them came from within thirty-five miles of the city. Other studies have shown that this was true also of the monasteries in Yorkshire and at Canterbury and Norwich cathedrals. Moreover, most of these individuals were drawn from the "middling ranks."[11] Further:

> A study of over 1,700 references to 542 nuns in eleven female monasteries in the diocese of Norwich between 1350 and 1540 concluded that far more nuns came from middling (and lower) ranks of society than from aristocratic and upper gentry families. Only seven came from titled families; eighty-one (15 per cent) from upper gentry; 345 (64 per cent) from parish gentry; eighty-six (16 per cent) from townsfolk and twenty-three (4 per cent) from yeomen.[12]

---

one-third and two-fifths of the English population, so the number of monastics in the mid-fourteenth century was likely as high as the number in 1500.

8. Though the dissolution of the monasteries under Henry VIII erased monasticism from the landscape of England for the next three hundred years, it did not directly affect monasticism in other countries of Europe. That is, Henry's extreme actions were not copied by other monarchs.

9. Bernard, *Late Medieval English Church*, 165–66.

10. Clark, "Religious Orders in Pre-Reformation England," 14.

11. Bernard, *Late Medieval English Church*, 166.

12. Ibid., 166–67; citing Marilyn Oliva, *The Convent and the Community in Late Medieval England: Female Monasteries in the Diocese of Norwich, 1350–1540* (Woodbridge, UK: Boydell Press, 1998).

Other studies corroborate these findings, leading to the conclusion that monasteries were not the dumping grounds for unwanted children, nor were they the home of the financially and morally dissolute. Though the reception of child oblates (children given to the service of the monastery) had been outlawed in the thirteenth century (see chap. 14), the practice endured throughout the Middle Ages. However, during the fifteenth century, most monks and nuns joined the monastery in their late teens or early twenties, suggesting that they did so voluntarily. According to canon law, the minimum age for entrance to a monastery was sixteen, and this seems to have been honored, even if there were occasional exceptions.

Intellectual Life and the Printing of Books

The intellectual life of late medieval English monasteries is also evidence of their vitality. The Benedictines had founded a *studium* at Oxford in 1277 and, in time, at Cambridge too. In Clark's estimation, "By the turn of the fifteenth century, the Black Monks undoubtedly formed the largest community, religious or secular, at either university."[13] There were 324 monastic graduates from Oxford between 1500 and 1540, representing forty-two communities. Though women were not allowed to study at the universities, there was a higher rate of vernacular literacy in women's communities in the late Middle Ages than in earlier periods. Thomas Gascoigne (d. 1458), a theologian at Oxford, translated into English the daily divine office for the Brigittine nuns of Syon Abbey, and Richard Foxe (d. 1528), bishop of Winchester, translated the *Rule of Benedict* (RB) into English at the request of the nuns of Wherwell and Witney. Within the monasteries themselves, the university-educated monks would often give lectures and sermons. From the time of their entrance to the community, monks were expected to be active learners. The fourteenth-century customary for St. Augustine's Canterbury legislated for the novices that the times between the canonical offices should be spent in their cell or the school (*scolam*) under instruction from the novice master, who would lecture on the RB and ensure that the novices knew the Psalter and a number of liturgical texts by heart. The 1337 Constitutions of Pope Benedict XII (d. 1342) also prescribed the study of grammar, logic, and philosophy for all Benedictines in England and not just for those attending university.[14]

13. Clark, "Religious Orders in Pre-Reformation England," 20.
14. Joan Greatrex, *The English Benedictine Cathedral Priories: Rule and Practice, c. 1270–c. 1420* (Oxford: Oxford University Press, 2011), 65 and 70.

Not only were monks students at English universities and active scholars within their own communities, but they were also participants in the printing of religious books. "In early Tudor England some of the earliest and most prolific presses operated under the patronage of monasteries."[15] There was an active printing press associated with St. Albans from 1479, and in the 1520s and 1530s presses were set up at Abingdon, Tavistock, and St. Augustine's Canterbury. Though each of these presses printed books written by monks, perhaps the best example of vital pre-Reformation monasticism is the monks of Syon Abbey. Though Syon Abbey did not have its own printing press, between 1525 and 1534 the abbey sent eleven works to printers in London. All of these works were written by three Syon brothers, each of whom graduated from Cambridge University: Richard Whitford (d. ca. 1543), William Bonde (d. 1530), and John Fewterer (d. 1536). With these works, "the Abbey presented itself as part of the vanguard of the Church, fighting heresy [i.e., Protestantism] with a threefold commitment to reformed spiritual leadership, vernacular theology, and the spiritual education of the laity."[16] Based on one's theological proclivities, it could be argued that the Syon Abbey monks were not advocating a healthy theology and, therefore, are not illustrative of a vital pre-Reformation English monasticism. Yet, as Alexandra da Costa argues convincingly, these monks were actively seeking to reform the church and were doing so through the medium of printed books geared toward the laity, in the language of the laity. Two examples will suffice. First, in 1527 Bonde published *The Directory of Conscience*, a book aimed at those in the early stages of the Christian life, particularly devout laypeople. The book "addressed the problem of scrupulosity, over-anxious adherence to regulations through fear of God, common among the religious, and also melancholy, or depression. It offered clear guidance and practical remedies."[17] The *Directory* was written in response to a request from a "devout religious woman" and, along with Whitford's *A Daily Exercise of Death* (published in 1534), was written for a female audience.[18] Bonde begins by stressing that the book is intended to cultivate wisdom and the fear of God in the reader in order to attain perfection. To do this Bonde says he will make use of the Holy Scriptures and the writings of the "holy doctors and fathers" of the church. According to this description, it is unmistakable that the *Directory* was not only a devotional

15. Clark, "Religious Orders in Pre-Reformation England," 24.

16. Alexandra da Costa, *Reforming Printing: Syon Abbey's Defence of Orthodoxy 1525–1534* (Oxford: Oxford University Press, 2012), 1.

17. Virginia R. Bainbridge, "Bonde, William (d. 1530)," *Oxford Dictionary of National Biography* (Oxford: Oxford University Press, 2004).

18. Da Costa, *Reforming Printing*, 31 and 36.

guide but also served as a primer on the theology and history of the Christian tradition. That is, Bonde's task was as much catechetical as it was exhortatory, as much theological as it was devotional.

A second example of monks reforming the church through books for the laity is Whitford's *The Work for Householders*. This book went through five editions in Whitford's lifetime and was also written by request, this time for a "private person and special friend." It was geared explicitly toward the laity and was meant for all classes of people, not just the nobility. The *Work* provided a form for daily devotions and included "advice on how to teach the Christian rudiments to children and servants," who were all sinners and therefore equal in stature before God.[19] Though householders would be preoccupied with the many things they needed to do and with routine business, Whitford assured his readership that they could have a robust spiritual life nonetheless. These daily occupations would help the reader avoid idleness, which Whitford viewed as the "mother and nurse of all evil." The readers were admonished to take as much rest as possible on a Sunday, to attend Mass regularly, and to listen to orthodox (i.e., non-Protestant) preaching as often as possible. Likely influenced by the communal nature of monasticism, Whitford instructed his readers that their secular life was communal too. He encouraged his reader to gather with neighbors on Sunday for basic catechesis, to eat together while someone read aloud in English and Latin, and to go together from their homes to the church.[20] Whitford was not suggesting that everyone should become a monk or nun, but he was hoping to cultivate the spiritual life of the laity in the midst of their secular vocations, a common notion in late medieval England, as will be seen below. He was concerned that laity understood something as simple as making a proper sign of the cross, in addition to understanding the fundamentals of Christian faith and practice. In short, "He saw the teaching, as well as the absorption, of the basic tenets as a key part of the pious layman's life. He rejected the idea that the education of the laity was the responsibility of the clergy alone and emphasized the role the laity was meant to play in the transmission of the basic tenets."[21] For Whitford, and for Bonde and Fewterer as well, the apostolate of writing and publishing books for the laity was motivated by their commitment to the *cura animarum* (care of souls) inasmuch as it was a defense of traditional

19. Ibid., 73.
20. Ibid., 74. The *Work* contained a "poor lesson" for public reading on Sundays, containing an explication of the Lord's Prayer, Ave Maria, and the Nicene Creed, along with "succinct treatments of the Ten Commandments, Seven Deadly Sins, Five Wits, and Seven Works of Mercy" (ibid., 76).
21. Ibid., 76.

religion. But the writing and printing of books was not the only way in which late medieval English monks practiced the care of souls.

The Care of Souls

In previous chapters we saw how the canons and the friars engaged in the care of souls primarily through the medium of preaching. Thanks to the scholarship of Joan Greatrex, we know that late medieval Benedictine monks were also actively engaged in preaching, often outside their cloisters.[22] Benedictine monk Henry Henfeld (d. 1396) is described as the "greatest preacher of God's word," and one Benedictine chapter boldly stated that monks "should study the art of presenting the word of God before others in order to become more efficient and well qualified in disputation and in preaching."[23] After examining manuscripts of sermons from the Benedictine's at Worcester, Greatrex concludes, "While there are in these collections a few sermons intended for monastic or clerical audiences . . . most appear to have been intended for general use."[24] She also concludes that though many of the sermons were written in Latin, they were most likely delivered in the vernacular, making them accessible to the average layperson.

That Benedictine monks were preaching to both clergy and laity is further demonstrated in an early fourteenth-century sermon collection. Patrick Horner believes these sermons were written by a Benedictine monk;[25] furthermore, he and others have demonstrated that these sermons were directed at both a clerical and a lay audience.[26] An examination of one of these sermons shows that the preacher is trying to impress upon his ordained and lay audience that the creed is meant for them all and that they must know and believe it for their own salvation. From these sermons it appears that the Benedictine

22. Joan Greatrex, "Benedictine Monk Scholars as Teachers and Preachers in the Later Middle Ages: Evidence from Worcester Cathedral Priory," *Monastic Studies* 2 (1991): 213–25; and idem, "Benedictine Sermons: Preparation and Practice in the English Monastic Cathedral Cloisters," in *Medieval Monastic Preaching*, ed. Carolyn Muessig (Leiden: Brill, 1998), 257–78.

23. Greatrex, "Benedictine Sermons," 258; and William Pantin, ed., *Documents Illustrating the Activities of the General and Provincial Chapters of the English Black Monks, 1215–1540* (London: Royal Historical Society, 1931–1937), 2:75.

24. Greatrex, "Benedictine Monk Scholars," 224.

25. Patrick J. Horner, ed. and trans., *A Macaronic Sermon Collection from Late Medieval England: Oxford, MS Bodley 649* (Toronto: PIMS, 2006), 4–6.

26. Ibid., 6–7. See also Siegfried Wenzel, *Macaronic Sermons: Bilingualism and Preaching in Late-Medieval England* (Ann Arbor: University of Michigan Press, 1994), 51–52. For a summary of the content of these sermons and other forms of late medieval monastic pastoral care, see Greg Peters, "Religious Orders and Pastoral Care in the Late Middle Ages," in *Pastoral Care in the Late Middle Ages*, ed. Ronald J. Stansbury (Leiden: Brill, 2010), 263–84.

preacher was directing much of his exhortation to laypeople listening to his sermons. It was becoming common in the late Middle Ages for monks, including those who were not friars and were traditionally cloistered (like the Benedictines), to preach in the vernacular to laypeople. In these sermons, the preacher included ordained persons in the same categories of sin and struggle as laypersons, demonstrating his understanding that though society may be divided into unique orders (ordained vs. lay, monk vs. knight, etc.), no one was immune from the snares of heresy. The preacher's message in these sermons is consistent: confess the creed, be baptized, and submit oneself to the sacrament of penance. Thus these sermons and others like them should be viewed as a form of pastoral care from monks to laypeople.

Certainly these sermons enhanced the religious life of the laity, or, owing to humankind's fallen nature, at least some of the laity. But late medieval monasteries influenced lay religious life in multiple ways, and to investigate lay religious life is oftentimes to consider the activities of monks and nuns. For example, it was common for monasteries to run different types of schools. The Benedictines in Durham, for example, ran an almonry (or grammar school) and a "song school," a specialist track within the grammar school for boys who could sing well.[27] The almonry school took its name from the fact that it was a charitable institution run with general oversight from the monastery almoner. In Durham, "certain poor children, called the children of the Almery [sic] . . . were maintained with learning . . . and . . . went dayly [sic] to school to the Farmary school, without the Abbey gates."[28] Oftentimes these schools were populated with the relatives of the monastery's monks, but non-relatives could also be recommended as pupils, especially those students who were apt to become monks. These schools were one of the many ways in which a monastery could influence the spiritual lives of the laity, though the laity had a unique spirituality of their own, centered primarily around the local parish, guilds and confraternities, and, in late medieval England, chantries (small, private chapels built for the purpose of having priests say Masses for the founder and his or her friends).

After describing what is known about the parishes of late medieval Durham, along with their affiliated facilities (such as chapels and hospitals), Margaret Harvey concludes, "The object of all the institutions which have hitherto been described was to help the salvation of souls. Essential to that, of course,

---

27. Margaret Harvey, *Lay Religious Life in Late Medieval Durham* (Woodbridge, UK: Boydell Press, 2006), 120.

28. From the *Rites of Durham*, quoted in Greatrex, *English Benedictine Cathedral Priories*, 189.

was that Christians should regularly worship God and live holy lives."[29] This was most naturally worked out in one's local parish. Early sixteenth-century Durham, for example, had six parish churches serving its population of approximately four thousand people. The church year was observed by these parishes, with certain feast days receiving particular attention. Yet "the feasts and seasons of the Christian calendar were not just dates: they impacted on daily life in dietary and other restrictions—the abstinence from meat on Friday and Lent; a ban on sexual activity at certain seasons (notably during Advent and Lent) or on particular days, prohibitions on trade and labour, the halting of judicial processes."[30] Further, during the Easter season, adults (anyone over twelve years old) were required by canon law to make a proper confession to the parish priest and to receive Holy Communion. Complementing their parish liturgical life was the use of Books of Hours, which were illustrated prayer books meant for private, individual use. They "offered sequences of psalms and prayers, including the Office for the Dead, and various devotions to the Virgin, which could be consulted in private or used to bolster devotions during church services."[31] Though these Books of Hours required the user to be literate, they were popular before the advent of printing and became ubiquitous after the introduction of the printing press.

It was also common for laypeople to join local guilds and confraternities, as well as devotional and charitable associations. Though these groups varied widely across Europe in their purpose, membership, and expectations, they can be defined as a voluntary association of people who met together at regular intervals, under the guidance of certain rules, to promote a common religious life and to engage in pious and charitable works. A main concern of these organizations was to provide their members with an appropriate funeral and a "guaranteed *post mortem* remembrance."[32] In Italy the confraternities fit into one of three categories: (1) charitable and devotional associations, known as *misericordia*; (2) the *laudesi*, devotional groups that engaged "in the public singing of praises to the saint"; and (3) the *disciplinati*, penitential associations "characterised by a Passion-centred devotion which manifested itself in flagellation."[33] The guilds were made up of people engaged in a common trade who came together to commemorate a particular saint or worship at a particular church.

29. Harvey, *Lay Religious Life*, 27.
30. R. N. Swanson, *Religion and Devotion in Europe, c. 1215–c. 1515* (Cambridge: Cambridge University Press, 1995), 96.
31. Ibid., 97.
32. Ibid., 117.
33. Ibid., 119–20.

Yet another way in which the laity demonstrated their devotion was in the creation of chantries. Though the exact origin of chantries is uncertain, they were foundations that provided for Masses to be said for the souls of the dead. They fall into several types:

> The first was the simple chantry where a benefactor gave a legacy to a corporation or parish to provide a priest to say the mass, with the corporation or the parish to pay the priest out of the funds provided, which became the property of the corporation, not of the chantry priest. The second type was the chantry proper, where the founder provided a benefice, with an endowment for the priest and with patronage like any other. The third type was the "service" or perpetuity, where a stipend was created without a benefice, whereby the funds were managed by trustees, on condition that they paid a priest.[34]

Depending on the financial status of the person setting up the chantry, it could call for one Mass to be said after the death or for Mass to be said on the anniversary of the person's death for a fixed number of years, or even in perpetuity. Throughout the thirteenth to fifteenth centuries, thousands of chantries were set up across Europe, making the chantry a particularly popular focus of lay piety.

Monastic and Non-monastic Spirituality

One of the clearest ways that monastic practice and spirituality and lay practice and spirituality came together was in treatises dedicated to the so-called mixed life. Two texts from late medieval England in particular illustrate this well: the anonymous *The Abbey of the Holy Ghost* and Walter Hilton's (d. 1396) *Epistle on the Mixed Life. The Abbey of the Holy Ghost* has historically been attributed to Richard Rolle (d. 1349) but is actually a translation of an original French text whose authorship is unknown. The purpose of the text, which the author lays out at the start, is to provide a kind of spiritual monastery for those who cannot enter an actual monastery: "I here draw up a book of religion of the heart, that is, of the Abbey of the Holy Ghost, so that all those who may not physically enter religion may do so spiritually."[35] This

---

34. Harvey, *Lay Religious Life*, 132–33. It is thought that chantries came into existence because the monastic orders were unable to meet the growing need for a priest to offer intercessory Masses for the dead. The need for these intercessory Masses seems to be connected to a rise in belief in purgatory and a fear of postmortem punishment.

35. R. N. Swanson, trans., *Catholic England: Faith, Religion and Observance before the Reformation* (Manchester, UK: Manchester University Press, 1993), 96.

monastery will be built in a person's conscience, after it has been cleansed by righteousness and "the maiden Love-of-cleanness" and constructed on the firm foundations set down by humility and poverty. The walls are built by Lady Obedience and Lady Mercy with the stones of good deeds. The monastery's pillars are erected by Lady Patience and Lady Fortitude, and the cloister is enclosed so as to keep foul sights, hearings, speech, and thoughts from entering. Further, Penance constructs the chapter house, since that is the place in a monastery where the monks name offences committed against one another, and Prayer builds the chapel. The monastic offices will be populated with virtues: the infirmarer is Pity, since infirmarers exercise pity and care for the sick, whereas Lady Discretion is the treasurer, since the monastery's finances must be cared for with prudence. For obvious reasons, she who chants the daily office (the chantress) is Prayer, while Temperance serves in the refectory because the nuns must never eat more than required for physical sustenance and health. Mercy is almoner so that all alms given in support of the poor and destitute are distributed with compassion, and the hosteller is Lady Courtesy so that all who come to the monastery will be received with graciousness as the person of Christ. The Holy Spirit is the episcopal warden (i.e., the one who gives oversight) and visitor of the abbey, and Lady Charity is its abbess, for everything must be done with her permission;[36] that is, all that we do in our spiritual lives must be done in love. The prioress of the monastery is Lady Wisdom, who should be consulted for all decisions, and the sub-prioress is Lady Humility, who shall be honored with obedience.

The purpose of this interior monastery is to ensure that she who possesses it engages in contemplation, which the anonymous author defines as a "burning to dwell with God in love, and with his delights to enhance the soul, and have a partial taste of the sweetness that God's chosen shall have in Heaven."[37] Such contemplation is aided by meditation, "good thoughts of God and of his works, of his words, and of his creation, of the pains he suffered, and of the heart-felt love that he had and has for us for whom he endured death."[38] The beginning of all perfection, according to the anonymous author, is to think and meditate deeply on God and his works, which then develops into a devout longing love for God that brings tears. In response, God offers his comfort, which ultimately leads to contemplation. It appears that the author thought of this inner abbey as similar to the ideal, pre-fall state of humankind, because it is Satan's activities that bring decline to the abbey when he allows

36. That Lady Charity is the abbess suggests that the text was written initially for pious laywomen.
37. Swanson, *Catholic England*, 97.
38. Ibid., 101.

his four daughters of ill will to enter the house: Envy, Pride, Complaint, and False-witness. Their purpose and intent is to disturb and harm the convent through wickedness. However, the prioress Lady Wisdom and sub-prioress Lady Humility counsel with Lady Discretion so that "they should all fall into prayer to the Holy Ghost, who is visitor of this abbey, that he should hurry to come, as they had great need, to help them and visit them with his grace."[39] The Holy Spirit responds to their request by visiting the house and cleansing it of Satan's daughters.

In short, this treatise implicitly views monasticism as superior to the non-monastic estate because it encourages everyone to enter a monastery, be it a physical one or an interior, spiritual one. However, the text also shows the closeness of these forms of life. The monastic life is no longer so lofty that it can be reached only by the elect few, but is accessible and beneficial to everyone. The text advocates that all people, whether lay or monastic, can attain the heights of divine contemplation, assuming that they erect an Abbey of the Holy Ghost in their conscience. This is a robust vision of lay spirituality.

Hilton's *Epistle on the Mixed Life* lays out a similar monastic vision of lay spirituality. Hilton, an Augustinian canon, begins the text by establishing that the person who wants to be spiritual must begin with the physical. That is, he or she must fast, watch, restrain fleshly lusts through penance, perform the corporal works of mercy, and endure all physical discomforts, because "whoever wishes to be spiritually engaged, it is surer and profitable for him first to be tested for a long time by this physical activity, for these bodily deeds are a sign and demonstration of moral virtues, without which a soul is incapable of spiritual labours."[40] This vision is then distilled in twenty-eight chapters, all of which are aimed at the person who cannot and should not abandon his or her active life to act like a monk or friar. Hilton recognizes that not everyone is called to the monastic life, so he assures his readers that those who are not called have, nonetheless, a responsibility and godly obligation to live a robust spiritual life. People in this estate should "mix the works of the active life with spiritual works of the contemplative life."[41] They are to live a Martha-Mary life, a balanced combination of both action and contemplation. According to Hilton, there are three ways of living: the active life, the contemplative life, and the mixed life. The active life characterizes the uncouth and fleshly, whose only motivation to act spiritually in any capacity is the avoidance of hell and

39. Ibid., 103–4.
40. Ibid., 105.
41. Ibid., 107.

the dread of God, though they do have a desire to please God, get to heaven, and show goodwill to fellow Christians. Contemplatives, however, are those "who for the love of God forsake all overt sins of the world and of their flesh, and all business, duties and oversight of worldly goods, and make themselves poor and naked, down to the bare necessities of bodily nature, and flee from authority over other men into the service of God."[42] Contemplatives labor and occupy themselves inwardly with those things that lead to cleanness of heart and a peaceful conscience by means of destroying sin and cultivating the virtues. The contemplative life is characterized by devout prayers, fervent longing, and spiritual meditation.

The mixed life, Hilton writes, is particularly apropos for prelates of the church and secular lords simply because these vocations have both active and contemplative aspects. He notes that to "these men it sometimes pertains to employ works of the active life, to assist and sustain themselves and their subjects and others as well, and sometimes to leave all external business and give themselves up for a time to prayers, meditations, readings of holy writ, and other spiritual activities."[43] Hilton assures his readers that this form of life is nothing new; it was modeled for the church by Jesus himself, along with other holy men and women. Though Hilton's text is not as explicit as *The Abbey of the Holy Ghost* in its use of monastic terms, Hilton was certainly working from the age-old distinction that the active life is primarily the purview of the laity, friars, and canons and that the contemplative life is exclusively reserved for cloistered monastics. He implicitly rejects this division and instead sees in the life of Christ a model for the mixed life. By appealing to the example of Jesus Christ, Hilton has established that the mixed life is principally christological and therefore most worthy of emulation. He has essentially leveled the spiritual playing field of late medieval spirituality.

Ressourcement: Complementarity of Monastic and Non-monastic Spiritual Life

Anyone who posits that there has always been a deep divide between monastic and non-monastic lifestyles and spirituality is not familiar with the history of spirituality of late medieval England. Though there are certainly important distinctions between monastic and lay faith and practice, there are also many similarities, and a healthy understanding of both will result in a robust vision of the spiritual life. Today the complementarity of these kinds

42. Ibid., 107–8.
43. Ibid., 108.

of life manifests itself in the plethora of oblates and associates affiliated with monasteries (see chap. 14). These oblates and associates are non-monastic laypeople and clergy who affiliate with a particular monastery for the purpose of spiritual edification and to intentionally incorporate into their life monastic disciplines and practices. Though this is one way in which monasticism has found a home in non-monastic spirituality, it is not the only way. Many aspects of "everyday" spirituality are monastic-like, whether or not they are directly borrowed from monastic history. For example, the modern movement, especially in evangelical Protestant churches, toward an emphasis on churchly community is certainly monastic in sentiment, as is the Eucharistic-focused ecclesiology of the post–Vatican II church. Though the lines of influence may not run directly from the institution of monasticism to these modern ecclesial practices, they run between the two nonetheless.

In Fyodor Dostoevsky's *The Brothers Karamazov*, Fr. Zosima, a monastic elder at the local monastery, says to the young Alyosha Karamazov, "You will go forth from these [monastery] walls, but you will sojourn in the world like a monk."[44] This sentiment, that a non-monastic person could live in the world as a monk or nun, is known as interiorized (or untonsured) monasticism. This unconventional vision of monasticism is generally associated with the later eighteenth-century Russian monk Tikhon of Zadonsk (d. 1783), who writes, "The one who wears a white habit [the clothing of ordinary people] and who is clothed in obedience, humility and purity, such a one is a true monk, though untonsured."[45] This concept of interiorized monasticism, made more widely known by Dostoevsky and then popularized in the twentieth century by the Russian-born, French Orthodox theologian Paul Evdokimov, gets at a theology of monasticism by suggesting that it is not *just* monastic vows that make the monk but that all Christians, in a sense, are monks and nuns. Evdokimov did not deny the legitimate, divine calling of men and women into the monastic life as traditionally understood, but he strove to root the essence of monasticism in the Christian's baptismal vows.[46] More important, what Tikhon and Evdokimov both understood is that there is a fine line between monastic spirituality in particular and Christian spirituality generally. In reality, there is no distinct monastic spirituality. Instead, all Christians are called to the same *telos* of the spiritual life: holiness (see 1 Pet. 1:14–16). What is distinct between monastics and non-monastics is the means to this end, but the end is

44. Fyodor Dostoevsky, *The Brothers Karamazov*, trans. Richard Pevear and Larissa Volokhonsky (New York: Farrar, Straus and Giroux, 1990), 285.

45. Michael Plekon, "Interiorized Monasticism: Paul Evdokimov on the Spiritual Life," *American Benedictine Review* 48, no. 3 (1997): 227.

46. See Plekon, "Interiorized Monasticism," 227–53.

the same for all believers. Men and women become monks and nuns because they are called by God to be monks and nuns, not because they are joining an institution that is inherently more holy or a surer guarantor of holiness. Because of this, monastic practices can be used by non-monastics on their own journey to God and vice versa.

Part IV

LUTHER *to* MERTON

12

The Reformers and Counter-Reformers

n May 1936 the great poet T. S. Eliot, an Anglican and American expatri-
ate, visited St. John's Church in Little Gidding, Huntingdonshire, England.
Though the church itself had been rebuilt in 1714, the location had been home
in the seventeenth century to a small Anglican religious community. In 1625
Mary Ferrar purchased a house with an abandoned chapel in Little Gidding
and was joined there by her sons Nicholas and John, along with John's wife
and children, as well as Mary's daughter and son-in-law with their sixteen
children. Nicholas, a former Member of Parliament and ordained deacon in
the Church of England, was the spiritual head of the community. The small
community remained a family affair, dedicated to unceasing prayer (someone
was always praying in the church) and a strict routine of Sabbath observance
and the recitation of the daily offices, which began at 4:00 a.m. in the summer and 5:00 a.m. in the winter. Beyond the community, the family helped to
educate and care for poor local children and produced spiritual books. The
experiment was short-lived but is remembered as one of the first attempts to
reinstitute monasticism into England after the sixteenth-century dissolution
of the monasteries. Six years after his visit, Eliot published his poem "Little
Gidding," the last of the *Four Quartets*. One of the main themes of this poem
is the notion that all time (past, present, and future) exists in the ever-present
now. Because of Little Gidding's connection to the history of monasticism,

it suggests that the institution of monasticism is also timeless, that its spirit lives on even in those places where it was (violently) removed as a result of the Protestant Reformation, and that these very places hold promise for a future monasticism.

It is often understood that the Protestant Reformers by and large rejected the institution of monasticism. This is true, though not without some significant qualifications. For example, Martin Luther and John Calvin rejected monasticism primarily because it was thought to be salvific and because it was based on the taking of lifelong vows. Both Reformers, however, had room for monasticism if it could be construed as the fruit of one's salvation and if it was practiced without permanent vows. Furthermore, many other Reformers did not entirely reject monasticism and did not see it as inconsistent with a reformed theology, whether Lutheran, Calvinistic, Anglican, or other.[1] At the same time that the Protestant Reformers were debating the validity of monasticism, the Roman Catholic Church was experiencing a renaissance in monastic life primarily by way of the founding of the Jesuits by Ignatius of Loyola and the reform of the Carmelites by Teresa of Avila and John of the Cross. This chapter will concern itself with Protestant conceptions of the monastic life and how it was not rejected wholesale. Attention will also be given to the formation and spirituality of the Jesuits and the Discalced Carmelites and the important role that they played in the Catholic Reformation.

Protestant Views of Monasticism

Though the institution of monasticism was certainly considered suspect by most magisterial Protestant Reformers, it was never rejected across the board even by the most prolific and influential of these Reformers, namely, Luther and Calvin. As shown in the last chapter, the state of monasticism at the turn of the sixteenth century was not as desperate as is often depicted in both primary and secondary literature. Though it may have been healthier in one location than another, it was nonetheless not as debauched as the polemical literature often depicts. As well, there was a steady stream of Protestants who continued to support the presence or reestablishment of monasticism in the church and who lamented that the baby of monasticism had been thrown out with the bath water of the Roman Catholic Church. An overview of Luther's and Calvin's views shows that they had not altogether rejected monasticism.

1. For an overview of Protestantism and monasticism, see Greg Peters, *Reforming the Monastery: Protestant Theologies of the Religious Life* (Eugene, OR: Cascade, 2014).

Luther

Martin Luther (d. 1546) entered the Augustinian friary at Erfurt in July 1505 but walked out of it forever on January 3, 1521, when he was excommunicated by Pope Leo X (d. 1521). Though Luther entered the monastic life because of a vow he made to God when fearful for his life during a thunderstorm, he was a good monk, albeit an overly scrupulous one. His commitment to the monastic life (as well as his over-scrupulosity) was intimately connected with the erroneous late medieval understanding of how one is saved. By the early sixteenth century it was commonly believed that most people were going to spend a large part of their afterlife suffering in the fires of purgatory; therefore, one should spend a great deal of time and energy in this life to alleviate this future suffering and ultimately secure a place in heaven. For example, the benefits for joining the fraternity of St. Chad in Lichfield, England, whose purpose was to provide income for the upkeep of the cathedral, included 4,040 "days of privilege" granted by the bishop of Lichfield; 12,000 "days of privilege" granted by other bishops; and twenty-one "years of privilege" granted by the popes.[2] In short, the main motivation for giving one's money to the fraternity was to buy time out of purgatory. Famous, of course, was Luther's run-in with the now infamous indulgence peddler Johann Tetzel (d. 1519). Tetzel, a Dominican friar, played into the fears of the average Christian regarding future punishment by letting the populace think that through the purchase of indulgences they were, in essence, procuring a ticket to heaven. With the slogan "As soon as the coin into the box rings, a soul from purgatory to heaven springs" serving as his tagline, Tetzel entered towns "accompanied by a fanfare of trumpets and drums and a procession complete with flags and symbols of the papacy. After a vivid sermon on hell and its terrors in the town square, he proceeded to the largest church and gave an equally vivid sermon on purgatory and the sufferings not only awaiting the audience but presently endured by their dead relatives and loved ones."[3] He would then sell indulgences on a sliding scale depending on each person's ability to pay. This "saved by indulgence" soteriology was outlawed in Wittenberg by the city's patron, Frederick the Wise, but Luther's parishioners went out to meet Tetzel wherever they could nonetheless. Luther, a man of quick mind and biting tongue, did not hesitate to speak out against this scheme, the proceeds of which supported the construction of the grandiose St. Peter's Basilica in Rome.

2. R. N. Swanson, trans., *Catholic England: Faith, Religion and Observance before the Reformation* (Manchester, UK: Manchester University Press, 1993), 218.
3. Carter Lindberg, *The European Reformations* (Oxford: Blackwell, 1996), 75.

Having begun a course of events that was impossible to harness and would ultimately change the world, Luther, in 1520, published *The Freedom of a Christian*, in which he lays out his initial thoughts on the validity of the institution of monasticism in relation to his soteriology. *The Freedom of a Christian* was written in both German and Latin so that it was fully accessible to both the laity and the educated reader. In the German edition, Luther writes that his purpose is "to discern what a Christian person is and what freedom Christ has acquired and given this person."[4] For Luther, a Christian believer possesses free will above all things and thereby is subject to none, while at the same time he affirms that a Christian is also a dutiful servant in all things and thereby subject to everyone. These two contradictory positions are held in balance by the fact that the former is true of the soul and is spiritual, whereas the latter statement is made in relation to the flesh and is thus physical. The Christian's freedom belongs to the inward, spiritual person because nothing external makes a person free. Luther's point here is that there is dissimilarity between the spiritual and the material. Luther is not espousing a dualistic anthropology, but he does affirm that this is how we are as believers. As he writes, "What help is it to the soul if the body is not captive, fresh, and healthy, and eats and drinks, and lives as it wants? From the other perspective, what harm comes to the soul if the body is confined, sick, and weary, and hungers, thirsts, and suffers in the way it does not like?"[5] This conclusion allows Luther to argue that how one behaves outwardly, that is, one's state of life, does not have a direct bearing on one's soul and, by extension, on one's level of justification or holiness. To illustrate this point he immediately looks to churchly ostentation, assuring his readers that the soul receives no benefit if the body puts on holy clothing like the priests and clergy, nor is it helpful to be in churches and sacred places. The only thing that can make the soul righteous and therefore free and Christian is the gospel and the word of God preached by Christ.

This creates the space necessary for Luther to discuss the contents of the word of God, which "is nothing but the preaching of Christ in accordance with the gospel, spoken in such a way that you hear your God speaking to you. It shows how your whole life and work are nothing before God but must eternally perish with everything that is in you."[6] Thus Christians are able to see their depravity and that they are headed for damnation. Luther also says that it is the word of Christ that brings assurance to the Christian so that she can

---

4. Martin Luther, *The Freedom of a Christian* 1; Philip D. W. Krey and Peter D. S. Krey, eds., *Luther's Spirituality* (New York: Paulist Press, 2007), 70.

5. Luther, *Freedom of a Christian* 3; Krey and Krey, *Luther's Spirituality*, 71.

6. Luther, *Freedom of a Christian* 6; Krey and Krey, *Luther's Spirituality*, 72.

move beyond the state of destruction to the state of redemption. To this end, God places Jesus Christ before the believer and allows her to be addressed by the living and comforting Word. The purpose of this revelation of the Son of God is that each person will surrender to the Word and trust in God alone for salvation. In this way destruction will be overcome, and the Christian will be "righteous, genuine, satisfied, upright, and fulfill all the commandments and be free of all things."[7] For Luther, true freedom is found in one's justification by faith in Jesus Christ, making good works no longer *necessary* for salvation but instead the *result* of a person's justification. Good works become the way in which Christians practice and strengthen their faith. In Luther's assessment no other work can make a Christian; he assures his readers that salvation is by faith alone apart from works. Thus, "This is Christian freedom: faith alone, which brings about not that we might become idle or do evil but that we have need of no works to attain righteousness and blessedness."[8]

Having established this foundation regarding the spiritual and that which is of the soul, Luther turns to the outward person in the second part of *The Freedom of a Christian*. Because faith alone is sufficient to make one righteous, Luther imagines that a true believer could be tempted to simply "relax, eat, drink, be merry" (Luke 12:19). Why should one go about doing good works if one is already justified? Since a believer's perfection is eschatological—and therefore, in the future—the Christian should be a dutiful servant and subject to everyone in the course of this life. Again, though the Christian is free, she is also a servant under obligation to perform many kinds of good works. From the perspective of the soul, one is justified through faith and has everything necessary for salvation even while one's faith and trust in God should continue to grow until she reaches heaven. While still remaining in this body on earth, the Christian must rule her own life and relate to people. This is where works begin to play a role, so one should not be idle. For Luther, and for the Reformers in general, works are the *result* of faith and are not constituent parts of or necessary to faith. The good works that result from faith are manifested in the life of each believer.

In the doing of good works, however, the Christian soon "discovers a recalcitrant will that wants to serve the world and seek its own pleasure."[9] Faith does not tolerate this disobedient will, so it endeavors to discipline it. Quoting from 1 Corinthians 9:27 ("I discipline my body and keep it under control") and Galatians 5:24 ("Those who belong to Christ . . . have crucified

---

7. Luther, *Freedom of a Christian* 6; Krey and Krey, *Luther's Spirituality*, 72.
8. Luther, *Freedom of a Christian* 10; Krey and Krey, *Luther's Spirituality*, 75.
9. Luther, *Freedom of a Christian* 20; Krey and Krey, *Luther's Spirituality*, 81.

the flesh with its passions"), Luther shows that this disciplining of the will often requires a physical, bodily form. But in spite of the believer's need to discipline her body, these works must never be seen as salvific. Since the believer is already found by God to be righteous by faith, these good works are the result of that faith; they do not instill or activate faith. Thus these works should be done only with the understanding that the body becomes obedient and purified of its evil passion when it is disciplined. We see in Luther the close connection between works and the mortification of the body because as the soul is purified it longs to see the body purified too. Luther writes, "Thus these two verses are true: Good and righteous works will never make a good and righteous person, but a good and righteous person does good and righteous works. Evil works never make an evil person, but an evil person does evil works. Therefore, the person must always be good and righteous beforehand, ahead of all good works, and good works follow and flow out of a righteous and good person."[10]

In the third section of the book, Luther turns from bodily good works to consider good works that are useful and serve others. Keeping in mind others' needs is evidence of a genuine Christian life, writes Luther. Because believers are slaves, they become servants in order to help their neighbor. This others-centeredness flows from faith and is evidenced by love for neighbor, not by a fixation on one's own spiritual life. From this perspective Luther commends monasticism, as long as it has the good of others in mind: "All the works of priests, monasteries, and religious foundations should be done in the same way too, that all do the work of their position in life or order for nothing else than the welfare of others."[11] Monks and nuns should govern their bodies to be an example for others, who in turn do the same. Yet this beneficial aspect of monasticism is often destroyed by the laws of the pope, overzealous monastic rules, and even well-meaning secular rulers who stipulate and insist that these good works—done for the example and benefit of others—do not result from the Christian's justification but are necessary for it. Because of this the believer must judge rightly between the commands "of the blind and mad prelates and the right-minded ones" regarding his involvement in living the monastic life, since any work that is not oriented toward serving another is not a good, Christian work. "I worry," writes Luther, "that few foundation churches, monasteries, altars, masses, and testaments are Christian and, along with that, the special fasting and prayers to some of the saints. For I fear that in all of these works each person seeks

10. Luther, *Freedom of a Christian* 23; Krey and Krey, *Luther's Spirituality*, 83.
11. Luther, *Freedom of a Christian* 28; Krey and Krey, *Luther's Spirituality*, 88.

only his or her own benefits, presuming thereby to do penance for his or her sins and be saved."[12]

Though Luther's strongest assessment of monasticism is not offered in *The Freedom of a Christian*, he is concerned that many who practice it or may practice it will come to see it as salvific rather than as a fruit or good work of saving faith. The result of justification must be the doing of good works for the benefit of others. Though Luther believes that this is laid out in the Scriptures, he insists that the Roman Catholic Church reverses the *ordo salutis* (order of salvation) from justification by faith leading to good works, to good works leading to justification. This is *the* error of the late medieval Roman Catholic Church, according to Luther, and it leads him to conclude that many monastics joined the monastery only because they were convinced to do so by someone who thought monastic life was salvific. They became a monk or nun for the sake of being saved and not for the good of the world and neighbor. Luther's soteriological concern about monasticism grew out of his rejection of the late medieval practice of buying time out of purgatory and, for salesmen like Tetzel, buying heaven itself. The reward of heaven, as Luther knew, comes about through faith alone, and he did not want to see the institution of monasticism support the Roman Catholic Church's erroneous theology. He did not reject monasticism in toto, but he certainly rejected any conception of monasticism that involved the earning of merit and salvation.

Luther's fuller treatment of monasticism is found in his *On Monastic Vows*, published in 1522.[13] In this text Luther acknowledges that what makes the monk is not that he is under vows but rather that he has freely chosen to become a monk. At this point Luther goes so far as to say that he himself is both a monk yet not a monk. God is Luther's abbot, not any church-appointed authority. The main question Luther seeks to answer in *On Monastic Vows* is whether monastic vows are truly vows. He acknowledges that the Scriptures teach vow-keeping, but he questions the validity of monastic vows. His argument consists of five points: (1) Scripture does not command monastic vows; (2) monastic vows conflict with faith; (3) the compulsory and perpetual nature of monastic vows violates a Christian's freedom; (4) monastic vows go against the Ten Commandments; and (5) monastic vows are contrary to common sense.

In proving his first point that Scripture does not command monastic vows, Luther argues that (1) monastic vows are the equivalent of one's baptismal

---

12. Luther, *Freedom of a Christian* 29; Krey and Krey, *Luther's Spirituality*, 89.

13. A full analysis of the contents of this treatise can be found in Peters, *Reforming the Monastery*, 24–37. The text itself is available in James Atkinson, ed., *Luther's Works*, vol. 44, *The Christian in Society I* (Philadelphia: Fortress Press, 1966), 243–400.

vows; (2) biblical commandments apply to all Christians because God makes no distinction (contra the Roman Catholic Church) between counsels and precepts; and (3) virginity and celibacy are commandments given to all Christians, though they are worked out in the midst of one's vocational calling.

Luther's second point, that monastic vows conflict with Christian faith, is largely based on Luther's assessment that the permanency of monastic vows goes against Romans 14:23, which states that everything that is not of faith is sin. If one is under permanent monastic vows but not from a place of faith, then one sins by keeping those vows. Thus monastic vows should allow someone "to keep them at one time or to renounce them at another."[14] Luther then returns to the theme of *The Freedom of a Christian* and argues that choosing to be a monastic is the fruit of one's faith and is not salvific. The permanency of monastic vows undercuts this by suggesting that one cannot leave the monastic life because it is superior to and, thereby, more meritorious than a non-monastic life.

Luther's third main point, that monastic vows are against evangelical freedom, is based on his assessment that the vows resist the fruit of faith and the word of God. Given their non-salvific nature, monastic vows must be, by definition, "a matter of free choice and can be laid aside."[15] To say otherwise would be to rob a person of their God-given freedom in Christ. But this does not mean, writes Luther, that one's freedom annuls the imperative of biblical commandments. Rather, Christians must perform good works, and as long as one's decision to be a monk or nun is the fruit of faith and a good work, then one can freely become a monastic; yet taking any kind of permanent vow automatically removes the very freedom that the Christian has been given by God, for true Christian freedom is "a freedom of conscience which liberates the conscience from works."[16] Again, this comes back to Luther's insistence that justification is not by works but by faith alone.

Luther's fourth point is expressed as follows: because monastic vows are contrary to the Christian faith and to evangelical freedom, as well as against Scripture, then monastic vows "cannot be anything else but contrary to all divine commandments when they are contrary to the One from whom and through whom and in whom all things exist."[17] For Luther, monastic vows are against the first three of the Ten Commandments in particular. The first commandment commands faith, the second commands praise and confession of the name of God, and the third commands the work of God

14. Atkinson, *Luther's Works*, 44:273.
15. Ibid., 44:297.
16. Ibid., 44:298.
17. Ibid., 44:317.

in us. Monastic vows transgress the first commandment because they teach works. They go against the second commandment because monastics no longer offer praise to God by calling themselves "Christians" but by calling themselves Benedictines, Dominicans, Franciscans, and so on. The third commandment is violated when monastics are happier about keeping their order's rule than they are about keeping their baptismal vows, which are binding on all Christians.

Finally, Luther's fifth point is that monastic vows are contrary to common sense and reason because if one vow can be set aside, then all vows are able to be set aside under the proper circumstances. One of his examples is a vow of celibacy. If a person takes a vow of celibacy but then realizes he is unable to keep it, he is free to marry for "it is better to marry than to burn with passion" (1 Cor. 7:9). Therefore, if a vow as serious as celibacy can be laid aside, then certainly all vows that are unreasonable can also be laid aside. The distinction between vows that are reasonable and those that are not is what allows Luther to still posit the good of marriage vows, for example, because they are reasonable and therefore cannot be laid aside. Permanent monastic vows, however, are unreasonable.

Calvin

John Calvin (d. 1564) was a second-generation Protestant Reformer, but he too rejected monasticism largely due to the nature of monastic vows, which he lays out in his *Institutes of the Christian Religion*. Calvin believed that vows, including monastic vows, served one purpose: to ensnare humankind so as to keep them from the worship of and service to God. He believed that whatever Christians needed to guide them to piety and holiness was already found in the biblical law and in God's call for all believers to be obedient to his will. Thus monastic vows were unnecessary and superfluous. Calvin went so far as to suggest that vow-making was more pagan than Christian since it implied that God was fickle and entered into individual contracts as opposed to legislating one godly law for all people. Calvin established three criteria to determine the legitimacy of a vow: (1) it must be made to God; (2) the person making the vow must be able to keep it; and (3) the person's intention for making the vow should be either thanksgiving or repentance. Regarding the first criterion, all legitimate vows are made to God; therefore, any vow made to someone other than God is objectionable. Futhermore, legitimate vows are made at the instigation of God and not from someone's own initiative. Thus Calvin writes, "Let us not take to ourselves such license as to dare to vow to God that which bears no evidence as to how he may esteem it."[18] The most appropriate vows are those dictated by God's word. Concerning Calvin's second criterion, the person making the vow must be up to the task of keeping the vow, which is a matter of one's strength, albeit assisted by God. If the believer makes a rash vow that she is unable to keep, then she is neglecting the liberty given the Christian by God. This also shows a person's ungratefulness to God's beneficence since one should never make a promise to God if the promise is intended to be kept in one's own strength. Vows are something that are given back to God, since he is the giver of all good and perfect gifts. Therefore, vows are gifts to God, intended as an offering to God for the strength that he provides to keep the vow. In particular, Calvin views the vow of celibacy as particularly problematic since the book of Genesis commands all people to be fruitful and multiply. To vow celibacy spurns God's nature because it goes beyond God's divinely established law.

Regarding the third and final criterion, "your intention in making a vow is important if you would have God approve it,"[19] Calvin says that there are four ends to which vows ought to be directed, and these fall into two categories: (1) vows that attest gratitude to God for something received, and (2) vows entered into to punish oneself for offenses committed against God. The first kind of vows are exercises of thanksgiving, and the latter are exercises of repentance. As well, there are future ends to which vows can be directed: (1) to make the believer more cautious in how he lives, and (2) to arouse the believer to Christian duty. Nonetheless, all believers primarily fall under one vow in particular, and that is the baptismal vow to renounce Satan and yield oneself to God's holy commandments. This baptismal vow is renewed at catechism and in the partaking of the Lord's Supper. Other vows, even if lawful, are not to be a daily practice, writes Calvin. Rather, without offering a direct prescription about number or time, Calvin believes that anyone who follows his advice will enter into only sober and temporary vows. Making too many vows results in a cheapened religious character by way of repetition and results in superstition. In short, "If you bind yourself to a perpetual vow, either you will fulfill it with great trouble and tedium, or else, wearied by its long duration, you will one day venture to break it."[20] In other cases, vows are simply perverse and should never be entered into, such as vows regarding fasting, abstinence from wine or meat on certain days, and pilgrimages to religious sites. All of these vows, according to Calvin's rules, will be deemed empty and fleeting and full of marked impiety. Such perverse vows give the

18. John Calvin, *Institutes of the Christian Religion* 4.13.2; Ford Lewis Battles, trans., *Institutes of the Christian Religion* (Philadelphia: Westminster, 1960), 1256.

19. Calvin, *Institutes* 4.13.4; Battles, *Institutes*, 1258.

20. Calvin, *Institutes* 4.13.6; Battles, *Institutes*, 1260.

impression that they are the result of exceptional righteousness, which places true piety in outward forms and observances, despising others who do not engage in such activity. Undoubtedly, Calvin is very much against the taking of perpetual vows that carry any connotation of being superior to biblical Christian duty or to the baptismal vows of all Christians. He is not against all vows but views as valid only those vows that are temporary and for the purpose of correcting wrong behavior and showing gratitude to God, as well as vows that serve as a kind of punishment for sinning against God.

Calvin also rejects monasticism, at least sixteenth-century monasticism, because it was nothing like early Christian monasticism. He believes that the institution of monasticism is legitimate because of its antiquity, and he believes that the early monks showed this legitimacy by sleeping on the ground, eating a simple diet, and avoiding all bodily pomp and sumptuousness. Sixteenth-century monks, however, do none of these things and are given over primarily to idleness. Monks and nuns no longer serve the church but instead claim to be living a superior form of the Christian life, all the while enjoying the pleasures of this world. Calvin rejects wholeheartedly this false claim that monasticism is a superior state of perfection. In his estimation, "the character of present-day monasticism is so different that you could scarcely find things more unlike, not to say contrary."[21]

Again, Calvin was not wholly against monasticism since he was capable of seeing the goodness in ancient patterns of monasticism. Like Luther, he was certainly against any view of monasticism that implied it was more meritorious or holy than other forms of Christian life, and he rejected, along with Luther, the concept of permanent monastic vows. At the same time, however, Calvin was capable of speaking positively of monasticism and individual monastics, and Luther could also see the good in a monasticism that did not consider itself salvific but saw itself as a result of someone's justification by faith. While these two Reformers were spilling quite a bit of ink on the topic of monasticism (set against the background of King Henry VIII's destruction of the monasteries in England), the Roman Catholic Church was undergoing a monastic reformation not unlike the monastic renaissance of the twelfth century.

The Counter-Reformers

Though the official response to Protestantism from the Roman Catholic Church developed slowly, with the first session of the Council of Trent opening in 1545,

21. Calvin, *Institutes* 4.13.10; Battles, *Institutes*, 1265.

there was a renewal in organized monastic life that had little to do, it appears, with the Protestant Reformation and more to do with an internal renewal of the Roman Catholic Church. The sixteenth century gave rise to a number of influential religious orders, not all of which were technically monastic, such as the Theatines, Capuchins, Barnabites, Ursulines, Oratorians, Jesuits, and reformed Carmelites. This organic renewal of religious life lends credence to the idea that it is appropriate to speak of the "Catholic Reformation" of the sixteenth century and not just of the "Counter-Reformation." The Church of Rome was undergoing spiritual renewal at the same time that the Protestants were forcing it to counter their theological claims. Of these newly founded religious orders, the most well-known and influential in monastic history are the Jesuits and the reformed Carmelites, both a product of Spanish Roman Catholicism.

The Jesuits

On September 27, 1540, Pope Paul III (d. 1549) approved the new religious order known as the Society of Jesus, or the Jesuits. The founder of this order, Ignatius of Loyola (d. 1556), was immediately elected superior and oversaw the rapid expansion of the order. Before his death, Ignatius dictated an account of his life in which he recounts his birth into nobility and the subsequent education that came with such a station in life. He tells of how he was injured around the age of thirty at the battle of Pamplona in 1521 and how he entered into a long convalescence during which he experienced a profound religious conversion. The impetus for his conversion was the result of his reading Ludolph of Saxony's *Life of Christ*, written in the fourteenth century, coupled with Jacob of Voragine's *The Golden Legend* from the thirteenth century. These texts brought Ignatius a profound sense of consolation, as opposed to the bellicose form of life he was living before. So moved by this experience, he spent a year in prayer and reflection at Manresa, near Barcelona, from 1522 to 1523. During this year, Ignatius reports that he underwent a number of mystical experiences, and he began setting out his spiritual vision in his masterpiece, the *Spiritual Exercises*, though it would not be published in its final form until 1548. In 1524 he made a pilgrimage to the Holy Land, and in 1526 he entered the University of Alcalá before attending the University of Paris from 1528 to 1535. It was in Paris that he gathered around him the group of men who would form the nucleus of the Society.

In August 1534 Ignatius and six companions covenanted together to make a pilgrimage to Jerusalem, where they intended to minister for the rest of their lives, and they were soon joined by three others. The group agreed, however, that if they could not find passage from Venice to Jerusalem within a year's time, they would then present themselves to the pope for service anywhere in the church. By 1537 they were all in Venice, where those who were not already priests were ordained. They spent their time preaching, hearing confessions, catechizing, and caring for the sick. As an easy way to identify themselves to inquirers, they adopted the name "Company of Jesus." Their life was formed in large part by the *Spiritual Exercises*, but it is unlikely at this point that they thought of themselves as a new monastic order. Unable to make it to Jerusalem by 1538, they traveled to Rome, where they secured an audience with the pope and continued performing the ministries that characterized their lives in Venice. As well, they guided others through Ignatius's *Spiritual Exercises*, including the influential Cardinal Gasparo Contarini, who is largely responsible for the pope's approval of the Jesuits. In the spring of 1539 the companions discussed and prayed about their future, eventually deciding to form a new order. They drew up a short form of life, called the "Formula of the Institute," that was approved by Paul III. According to the "Formula," the society is

> founded chiefly for this purpose: to strive especially for the defense and propagation of the faith and for the progress of the souls in Christian life and doctrine, by means of pubic preaching, lectures, and any other ministration whatsoever of the word of God, and further by means of the Spiritual Exercises, the education of children and unlettered persons in Christianity, and the spiritual consolation of Christ's faithful through hearing confessions and administering the other sacraments.[22]

As well, they were dedicated to "reconciling the estranged, in holily assisting and serving those who are found in prisons or hospitals, and indeed in performing any other works of charity, according to what will seem expedient for the glory of God and the common good."[23]

Though a religious order, the Jesuits never adopted a distinct habit, and many Jesuits simply wore black cassocks held together with a cincture. They were governed by General Congregations (similar to the traditional monastic General Chapter), whose decisions were enforced by the general of the order, who was elected for life and who appointed all other major superiors. From the start, obedience to the superior was a hallmark of the order, as was the fact that the order answered directly to the pope. In the words of the "Formula of the Institute": "This entire Society and the individual members who make their profession in it are campaigning for God under faithful obedience to His Holiness Pope Paul III and his successors in the Roman pontificate."

22. George E. Ganss, trans., *The Constitutions of the Society of Jesus* (St. Louis: Institute of Jesuit Sources, 1970), 66–67.
    23. Ibid.

This devotion to the pope went so far as to include "a special vow to carry out whatever the present and future Roman pontiffs may order."[24] Regarding the order's general, he was given all the "authority and power over the Society which are useful for its good administration, correction, and government."[25] The order expanded rapidly so that by 1615 there were 13,000 members in 32 provinces running 372 schools and 123 residences.[26] All this growth and expansion, no doubt, was largely attributable to the formation each Jesuit received by way of Ignatius's *Spiritual Exercises*, arguably the most influential sixteenth-century Catholic Reformation spiritual text.

The *Spiritual Exercises* is not a traditional spiritual text meant to be read for spiritual benefit. Rather, it is a manual to guide a set of exercises carried out by an exercitant, coupled with advice from a spiritual director. The text guides both the exercitant and the director over the course of their time together, ideally several times a day for a month, though it has always been adapted to the exercitant's needs and availability. The topics and directions were given in the form of conversations between the director and the exercitant with the purpose of ordering a person's life to God through discernment (confirmed with consolation) and training the exercitant to contemplate the presence and action of God in all created things and in all of life's circumstances. Ignatius believed that God spoke directly to each person and that it was possible for each person to hear God's words clearly. This word from God was discerned in the soul and then acted upon. That a person discerned rightly was confirmed by the presence of consolation, defined as "that which occurs when some interior motion is caused within the soul through which it comes to be inflamed with love of its Creator and Lord."[27] The book opens with twenty introductory explanations followed by the "Principle and Foundation,"

> which presents the principles for the logic which functions through the rest of the book. It presents (1) an inspiring goal, eternal self-fulfillment as the purpose of life on earth; (2) the means to the goal, creatures rightly used; (3) a preliminary attitude for their wise use: making oneself "indifferent" or undecided until the sound reasons for choice appear; (4) a criterion of choice: Which option is likely to be more conducive to the end, greater praise or glory to God?[28]

24. Ibid., 68.

25. Ibid., 69.

26. John W. O'Malley, "The Society of Jesus," in *Religious Orders of the Catholic Reformation: In Honor of John C. Olin on His Seventy-Fifth Birthday*, ed. Richard L. DeMolen (New York: Fordham University Press, 1994), 157.

27. Ignatius of Loyola, *Spiritual Exercises* 316; George E. Ganss, ed., *Ignatius of Loyola: Spiritual Exercises and Selected Works* (New York: Paulist Press, 1991), 202.

28. Ganss, *Ignatius of Loyola*, 51.

The *Exercises* are then divided into four "Weeks." The first week of exercises is meant to assist the exercitant on the purgative way through the understanding of sin and its consequences as well as humanity's role in this. The second week concerns itself with the illuminative way—how to acquire Christlike virtues. The third and fourth weeks help the exercitant achieve the unitive way through exercises that establish habitual and intimate union with God. The *Exercises* close with a number of additional teachings, such as the "Three Methods of Praying" and the "Rules for the Discernment of Spirits."

The Carmelites

Another influential Catholic Reformation movement was the reformed Carmelites who came to be known as the Discalced ("Barefoot") Carmelites. The main protagonists in the reform of the Order of the Brothers of Our Lady of Mount Carmel, an order founded in the twelfth century, were Teresa of Avila and John of the Cross. Teresa of Avila (d. 1582) was born in 1515 into a merchant-class family who were descendants of Spanish Jews who converted to Christianity. At the age of twenty she entered the Carmelite Convent of the Incarnation in Avila, but she did so out of a fear of hell and not because she sensed, as yet, a monastic calling. The convent was home to the daughters of many of the city's wealthiest and most influential men, many of whom arrived at the monastery with their personal servants. This did not mean that they were not good nuns; it was simply a reflection of the times that Carmelite monastic life was more of an option for the well-to-do, who lived fairly well in the monastery. In 1538 Teresa fell seriously ill, spending three days in a coma. Upon awakening and regaining strength, Teresa read Francisco de Osuna's (d. 1540) *The Third Spiritual Alphabet*, from which she learned the concept of recollection, "a method of prayer based on a passive or quiet negation of self in order to receive God's communication without obstruction or distraction."[29] Despite her newfound spiritual vitality, Teresa was still forced to live in the unique social constraints of her convent. In her own words, "On the one hand God was calling me; on the other hand I was following the world."[30]

Nonetheless, Teresa threw herself into monastic life, and by 1554 she reports that a new conversion occurred within her as a result of two profound experiences: identifying with Jesus's sufferings after seeing a statue and reading

29. Jodi Bilinkoff, "Teresa of Jesus and Carmelite Reform," in DeMolen, *Religious Orders*, 168.

30. Teresa of Avila, *The Book of Her Life* 7.17; Kieran Kavanaugh and Otilio Rodriguez, trans., *The Collected Works of St. Teresa of Avila*, vol. 1, *The Book of Her Life, Spiritual Testimonies, Soliloquies* (Washington, DC: ICS Publications, 1976), 62.

about Augustine of Hippo's conversion in his *Confessions*. By the following
year she began to chronicle a series of frequent and profound religious experiences that included seeing visions, hearing voices, and entering into states of
mystical union with God. Though her spiritual director and confessor were
skeptical of these mystical visitations, Teresa's influence began to grow. The
final push in Teresa's journey that led her to reform the Carmelites was a vision of hell. She writes, "While I was in prayer one day, I suddenly found that,
without knowing how, I had seemingly been put in hell."[31] As a result of this
terrifying vision, she determined to follow the Carmelite rule more faithfully,
which led to her founding the Convent of St. Joseph in Avila in 1562. She
was joined there by eleven other nuns desirous, like Teresa, of following the
Carmelite rule faithfully and living a devoted life of Christian prayer. Soon
thereafter Teresa desired to found other monasteries dedicated to reform and
was given permission to do so, for both men and women, by the general of
the Carmelite order in 1567. As a result of this permission, she arranged to
meet John of the Cross.

John de Yepes (d. 1591) was born in 1542 in a small town near Avila, but
after the death of his father when he was three, his mother moved the family
to Medina, where John obtained a basic education and worked as a nurse
and alms seeker for the hospitals of Medina. At the same time he studied at
the local Jesuit school, demonstrating an intellectual acumen. When he was
twenty-one years old he was offered ordination to the priesthood so that he
could serve as chaplain at a hospital. He rejected this offer and instead joined
the Carmelites of Medina. After his profession he was sent to Salamanca,
where he studied philosophy and theology for four years. Because of his
intellectual giftedness, John was made prefect of studies at the Carmelite
College of San Andrés in Salamanca, but he continued to pursue his vision
of a monastic vocation by practicing austerity and following a contemplative
way of life. This strong ascetical, contemplative bent led John to consider
joining the Carthusians, but a move back to Medina in 1567 allowed him to
meet Teresa, who was looking for friars to adopt the reform that she had
initiated among the Carmelite nuns.

Teresa and John, along with a small group of other Carmelites, set off
on August 9, 1568, from Medina to Valladolid with the intention of making
another reformed foundation. After a few months under Teresa's teaching,
John left Valladolid to found the first reformed Carmelite friary in Duruelo,
midway between Avila and Salamanca. The beginning of this foundation is
dated to November 28, 1568. John was chosen as the house's novice master,

---

31. Teresa of Avila, *Book of Her Life* 32.1; Kavanaugh and Rodriguez, *Collected Works*, 1:213.

beginning his apostolate of spiritual direction that became a hallmark of the remainder of his life. Despite many more years of personal difficulties and challenges, such as John's imprisonment in 1577, the Carmelite reform solidified itself, gaining approval from Pope Gregory XIII (d. 1585) in June 1580 to form a separate province of Carmelites and become self-governing. In the understated words of Teresa, "Now we are all at peace, calced and discalced; no one can hinder us from serving our Lord."[32]

Teresa's spirituality is summed up well by the way in which she understands the degrees of prayer and her conception of spiritual growth as distilled in her mature work *The Interior Castle*, conceived in 1577. For Teresa there are four degrees of prayer—vocal prayer and discursive meditation, recollection, prayer of quiet, and mystical union—and the soul is more dependent on God with each successive stage. The first stage, vocal prayer, is just that, speaking to God with the mouth; with discursive meditation one works to control the senses by meditating on one's life and the life of Christ. With the second stage, recollection, the one who prays enters into herself to be with God; the pray-er begins to move beyond the use of the senses. The third stage, prayer of quiet, is a type of mystical, infused contemplation in which the faculties are stilled and have no wish to move because any movement hinders the soul from loving God. Finally, the fourth stage of prayer, mystical union, occurs when all the faculties are centered on God. Teresa also lays out the paradigmatic Christian journey by way of seven steps, the last four of which are understood to be mystical experience: (1) a state of grace in which the believer still loves the world; (2) an opening to the practice of prayer (while still in the world) through edifying books, sermons, and friendships; (3) a life of virtue by way of ascetical practices, times of recollection, opportunities to love neighbor, and good management of households; (4) experiencing spiritual consolations, as in the prayer of quiet; (5) an initial union with God; (6) growth in intimacy with God; and (7) spiritual marriage, defined as an experience of God that is not imaginative but intellectual in nature, resulting in forgetfulness of self, a great desire to suffer, no more longing for consolations, and a detachment from everything that does not benefit the soul.

John's spiritual theology is best distilled in the threefold path of purgation, betrothal, and spiritual marriage. John posits a ladder of ten steps to God: (1) the soul becomes sick for the glory of God; (2) the soul searches unceasingly for God; (3) the soul does good works; (4) the soul suffers and the flesh

32. Teresa of Avila, *The Foundations* 29.32; Kieran Kavanaugh and Otilio Rodriguez, trans., *The Collected Works of St. Teresa of Avila*, vol. 3, *The Book of Her Foundations, Minor Works* (Washington, DC: ICS Publications, 1985), 279.

is conquered; (5) the soul develops an impatient desire and longing for God; (6) the soul moves toward God, sensing his touch; (7) the soul is emboldened; (8) the soul lays hold of God as beloved; (9) the soul burns with love; and (10) the soul becomes one with God after death. Along the way the believer will experience the dark night of the senses wherein she will renounce all good things that she desires, as well as the dark night of the Spirit, characterized by alienation and isolation, so much so that the Christian is unable to pray and perform her usual duties. Both of these dark nights, however, are gifts from God and are used in a person's life to help bring one to union with God.

Ressourcement: Institutional Monasticism Can Be Consistent with Protestantism

While the Protestant Reformers were working out their theology of monasticism in light of soteriology, the Roman Catholic monastic reformers in Spain were concerning themselves with how monks and nuns could achieve intimate union with God. Though there are occasional hints in the Spanish mystics that monasticism is salvific, this was never a central focus of their monastic vision. Whereas Luther and Calvin were certainly right in their assessment of individual aspects of late medieval monasticism, it must always be kept in mind that they were also highly motived by their anti-Roman Catholic biases and polemics. For both Protestants and Roman Catholics of the sixteenth century, there was some good to be found in the institution of monasticism. Luther could imagine a monasticism that was the result of one's salvation, characterized by service to others and temporary vows. Calvin's vision of monasticism looked like the monasticism of the early church, with a strong ascetical bent; it was also characterized by the taking of temporary vows. For Calvin monasticism must be an extension of one's baptismal vows—not an "improvement" on one's baptismal vows—and certainly not a sign of someone's greater level of perfection. For Luther and Calvin salvation came first, with the good work of monasticism following as a fruit of one's faith and not a necessary condition of one's faith. Contrary to popular opinion, Luther and Calvin did not reject monasticism wholesale but re-envisioned it through a Protestant theological lens. This being the case, what prevents the Protestant church of today, especially the evangelical church, from championing a reinstitution of monasticism along the lines of Luther and Calvin?

The main impediment, it seems, to a Protestant reappropriation of institutionalized monasticism is the ongoing animosity of many Protestants toward the Roman Catholic Church. Though such anti-Roman and anti-Protestant polemic like that of the Reformation is now mostly witnessed only in evangelical fundamentalism and in traditionalist Catholicism, there is still an underlying suspicion of Roman Catholicism by many (though certainly not all) Protestant Christians. Despite the many positive steps over the past twenty years to overcome much of this suspicion and division (e.g., the Evangelicals and Catholics Together movement and the 1999 *Joint Declaration on the Doctrine of Justification* of the Roman Catholic Church and the Lutheran World Federation), there is still much work to be done. The ecumenicity born out of Vatican II continues to make ground while more and more Protestants are receptive to the practices of historical Roman Catholicism, including monasticism (along with spiritual direction and retreats, as discussed above).

Another positive sign of Protestantism's potential readoption of monasticism is the recovery of the teaching and practice of the ancient church, of which this book is but one example. Within Protestant evangelicalism, significant steps have been made in recovering the history of the Christian church, though there is more work to be done.[33] The outdated Protestant historiographies of the early and medieval church are now largely relegated to the dustbins of scholarship,[34] and the church's history is showing itself to be a rich source of renewal, a rediscovery that is paralleled in the post–Vatican II Roman Catholic Church. It seems unreasonable to think that the institution of monasticism would be wholly embraced by Protestants writ large, and evangelicals in particular, if the history of the church was not a rich, valid source from which to draw insight.[35] Hence, evangelicalism's newfound appreciation for Christian history seems to bode well for the potential adoption of historical monastic institutions.

33. InterVarsity Press's Ancient Christian Commentary on Scripture series and Reformation Commentary on Scripture series are examples of this *ressourcement*, along with Christopher Hall's *Reading Scripture with the Church Fathers* (Downers Grove, IL: InterVarsity, 1998) and *Learning Theology with the Church Fathers* (Downers Grove, IL: InterVarsity, 2002), and Timothy George's *Reading Scripture with the Reformers* (Downers Grove, IL: InterVarsity, 2011). The Bible in Medieval Tradition series, published by Eerdmans, is attempting to do for the Middle Ages what InterVarsity has done for the early church and Reformation-era church.

34. See Daniel H. Williams, *Retrieving the Tradition and Renewing Evangelicalism: A Primer for Suspicious Protestants* (Grand Rapids: Eerdmans, 1999).

35. On the value of the church's history for evangelical spirituality and spiritual formation, see Greg Peters, "Historical Theology and Spiritual Formation: A Call," *Journal of Spiritual Formation and Soul Care* 7, no. 2 (2014): 203–9.

13

Protestants and Monasticism
after the Reformation

Institutions do not die easily, especially if they are deeply rooted in the societal structures and mentality of culture. One of the most glaring examples that continues to be discussed in the American context is the institution of slavery and its effects throughout the past two centuries in the form of either explicit or implicit racism. Scholars debate about how entrenched racism is in the psyche of the American populace, but it seems plain from the recent immigration debates, for example, that racism still exists in the United States (and around the world). There is a longing in the fabric of the United States that hopes for and prays for an end to racism, that God's will would be done on earth as in heaven. Nonetheless, the deep-rootedness of American racism certainly goes back to the institution of slavery; though it was outlawed in the United States 150 years ago, its effects continue. Institutions and their accompanying mentalité die hard. The same is true of the institution of monasticism. Though it was entirely wiped out in England in the sixteenth century and though it did not find a sympathetic hearing among the Protestant churches writ large, there were still those who lamented its demise: "the removal or throwing away of many things [in the Reformation], and what had followed that, had thrown out the good with the evil and also done great harm to the truth . . . for example . . . the manifold orders and monasteries of monks and spirituals. . . . Alas, that men have stamped out the grand."[1] This chapter will concern itself with the ongoing monastic presence within Protestantism from the late sixteenth century down to the present, discussing the monastic theology of such authors as Karl Barth, Dietrich Bonhoeffer, Donald Bloesch, Jonathan Wilson-Hartgrove, Shane Claiborne, and Scott Bessenecker. In addition, the reintroduction of institutionalized monasticism into the Anglican church in the nineteenth century will be examined, as will the current movement within the larger evangelical Protestant church known as the "New Monasticism." This chapter will demonstrate that in spite of the Reformation's measured reaction against monasticism, it never fully ceased to exist in the Protestant churches.

Protestant Monastics

Space constraints limit a full investigation into Protestant thought concerning monasticism since the time of the Reformation.[2] Suffice it to say that even in those areas where the institution itself went away, a consistent sentiment still expressed that the loss of the institution of monasticism should be mourned and even that it should be reinstituted along lines consistent with Reformational theology. For example, the twelfth-century Cistercian abbey of Loccum became a "Protestant monastery" in 1593. Once the monastery converted to Protestantism and adopted the Augsburg Confession, the monks no longer took vows of poverty, chastity, and obedience. Rather, the community was composed of married Lutheran clergyman. Here and elsewhere, especially in Germany, many monasteries came over to the Reformation, continuing to live according to the rules of the Cistercians, Augustinians, and Benedictines, or at least adopting versions of these monastic rules. According to a sermon from the Protestant monastery of Loccum, it is a contradiction in terms to talk about a monk without a rule. Therefore, the Loccum abbey followed the *Rule of Benedict* (RB) along with the statutes of the Cistercian order in such a way that the "Protestant religion is not revoked or changed." In the words of Dorothea Wendebourg, "These communities followed strict rules in the tradition of the old orders, which included obedience toward the abbot/abbess or prior/prioress, celibacy, monastic hours, and a monastic habit. There were

---

1. Jodocus van Lodenstein, *The Contemplation of Zion* (1674), quoted in Carl J. Schroeder, *In Quest of Pentecost: Jodocus van Lodenstein and the Dutch Second Reformation* (Lanham, MD: University Press of America, 2001), 83.
2. See Greg Peters, *Reforming the Monastery: Protestant Theologies of the Religious Life* (Eugene, OR: Cascade, 2014).

no vows."[3] The rejection of vows, of course, was one of the sticking points of monasticism according to Martin Luther and John Calvin, so it is not surprising that a Protestant monasticism would not have vows and would include married couples. The Little Gidding community, mentioned briefly in the last chapter, was an attempt to bring monasticism back into the Church of England, demonstrating that not everyone in the British Isles was against the institution. John Bramhall (d. 1663), archbishop of Armagh in Ireland, writes that under certain conditions he did "not see why monasteries might not agree well enough with reformed devotion."[4]

Yet it was only in the nineteenth century that monasticism was permanently reintroduced into the Church of England, with other Protestant traditions following the next century. Marion Hughes (d. 1912) was the daughter of an Anglican priest who had heard John Henry Newman (d. 1890) preach and had read his *The Church of the Fathers*. As well, Hughes came to know Edward Pusey (d. 1882) through a mutual friend and through her cousin, the rector of an Oxford parish. These friendships were significant because Newman and Pusey, founders and leaders of the Oxford Movement (or Tractarians), were the most vocal supporters of the reintroduction of monasticism into the Church of England. Despite access to a monastery that she could enter, Hughes took the traditional monastic vows of poverty, chastity, and obedience before Pusey at a private home on Trinity Sunday (June 6) 1841. After making her vows she received communion from Newman at St. Mary's Church, Oxford, with Newman aware that she had just taken vows. Hughes wrote in her diary that evening:

> This day Trinity Sunday, 1841, was I enrolled one of Christ's Virgins, espoused to Him and made His handmaid and may He of His infinite mercy grant that I may ever strive to please Him, and to keep myself from the world though still in it, and should it be most mercifully granted that an opportunity may be given me to separate myself entirely from it, make me to rejoice in the means of taking the burden of His cross more closely to myself.[5]

Because of Hughes's family obligations she was unable to immediately found an institution, which was her only option given the lack of Anglican monasteries. In the meantime she traveled to France, visiting various Roman Catholic communities of nuns to study their rules and constitutions. Ten

---

3. Dorothea Wendebourg, "Luther on Monasticism," in *The Pastoral Luther: Essays on Martin Luther's Practical Theology*, ed. Timothy J. Wengert (Grand Rapids: Eerdmans, 2009), 351.

4. John Bramhall, *The Works of the Most Reverend Father in God, John Bramhall, D.D.*, vol. 1 (Oxford: John Henry Parker, 1842), 120.

5. Quoted in A. M. Allchin, *The Silent Rebellion: Anglican Religious Communities 1845–1900* (London: SCM Press, 1958), 59.

years later, in 1851, she was able to establish the community of the Society of the Holy and Undivided Trinity in Oxford, of which she remained the head until her death.

Yet before Hughes was able to set up her community, other Anglican sisterhoods came into existence. Although Hughes was the first woman to take monastic vows in the Church of England since the sixteenth century, there was a rush of new nuns during the 1840s. To illustrate, on March 26, 1845, two sisters arrived in London to form the nucleus of a new foundation being set up under the direction of a committee who concluded that a women's community should visit the poor and the sick in their own homes; visit hospitals, workhouses, and prisons; feed, clothe, and instruct destitute children; and assist in burying the dead. These two women were joined by the bishop of Edinburgh's daughter, and soon thereafter four more women arrived. The community took the name Sisterhood of the Holy Cross. Elsewhere, Henry Phillpotts (d. 1869), bishop of Exeter, placed an appeal in the *Guardian* newspaper on January 1, 1848, asking for additional workers to minister to the vast population of Devonport, a suburb of Plymouth, in the southwest of England. Priscilla Lydia Sellon (d. 1876) replied to the letter, setting up a home for orphaned daughters of poor sailors, with assistance from another young woman. Bishop Phillpotts approved the effort, giving the two women the name The Church of England Sisterhood of Mercy of Devonport and Plymouth and blessing them on October 27, 1848, during which the two women consecrated themselves to God, regarding this as their formal profession and consecration as Sisters of Mercy. In 1856 the nascent communities of Hughes and Sellon merged together to form the Congregation of Religious of the Society of the Most Holy Trinity. By the end of the twentieth century, there were many Anglican communities of both men and women, with hundreds of monastics. Without a doubt the institution of monasticism was fully restored in the Church of England, though the hope for such a reinstitution had never gone away completely.

In Lutheran Germany and among the Reformed (i.e., Calvinistic) churches, a fully mature monasticism returned only in the twentieth century. In 1836 pastor Theodor Fliedner (d. 1864) established an order of deaconesses in the United Church of Prussia after being exposed to Moravian deaconesses. These single women spent their days in prayer and work (either medical, domestic, or educational) and have subsequently been judged to be "a Protestant religious community, modelled in many ways upon the Roman Catholic Sisters of Charity."[6] But it was the Lutheran Wilhelm Loehe (d. 1872), building upon

6. Frederick S. Weiser, "Communal Ministries in Lutheranism: The Historical Precedent," *American Benedictine Review* 19 (1968): 309.

the work of Fliedner, who made the deaconess movement part of the Lutheran church in Germany. Despite his strong Protestantism, Loehe came to accept the concept of a Protestant sisterhood: "Brotherhoods and sisterhoods are not a sign of a dead church, but rather of the still existing good will. Thus, the present diaconate, at a time of corruption in the folk churches, is the support and pillar of spiritual life."[7] Adopting monastic poverty and obedience, Loehe's deaconesses wore black dresses to announce their renunciation of the world and spent their days in prayer and acts of charity.

By the 1940s the Lutheran church of Germany was ready for yet an even more traditional form of monasticism. In 1942, a group of young women resolved to engage in evangelistic outreach to other women despite being outlawed by the Nazis. On Easter night of that year they promised fidelity to Jesus Christ, vowing that the gospel would be their rule of life. In time members began to live in community under the direction of a Roman Catholic Benedictine monk. By 1950 this group was living together as a community, and in 1958 it was received as a monastery by the council and bishop of the Lutheran church in Bavaria under the name of Communität Casteller Ring. This community, which still exists today, follows the RB, taking vows of chastity, common ownership of all property, and obedience. The sisters have four fixed prayer times each day and worship together as a community three times each week (Sunday, Tuesday, and Friday), celebrating the Eucharist together at each of these services. Their apostolate consists of educational ministries, spiritual direction, and, since 1996, the operation and maintenance of Martin Luther's former Augustinian priory in Erfurt, Germany. Similarly, from 1936 to 1944, Clara Schlink (d. 2001) and Erica Madauss (d. 1999) started several Bible study groups near Darmstadt for young women, which were so successful that by 1944 about 150 young women were involved. On the night of September 11–12, 1944, an air raid on Darmstadt by Allied forces nearly wiped out the city in twenty minutes, killing thirty thousand people. Many of the women in the Bible studies saw this as God's judgment and a sign that he was calling them to repentance and prayer for their sins and for the sins of the German nation. Organizing itself as the Ecumenical Community of the Sisters of Mary, this community was officially founded on March 30, 1947; it gathers daily for prayer (historically gathering for the full sevenfold monastic office) and is involved in various forms of ecumenical work and reconciliation ministries. They have spread across the world with communities in the United States, Canada, Australia, Brazil, Japan, and elsewhere.

7. Quoted in ibid., 311.

Karl Barth

While these communities were coming into being, there was an effort afoot, though not necessarily intentional, to provide a theological rationale for the reinstitution of monasticism into the Protestant church. The two most well-known advocates were Karl Barth and Dietrich Bonhoeffer. Karl Barth (d. 1968), who served as both a pastor and as a university professor, offered his most mature reflection on the institution of monasticism proper in volume 4, part 2, of his *Church Dogmatics*, published in 1955. This volume is dedicated to a theology of the reconciliatory work of Jesus Christ, which is a movement from above to below (Jesus's incarnation) but also a move from below to above (humankind's response to Jesus's incarnation). Barth discusses tendencies and movements connected to Jesus's reconciliatory ministry that are predominantly or even exclusively criticized, so he first turns his attention to the institution of monasticism. Why? Because in monasticism Barth sees a movement that is particularly significant to the question of humankind's role or response to God's act of reconciling the world to himself and because monasticism is characterized by a "wealth and complexity of continually new forms" that have asserted themselves almost since the beginnings of the church.[8] For Barth, the historicity of monasticism commends itself as an object of study, but the future, forward-looking aspect of monasticism is also commendable. Barth does not defend the sixteenth-century Reformers for the ways in which they rejected monasticism, but he is concerned that monasticism's reintroduction into evangelical Christianity does not swing back to the imbalance prevalent in monasticism prior to the Reformation, as highlighted by Luther and Calvin. Barth lays out his argument in several steps.

First, he considers the etymology of the word "monk," noting that it comes from the Greek word *monos* (alone). The need to be alone, for Barth, is natural, so he rejects any reading of early Christian monasticism that accounts for it in dualistic terms—that is, believing that the spiritual is better than the material. A desire to flee the world is evident outside of Christianity as well, so such a desire does not necessarily mean that a flight from the world is a flight to God. The well-populated deserts of the third century, says Barth, were not culturally motivated but were the result of a human response to the transitory nature of life, which often feels empty. The deserts grew out of the apostolic urge toward ascetic activity that benefitted the whole church. Yet this communal tendency did not materialize into particular forms of

8. Karl Barth, *Church Dogmatics*, vol. 4, *The Doctrine of Reconciliation*, part 2, trans. G. W. Bromiley (Edinburgh: T&T Clark, 1958), 11.

community; that came later "with the special assistance of grace."[9] Barth then turns his attention to the "material question" of monasticism, that is, whether the need to withdraw from the world has only a negative connotation. For Barth, there are positive reasons to retreat from the world, such as protest against the world or flight from the worldly church.[10] This allows the one who flees to mount an effective counterattack against the world and the worldly church. For example, Barth sees this as characteristic of Benedictine monasticism throughout the ages as it stood up to misguided politicians. For Barth, however, the most germane question is whether all genuine Christian commitment involves some sort of separation from the world for the purpose of reengaging it more critically and Christianly: "Can there be either for the Church or for individuals any genuine approach to the world or men unless there is an equally genuine retreat?"[11] Yet Barth does not view monasticism through rose-colored glasses; he is fully aware of monasticism's inordinate emphasis on asceticism, including withdrawal for all the wrong reasons—perhaps as a result of an implicit dualism.

This dualistic tendency often worked itself out in monasticism's fear of engaging in unlawful sexual activity, fear that money and possessions keep one sinfully involved in the world, and fear that the traditional vows of chastity and poverty become meaningless if not entered into in the most ascetical manner manageable. Barth views this as a distorted understanding of asceticism and believes that if a proper understanding of asceticism could be achieved, then helpful ascetical practices would maintain a proper balance and serve one's greater end of flight from the world. Asceticism helps the Christian overcome sin and brings liberation, so that the believer is better prepared to serve God and his neighbor. Those who have fled the world and the church for right reasons and who engage correctly in asceticism are properly called monks and nuns. Though institutionalized forms of monasticism fail at times to maintain this balance, they should not detract from the fact that monasticism's true nature is one of flight and *askēsis*, says Barth. Monasticism is a "consistent orientation" of grace that ministers to grace-filled individuals, which "cannot be suppressed" because it was the church's response to the early problem of the "de-eschatologising and secularizing of [the church's] life and message."[12] Monks and nuns exist so that when some church members choose sleepiness and indolence, the church still has her vigilant and diligent members by way

9. Ibid., 13.
10. The worldly church for Barth was certainly the Nazi-infected German state churches of the 1930s and 1940s.
11. Barth, *Church Dogmatics*, 4:14.
12. Ibid., 4:15.

of her monks and nuns. Any other kind of monasticism is not true monasticism. For Barth the "normal monk" is one

> whose life did not at all consist in an unceasing conflict with the different *libidines* [i.e., lusts] of the flesh, but could and can be relatively quiet and continuously and richly and fruitfully occupied with spiritual and physical labour, with all kinds of arts and serious scholarship, with the exercise of hospitality and works of charity, even with preaching and pastoral work among the people, with social work and teaching, and above all with the supremely monastic *opus Dei* [i.e., work of God], the *officium* [i.e., the daily office of prayer], the adoration of God in private and communal worship, and above and beyond all this . . . with a whole range of other and very inward problems of individual and social morality.[13]

In short, Barth does not reject the institution of monasticism; rather, he commends it as a correction to the corrosive effects of the world and a worldly church. Monasticism reforms the church and is necessary for its well-being.

Dietrich Bonhoeffer

Dietrich Bonhoeffer (d. 1945) (Barth's colleague and confrere in the Confessing Church, which stood up to the Third Reich) outlined his vision of monasticism in two works: the *Cost of Discipleship* and *Life Together*. *Discipleship* (published in 1937) was written to address the tension between what Bonhoeffer calls "costly grace" and "cheap grace." Cheap grace "is preaching forgiveness without repentance; it is baptism without the discipline of community; it is the Lord's Supper without confession of sin; it is absolution without personal confession. Cheap grace is grace without discipleship, grace without the cross, grace without the living, incarnate Jesus Christ."[14] Costly grace calls the believer to true discipleship and into a life of following Jesus Christ no matter the circumstances or consequences. Costly grace, says Bonhoeffer, is characteristic of Jesus and his disciples and thereby should be characteristic of all Christianity. Bonhoeffer believes that costly grace fell out of favor once the church expanded and was secularized. This cheapened grace, but a form of costly grace endured: monasticism. He writes, "It was decisive that monasticism did not separate from the church and that the church had the good sense to tolerate monasticism. Here, on the boundary of the church, was the place where the awareness that grace is costly and that grace includes

13. Ibid., 4:15–16.
14. Dietrich Bonhoeffer, *Discipleship*, trans. Barbara Green and Reinhard Krauss (Minneapolis: Fortress Press, 2001), 44.

discipleship was preserved."[15] By allowing monasticism, however, the church actually created a kind of two-tier Christianity, one for the spiritual elite who lived according to costly grace (e.g., monks and nuns) and everyone else who chose cheap grace instead. The mistake of monasticism was that it created a way for a select few to become extraordinary, and it was only a matter of time before these overachievers claimed a special merit for their lifestyle.

Bonhoeffer believed, however, that this division was done away with, ironically, by the monk Martin Luther. Luther's overscrupulosity and "failure" as a monk led him to see that discipleship is not about meritorious actions but is a commandment for all Christians. Thus "Luther had to leave the monastery and reenter the world, not because the world itself was good and holy, but because even the monastery was nothing else but world."[16] Elitist monasticism was the enemy of the church since it perpetuated a dualistic view of the spiritual life. Luther made the church a monastery. Bonhoeffer did not think that this negated a place for monasticism in the church, but any future monasticism would have to resist becoming an instrument of cheap grace. Bonhoeffer viewed monasticism positively enough to famously quip (in another work) that the "restoration of the church will surely come from a sort of new monasticism which has in common with the old only the uncompromising attitude of a life lived according to the Sermon on the Mount in the following of Christ. I believe it is now time to call people to this."[17]

Bonhoeffer's most mature thoughts on the monastic life are found in the pages of *Life Together* (published in 1939), a work that grew out of his oversight of a seminary set up at Finkenwalde to train pastors for the Confessing Church. Bonhoeffer believed that the divinity schools of the 1930s were inadequate to train pastors, who needed to be in "church-monastic schools" in order to learn pure doctrine, be trained in prayer, and become Sermon on the Mount–kind of disciples.[18] Within the seminary Bonhoeffer created a subgroup of students known as the House of Brethren. One of the former members of this group later referred to it as a monastery with four goals: to make members better preachers; to further the discipleship of its members; to renounce personal prerogative for the purpose of serving others; and to create a spiritual refuge for pastors who needed to regain strength through retreat. Though the seminary and the House of Brethren were closed by the Gestapo in 1937, the experiment gave Bonhoeffer the ideas that would be included in *Life Together*, distilled in five

15. Ibid., 46.
16. Ibid., 48.
17. Geffrey B. Kelly and F. Burton Nelson, eds., *A Testament to Freedom: The Essential Writings of Dietrich Bonhoeffer*, rev. ed. (San Francisco: HarperSanFrancisco, 1995), 424.
18. Ibid.

chapters: Community, The Day with Others, The Day Alone, Ministry and Confession, and Communion. For Bonhoeffer this community would not be a life dedicated to contemplation but would be characterized by love of God and service to others. Christian community was natural, so a life together only strengthened the Christian in her life of discipleship. True community is a spiritual community, characterized by common worship, common praying, common hearing of the Word of God, and common meal-taking. The full day of work, educational endeavors, and pastoral ministries were also set up so as not to hinder one's prayer life. Members of the community were expected to find time to practice silence and solitude, out of which grows meditation, prayer, and intercession. By the end of *Life Together* it is obvious that Bonhoeffer has laid out a rule of life similar to the RB. There is a lot of overlap in Bonhoeffer's and Benedict's visions of communal living:[19]

Bonhoeffer's *Life Together*	*Rule of Benedict*
Psalm reading	Chapters 8–19
Scripture reading (Old and New Testaments)	Chapters 9.8; 10.2; 11.6–9; 12.4; 13.9–11; 73.3
Hymn singing	Chapters 9.4; 11.8, 10; 12.4; 13.11; 17.3–5; 18.8
Common/Free prayer	Chapter 20
Work	Chapter 48
Mid-day devotion	Chapter 16
Evening devotion	Chapters 16; 17.7–10; 42
Solitude/Silence	Chapters 6; 7.56–58; 38.5; 42.1; 52.2
Meditation	Chapters 8.3; 48.23; 58.5
Personal prayer	Chapter 52

Without a doubt, Bonhoeffer's vision of life together for Christians was monastic in its inspiration and in its structure. Though Bonhoeffer's life was cut short by the Nazis, it is likely that he desired to set up a proper monastic community based on the principles in *Life Together*.

Revaluing Monasticism

By the mid-twentieth century Protestant monasticism was flourishing in Europe (Anglican monasticism in England, Lutheran monasticism in Germany, and Reformed monasticism at Taizé in France and Iona in Scotland), the United

19. The chart is taken from Peters, *Reforming the Monastery*, 120.

States, and in many other countries of the world, especially where Anglicans and Lutherans were predominant. Its existence brought it into the mainstream of Protestant thought. For example, Peter Monkres, a pastor in the United Church of Christ writing in the popular magazine *The Christian Century* in 1979, said that the mainline Protestant churches of North America needed to reintroduce monasticism in order to provide unemployed clergy an opportunity to fulfill their ministerial calling. He writes, "One possibility for achieving this goal is by creating networks of religious communities—a new monastic order for ministers and their families who either cannot find parishes or who seek alternatives to traditional forms of parish ministry."[20] The communities would be a place in which to undertake a search for God in meditation, prayer, and liturgy. They would also be centers for the care of souls. In the following year the same publication published another call to Protestants to reintroduce monasticism into its ranks. James Baker, a Southern Baptist professor at Western Kentucky University, writes, "Protestantism is not necessarily antimystical, but it has always been antimonastic. . . . Every church needs bishops, preachers, counselors, scholars and monks. Protestants, most of us, have all but the last of these, and in their absence could lie the key to one of our most debilitating deficiencies: our spiritual witness." Baker, however, notes that Protestants are certainly not interested in the three qualities that define monasticism: poverty, obedience, and chastity. This leaves us with a "chronic Protestant spiritual deficiency": we are not an "authentically prayerful people."[21] Thus Protestants need a form of monasticism that will restore this lost dimension of spirituality, says Baker.

By the mid-1980s the evangelical church also began to see value in monasticism. In 1988 Rodney Clapp wrote an editorial for *Christianity Today* titled "Remonking the Church." This editorial distills the vices of the contemporary church such as violence, sensuality, and materialism, noting that the evangelical church adopts softer versions of the larger culture. To counteract this tendency, writes Clapp, the evangelical church needs to engage in a process of remonasticization:

> The remonasticization we would support would not be as tightly defined as traditional monasticism. It would not, for example, mean the stereotypical cluster of people retiring to desert solitude. Rather, it would look to the biblical antecedents for a select group of holy persons set apart to call all persons to holiness, such as the Old Testament Nazirites, Israel's witness as a light to all nations, and Jesus' calling of disciples to train and teach with the goal of

20. Peter R. Monkres, "An Innovative Ministry for Surplus Clergy," *Christian Century*, February 7–14, 1979, 148.
21. James T. Baker, "Benedict's Children and Their Separated Brothers and Sisters," *Christian Century*, December 3, 1980, 1192–93.

drawing all Israel to the same discipleship. And, of course, there is the church itself—which is supposed to be no more than it hopes the world will someday be. In this context, remonasticization might take several forms, all oriented towards service in and to the world.[22]

Unmarried believers would live together in community, witnessing together against violence, materialism, and a sinful sexuality. As well, families could purchase homes in the same neighborhood to meet daily for common worship and mutual discipleship. Older, retired Christians could form communities of worship, Bible study, and service in the world. For Clapp, evangelical monastics would resist the church's secularization and recover a life of prayer.

A good portion of this newfound familiarity with monasticism among American Protestants came through the work of Donald Bloesch (d. 2010), particularly by way of his *Centers of Christian Renewal* and *Wellsprings of Renewal.*[23] After exposure to a number of Anglo-Catholic monastic communities in England during a post-doctoral year abroad, Bloesch made his way to France, Switzerland, Italy, and Germany, visiting a number of communities on the way.[24] This exposure to Protestant monastic life in the mid-1950s remained with Bloesch throughout his life, and he returned to discussions of monasticism throughout his publishing career. Simply put, Bloesch viewed these communities as centers for genuine spiritual renewal in the Christian church and always maintained that these institutions are necessary in the Protestant church. Yet Bloesch was cautious about his approbation of monasticism given his concerns that monasticism often gave way to an erroneous mysticism, Pharisaism, and rigorism:

> The eremitic and monastic ways are constantly threatened by a false kind of mysticism in which one's attention is turned away from the anguish of the world to the vision of God. The call to the cloister is also bedeviled by Pharisaism, in which one falls into the delusion that one is making oneself morally acceptable to God and therefore superior to the ordinary Christian. Closely related are the pitfalls of legalism, where monastic works are made a condition for salvation, and of rigorism, in which strictness of living is deemed necessary to arrive at life's spiritual goal.[25]

22. Rodney Clapp, "Remonking the Church," *Christianity Today*, August 12, 1988, 20.

23. Donald Bloesch, *Centers of Christian Renewal* (Philadelphia: United Church Press, 1964); and idem, *Wellsprings of Renewal: Promise in Christian Communal Life* (Grand Rapids: Eerdmans, 1974).

24. For a full exploration of Donald Bloesch's theology of monasticism, see Greg Peters, "The Place of Monasticism in the Thought of Donald Bloesch," in *Church, Society and Monasticism: Acts of the International Symposium, Rome, May 31–June 3, 2006*, ed. Eduardo López-Tello García and Benedetta Selene Zorzi (St. Ottilien, Ger.: EOS Klosterverlag, 2009), 261–74.

25. Donald Bloesch, *The Struggle of Prayer* (San Francisco: Harper & Row, 1980), 144.

In short, Bloesch's concerns center around three important tensions: (1) substituting a mystical-based soteriology for that of the Reformational justification by faith; (2) falsely creating a spiritual dichotomy between those who enter the monastic life and those living a non-monastic Christian life; and (3) mistaking the nature of the monastic life as somehow more salvific than God's offer of free grace extended to all believers. In reaction to these perceived understandings, Bloesch attempted to craft a theology of the monastic life that would avoid these tendencies.

Though Bloesch understood the history of monasticism, he had little room for a monasticism dedicated to a cloistered, contemplative life. For Bloesch, monasteries should be centers of mission and evangelism, built around the natural family and set within the doctrinal context of justification by grace. Bloesch's most mature presentation of an evangelical, Protestant monasticism is found in his *The Church: Sacraments, Worship, Ministry, Mission* (published in 2002). He offers six "guiding principles" for a Protestant monasticism. First, the natural family should be the paradigm for monastic life contra the inherent anti-sex stance in much of monastic history. Whereas the Bible commands humankind to be fruitful and to multiply, historical monasticism has often said not to be fruitful and not to multiply. It appears, then, that Bloesch has a vision for Protestant monasticism that would welcome not only married couples but also children. Second, in agreement with Luther and Calvin, Bloesch rightly insists that monasticism is not salvific but is built on the Protestant doctrine of justification by grace alone. Monasticism is "a sign that justification has already been accomplished through the atoning death and glorious resurrection of our Lord Jesus Christ."[26] Given that all Christians are bound by the gospel's imperative of living wholly unto God, monasticism is not a superior way of life but just a different vocational calling for some. In Calvin's parlance, we are all bound by our baptismal vows. Third, Protestant monasteries will be centers of evangelism and world mission: "It will be both a training center for mission and a locus of mission. A concerted attempt will be made to draw those who come for retreats into personal faith in Jesus Christ."[27] Thus the spiritual center of the monastery, the chapel, will be not just a place for prayer but also a place for proclamation because faith comes through hearing the Word of God (Rom. 10:17). Fourth, the community's prayer will be both personal and corporate, including adoration, confession, thanksgiving, and petition. Any sense of mystical prayer is rejected by Bloesch due to its Neoplatonic heritage.

26. Donald Bloesch, *The Church: Sacraments, Worship, Ministry, Mission* (Downers Grove, IL: InterVarsity, 2002), 215.
    27. Ibid., 216.

The praying monk in a Protestant monastery intercedes with God on behalf of the world, not because he searches for God, but because God has already found him and he desires for others to come to God too. Prayer is our response to God's coming down to us in humility. Fifth, a Protestant monastery "will not claim to be an embodiment of the kingdom of God, nor will it set out to build the kingdom of God on earth."[28] Rather, it will be a sign of and a witness to the kingdom that is yet to come. The monastery stands under God's judgment in the kingdom; therefore, it must be ever mindful of reforming itself and of being purified by the Holy Spirit. Finally, Protestant monasteries must be intimately connected to local Protestant churches. They must be accountable to the local church and be a full partner in mission. In short, and as an echo to the thought of Barth, "The purpose is not to sunder the lines of communication with the wider church but to make an impact on the church through word and life and thereby contribute to its revitalization. The community must sound the call to periodic withdrawal from the tempests of the world but withdrawal only for the sake of return, this time on a deeper level."[29]

New Monasticism

As can be seen from the preceding, there is a remarkable continuity of thought from Luther and Calvin down to Barth, Bonhoeffer, and Bloesch. This is not surprising given that the latter three were all faithful students of Reformation thought, that Barth and Bonhoeffer worked together in the Confessing Church, and that Bloesch had studied with Barth in Basel during a sabbatical. This consistent representation and vision of Protestant monasticism, however, took a more radical turn beginning in 2004. In June of that year a conference was held in Durham, North Carolina, at which sixty practitioners of communal living, along with a number of academics, gathered together to give shape to an emerging movement that beforehand was composed of disparate and unrelated individuals and intentional communities. At the conference the "12 Marks of New Monasticism" were discussed and elaborated on:

1. Relocate to the abandoned places of Empire.
2. Share economic resources with fellow community members and the needy among us.
3. Provide hospitality to the stranger.

28. Ibid.
29. Ibid., 217.

4. Lament for racial divisions within the church and our communities, and actively pursue a just reconciliation.

5. Humbly submit to Christ's body, the church.

6. Provide intentional formation in the way of Christ and the rule of the community along the lines of the old novitiate.

7. Nurture common life among members of the intentional community.

8. Support celibate singles alongside monogamous married couples and their children.

9. Live in geographical proximity with community members who share a common rule of life.

10. Care for the plot of God's earth given to us and support local economies.

11. Practice peacemaking and conflict resolution in the midst of violence within communities along the lines of Matthew 18.

12. Commit to a disciplined, contemplative life.[30]

It must be noted that this movement grew out of intentional communities, and only after this conference did they come to be known as the New Monastics, practicing the so-called New Monasticism.[31] Three of the main proponents of this movement have offered reflections on monasticism.

The most well-known and vocal supporter and practitioner of the New Monasticism is Jonathan Wilson-Hartgrove (b. 1980), who articulates his vision of monasticism most succinctly in his *New Monasticism* of 2008. First, monasticism's place is at the margins of cities and towns, not in the center of corporate America but in "the abandoned places of Empire," to borrow a phrase from the "12 Marks of New Monasticism." It is here, says Wilson-Hartgrove, that the church discovers that God is at work in the people and in the places that have been given up on by society. New monastics move into these locations in order to offer compassion and hope for those who rarely receive compassion and are often hopeless. The purpose of moving to these locations is not just to offer something to the populace but to learn from them. Unlike a large percentage of monks and nuns in Christian history who fled to the desert (whether this desert was real or imagined) in order to move away from people, the new monastics commend moving somewhere between the city and the desert, finding there the easily forgotten who are in need of

---

30. The Rutba House, ed., *School(s) for Conversion: 12 Marks of a New Monasticism* (Eugene, OR: Cascade, 2005), xii–xiii.

31. For an overview of the movement, see Erik C. Carter, "The New Monasticism: A Literary Introduction," *Journal of Spiritual Formation and Soul Care* 5, no. 2 (2012): 268–84.

assistance and redemption. This is a vision of monasticism more akin to the canons and friars. Second, new monastics adhere to God's economy and not the economic structures of society. Given the large divide between those who have and those who do not, new monastics commit themselves to organizing their communities around a vision of God's economy, which involves having one's daily needs met as well as being the agent for helping to meet others' daily needs. The biblical image for this, writes Wilson-Hartgrove, is the Lord's Table, where the church is fed by God with Christ's body and blood. Thus whomever one shares the Eucharist with must also be one whom one is willing to feed with material food. For some new monastic communities this means maintaining a strict common purse à la Acts 4:32. Others adopt a common standard of living wherein each community member contributes a set amount of his or her income to the community and then is allowed a fixed amount for discretionary spending. Despite these differing ways of practicing their economics or, to use more traditional language, practicing their poverty, it is important that each community "share a conviction that it really is possible to share what we have in common and trust God for our daily bread."[32]

Third, new monastics will also serve as a new kind of Peace Corps, albeit one that fights evil with the weapons of the Spirit, all the while calling the church back to practices of peace. This will often be worked out at the local level where the new monastics fight against implicit and explicit racism, but it will, on occasion, rise to the level of international warfare when the new monastics join organizations, such as Christian Peacemaker Teams, to stand against violent warfare around the globe. Wilson-Hartgrove refers to this as "getting in the way," emphasizing that it takes courage and citing as an example his many arrests for trespassing related to the public execution of four men in North Carolina. In Wilson-Hartgrove's estimation, "a concerted effort to invest in peacemaking would go a long way toward making real the alternative that Jesus taught and practiced."[33] Fourth, a new monastic community will nurture a culture of grace and truth. They will do this by grassroots ecumenism and by engaging in good works through service to one another in the community and beyond. Wilson-Hartgrove sees the primary work of the communities to be the proclamation and distribution of God's grace. Finally, in line with Bloesch, Wilson-Hartgrove writes that the new monastics will be fully integrated into the church and work alongside the church, not as parachurch organizations, but as "a *prochurch* movement."[34] True discipleship

32. Jonathan Wilson-Hartgrove, *New Monasticism: What It Has to Say to Today's Church* (Grand Rapids: Brazos, 2008), 96.
33. Ibid., 124.
34. Ibid., 147, emphasis in original.

happens in the church, and to assume otherwise is to trivialize the church as God's agent of defeating the powers of darkness in this world.

Wilson-Hartgrove's move toward intentional community and ultimately to the New Monasticism was initiated by the time he spent at Shane Claiborne's Simple Way community in Philadelphia. Claiborne (b. 1975) founded the community in 1998 after being exposed to the plight of people in Philadelphia's Kensington neighborhood in 1996, when he and a number of other students from Eastern University worked with the local homeless community to stop the eviction and destruction of a former church building that was housing a host of homeless persons. Their way of life, described in a 2005 *Christianity Today* article, includes working part-time jobs and returning a portion of this income to the community to pay for living expenses.[35] Members devote themselves to personal Bible study and prayer, Simple Way activities, or local ministries. A hallmark of the community is their advocacy on behalf of the poor and homeless, though they also spend time tutoring local schoolchildren. At the end of the day, Claiborne views himself as someone who lives "authentically small and evangelically large," to use his words.

Though Claiborne was featured on the cover of the *Christianity Today* issue dedicated to the new monasticism, the accompanying article also made reference to the "new friars." These new friars have been given definition in the writings of Scott Bessenecker. Bessenecker understands "friar" as someone who ministers incarnationally, that is, someone who rejects the comforts of the so-called developed world and adopts the majority world's perspective(s), engaging in intentional ministry. The book *Living Mission*, edited by Bessenecker, describes the new friars: in addition to being incarnational, they are devotional, communal, missional, and marginal.[36] In today's world this intentional, incarnational ministry often takes the form of people moving into slum communities, living alongside and in a similar manner to those who are from the slums and relegated to the slums because of poverty. In his *The New Friars*, Bessenecker uses the same five adjectives to describe the new friars: incarnational, devotional, communal, missional, and marginal.

To be incarnational is to break "out of the padding that separates and protects us from the harsh realities of poverty by embracing it voluntarily and stepping into relationship with the poor without the power dynamic that is usually present between poor and nonpoor."[37] For Bessenecker, "devotional" primarily means

---

35. Rob Moll, "The New Monasticism," *Christianity Today*, September 2005, 38–46.

36. Scott A. Bessenecker, *Living Mission: The Vision and Voices of New Friars* (Downers Grove, IL: InterVarsity, 2010).

37. Scott A. Bessenecker, *The New Friars: The Emerging Movement Serving the World's Poor* (Downers Grove, IL: InterVarsity, 2006), 76.

sharing in the sufferings of Jesus Christ, who himself was homeless and voiceless. Thus to live among the poor and marginalized is to suffer and identify with Jesus in ways that would be difficult to achieve when living in material overabundance. The new friars value a devotional life because "without intimacy with Jesus we have nothing to give away to others."[38] The communal aspect of being a new friar is worked out by living in community with and sharing one's possessions with those in need. Bessenecker and the new friars reject a philosophy of service that would recommend living apart from those to whom one ministers. It is not communal to live in material abundance in a private neighborhood twenty miles from the slums of Manila and expect to have a fruitful ministry to those who live daily in the slum itself. Bessenecker understands that it goes against Western sensibilities to live closely intertwined lives with those who are not blood relatives. Sharing possessions, space, and time with the poor and outcast does not fit with a Western mentality. But the new friars believe that by doing this they are demonstrating that there is enough material means for everyone to live well if no one lives extravagantly. Their missional commitment takes the form of leaving their family and comfort zones and moving to places of real need. This is modeled on Jesus's own post-resurrection ministry to his followers, in which he taught them to bring people into his kingdom. Finally, the new friars strive to be at the margins of society, those places "just on the outside of acceptability."[39] They live among the displaced and the nomadic, ministering to the prostitute, the former sex slave, and the drug addict. They search the darkest alleys and dirtiest streets for those in need. Bessenecker summarizes:

- incarnational—tearing down the insulation and becoming real to those in trouble
- devotional—making intimacy with Christ our all-consuming passion
- communal—intentionally creating interdependence with others
- missional—looking outside ourselves
- marginal—being countercultural in a world that beckons us to assimilate at the cost of our conscience[40]

Unapologetically, the new friars' way of life is loosely based on Francis of Assisi's rejection of his father's lucrative cloth business in order to live among the poor, the sick, and the marginal. The new friars are mostly trying to emulate the friars of old.

38. Ibid., 104.
39. Ibid., 135.
40. Ibid., 172.

Ressourcement: Ongoing Presence of Monasticism in Protestant Churches

Without doubt, there has always been a monastic impetus and impulse in the Protestant church. At times this has manifested itself in the foundation and propagation of traditional monastic communities, especially in the Anglican, Lutheran, and Reformed churches. More recently this monastic presence has begun to appear in the evangelical churches in the form of the New Monastic movement—including the new friars—and among individuals who have taken traditional monastic vows and are in conversation with others regarding their vocational calling. In time these individuals will birth more traditional (i.e., historical) forms of monastic life. Though the new monastics seem at times to have only a tenuous connection to historical monasticism, the spirit and the work of the movement have much in common with historical forms of monasticism.[41] For example, the new friars fancy themselves to be walking in the footsteps of Francis and Clare. Regardless of whether the new monastics are "new" or "monastic," institutionalized monasticism has been a part of the Protestant church for nearly two hundred years. In spite of this, many Protestants (especially evangelicals) are still unaware of the history of monasticism and the role that it has played in the larger history of the Christian church, as well as in the Protestant church. The question is not "Should monasticism exist in the Protestant church?" but "Why is monasticism not more prevalent among Protestants?" As it turns out, monasticism is as Protestant as the sermon or hymn-singing, and to think otherwise is to ignore the historical facts. To paraphrase Rodney Clapp, it is time to remonk the church.

---

41. For example, one is hard-pressed to find a basic definition of monasticism in the writings of the New Monastics, which begs the question of whether they are monastic at all, as opposed to being merely non-monastic intentional communities. On intentional communities in general, see David Janzen, *The Intentional Christian Community Handbook: For Idealists, Hypocrites, and Wannabe Disciples of Jesus* (Brewster, MA: Paraclete Press, 2013).

14

Continuing Roman Catholic Monastic Practice

On October 19, 1846, a Benedictine monk named Boniface Wimmer from St. Michael's Priory in Metten, Germany, arrived at Saint Vincent Parish, forty miles southeast of Pittsburgh. Though the new parish only had a few rudimentary buildings, Wimmer had come not only to serve as the local priest but also to found a Benedictine monastery. So on October 24, 1846, Boniface Wimmer was installed as pastor of Saint Vincent Parish and founded what would later become St. Vincent's Archabbey, the first Benedictine monastery in the United States. Five years later the monastery had over a hundred monks, and when Wimmer died on December 8, 1887, his initial group of fourteen monastic candidates had grown into a Benedictine congregation of five abbeys and two priories, with another 150 parishes, missions, and stations. Within the congregation were three bishops, four abbots, two priors, more than two hundred priests, and another two hundred non-ordained monks. In the Roman Catholic Church, the modern Order of St. Benedict was established in 1893 by Pope Leo XIII (d. 1903) in the brief *Summum semper*. The brief created the office of Abbot Primate, headquartered in Rome at Sant'Anselmo, the international Benedictine house of studies. The Abbot Primate was given limited jurisdiction over the Benedictine congregations and abbeys so as to preserve the autonomy of individual monasteries. A "Proper Law," ordered by Pope Pius XII (d. 1958) and renewed after the Second Vatican Council (held from 1962 to 1965), currently guides the Benedictine Confederation, as the order is now called. There are presently more than twenty congregations of men with approximately eight thousand monks, and more than sixty congregations and federations of approximately sixteen thousand Benedictine nuns. The rise of the Benedictines and other monastic orders around the world, and in the United States in particular, shows that without a doubt the institution of monasticism has continued unabated within the Roman Catholic Church throughout the centuries since the Reformation. Monastics such as Thomas Merton have "popularized" the ethos of monasticism to those outside the Roman Catholic Church, and Merton's influence has reached far beyond the cloister. Yet the number of monks and nuns in the Roman Catholic Church has declined sharply and steadily since Vatican II. This chapter will investigate the ongoing presence of monasticism in the Roman Catholic Church, looking at the important personality of Merton and discussing the language of monastic renewal promulgated by Vatican II. The influence of Roman Catholic monastic practices on Protestants will also be detailed, especially in terms of "oblate" and "associate" programs.

According to Rodney Stark and Roger Finke, "In 1965 there were 181,421 nuns, 12,255 brothers and 48,046 male seminarians in the United States. Just five years later, in 1970, there were only 153,645 American nuns. . . . Meanwhile, the number of seminarians had declined by 40 percent to 28,819 and the number of brothers had dropped to 11,623. By 1995 the number of American nuns had dropped to 92,107, brothers to 6,578 and seminarians to 5,083."[1] As a point of comparison, the number of nuns in Canada declined 46 percent between 1965 and 1995, and the number of male brothers dropped 77 percent. European countries experienced similar levels of decline.[2] This amazing and rapid decline in the numbers of monks and nuns in Roman Catholic monasteries is attributable to Vatican II and the changes that it introduced vis-à-vis religious life. But in many ways the institution of monasticism was at the apex of its influence in the early 1960s, just prior to Vatican II. The writings of Merton (d. 1968), a Trappist Cistercian from the Abbey of Our Lady of Gethsemani in Kentucky, were popular in mainstream American literary culture and even more so among spiritual seekers in the Roman Catholic Church, the Protestant church, or no church at all. Merton's influence continued to grow until his untimely death, and his writings have remained popular since then. In the words of Patrick Hart, "He is perhaps the most widely read of 20th-century Christian monastics."[3]

1. Rodney Stark and Roger Finke, "Catholic Religious Vocations: Decline and Renewal," *Review of Religious Research* 42, no. 2 (2000): 125.
2. Ibid., 126.
3. Patrick Hart, "Merton, Thomas," in *Encyclopedia of Monasticism*, ed. William M. Johnston (London: Fitzroy Dearborn, 2000), 857.

Merton was born in France in 1915 to a father from New Zealand and a mother from the United States. Because of World War I, the family soon moved to New York, where Merton's mother died of cancer when he was only six years old. Merton's father moved the family back to France, then to England, and finally to Rome. In 1933 Merton entered Clare College, Cambridge, but left after one year, enrolling in Columbia University in New York in January 1934 and graduating in January 1938. Merton stayed at Columbia to do graduate work in English on William Blake, for which he took his master of arts; he began a doctorate on the poetry of Gerard Manley Hopkins that he never finished. Having been encouraged by a Hindu monk to read Augustine of Hippo's *Confessions* and *The Imitation of Christ* by Thomas à Kempis in order to reconnect with his own faith tradition, Merton experienced a profound conversion and entered the Roman Catholic Church in 1938. In December 1941 he entered the Abbey of Gethsemani, spending his life in the community publishing books on a variety of topics and engaging in the study of contemplation in Western and Eastern religions. Merton died by accidental electrocution in December 1968 in Thailand while attending an interreligious conference on monasticism and contemplation.

Merton published a number of books on monasticism throughout his career. In his autobiography *The Seven Storey Mountain* (published in 1948), having just entered the Abbey of Gethsemani, Merton describes the monastery in language reminiscent of Benedict of Nursia: "The Monastery is a school—a school in which we learn from God how to be happy. Our happiness consists in sharing the happiness of God, the perfection of His unlimited freedom, the perfection of His love." Merton continues by saying that we enter the monastery in order to be healed and restored to our true nature, which has been made in the likeness of God. The monastery teaches the monastic how to love disinterestedly—that is, "the love of God for His own sake, because He is God." In order for God to give us his love, we must detach ourselves from ourselves, so he makes us detest ourselves so that we can be remade. This, for Merton, is the essence of the monastic (i.e., contemplative) life that gives meaning to "all the apparently meaningless little rules and observances and fasts and obediences and penances and humiliations and labors that go to make up the routine of existence in a contemplative monastery."[4] All of these activities remind the monks and nuns who God is, creating space for them to turn to God and find themselves.

4. Thomas Merton, *The Seven Storey Mountain* (New York: Harcourt, Brace, 1948), 372. See the *Rule of Benedict* (RB), Prologue 45, where Benedict writes, "Therefore we intend to establish a school for the Lord's service."

For Merton, the monastic life is essentially a contemplative life that over-flows itself so as to benefit others. He rejects the distinction, made by Thomas Aquinas and others, that there are active orders, contemplative orders, and so-called mixed orders. For Merton, all monks and nuns are contemplatives, and all monks and nuns are engaged in active works. For example, even the Carthusians, who make "elaborate efforts to preserve the silence and solitude of the hermit's life in their monasteries, definitely wrote into their original 'Customs' the characteristic labor of copying manuscripts and writing books in order that they might preach to the world by their pen even though their tongues were silent."[5] The active life is sterile without the contemplative life, believes Merton. Thus in all religious orders there is the possibility and necessity of pursuing a life of contemplation, which is then shared with others through a variety of means. At its essence monastic life is a life lived in contemplation of God for the purpose of actively returning the fruits of this contemplation back to the church and the world. The contemplative life, however, is not exclusive to monks and nuns. Rather, it is the God-ordained life for all people. Sounding very much like the Protestant Reformers, Merton writes:

> There is only one vocation. Whether you teach or live in the cloister or nurse the sick, whether you are in religion or out of it, married or single, no matter who you are or what you are, you are called to the summit of perfection: you are called to a deep interior life perhaps even to mystical prayer, and to pass the fruits of your contemplation on to others. And if you cannot do so by word, then by example.[6]

Merton's vision of the monastic life is rooted in God's universal call to holiness and in the baptismal vows of all Christians, something that is echoed in the teaching on monasticism at Vatican II.

In a work published just after his death, *The Climate of Monastic Prayer*, Merton writes that a "monk is a Christian who has responded to a special call from God, and has withdrawn from the more active concerns of a worldly life, in order to devote himself completely to repentance, 'conversion,' *metanoia*, renunciation and prayer." The monastic life is one of prayer where ascetical practices "fill the space created by the abandonment of other concerns."[7] Elsewhere, Merton says that this vocation, this calling from God, is one of the

---

5. Merton, *Seven Storey Mountain*, 417.
6. Ibid., 419.
7. Thomas Merton, *The Climate of Monastic Prayer* (Kalamazoo, MI: Cistercian Publications, 1969), 29.

most beautiful in the church of God, one in which a monk gives himself wholly to God, to a life of "self-obligation to God."[8] Merton recognizes that in all the great religious traditions of the world there are men and women called to separate themselves from ordinary life and devote themselves to "one task above all: to deepening their understanding and practice of their own religion in its most basic implications."[9] The monk's actions are directed toward achieving purity of heart by way of prayer, praise, and labor. For Merton monasticism is a life of asceticism, but the monk must not mistake the means for the end. Ascetical disciplines are for the greater end of contemplation and intimacy with God; they make up the daily life of the monk, but Christ is the center of monastic living. Though the monastic vocation is an ascetic charism, the work of the monk is to seek God alone.[10] Merton is attempting to turn the clock back to an understanding of monasticism that is more at home in the Egyptian desert of early Christianity, while also pointing a way forward.

On January 25, 1959, less than three months into his papacy, Pope John XXIII (d. 1963) called for a new ecumenical council of the Roman Catholic Church for the "good of souls" and to address the spiritual needs of the times. In his speech, delivered in Italian at the end of the Week of Prayer for Christian Unity on the Feast of the Conversion of St. Paul (January 25), the pope used the word *aggiornamento* ("a bringing up to date") to describe the program for his pontificate—that he was open-minded and looking to make necessary changes in the church. This word would later become the keyword for the whole council and the spirit of the modern Roman Catholic Church. Merton, writing sometime after this speech but before the pope's death, composed a short work that was originally titled "Monastic Reform: Memorandum to Pope John XXIII." Though this work, along with several letters, was never sent to the pope, a later version was published as "Monastic Renewal: A Memorandum." In this work Merton warns that despite the task of *aggiornamento*, monastics must not adopt practices that are foreign to monasticism. He writes that the first concern of monastic reform is to clarify monastic principles through a return to the sources of monastic history. A return to these sources provides the broader and more appropriate context from which to reform monasticism. True monastic reform is not authentic if it is only an adjustment to the community's liturgy or regular observance coupled with "exhortations to a greater spirit of prayer and a more exact

8. Thomas Merton, *Basic Principles of Monastic Spirituality* (Springfield, IL: Templegate, 1996), 7.

9. Patrick Hart, ed., *The Monastic Journey of Thomas Merton* (Kansas City: Sheed Andrews and McMeel, 1977), 5–6.

10. Ibid., 165.

observance of silence and enclosure."[11] According to Merton, true monastic *aggiornamento* will not view familiar monastic structures as the norm but will be open to new forms of monastic life that arise out of specific occasions, which are themselves an overflow of a life of silence and prayer. In short,

> The monastic life is a life of love for God and for man. The social aspect of the monastic life is therefore very important, but its importance must not be overemphasized to the detriment of the spirit of prayer and solitude. The apostolate of the monk need not necessarily be confined to prayer and reparation, but if in active work the monk merely imitates what can be done better by other orders or by the secular clergy, his apostolate loses its meaning and justification.[12]

An ideal monastic apostolate, says Merton, is for monasteries to offer retreats and conferences given by members of the community that are deeply imbued with a traditional monastic spirit. In this way, Merton was imbibing the spirit of Vatican II, though history would later show that for many monastics this re-envisioned monastic charism was not to their liking.

On October 28, 1965, Pope Paul VI (d. 1978) proclaimed *Perfectae Caritatis*, Vatican II's "Decree on the Adaptation and Renewal of Religious Life." The decree is meant for anyone who lives in an institute that makes a profession of chastity, poverty, and obedience, including, for example, the Benedictines who do not take those three vows. From the start it is possible to glimpse the limitations of the decree despite its applicability to all members of monastic and religious communities. Though not stated explicitly, it appears that the council's understanding of a monastic, at least juridically, is one who vows chastity, poverty, and obedience. Elaborating further, however, the council fathers acknowledge the antiquity of monastic life, seeing it as a life dedicated to God under the inspiration of the Holy Spirit. Monasticism builds up the body of Christ, enriching it with good works. In light of this and "in order that the great value of a life consecrated by the profession of the counsels and its necessary mission today may yield greater good to the Church, the sacred synod lays down" a number of prescriptions that provide "the general principles of the adaptation and renewal of the life and discipline of Religious orders" (1).[13] First, the adaptation and renewal of monastic life is accomplished only through a "constant return to the sources of all Christian

---

11. Ibid., 166.
12. Ibid., 168.
13. This and all subsequent quotations from *Perfectae Caritatis* are taken from the Roman Catholic Church's official English translation of the decree found on the Vatican's website: www.vatican.va. Numbers in parentheses indicate the section of the decree from which the quotation is taken.

life and to the original spirit of the institutes and their adaptation to the changed conditions of our time" (2). A twofold movement can be seen here regarding monasticism's sources. In the first place monks and nuns need to return to the Scriptures since "the ultimate norm of the religious life is the following of Christ set forth in the Gospels" (2a). Moreover, the foundation documents must be studied in order to understand the original impetus and apostolate of the order. Echoing Merton's sentiment, the decree states, "The purpose of the religious life is to help the members follow Christ and be united to God through the profession of the evangelical counsels. It should be constantly kept in mind, therefore, that even the best adjustments made in accordance with the needs of our age will be ineffectual unless they are animated by a renewal of spirit. This must take precedence over even the active ministry" (2e).

The second prescription the synod gave was that the way in which a nun lives out her vocation must be adapted to local culture. One size does not fit all; therefore, the order's custom books, liturgies, and so on must be adapted, suppressing any obsolete practices. Not only would this align the monastery to its cultural situatedness, but it would also bring to an end any archaic, noncultural practices that had been instantiated in the monastery by its founders. For example, though Western Europeans founded Benedictine monasticism in India, the monks there would no longer have to observe traditions that were not natural or culturally appropriate to the Indian setting. Third, though superiors had the right to introduce the norms of adaptation and renewal, they should take counsel from members of the order as well as from the Holy See or the local bishop as appropriate. In simple terms, changes should have the buy-in of everyone affected by the changes and should not come only from the top down. Fourth, monks and nuns must keep in mind that they are in the monastery because "they responded to a divine call so that by being not only dead to sin (see Rom. 6:11) but also renouncing the world they may live for God alone." This special consecration to God is rooted in one's baptism but "expresses itself more fully" (5). It appears that this element of the decree is addressing the council's foresight that change is never easy and that many of the re-envisioned orders might not look all that familiar to their members once the process of adaptation and renewal was completed. Though it is unlikely that the council fathers could have imagined the great exodus from the monasteries that occurred after Vatican II, they seem aware enough to suggest to members of the religious orders that the primary reason for being in the monastery is based on a response to God's call and not because of the outward trappings of the monastic life. Monks and nuns are to seek "God solely and before everything else" and to "fix their minds and hearts on Him, with apostolic love, by which they strive to be associated with the work of redemption and to spread the kingdom of God" (5). They are to be primarily committed not to the order's rule and customs but to God himself.

Fifth, the religious life is first and foremost a life of prayer involving the reading of and meditation on the Scriptures, along with participation in the liturgy, specifically the Eucharist. Sixth, contra Merton, those orders dedicated to contemplation should remain so, and those devoted to the apostolic, active life should continue to be so. Both kinds of religious life should be pursued appropriately, and the one should not be confused with the other. Then, turning its attention squarely to monasticism, the decree states that the

> principal duty of monks is to offer a service to the divine majesty at once humble and noble within the walls of the monastery, whether they dedicate themselves entirely to divine worship in the contemplative life or have legitimately undertaken some apostolate or work of Christian charity. Retaining, therefore, the characteristics of the way of life proper to them, they should revive their ancient traditions of service and so adapt them to the needs of today that monasteries will become institutions dedicated to the edification of the Christian people. (9)

This seems consistent with Merton's recommendation that monasteries should become places of pilgrimage and retreat in order to distill an authentic monastic spirituality. Without a doubt, this more outward-looking vision of monastic life is what has had the greatest impact in post–Vatican II monasticism.

As mentioned before, there was a vast exodus of monks and nuns from their monasteries after Vatican II. Though there are likely as many reasons for this as there are former monks and nuns, it appears obvious that the decisions of Vatican II had an effect wherein many people were no longer interested in the monastic life. The past fifty years has seen an endless analysis of the causes of this pattern, but simply put, many men and women no longer saw a raison d'être for the monastic life. The proverbial leveling of the playing field that occurred with vernacular liturgies and the council's theology of God's universal call to holiness took the wind out of the monastic sails. Despite this drastic decrease in the number of professed monks and nuns, however, there has been a dramatic increase in the number of laypeople with formal ties to monasteries through various oblate and associate programs, many of which existed prior to Vatican II but gained traction only after the council.

In early and medieval monastic history, an oblate (Latin: *oblatus*) was a child who was offered to the monastery by his or her parents. Benedict's rule is the only early Christian rule that mentions oblates; he records that at times "a member of the nobility offers his son to God in the monastery."[14] In the early ninth century the Benedictine monk Rabanus Maurus (d. 856) wrote a treatise *On the Oblation of Children* in which he asserts the biblical nature of oblation (e.g., Hannah's dedication of Samuel to God) and says that because the monastic life is the most perfect form of Christian discipleship, giving a child to a monastery is a godly and virtuous act. Not only were children often given to monasteries in the early and high Middle Ages; there were also groups of adults connected to the monastery, though not always by formal profession. William of Hirsau (d. 1091), also a Benedictine monk, established rules for two types of oblates: the Regular Oblates (or Interns) lived in the monastery without making formal vows, and the Secular Oblates (or Externs) lived outside the monastery but were affiliated with it. Both kinds of oblates promised obedience—and sometimes chastity—and gave financially to the monastery. During the fourteenth century the Olivetans, the Benedictine re-form movement founded by Bernard Tolomei (d. 1348) in Italy, established a Brotherhood of Oblates, and soon thereafter Frances of Rome (d. 1440), a laywoman under the spiritual direction of an Olivetan monk, joined together with a number of other women to renounce their lives of extravagance and engage in service to the poor. By the close of the Middle Ages, however, the practice of child oblation had fallen out of favor, and most monastic orders, including the Cistercians and Cluniacs, had legislated against the custom. The decline of the monastic orders in subsequent centuries, due to the Refor-mation and the Enlightenment, further eroded the presence of adult oblates connected to the monastery.

In the American context, it was Boniface Wimmer of St. Vincent's who envisioned a kind of third order of St. Benedict that would be open to men and women.[15] A "certificate of Oblation states that the 'Institute of Secular Oblates of the Benedictine Order' was introduced to the United States with papal approval by Abbot Boniface on August 6, 1865," and the first *Manual for Benedictine Oblates* was published at St. Vincent's in 1898.[16] Colman

14. RB 59.1; Timothy Fry, ed., *RB 1980: The Rule of St. Benedict in Latin and English with Notes* (Collegeville, MN: Liturgical Press, 1981), 271.

15. Third orders were a common feature of monastic life beginning in the Middle Ages. They were open to persons who desired to have a formal connection to a particular religious order without taking formal vows. The name "third order" comes from the fact that vowed men were seen as the first order; vowed women were the second order; and non-vowed persons constituted the third order. One of the most well-known members of a third order is Catherine of Siena (d. 1380), a member of the Third Order of St. Dominic. Members of third orders are sometimes known as tertiaries.

16. Roberta Werner, *Reaching for God: The Benedictine Oblate Way of Life* (Collegeville, MN: Liturgical Press, 2013), 89.

Barry tells a slightly different story when he says that the oblate program "had been revived in the United States in 1894 by Archabbot Leander Schnerr of St. Vincent."[17] Regardless, in 1937 St. Vincent's daughter abbey of St. John's in Collegeville, Minnesota, wrote a *Manual for Oblates of St. Benedict* in which abbot Alcuin Deutsch says that the "Secular Oblates of St. Benedict" were organized at the request of Hildebrand de Hemptinne, primate of the Benedictine Order. Deutsch goes on to say that Hemptinne had obtained two documents from Pope Leo XIII in 1898: a brief granting spiritual favors and privileges to Benedictine oblates and a decree from the Sacred Congregation of Bishops and Regulars approving the Statutes and Rules for Secular Oblates of St. Benedict.

Today, St. Vincent's Archabbey writes that Benedictine oblates are Christian men and women who choose to associate themselves with a religious community of Benedictine monks or nuns in order to strengthen their baptismal commitment and enrich their Christian way of life. These oblates do not take vows, nor do they live in a monastery. Rather, they continue to live in the world, eagerly striving to live out the values of the gospel. These men and women enter into an intentional period of discernment, usually of one year's duration, regarding their vocation to be an oblate, during which they engage in active reading and reflecting on the *Rule of Benedict* (RB) and attend oblate gatherings. These gatherings are usually led by a monk or nun who prays the daily office with those gathered and teaches on a topic of monastic life or spirituality adapted to an oblate context. After this novitiate period, the aspirant, with the monastic community's agreement, may make his or her final oblation according to the monastery's oblate ceremony.

Other religious orders have similar third orders, such as the International Association of Lay Cistercian Communities. According to the website of the Abbey of Our Lady of the Holy Spirit—a Cistercian community in Conyers, Georgia—Cistercian lay associates arose in the 1970s. The movement began in Nigeria at Awhum Monastery but was brought to the United States by the Cistercian monk Anthony Delisi, who, while assisting in novice formation at Awhum, took notice of the movement. Under the guidance of Delisi and the abbot of the Holy Spirit Abbey, five people came together to establish the Associate Oblates of Our Lady of the Holy Spirit in 1987, the first Lay Cistercian community in the United States. After two and a half years in formation this small group made their oblation on March 25, 1990. In 1998, during the nonacentenary of the founding of Cîteaux, Pope John Paul II (d. 2005)

17. Colman Barry, *Work and Worship: Saint John's Abbey and University 1856–1992* (Collegeville, MN: Liturgical Press, 1994), 261.

acknowledged the existence of the Cistercian Lay Associates. Beginning in 2000 the Lay Associates began to organize themselves intentionally, meeting triennially. In 2008 they issued a document titled "Lay Cistercian Identity" in which they write, "We are convinced that it is possible to adapt Cistercian spirituality to the lifestyle of a lay person though it is very clear that there are two different ways to live it, monastic and lay, and both are complementary. Lay people have found in Cistercian spirituality a way to live in the world with greater commitment and spiritual depth. We are unanimous in our belief that the Cistercian charism can be lived outside the monastery." Just like the Benedictine oblates, the Cistercian Lay Associates exist to incorporate monasticism into the daily lives of men and women who are not called to make a formal monastic profession.

Ressourcement: Ongoing Charism and Tenacity of Monasticism

Despite the many setbacks experienced by Roman Catholic monasticism in the past five hundred years (e.g., the Reformation, the Enlightenment, the wars of religion, and the shake-up of Vatican II), it continues to endure and, in its own way, thrive. Despite the sharp decrease in the number of Roman Catholic monks and nuns since the late 1960s, individuals continue to be drawn to the monastic profession, finding their way to the many monasteries that continue to survive despite their reduced numbers. At the same time most monasteries now have many more oblates or associates than they have monastics, a sign that though the monastic lifestyle is not as attractive as it once was, there is still a great interest in monasticism, its spirituality, and its applicability and adaptability to modern lifestyles. Because of this close connection between the monastery and non-monastics by way of oblate programs and retreat ministries, there is no end to books written for the purpose of learning how to have monastic principles guide one's spiritual life or even one's business.[18] Due to this shift in numbers, monasteries are learning how to adjust to their reduced populations while also capitalizing on the influx of non-monastics interested in visiting and being in relationship with the monastery. Heeding Merton's admonition that monasteries should offer retreats and conferences, many monasteries today run retreat centers where guests can simply come away for a time of silence and solitude or where they can enjoy teaching on monastic topics from one of the monastery's monks or nuns. Though it is

18. See, for example, Kit Dollard, Anthony Marrett-Crosby, and Timothy Wright, *Doing Business with Benedict: The Rule of Saint Benedict and Business Management: A Conversation* (New York: Continuum, 2002).

certainly a new day for Roman Catholic monasticism, its future is bright; the charism of monasticism has yet to die, and God continues to call men and women into the monastery. Though there will certainly be fewer monasteries in the future, there will be monasteries nonetheless. Though there will be fewer monks and nuns, there will be monks and nuns nonetheless. And it is to be hoped that these monks and nuns will live not only in Roman Catholic monasteries but also in newly founded Protestant monasteries.

Epilogue

Monasticism Today and Tomorrow

Monasticism's Potential and the Future

This book has recounted the story of Christian monasticism across the past two millennia. It has not presented an exhaustive survey of the history of monasticism, for "I suppose that the world itself could not contain the books that would be written" on monastic history (John 21:25), but it has touched on all of the significant monastic movements and has mapped out a trajectory of monastic history that demonstrates its continual presence within the church. This book has also been an attempt at *ressourcement*, a recovery of the biblical impulse and evangelical (i.e., gospel-centered) nature of monasticism. Thus I want to end with a look to the future and a challenge to the Christian church, especially to the Protestant evangelical church. Though I do not advocate unequivocally for an uncritical reintroduction of monasticism into the evangelical church, I suggest, as I hope it has already become clear, that monasticism itself is not contrary to the spirit of evangelicalism and has been a consistent presence in Christian history.

The concept of reform, renewal, or rebirth is a well-established one, not only for the Middle Ages in general and the twelfth-century in particular,[1]

---

1. Charles Homer Haskins, *The Renaissance of the Twelfth Century* (Cambridge, MA: Harvard University Press, 1927); and Robert L. Benson, Giles Constable, and Carol D. Lanham, eds., *Renaissance and Renewal in the Twelfth Century* (Cambridge, MA: Harvard University Press, 1982).

but also in medieval monastic scholarship.[2] Many words in extant monastic literature express the concept, such as re-create, convert, correct, remake, restore, repair, return, revert, regenerate, recover, recuperate, revive, resuscitate, reflower, regrow, reflourish, rewarm, relight, and rekindle.[3] For example, the abbot Hugh of Cluny (d. 1109) was said to be a reformer (*reformator*) of monasticism,[4] and a monastery was given to Cluny in 1082 for the purpose of reviving (*reviviscat*) its monastic order.[5] The biographer of William of Hirsau (d. 1091) writes, "By the effort of this holy man, the monastic religion, which among those who had assumed the religious habit had almost grown cold in the Teutonic regions, began to grow warm again [*recalescere*] and to recover [*recuperari*]."[6] Peter the Venerable (d. 1156), in a letter to the archbishop of Lyons, writes that the monastic life had been renewed (*renovantur*) throughout the Western church, especially within Gaul.[7] Finally, Philip of Harvengt (d. 1183) in his *On the Institution of Clerics* writes that the monasteries of the middle of the twelfth century were

> seen to flower again [*reflorere*] and, after having been almost overwhelmed by the winter frost and desiccated by the constant northern winds, are restored [*revertuntur*] to their pristine state by the new sun and warmed by the favoring breezes. . . . When the new dew had fallen the claustral region flowered again [*reflorescit*]. In the cloisters, as in trees, a rare fruit grew ripe. A workshop of total sanctity was set alight by the fire sent from above and fanned by violent winds.[8]

The point of this use of language is unmistakable: monasticism was in need of a renewal, and so it was being renewed. But a *ressourcement* of the tradition was needed in order to give impetus to fresh expressions of the monastic life—hence the return to the idea by the Templars of the early Christian monks as "knights of Christ" (*miles Christi*) or to the wholesale adoption of language meant to legitimate one's form of monastic life above others (e.g., the "apostolic life" as superior to non-apostolic forms of monastic life).

It is time for the evangelical church to engage in an intentional and serious *ressourcement* of the Christian tradition, including (and perhaps especially)

2. Giles Constable, *The Reformation of the Twelfth Century* (Cambridge: Cambridge University Press, 1996).

3. Ibid., 39.

4. Marquard Herrgott, ed., *Vetus disciplina monastica* (Paris, 1726), 134.

5. Auguste J. Bernard and Alexandre Bruel, eds., *Recueil des chartes de l'abbaye de Cluny, Tome Quatrième* (Paris, 1888), 4.756 no. 3598.

6. Cited in Constable, *Reformation of the Twelfth Century*, 41.

7. Giles Constable, ed., *The Letters of Peter the Venerable*, vol. 1 (Cambridge, MA: Harvard University Press, 1967), 130.

8. Cited in Constable, *Reformation of the Twelfth Century*, 43.

the monastic tradition. Though the early, patristic era has received renewed attention by evangelical scholars in the past fifteen years or so,[9] the Middle Ages continue to be neglected. In the words of D. H. Williams, "Tradition is not something evangelicals can take or leave," though we have often tried harder to leave it than to take it.[10] Nonetheless, a new day is dawning in which this stance is no longer viewed as the wisest way forward. Despite popular evangelicalism's fascination with all things shiny and new, more and more evangelicals are turning to the Christian church's past to map a way forward.[11] The very presence of this book is evidence of the shift.

Yet why should monasticism be a part of this *ressourcement*? As I have written elsewhere:

> For two thousand years the Holy Spirit has been calling Christian men and women into monastic communities that are dedicated to prayer, the cultivation of holiness, sacrificial service, and mission (both within and outside the Christian church). Yet, after the Reformation of the sixteenth century, this divine instrument of renewal largely disappeared from the Protestant landscape. Recently, however, the Holy Spirit has been breaking through the five-hundred-year-old boundaries (theological and otherwise) that have kept the institution of monasticism from reemerging in Protestant Christianity, calling a new generation of men and women to dedicate themselves to a monastic life.[12]

I believe that the institution of monasticism has been a historical instrument of the Holy Spirit used in the life of the church. This is not quite the same as saying that the Holy Spirit inspired monasticism (although that might be true too). Rather, it is to acknowledge the fact that regardless of the primary motivations for monasticism's genesis (though these motivations appear to be rooted in a response to the gospel), God the Holy Spirit has seen fit over and over again to use monks and nuns and the institution of monasticism itself to further his kingdom. In other words, God has used monasticism

9. See, for example, Daniel H. Williams, *Retrieving the Tradition and Renewing Evangelicalism: A Primer for Suspicious Protestants* (Grand Rapids: Eerdmans, 1999); and Bryan M. Litfin, *Getting to Know the Church Fathers: An Evangelical Introduction* (Grand Rapids: Brazos, 2007).

10. Williams, *Retrieving the Tradition*, 13.

11. A good example of this is in the area of biblical studies, where evangelical scholars are arguing for a theological interpretation of the Bible over against the merely critical-historical interpretive framework that has dominated evangelicalism for a century. See, for example, Daniel J. Treier, *Introducing Theological Interpretation of Scripture: Recovering a Christian Practice* (Grand Rapids: Baker Academic, 2008).

12. Greg Peters, "Monasticism: Instrument of the Holy Spirit in the Renewal of Today's Church," in *The Holy Spirit and the Christian Life: Historical, Interdisciplinary, and Renewal Perspectives*, ed. Wolfgang Vondey (New York: Palgrave Macmillan, 2014), 41.

providentially in carrying out his will for the church and for the world. To state the obvious, monasticism is not a fringe movement in Christian history but one of its main threads. To ignore monasticism is to ignore a large element of God's history of salvation; therefore, it deserves our attention. Simply put, monasticism is a work of God. So,

> let me return to the relative absence of monastic life in the larger Protestant tradition. If I have been convincing in my demonstration that the monastic life is a Christian practice, the presence of which can be attributed to the work of God, in particular the Holy Spirit, or if I have at least created space for that to be possible, then let me suggest that monasticism must be allowed to flourish in the Protestant and evangelical traditions in order for the Holy Spirit to use it as an instrument in his ongoing work in the life of the church and the world. If it is a gift of the Holy Spirit, then it must exist in the church. And if it exists in the church, and it is of God, then I believe that the institution of monasticism can serve as an instrument of renewal and revitalization.[13]

Of course, there will be some (or perhaps many) who will not agree with this assessment. That being the case, I can only say that I am hoping these individuals will have a change of heart. Yet I am certainly writing for those evangelicals who know that evangelicalism's ahistorical disrootedness is not a strength of the tradition but a weakness. Monasticism is a wellspring for our renewal, and we err if we do not drink from it liberally.[14] Monasticism has had and continues to have much to teach Christians who seek a deeper encounter with God and who wish to help the church continue to form its members spiritually. It deserves its rightful place in our lives and in the church.

13. Ibid., 52.
14. Here I am echoing Donald Bloesch's *Wellsprings of Renewal: Promise in Christian Communal Life* (Grand Rapids: Eerdmans, 1974).

Bibliography

Achelis, Hans. "Agapetae." In *Encyclopedia of Religion and Ethics*, edited by James Hastings. New York, 1910.

———. *Virgines Subintroductae: Ein Beitrag zu I Kor. VII.* Leipzig: J. D. Hinrich, 1902.

Allchin, A. M. *The Silent Rebellion: Anglican Religious Communities 1845–1900.* London: SCM Press, 1958.

Andrews, Frances. *The Other Friars: Carmelite, Augustinian, Sack and Pied Friars in the Middle Ages.* Woodbridge, UK: Boydell Press, 2006.

Angold, Michael. *Church and Society in Byzantium under the Comneni, 1081–1261.* Cambridge: Cambridge University Press, 1995.

Antry, Theodore J., and Carol Neel. *Norbert and Early Norbertine Spirituality.* Mahwah, NJ: Paulist Press, 2007.

Appleby, David. "Benedict of Aniane, St. c. 750–821." In *Encyclopedia of Monasticism*, edited by William M. Johnston, 2 vols. London: Fitzroy Dearborn, 2000.

Archambault, Paul J. *A Monk's Confession: The Memoirs of Guibert of Nogent.* University Park: Pennsylvania State University Press, 1996.

Armstrong, Chris. "The Future Lies in the Past." *Christianity Today*, February 2008, 22–29.

Armstrong, Regis J. "The Spiritual Theology of the *Legenda Major* of Saint Bonaventure." PhD diss., Fordham University, 1978.

Armstrong, Regis J., and Ignatius C. Brady, trans. *Francis and Clare: The Complete Works.* New York: Paulist Press, 1982.

Armstrong, Regis J., J. A. Wayne Hellmann, and William J. Short, eds. *The Francis Trilogy of Thomas of Celano.* Hyde Park, NY: New City Press, 2004.

Atkinson, James, ed. *Luther's Works.* Vol. 44, *The Christian in Society I.* Philadelphia: Fortress Press, 1966.

Bainbridge, Virginia R. "Bonde, William (d. 1530)." In *Oxford Dictionary of National Biography.* Oxford: Oxford University Press, 2004.

Baker, James T. "Benedict's Children and Their Separated Brothers and Sisters." *Christian Century*, December 3, 1980, 1191–94.

Barber, Malcolm. *The Trial of the Templars.* Cambridge: Cambridge University Press, 1978.

Barrett, C. K. *The First Epistle to the Corinthians.* New York: Harper & Row, 1968.

Barry, Colman. *Work and Worship: Saint John's Abbey and University 1856–1992.* Collegeville, MN: Liturgical Press, 1994.

Barth, Karl. *Church Dogmatics*. Vol. 4, *The Doctrine of Reconciliation*, part 2. Translated by G. W. Bromiley. Edinburgh: T&T Clark, 1958.

Battles, Ford Lewis, trans., *Institutes of the Christian Religion* (Philadelphia: Westminster, 1960), 1256.

Beattie, B. R. *Angelus pacis: The Legation of Cardinal Giovanni Gaetano Orsini, 1326–1334*. Leiden: Brill, 2007.

Bebbington, David. *Evangelicalism in Modern Britain: A History from the 1730s to the 1980s*. Grand Rapids: Baker, 1989.

Bellitto, Christopher M. *Renewing Christianity: A History of Church Reform from Day One to Vatican II*. Mahwah, NJ: Paulist Press, 2001.

Bellitto, Christopher M., and David Zachariah Flanagin, eds. *Reassessing Reform: A Historical Investigation into Church Renewal*. Washington, DC: Catholic University of America Press, 2012.

Benson, Robert L., Giles Constable, and Carol D. Lanham, eds. *Renaissance and Renewal in the Twelfth Century*. Cambridge, MA: Harvard University Press, 1982.

Berman, Constance Hoffman. *The Cistercian Evolution: The Invention of a Religious Order in Twelfth-Century Europe*. Philadelphia: University of Pennsylvania Press, 2010.

Bernard, Auguste J., and Alexandre Bruel, eds. *Recueil des chartes de l'abbaye de Cluny, Tome Quatrième*. Paris, 1888.

Bernard, G. W. *The Late Medieval English Church: Vitality and Vulnerability before the Break with Rome*. New Haven: Yale University Press, 2012.

Bertram, Jerome. *The Chrodegang Rules: The Rules for the Common Life of the Secular Clergy from the Eighth and Ninth Centuries. Critical Texts with Translations and Commentary*. Aldershot, UK: Ashgate, 2005.

Bessenecker, Scott A. *Living Mission: The Vision and Voices of New Friars*. Downers Grove, IL: InterVarsity, 2010.

———. *The New Friars: The Emerging Movement Serving the World's Poor*. Downers Grove, IL: InterVarsity, 2006.

Bilinkoff, Jodi. "Teresa of Jesus and Carmelite Reform." In *Religious Orders of the Catholic Reformation: In Honor of John C. Olin on His Seventy-Fifth Birthday*, edited by Richard L. DeMolen. 165–86. New York: Fordham University Press, 1994.

Bloch, Marc. *Feudal Society*. Translated by L. A. Manyon. Chicago: University of Chicago Press, 1961.

Bloesch, Donald. *Centers of Christian Renewal*. Philadelphia: United Church Press, 1964.

———. *The Church: Sacraments, Worship, Ministry, Mission*. Downers Grove, IL: InterVarsity, 2002.

———. *The Struggle of Prayer*. San Francisco: Harper and Row, 1980.

———. *Wellsprings of Renewal: Promise in Christian Communal Life*. Grand Rapids: Eerdmans, 1974.

Blum, Owen J. *Peter Damian: Letters 31–60*. Washington, DC: Catholic University of America Press, 1990.

Boersma, Hans. *Nouvelle Théologie and Sacramental Ontology: A Return to Mystery*. New York: Oxford University Press, 2009.

Bonhoeffer, Dietrich. *Discipleship*. Translated by Barbara Green and Reinhard Krauss. Minneapolis: Fortress Press, 2001.

Boyle, Leonard. "The Setting of the *Summa theologiae* of Saint Thomas." In *The Gilson Lectures on Thomas Aquinas*. 19–45. Toronto: PIMS, 2008.

Bramhall, John. *The Works of the Most Reverend Father in God, John Bramhall, D.D.* Vol. 1. Oxford: John Henry Parker, 1842.

Broshi, Magen, and Hanan Eshel. "Was Qumran Indeed a Monastery? The Consensus and Its Challengers: An Archaeologist's View." In *Bread, Wine, Walls and Scrolls*, edited by Magen Broshi. 259–73. London: Sheffield Academic, 2001.

Brown, Colin, ed. *The New International Dictionary of New Testament Theology*. Vol. 2. Grand Rapids: Zondervan, 1976.

Brown, Peter. *The Body and Society: Men, Women, and Sexual Renunciation in Early Christianity*. New York: Columbia University Press, 1988.

Burr, David. *The Spiritual Franciscans: From Protest to Persecution in the Century after Saint Francis*. University Park: Pennsylvania State University Press, 2001.

Burton, Janet, and Julie Kerr. *The Cistercians in the Middle Ages*. Woodbridge, UK: Boydell Press, 2011.

Bynum, Caroline Walker. *Docere Verbo et Exemplo: An Aspect of Twelfth-Century Spirituality*. Missoula, MT: Scholars Press, 1979.

Cabaniss, Allan, trans. *Benedict of Aniane: The Emperor's Monk*. Kalamazoo, MI: Cistercian Publications 2008.

Calvin, John. *Institutes of the Christian Religion*. Edited by John T. McNeill. Translated by Ford Lewis Battles. Philadelphia: Westminster, 1960.

Cantor, Norman F. "The Crisis of Western Monasticism, 1050–1130." *American Historical Review* 66 (1960): 47–67.

Capps, Walter. *The Monastic Impulse*. New York: Crossroad, 1983.

Carter, Erik C. "The New Monasticism: A Literary Introduction." *Journal of Spiritual Formation and Soul Care* 5, no. 2 (2012): 268–84.

Casey, Michael, trans. *Cistercians and Cluniacs: St. Bernard's Apologia to Abbot William*. Kalamazoo, MI: Cistercian Publications, 1970.

Castelli, Elizabeth. "Virginity and Its Meaning for Women's Sexuality in Early Christianity." *Journal of Feminist Studies in Religion* 2 (1986): 61–88.

Chadwick, Henry, trans. *Saint Augustine: Confessions*. Oxford: Oxford University Press, 1991.

Chan, Simon. *Liturgical Theology: The Church as Worshipping Community*. Downer's Grove, IL: IVP Academic, 2006.

Charanis, Peter. "Monastic Properties and the State in the Byzantine Empire." *Dumbarton Oaks Papers* 4 (1948): 51–118.

Clapp, Rodney. "Remonking the Church." *Christianity Today*, August 12, 1988, 20–21.

Clark, Francis. *The Pseudo-Gregorian Dialogues*. 2 vols. Leiden: Brill, 1987.

Clark, Gillian. *Women in Late Antiquity: Pagan and Christian Lifestyles*. Oxford: Clarendon, 1993.

Clark, James G. *The Benedictines in the Middle Ages*. Woodbridge, UK: Boydell Press, 2011.

———, ed. *The Religious Orders in Pre-Reformation England*. Woodbridge, UK: Boydell Press, 2002.

Clarke, W. K. L., trans. *The Ascetic Works of Saint Basil*. London: SPCK, 1925.

Claussen, M. A. *The Reform of the Frankish Church: Chrodegang of Metz and the Regula caononicorum in the Eighth Century*. Cambridge: Cambridge University Press, 2004.

Cloke, Gillian. *"This Female Man of God": Women and Spiritual Power in the Patristic Age, AD 350–450*. New York: Routledge, 1995.

Coleman-Norton, P. R. *Roman State and Christian Church: A Collection of Legal Documents to AD 535*. Vol. 2. London: SPCK, 1966.

Constable, Giles. "The Interpretation of Mary and Martha." In *Three Studies in Medieval Religious and Social Thought*. 1–141. Cambridge: Cambridge University Press, 1995.

———, ed. *The Letters of Peter the Venerable*. Vol. 1. Cambridge, MA: Harvard University Press, 1967.

———. *The Reformation of the Twelfth Century*. Cambridge: Cambridge University Press, 1996.

Constable, Giles, and Bernard S. Smith, eds. and trans. *Libellus de Diversis Ordinibus et Professionibus qui Sunt in Aecclesia*. Oxford: Clarendon, 1972.

Coulton, G. G. *Five Centuries of Religion*. Vol. 3, *Getting and Spending*. New York: Octagon Books, 1979.

———. *Five Centuries of Religion*. Vol. 4, *The Last Days of Medieval Monachism*. Cambridge: Cambridge University Press, 1950.

Cousins, Ewert, trans. *Bonaventure: The Soul's Journey into God, The Tree of Life, The Life of St. Francis*. New York: Paulist Press, 1978.

Currier, Charles Warren. *History of Religious Orders*. Boston: MacConnell Brothers, 1896.

Da Costa, Alexandra. *Reforming Printing: Syon Abbey's Defence of Orthodoxy 1525–1534*. Oxford: Oxford University Press, 2012.

D'Ambrosio, Marcellino. "*Ressourcement Theology, Aggiornamento*, and the Hermeneutics of Tradition." *Communio* 18 (Winter 1991): 530–55.

De Jong, Mayke. "Carolingian Monasticism: The Power of Prayer." In vol. 2 of *The New Cambridge Medieval History, c. 700–c. 900*, edited by Rosamond McKitterick. 622–53. Cambridge: Cambridge University Press, 1995.

DeMolen, Richard L., ed. *Religious Orders of the Catholic Reformation: In Honor of John C. Olin on His Seventy-Fifth Birthday*. New York: Fordham University Press, 1994.

De Seilhac, Lazare, and M. Bernard Saïd, trans. *Règles monastiques au féminin*. Bégrolles-en-Mauges: Abbaye de Bellefontaine, 1996.

De Vogüé, Adalbert. "The Cenobitic Rules of the West." *Cistercian Studies Quarterly* 12 (1977): 175–83.

———. *La Règle de Saint Benoît*. Vols. 1–6. Paris: Éditions du Cerf, 1971–1972.

———. *La Règle du Maître*. Vols. 1–3. Paris: Éditions du Cerf, 1964.

———. *Le Maître, Eugippe et saint Benoît: Recueil d'articles*. Hildesheim: Gerstenberg, 1984.

———. "Poverty in Western Monasticism: Fourth to the Eighth Century." *Monastic Studies* 13 (1982): 99–112.

Dickens, A. G. *The English Reformation*. 2nd ed. University Park: Pennsylvania State University Press, 1989.

Dickinson, J. C. *The Origins of the Austin Canons and Their Introduction into England*. London: SPCK, 1952.

Dollard, Kit, Anthony Marrett-Crosby, and Timothy Wright. *Doing Business with Benedict: The Rule of Saint Benedict and Business Management: A Conversation*. New York: Continuum, 2002.

Dostoevsky, Fyodor. *The Brothers Karamazov*. Translated by Richard Pevear and Larissa Volokhonsky. New York: Farrar, Straus and Giroux, 1990.

Dufeil, Michel-Marie. *Guillaume de Saint-Amour et la polémique universitaire parisienne, 1250–1259*. Paris: Picard, 1972.

Duffy, Eamon. *The Stripping of the Altars: Traditional Religion in England 1400–1580*. New Haven: Yale University Press, 2005.

Dunn, Marilyn. *The Emergence of Monasticism: From the Desert Fathers to the Early Middle Ages*. Oxford: Blackwell, 2000.

———. "Mastering Benedict: Monastic Rules and Their Authors in the Early Medieval West." *English Historical Review* 105 (1990): 567–94.

Eberle, Luke, trans. *The Rule of the Master*. Kalamazoo, MI: Cistercian Publications, 1977.

Egan, Keith J. "Contemplation." In *The New Westminster Dictionary of Christian Spirituality*, edited by Philip Sheldrake. Louisville: Westminster John Knox, 2005.

Elder, E. Rozanne, ed. *The New Monastery: Texts and Studies on the Earliest Cistercians*. Kalamazoo, MI: Cistercian Publications, 1998.

Elm, Susanna. *"Virgins of God": The Making of Asceticism in Late Antiquity*. Oxford: Clarendon, 1994.

Emergy, Andrée. "On Religious Poverty." *Communio* 9 (1982): 16–21.

Emmoni, V. "Agapètes." In *Dictionnaire d'histoire et de géographie eccclésastiques*, Tome 1. Edited by Alfred Baudrillart, Albert Vogt, and Urbain Rouziès. Paris: Letouzey et Ané, 1909.

Ernest, James D. "Athanasius of Alexandria: The Scope of Scripture in Polemical and Pastoral Context." *Vigiliae Christianae* 47 (1993): 341–62.

Evans, Christopher P., ed. *Writings on the Spiritual Life: A Selection of Works of Hugh, Adam, Achard, Richard, Walter, and Godfrey of St Victor*. Turnhout, Belg.: Brepols, 2013.

Feiss, Hugh. "Victorines." In *Encyclopedia of Monasticism*, edited by William M. Johnston, 2 vols. London: Fitzroy Dearborn, 2000.

Ferguson, Everett, and Abraham J. Malherbe, trans. *Gregory of Nyssa: The Life of Moses*. New York: Paulist Press, 1978.

Ford, J. Massingberd. "Levirate Marriage in St. Paul (1 Cor. 7)." *New Testament Studies* 10 (1963/64): 361–65.

Forman, Mary, and Thomas Sullivan. "The Latin Cenobitic Rules: AD 400–700: Editions and

Translations." *American Benedictine Review* 48, no. 1 (1997): 52–68.

Fraade, Steven D. "Ascetical Aspects of Ancient Judaism." In *Jewish Spirituality: From the Bible through the Middle Ages*, edited by Arthur Green. 253–88. New York: Crossroad, 1986.

France, James. *Separate but Equal: Cistercian Lay Brothers, 1120–1350*. Collegeville, MN: Cistercian Publications, 2012.

Frank, Hieronymus, ed. *Capitula qualiter observationes sacrae in nonnullis monasteriis habentur quas bonae memoriae Benedictus secundus in coenobiis suis alumnis habere instituit*. Siegburg: Schmitt, 1963.

Frank, Karl Suso. *Angelikos Bios: Begriffsanalytische und begriffsgeschichtliche Untersuchung zum "engelgleichen Leben" im frühen Mönchtum*. Münster im Westfalen: Aschendorff, 1964.

Franklin, Carmela Vircillo, Ivan Havener, and J. Alcuin Francis, trans. *Early Monastic Rules: The Rules of the Fathers and the Regula Orientalis*. Collegeville, MN: Liturgical Press, 1982.

Friesen, Garry. *Decision Making and the Will of God: A Biblical Alternative to the Traditional View*. Colorado Springs: Multnomah Books, 2004.

Fry, Timothy, ed. *RB 1980: The Rule of St. Benedict in Latin and English with Notes*. Collegeville, MN: Liturgical Press, 1981.

Ganss, George E., trans. *The Constitutions of the Society of Jesus*. St. Louis: Institute of Jesuit Sources, 1970.

———, ed. *Ignatius of Loyola: Spiritual Exercises and Selected Works*. New York: Paulist Press, 1991.

George, Timothy. *Reading Scripture with the Reformers*. Downers Grove, IL: InterVarsity, 2011.

Gilpin, William. *Observations on the River Wye*. 2nd ed. London: R. Blamire, 1789.

Ginzberg, Louis. *Legends of the Jews*. Vol. 1. Dulles, VA: Jewish Publication Society, 2003.

Godfrey, C. J. *The Church in Anglo-Saxon England*. Cambridge: Cambridge University Press, 1962.

Grafe, Eduard. "Geistliche Verlöbnisse bei Paulus." *Theologische Arbeiten aus dem rheinischen wissenschaftlichen Prediger-Verein*, N. F. III (1899): 57–69.

Greatrex, Joan. "Benedictine Monk Scholars as Teachers and Preachers in the Later Middle Ages: Evidence from Worcester Cathedral Priory." *Monastic Studies* 2 (1991): 213–25.

———. "Benedictine Sermons: Preparation and Practice in the English Monastic Cathedral Cloisters." In *Medieval Monastic Preaching*, edited by Carolyn Muessig. 257–78. Leiden: Brill, 1998.

———. *The English Benedictine Cathedral Priories: Rule and Practice, c. 1270–c. 1420*. Oxford: Oxford University Press, 2011.

Gregg, Robert C., trans. *Athanasius: The Life of Antony and the Letter to Marcellinus*. New York: Paulist Press, 1980.

Guillaumont, Antoine. "La conception du desert chez les moines d'Égypte." *Revue de l'Histoire des Religions* 188 (1975): 3–21.

———. "Le Nom des 'Agapètes.'" *Vigiliae Christianae* 23 (1969): 30–37.

Hall, Christopher. *Learning Theology with the Church Fathers*. Downers Grove, IL: InterVarsity, 2002.

———. *Reading Scripture with the Church Fathers*. Downers Grove, IL: InterVarsity, 1998.

Harmless, William. *Desert Christians: An Introduction to the Literature of Early Monasticism*. Oxford: Oxford University Press, 2004.

Hart, Patrick. "Merton, Thomas." In *Encyclopedia of Monasticism*, edited by William M. Johnston, 2 vols. London: Fitzroy Dearborn, 2000.

———, ed. *The Monastic Journey of Thomas Merton*. Kansas City: Sheed Andrews and McMeel, 1977.

Harvey, Margaret. *Lay Religious Life in Late Medieval Durham*. Woodbridge, UK: Boydell Press, 2006.

Haskins, Charles Homer. *The Renaissance of the Twelfth Century*. Cambridge, MA: Harvard University Press, 1927.

Hausherr, Irénée. *Penthos: The Doctine of Compunction in the Christian East*. Kalamazoo, MI: Cistercian Publication, 1982.

Herrgott, Marquard, ed. *Vetus disciplina monas-tica.* Paris, 1726.

Horner, Patrick J., ed. and trans. *A Macaronic Sermon Collection from Late Medieval England: Oxford, MS Bodley 649.* Toronto: PIMS, 2006.

Hunter, David, trans. and ed. *Marriage in the Early Church.* Minneapolis: Fortress Press, 1992.

Iogna-Prat, Dominique. *Order and Exclusion: Cluny and Christendom Face Heresy, Judaism, and Islam (1000–1150).* Translated by Graham Robert Edwards. Ithaca, NY: Cornell University Press, 2002.

Janzen, David. *The Intentional Christian Community Handbook: For Idealists, Hypocrites, and Wannabe Disciples of Jesus.* Brewster, MA: Paraclete Press, 2013.

Johnston, William M., ed. *Encyclopedia of Monasticism.* 2 vols. London: Fitzroy Dearborn, 2000.

Jordan, R. H., and Rosemary Morris. *The Hypotyposis of the Monastery of the Theotokos Evergetis, Constantinople (11th–12th Centuries): Introduction, Translation and Commentary.* Farnham, UK: Ashgate, 2012.

Kam, John. "A Cursory Review of the Biblical Basis of Monastic Life." *Asia Journal of Theology* 6 (1992): 183–86.

Kardong, Terrence G. *Benedict's Rule: A Translation and Commentary.* Collegeville, MN: Liturgical Press, 1996.

———. *The Life of St. Benedict by Gregory the Great: Translation and Commentary.* Collegeville, MN: Liturgical Press, 2009.

———. *Pillars of Community: Four Rules of Pre-Benedictine Monastic Life.* Collegeville, MN: Liturgical Press, 2010.

Kavanaugh, Kieran, and Otilio Rodriguez, trans. *The Collected Works of St. Teresa of Avila.* Vol. 1, *The Book of Her Life, Spiritual Testimonies, Soliloquies.* Washington, DC: ICS Publications, 1976.

———, trans. *The Collected Works of St. Teresa of Avila.* Vol. 3, *The Book of Her Foundations, Minor Works.* Washington, DC: ICS Publications, 1985.

Kavenagh, Terence. "Vallombrosans." In *Encyclopedia of Monasticism,* edited by William M. Johnston, 2 vols. London: Fitzroy Dearborn, 2000.

Kelly, Geffrey B., and F. Burton Nelson, eds. *A Testament to Freedom: The Essential Writings of Dietrich Bonhoeffer.* Rev. ed. San Francisco: HarperSanFrancisco, 1995.

Kierkegaard, Søren. *Fear and Trembling.* Translated by Alastair Hannay. London: Penguin, 1985.

Klinghardt, Matthias. "The Manual of Discipline in the Light of Statutes of Hellenistic Associations." *Annals of the New York Academy of Sciences* 722 (1994): 251–67.

Knowles, David. *Great Historical Enterprises and Problems in Monastic History.* London: Nelson, 1963.

———. *The Monastic Order in England: A History of Its Development from the Times of St. Dunstan to the Fourth Lateran Council 913–1216.* Cambridge: Cambridge University Press, 1950.

Kodell, Jerome. "Celibate because of the Kingdom." *Tjurunga: An Australasian Benedictine Review* 81 (2011): 23–27.

Krey, Philip D. W., and Peter D. S. Krey, eds. *Luther's Spirituality.* New York: Paulist Press, 2007.

Laboa, Juan María. "Old Testament Monasticism." In *The Historical Atlas of Eastern and Western Christian Monasticism,* edited by Juan María Laboa. 18–21. Collegeville, MN: Liturgical Press, 2003.

Lanne, Emmanuel. "La xeniteia d'Abraham dans l'oeuvre d'Irénée: aux origines du thème Monastique de la 'peregrinatio.'" *Irénikon* 47 (1974): 163–87.

Lapidge, Michael, and Michael Winterbottom, eds. *Wulfstan of Winchester: The Life of St. Æthelwold.* Oxford: Clarendon, 1991.

Lawless, George. *Augustine of Hippo and His Monastic Rule.* Oxford: Clarendon, 1987.

Lawrence, C. H. *The Friars: The Impact of the Early Mendicant Movement on Western Society.* London: Longman, 1994.

———. *Medieval Monasticism.* 3rd ed. Harlow, UK: Longman, 2001.

Lebreton, Jules, et al. "Contemplation." In *Dictionnaire de Spiritualité*, vol. 2, edited by Marcel Viller, Charles Baumgartner, and André Rayez. Paris: Beauchesne, 1953.

Lesne, Emile. *L'Orgine des menses dans le temporel des églises et des monastères de France au IXe siècle.* Lille: Rene Giard; Paris: Honoré Champion, 1910.

Leyser, Henrietta, trans. "Peter Damian, *Life of St. Romuald of Ravenna.*" In *Medieval Hagiography: An Anthology*, edited by Thomas Head. 296–316. New York: Garland, 2000.

Lindberg, Carter. *The European Reformations.* Oxford: Blackwell, 1996.

Litfin, Bryan M. *Getting to Know the Church Fathers: An Evangelical Introduction.* Grand Rapids: Brazos, 2007.

Little, Lester K. *Religious Poverty and the Profit Economy in Medieval Europe.* Ithaca, NY: Cornell University Press, 1978.

Luibheid, Colm, trans. *Pseudo-Dionysius: The Complete Works.* New York: Paulist Press, 1987.

Luibheid, Colm, and Norman Russell, trans. *John Climacus: The Ladder of Divine Ascent.* New York: Paulist Press, 1982.

Mansi, J. D., ed. *Sacrorum Conciliorum Nova et Amplissima Collectio, Tomus Tertius.* Venice: Antonio Zatta, 1759.

Mayr-Harting, Henry. *The Coming of Christianity to Anglo-Saxon England.* University Park: Pennsylvania State University Press, 1991.

McGinn, Bernard. ed. *The Essential Writings of Christian Mysticism.* New York: Modern Library, 2006.

———. "Withdrawal and Return: Reflections on Monastic Retreat from the World." *Spiritus: A Journal of Christian Spirituality* 6 (2006): 149–72.

McNamara, Jo Ann. *The Ordeal of Community.* Toronto: Peregrina, 1993.

McNeill, John T., ed. *Calvin: Institutes of the Christian Religion.* 2 vols. Translated by Ford Lewis Battles. Philadelphia: Westminster, 1960.

Merton, Thomas. *Basic Principles of Monastic Spirituality.* Springfield, IL: Templegate, 1996.

———. *The Climate of Monastic Prayer.* Kalamazoo, MI: Cistercian Publications, 1969.

———. *The Seven Storey Mountain.* New York: Harcourt, Brace, 1948.

Meyer, Robert T., trans. *Palladius: The Lausiac History.* Westminster, MD: Newman Press, 1965.

Meyvaert, Paul. "The Enigma of Gregory the Great's *Dialogues*: A Response to Francis Clark." *Journal of Ecclesiastical History* 39 (1988): 335–81.

Miller, Timothy S. *The Birth of the Hospital in the Byzantine Empire.* Baltimore: Johns Hopkins University Press, 1997.

Moll, Rob. "The New Monasticism." *Christianity Today*, September 2005, 38–46.

Monkres, Peter R. "An Innovative Ministry for Surplus Clergy." *Christian Century*, February 7–14, 1979, 146–51.

Morris, Leon. *The First Epistle of Paul to the Corinthians.* Grand Rapids: Eerdmans, 1958.

Morris, Rosemary. *Monks and Laymen in Byzantium, 843–1118.* Cambridge: Cambridge University Press, 1995.

Mullady, Brian. *The Call of God: A Short Primer on the Theology of Vocation.* Libertyville, IL: Institute on Religious Life, 2008.

Munro, Dana Carleton, ed. *Life of St. Columban.* Translations and reprints from the Original Sources of European History, vol. 2, no. 7. Philadelphia: Department of History of the University of Pennsylvania, 1895.

Nightingale, John. *Monasteries and Patrons in the Gorze Reform: Lotharingia c. 850–1000.* Oxford: Clarendon, 2001.

Ní Mheara, Róisín. *In Search of Irish Saints: The Peregrinatio pro Christo.* Dublin: Four Courts Press, 1994.

Ó Cróinín, Dáibhí. "A Tale of Two Rules: Benedict and Columbanus." In *The Irish Benedictines: A History*, edited by Martin Browne and Colmán Ó Clabaigh. 11–24. Dublin: Columba Press, 2005.

O'Donovan, Daniel, and Conrad Greenia, trans. *Bernard of Clairvaux: Treatises 3.* Kalamazoo, MI: Cistercian Publications, 1977.

Oliva, Marilyn. *The Convent and the Community in Late Medieval England: Female Monasteries in the Diocese of Norwich, 1350–1540*. Woodbridge, UK: Boydell Press, 1998.

Ó Maidín, Uinseann, trans. *The Celtic Monk: Rules and Writings of Early Irish Monks*. Kalamazoo, MI: Cistercian Publications 1996.

O'Malley, John W. "The Society of Jesus." In *Religious Orders of the Catholic Reformation: In Honor of John C. Olin on His Seventy-Fifth Birthday*, edited by Richard L. DeMolen. 139–63. New York: Fordham University Press, 1994.

O'Sullivan, Jeremiah F., trans. "A Dialogue between Two Monks." In *Cistercians and Cluniacs: The Case for Cîteaux*. 19–141. Kalamazoo, MI: Cistercian Publications, 1977.

———, trans. *Stephen of Sawley: Treatises*. Kalamazoo, MI: Cistercian Publications, 1984.

Pantin, William, ed. *Documents Illustrating the Activities of the General and Provincial Chapters of the English Black Monks, 1215–1540*. London: Royal Historical Society, 1931–1937.

Pate, C. Marvin. *Communities of the Last Days: The Dead Sea Scrolls, the New Testament and the Story of Israel*. Downers Grove, IL: InterVarsity, 2000.

Peters, Greg. "Cassian, John (c. 360–432)." In *Zondervan Dictionary of Christian Spirituality*, edited by Glen G. Scorgie. Grand Rapids: Zondervan, 2011.

———. "Coenobitism." In *The Oxford Dictionary of the Middle Ages*, edited by Robert E. Bjork, 2 vols. Oxford: Oxford University Press, 2010.

———. "Evagrius of Pontus (c. 346–399)." In *Zondervan Dictionary of Christian Spirituality*, edited by Glen G. Scorgie. Grand Rapids: Zondervan, 2011.

———. "Historical Theology and Spiritual Formation: A Call." *Journal of Spiritual Formation and Soul Care* 7, no. 2 (2014): 203–9.

———. "Monasteries." In *The Encyclopedia of Christian Civilization*, edited by George Thomas Kurian. Malden, MA: Wiley-Blackwell, 2011.

———. "Monasticism." In *Zondervan Dictionary of Christian Spirituality*, edited by Glen G. Scorgie. Grand Rapids: Zondervan, 2011.

———. "Monasticism: Instrument of the Holy Spirit in the Renewal of Today's Church." In *The Holy Spirit and the Christian Life: Historical, Interdisciplinary, and Renewal Perspectives*, edited by Wolfgang Vondey. 41–57. New York: Palgrave Macmillan, 2014.

———. "Monastic Orders." In *The Encyclopedia of Christian Civilization*, edited by George Thomas Kurian. Malden, MA: Wiley-Blackwell, 2011.

———. "The Place of Monasticism in the Thought of Donald Bloesch." In *Church, Society and Monasticism: Acts of the International Symposium, Rome, May 31–June 3, 2006*, edited by Eduardo López-Tello García and Benedetta Selene Zorzi, 261–74. St. Ottilien, Ger.: EOS Klosterverlag, 2009:

———. *Reforming the Monastery: Protestant Theologies of Religious Life*. Eugene, OR: Cascade, 2014.

———. "Religious Orders and Pastoral Care in the Late Middle Ages." In *Pastoral Care in the Late Middle Ages*, edited by Ronald J. Stansbury. 253–84. Leiden: Brill, 2010.

———. "Spiritual Marriage in Early Christianity: 1 Corinthians 7:25–38 in Modern Exegesis and the Earliest Church." *Trinity Journal* 23 NS (Fall 2002): 211–24.

Phipps, Colin. "Romuald—Model Hermit: Eremitical Theory in Saint Peter Damian's *Vita Beati Romualdi*, Chapters 16–27." In *Monks, Hermits and the Ascetic Tradition*, edited by W. J. Sheils. 65–77. Oxford: Basil Blackwell, 1985.

Plekon, Michael. "Interiorized Monasticism: Paul Evdokimov on the Spiritual Life." *American Benedictine Review* 48, no. 3 (1997): 227–53.

Prinz, Friedrich. *Frühes Mönchtum im Frankenreich. Kultur und Gesellschaft in Gallien, den Rheinlanden und Bayern am Beispiel der monastischen Entwicklung (4. bis 8. Jahrhundert)*. Rev. ed. Munich: R. Oldenbourg, 1988.

Rader, Rosemary. *Breaking Boundaries: Male/Female Friendship in Early Christian Communities*. New York: Paulist Press, 1983.

Ramsey, Boniface trans. *John Cassian: The Conferences*. New York: Paulist Press, 1997.

———, trans. *John Cassian: The Institutes*. New York: Newman Press, 2000.

Rees, Daniel, and members of the English Benedictine Congregation. *Consider Your Call: A Theology of Monastic Life Today*. London: SPCK, 1978.

Ribot, Felip. *The Ten Books on the Way of Life and Great Deeds of the Carmelites*. Translated by Richard Copsey. Faversham, UK: Saint Albert's Press, 2005.

Riley-Smith, Jonathan. *Templars and Hospitallers as Professed Religious in the Holy Land*. Notre Dame, IN: University of Notre Dame Press, 2010.

Robson, Michael. *The Franciscans in the Middle Ages*. Woodbridge, UK: Boydell Press, 2006.

Rordorf, Willy. "Marriage in the New Testament and the Early Church." *Journal of Ecclesiastical History* 20 (1969): 193–210.

Rutba House, The, ed. *School(s) for Conversion: 12 Marks of a New Monasticism*. Eugene, OR: Cascade, 2005.

Schroeder, Carl J. *In Quest of Pentecost: Jodocus van Lodenstein and the Dutch Second Reformation*. Lanham, MD: University Press of America, 2001.

Schuurman, Douglas J. *Vocation: Discerning Our Callings in Life*. Grand Rapids: Eerdmans, 2004.

Schwanda, Tom. "Contemplation." In *Zondervan Dictionary of Christian Spirituality*, edited by Glen G. Scorgie. Grand Rapids: Zondervan, 2011.

Seboldt, Roland H. A. "Spiritual Marriage in the Early Church: A Suggested Interpretation of 1 Cor. 7:36–38." *Concordia Theological Monthly* 30 (1959): 103–19.

Second Vatican Council, *Decree on the Adaptation and Renewal of Religioius Life, Perfectae Caritatis*. October 28, 1965.

S. Ephraemi Syri Commentarii in Epistulas Divi Pauli a patribus Mekhitaristis in latinum sermonem translate. Venice: Typogr. S. Lazari, 1893.

Sheldrake, Philip, ed. *The New Westminster Dictionary of Christian Spirituality*. Louisville: Westminster John Knox, 2005

Silvas, Anna M. *The Asketikon of St. Basil the Great*. Oxford: Oxford University Press, 2005.

Sinkewicz, Robert E., trans. *Evagrius of Pontus: The Greek Ascetic Corpus*. Oxford: Oxford University Press, 2003.

Sitwell, Gerard, trans. and ed. *St. Odo of Cluny: Being the Life of St. Odo of Cluny by John of Salerno and the Life of St. Gerald of Aurillac by St. Odo*. London: Sheed and Ward, 1958.

Stark, Rodney, and Roger Finke. "Catholic Religious Vocations: Decline and Renewal." *Review of Religious Research* 42, no. 2 (2000): 125–45.

Stevenson, Jane Barbara. "The Monastic Rules of Columbanus." In *Columbanus: Studies on the Latin Writings*, edited by Michael Lapidge. 203–16. Woodbridge, UK: Boydell Press, 1997.

Stewart, Columba. *Cassian the Monk*. New York: Oxford University Press, 1998.

———. "Introduction." In *Purity of Heart in Early Ascetic and Monastic Literature: Essays in Honor of Juana Raasch, O.S.B.*, edited by Harriet A. Luckman and Linda Kulzer. 1–15. Collegeville, MN: Liturgical Press, 1999.

———. "Monasticism and the New Testament: An Absent Phenomenon in Early Christianity." In *The Historical Atlas of Eastern and Western Christian Monasticism*, edited by Juan María Laboa. 22–25. Collegeville, MN: Liturgical Press, 2003.

Stöber, Karen. *Late Medieval Monasteries and Their Patrons: England and Wales, c. 1300–1540*. Woodbridge, UK: Boydell Press, 2007.

Stubbs, William, ed. *Memorials of Saint Dunstan, Archbishop of Canterbury*. London: Longman, 1874.

Sutcliffe, Edmund F. *The Monks of Qumran*. Westminster, MD: Newman Press, 1960.

Swanson, R. N., trans. *Catholic England: Faith, Religion and Observance before the Reformation*. Manchester, UK: Manchester University Press, 1993.

———. *Religion and Devotion in Europe, c. 1215–c. 1515*. Cambridge: Cambridge University Press, 1995.

Symons, Thomas, trans. *The Monastic Agreement of the Monks and Nuns of the English Nation*. London: Thomas Nelson, 1953.

Tanner, Norman P., ed. *Decrees of the Ecumenical Councils*. Vol. 1, *Nicea I to Lateran V*. London: Sheed & Ward; Washington, DC: Georgetown University Press, 1990.

Thomas, John Philip. *Private Religious Foundations in the Byzantine Empire*. Washington, DC: Dumbarton Oaks, 1987.

Thomas, John, and Angela Constantinides Hero, eds. *Byzantine Monastic Foundation Documents*. 5 vols. Washington, DC: Dumbarton Oaks, 2000.

Thurman, Robert A. F. "Tibetan Buddhist Perspectives on Asceticism." In *Asceticism*, edited by Vincent L. Wimbush and Richard Valantasis. 108–18. New York: Oxford University Press, 1995.

Tobin, John, ed. *George Herbert: The Complete English Poems*. London: Penguin, 1991.

Treggiari, Susan. *Roman Marriage: Iusti Coniuges from the Time of Cicero to the Time of Ulpian*. Oxford: Oxford University Press, 1991.

Treier, Daniel J. *Introducing Theological Interpretation of Scripture: Recovering a Christian Practice*. Grand Rapids: Baker Academic, 2008.

Tugwell, Simon. *Early Dominicans: Selected Writings*. New York: Paulist Press, 1982.

Turner, Andrew J., and Bernard J. Muir, eds. and trans. *Eadmer of Canterbury: Lives and Miracles of Saints Oda, Dunstan, and Oswald*. Oxford: Clarendon, 2006.

Tyers, John. "Not a Papal Conspiracy but a Spiritual Principle: Three Early Anglican Apologists for the Practice of Retreat." *Journal of Anglican Studies* 8, no. 2 (2010): 165–83.

Van Engen, John. "The 'Crisis of Cenobitism' Reconsidered: Benedictine Monasticism in the Years 1050–1150." *Speculum* 61 (1986): 269–304.

Veilleux, Armand., trans. *Pachomian Koinonia*. Vol. 1, *The Life of Saint Pachomius and His Disciples*. Kalamazoo, MI: Cistercian Publications, 1980.

———, trans. *Pachomian Koinonia*. Vol. 2, *Pachomian Chronicles and Rules*. Kalamazoo, MI: Cistercian Publications, 1981.

———. "Prayer in the Pachomian Koinōnia." In *The Continuing Quest for God: Monastic Spirituality in Tradition and Transition*, edited by William Skudlarek. 61–66. Collegeville, MN: Liturgical Press, 1982.

Venarde, Bruce L. "Premonstratensian Canons." In *Encyclopedia of Monasticism*, edited by William M. Johnston, 2 vols. London: Fitzroy Dearborn, 2000.

Vivian, Tim, and Apostolos Athanassakis, trans. *The Life of Antony: The Coptic Life and the Greek Life*. Kalamazoo, MI: Cistercian Publications, 2003.

Von Weizsäcker, Carl. *The Apostolic Age of the Christian Church*. Vol 2. Translated by James Millar. London: Williams and Norgate, 1895.

Waddell, Chrysogonus, ed. *Narrative and Legislative Texts from Early Cîteaux*. Cîteaux: Commentarii Cistercienses, 1999.

Wagner, Monica, trans. *Saint Basil: Ascetical Works*. Washington, DC: Catholic University of America Press, 1950.

Walker, G. S. M., ed. *Sancti Columbani Opera*. Dublin: Dublin Institute for Advanced Studies, 1957.

Walz, Angelus. *Saint Thomas Aquinas: A Biographical Study*. Westminster, MD: Newman Press, 1951.

Ward, Benedicta, trans. *The Sayings of the Desert Fathers: The Alphabetical Collection*. Kalamazoo, MI: Cistercian Publications, 1975.

Watson, Richard, ed. *A Biblical and Theological Dictionary: Explanatory of the History, Manners, and Customs of the Jews, and Neighbouring Nations*. New York: B. Waugh and T. Mason, 1832.

Wawrykow, Joseph P. *The SCM Press A–Z of Thomas Aquinas*. London: SCM Press, 2005.

Way, Agnes Clare. *Saint Basil: Exegetic Homilies*. Washington, DC: Catholic University of America Press, 1963.

Webber, Robert. *Evangelicals on the Canterbury Trail: Why Evangelicals Are Attracted to the Liturgical Church*. Waco: Word Books, 1985.

Weiser, Frederick S. "Communal Ministries in Lutheranism: The Historical Precedent." *American Benedictine Review* 19 (1968): 301–16.

Wendebourg, Dorothea. "Luther on Monasticism." In *The Pastoral Luther: Essays on Martin Luther's Practical Theology*, edited by Timothy J. Wengert. 327–54. Grand Rapids: Eerdmans, 2009.

Wenzel, Siegfried. *Macaronic Sermons: Bilingualism and Preaching in Late-Medieval England*. Ann Arbor: University of Michigan Press, 1994.

Werner, Roberta. *Reaching for God: The Benedictine Oblate Way of Life*. Collegeville, MN: Liturgical Press, 2013.

Williams, Daniel H. *Retrieving the Tradition and Renewing Evangelicalism: A Primer for Suspicious Protestants*. Grand Rapids: Eerdmans, 1999.

Williamson, G. A., trans. *Eusebius: The History of the Church from Christ to Constantine*. Edited by Andrew Louth. London: Penguin, 1989.

Wilson-Hartgrove, Jonathan. *New Monasticism: What It Has to Say to Today's Church*. Grand Rapids: Brazos, 2008.

Woods, Richard. "Columban, St. c. 543–615." In *Encyclopedia of Monasticism*, edited by William M. Johnston, 2 vols. London: Fitzroy Dearborn, 2000.

Zimmermann, Odo J. "An Unsolved Problem: The Rule of St. Benedict and the Rule of the Master." *American Benedictine Review* 10, no. 1 (1959): 86–106.

Index